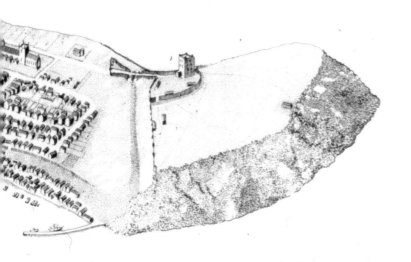

THE HISTORY OF SCARBOROUGH

From Earliest Times to the Year 2000

by

JACK BINNS

BLACKTHORN PRESS

Blackthorn Press, Blackthorn House
Middleton Rd, Pickering YO18 8AL
United Kingdom

ISBN 0 9535072 7 0

© Dr Jack Binns 2001

ILLUSTRATION CREDITS

The publisher and author are grateful to the following for help with
providing illustrations: British Library, David Pearson, Michael
Jaconelli, Andrew Avery, Scarborough Art Gallery, The Francis Frith
Collection, Scarborough Library.

PREFACE

Anyone setting out alone to write a history of Scarborough must be presumptuous and perhaps foolhardy. Firstly, the precedents are unpromising. Brogden Baker's *History of Scarbrough* (sic), published in 1882, claimed to start at 'the earliest date', yet it revealed nothing of the town's origins or existence before 1066. Moreover, because it lacked both index and references and, less excusably, factual accuracy, its raw content has frustrated and misled readers at least as often as it has enlightened them.

Although the second volume of the *Victoria County History of the North Riding of Yorkshire* contained a scholarly summary of Scarborough's past, it ran to only twenty pages and since its publication in 1923 it has become increasingly inadequate, even as an introduction.

More recent histories of the town, Rowntree's of 1931 and Edwards's of 1966, were carefully researched and well written, but both were the collective accumulations of several authors of unequal abilities. Arthur Rowntree farmed out six of his twelve chapters to a specialist archæologist and historians whose familiarity with Scarborough was at best brief and tenuous. Mervyn Edwards employed local men yet he did no more than edit the separate works of half a dozen contributors without attempting to bind them into a coherent narrative. Unfortunately, like Baker's *History*, *Scarborough 966 – 1966* was published without bibliography or index.

Readers will rightly protest that so far I have omitted the first and arguably the most accomplished of all Scarborough's historians – Thomas Hinderwell (1744-1825). However, even Hinderwell was honest enough to acknowledge the heavy debts he owed to a number of friends who had obliged him with their 'researches in the Tower [and] British Museum'. After the first pioneering work of 1798, his list of assistants grew longer for the second 1811 edition of his *History and Antiquities of Scarborough*. Finally, the third editions of 1832 and 1837, still described as Hinderwell's work, were in fact, posthumous: he had died in 1825. What these later versions added substantially to Hinderwell's original study was due largely to the research of Dr William Travis.

Secondly, what is known and can now be discovered of the history of Scarborough grows almost by the week. So much of the documentary evidence, such as correspondence, memoirs, court records and census returns, now accessible in county record offices and libraries, was once unavailable to Hinderwell and his aides, Baker or even Rowntree. Moreover, the science of archæology has made enormous progress since F.G. Simpson excavated Castle Hill between 1919 and 1927 and his findings were reported by Mortimer Wheeler and R.G. Collingwood in Rowntree's *History*. Today, the historian of a community even as small as Scarborough is confronted by a mountain of material, huge in quantity and varied in kind and quality. The principal problem is to decide what to leave out.

All too conscious of the massive weight of evidence about Scarborough's lengthy past and the wealth of significant events in it, I have tried to steer a middle course between superficiality and excessive detail. I have written for the general reader without, I hope, outraging the sensitivities of the professional historian and I have brought the story up to the end of the twentieth century to emphasise that contemporaries are just as much part of Scarborough's history as their predecessors.

Historians incur heavy debts and my debt is so extensive that it would be impossible to name here all those who have generously given to me their time and the benefit of their knowledge.

However, I feel obliged to record my particular gratitude to Mr Michael Ashcroft, chief archivist at the North Yorkshire County Record Office, whose dedication and industry have put all present and future students of Scarborough's history in his debt; Mr Bryan Berryman, whose comprehensive understanding of the resources of the Scarborough Room made my researches there most rewarding and fruitful; and Mr Trevor Pearson, whose continuing archæological work at Scarborough has added so much to our appreciation of the town's medieval past.

For the best photographic illustrations of contemporary Scarborough, from the air and at ground level, I am again grateful to Mr Michael Jaconelli and Mr Michael Marshall.

Of the many conscientious and helpful staffs who have given me assistance, I should like to thank in particular those of the libraries of Scarborough Central, Whitby Literary and Philosophical Society, York Minster and York City, the universities of Cambridge, Hull, Leeds, Oxford and York, the Public Record Office in London, the Borthwick Institute in York, and the County Record Offices of North and East Yorkshire at Northallerton and Beverley.

Last, but mostly, I am indebted to my wife whose loyal support has sustained me to the completion of this time-consuming enterprise.

CONTENTS

I. FROM BRONZE AGE TO HOLOCAUST.
First Summer Visitors P3, Roman Signal Station P4, Skarthi's Burg? P7, Holocaust 1066 P9.

II. GROWTH 1135 - 1307
Albemarle P15, Henry Plantagenet P18, St Mary's P19, John P21, Henry III P22, Friars P27.

III. DECAY AND DECLINE 1307 -1500
Riot and Rebellion P32, Falling Behind P36, Richard the Good P40.

IV. REFORMATION AND RECOVERY 1500 – 1642
Religious Reformation P44, Economic Revival P54, Oligarchy P60.

V. CIVIL WARS 1642 – 1660
Parliament's Outpost P64, Royalist Port P70, Castle Siege P73, Second War P77, Aftermath P80.

VI. RESTORATION AND REVOLUTION 1660 – 1699
Restoration P86, Quakers P87, Whigs versus Tories P91, The 'Spaw' P93.

VII. THE CONDITION OF THE PEOPLE
Public Health P105, Homes and Households P111, Crime and Punishment P115, Work and Trade P121, Oligarchy P128.

VIII. FIRST SEASIDE RESORT
Dicky Dickinson P133, The Great Schism P150, Invasion Scare 1745-6. P155.

IX. MARITIME RESORT.
Spa Waters P157, Law and Order P162, Lodgings, Gardens and Roads P165, Sea-Bathing P170, Amusements P173.

X. TRADE AND INDUSTRY: THE OTHER SCARBOROUGH
Ship Market P181, Coal and Piers P184, Lighthouse and Lifeboat P188, Commerce and Fishing P190.

XI. POPULATION, CHURCHES, CHARITIES AND NEW BUILDINGS.
Inhabitants P193, Anglicans P197, Nonconformists P202, Charity P206, Christ Church P208, Cliff Bridge P210, Rotunda Museum P212.

XII. POLITICS
Pocket Borough P215, Great Reform Act 1832 P219,
From 44 to 24 P223.

XIII. SCARBOROUGH ABOUT 1840
Walking the Boundaries P234, Getting There and Back P238, Granville's
Scarborough P239, The Other Scarborough P243, Crime and Punishment P247,
Schools and Churches P249, Summary P253.

XIV. STEAMPOWER
The Railway P255, Waterworks P257, Hotels and Lodging Houses P260,
Paxton's Music Hall P263, Market Hall and Eastborough P264, Cemetery and
Workhouse P266, Borough Gaol P269,

XV. MID-VICTORIAN HEYDAY
Valley Bridge P271, Grand Hotel P273, North Bay Rock Gardens and Pier
P274, Bathing and Baths P277, Aquarium and Foreshore Road P280, Verity's
Grand Hall P282, More Churches and Chapels P285, Summary P288.

XVI. 'DEVELOP SCARBOROUGH MAJESTICALLY'
Parks and Gardens P297, Roads and Rails P302, Schools P305,
 Sport P311, Politics P314, Fishing P321.

XVII. THE BOMBARDMENT AND AFTER
The Bombardment 1914 P329, Aftermath P335,
Health and Homes P337, North Side P342, Entertainment P346, Enlightenment
P351, Adshead Revisited P355.

XVIII.   FROM BLITZ TO BINGO
Blitz P361, Recovery P365, Health and Homes P373,
Ominous Signs P378.

XIX. FIN DE SIECLE 1974-2000
Reorganisation: Winner or Loser? P387, Town Centre: Supermarkets,
Pedestrians and Parking P393, South Side P398, North Side P402, Theatres
P406, Schools and Colleges P410, Parliamentary Politics P415, Prospects P418,
Conclusion P423.

SELECT BIBLIOGRAPHY P427.

INDEX P440.

PLATES, MAPS & ILLUSTRATIONS

PLATES

Plate 1. The Headland. Aerial view taken from out at sea.
Photo, Michael Jaconelli.

Plate 2. A reconstruction of the Roman watchtower.
Scarborough Art Gallery

Plate 3. The burning of Scarborough by Hardrada in 1066.
David Pearson

Plate 4. Scarborough castle. Henry II's great keep.
Michael Marshall

Plate 5. Engineer's plat. The first image of Scarborough circa 1538.
British Library.

Plate 6. 'Holiday-makers on Scarborough Beach' 1770 painted by
T. Ramsey. Scarborough Art Gallery

Plate 7. The Grand Hotel.
Photo, Alan Avery

Plate 8. The Stephen Joseph Theatre.
Photo, Andrew Avery

MAPS

Roman Yorkshire *P5*

A plan of Scarborough 1811, *P159*

Street Map of Modern Scarborough *P291*

John Cossins's 'New and Exact Plan' of Scarborough drawn in 1725,
back end paper

ILLUSTRATIONS

Reconstruction of Late Medieval Scarborough, *Front end paper*

Reconstruction of Albemarle's castle, *P15*

The castle keep, drawbridges and barbican walls, *P23*

The Three Mariners House, *P39*

Richard III's house, Sandside, *P41*

St Mary's medieval chantry chapels and south transept, *P46*

Reconstruction of St Mary's at its fullest extent, *P49*

Sir Hugh Cholmley 1600-57, *P67*

Capt Browne Bushell 1609-51, *P81*

Admiral Sir John Lawson c. 1615-65, *P83*

Scarborough harbour and Spaw about 1685 according
to the coastal survey of Captain Greenville Collins, *P86*

George Fox, *P88*

Lady Cholmley, *P103*

17th Century Street Scenes, *P129*

Dicky Dickinson first 'Governor' of Scarborough Spa, *P141*

South-west view of Scarborough
engraved by John Haynes for Thomas Gent in 1735, *P143*

Scarborough town and South Bay from castle dykes
by T Ramsey 1770, *P147*

Scarborough's lifeboat heading off in a rough sea, 1801, *P189*

Victoria Street, *P192*

Westwood, *P192*

The newly-built Cliff Bridge, by J Stubbs, 1827, *P211*

The Rotunda Museum 1829, *P213*

Sir George Cayley at the age of seventy, *P221*

Gothic Newborough Bar 1847-1890, *P235*

South Steel battery and Weddell's bath-house from East Pier, by J Stubbs, 1827, *P242*

Old Sandside in the late nineteenth century, *P245*

North Bay 1897, *P276*

South Cliff United Reformed Church, *P287*

Albion Road, South Cliff, *P289*

Ramsdale mill dam and plantation, by J Stubbs, 1827, *P299*

Sir George Reresby Sitwell, baronet, 1860-1943, *P317*

Thomas Whittaker 1813-99, *P319*

Part of the herring fleet off Scarborough, *P323*

Direct hit received by Scarborough Lighthouse, *P329*

Hits received at the back of St Nicholas Parade, *P331*

The Butter Cross, West Sandgate, *P375*

Railway Poster from the 1930s by Andrew Johnson, *P383*

Broxholme – Scarborough's Art Gallery, *P383*

Pedestrian Precinct, *P396*

South Bay and Oliver's Mount in 2000, *P398*

Donkey Rides on North Bay Beach, *P402*

North Bay in 2000, *P405*

1

FROM BRONZE AGE TO HOLOCAUST

For convenient simplification, archaeologists divide the prehistoric past into distinct periods - the Old Stone (Palaeolithic), Middle Stone (Mesolithic), New Stone (Neolithic), Bronze and Iron Ages.

During the Old Stone Age our very small number of ancestors were migrant hunters and food gatherers; in the Mesolithic, about 10,000 to 6,000 years ago, during the final stages of the last Ice Age when Britain became an island, they first built boats, domesticated dogs, and fashioned improved tools and weapons from flint, bone and antler.

During the New Stone Age, between 6,000 and 4,000 years ago, our ancestors learned to farm: they cultivated cereals, husbanded animals, made pots, built permanent houses, buried their dead collectively in long barrows and erected stone monuments. The great stone circle at Avebury was originally the work of Neolithic farmers.

Bronze metal-working was brought into Britain soon after 4,000 BC. Communal burials gave way to individual interments in round barrows; inhumation was gradually replaced by cremation; and the dead were provided with pots, food and weapons. Stonehenge was the achievement of the organising ability and wealth of Bronze Age people.

Finally, from about 700 BC onwards, knowledge of iron-working was imported into Britain by Celts whose culture is known as Hallstatt from the place in Austria where their cemeteries were first excavated. The only local settlement of this early Iron Age so far discovered was on Scarborough's Castle Hill.

Between the third and first centuries BC the whole of Britain was divided into tribal districts and east Yorkshire was occupied by people called by Ptolemy, the Greek geographer, the Parisi. Whether these Parisi where of the same Gallic tribe that gave their name to the capital of France remains a controversial question. They buried their

1

dead in the centre of a square ditch along with weapons, jewellery, joints of meat and sometimes between a two-wheeled cart or 'chariot'.

The Roman conquest of Britain began in AD 43 and had reached the Humber within five years. The revolt of the Iceni tribe under Queen Boudicca halted further expansion, but in AD 71 the Ninth Legion based at Lindum (Lincoln) advanced northwards, overran the Parisi, established forts at Derventio (Malton) and Eboracum (York), before destroying the last resistance of the Brigantes.

For most of the 350 years that Britain remained part of the Roman Empire it enjoyed almost uninterrupted peace and prosperity. What had been more than 30 warring kingdoms became one secure colonial province. Besides new vegetables such as carrots and turnips, iron ploughshares and wheeled ploughs, the Romans brought lavatories and underground sewers which made urban life not merely possible but comfortable and hygienic. Britain's earliest towns grew up alongside the military garrisons and Britain's first metal roads were laid in straight lines to link them. In east Yorkshire Iron Age villages continued through the Roman period, sometimes associated with new Roman villa farms. With their mosaic floors, central heating, hot-water baths, stone walls and tiled roofs, the villas contrasted with the wattle and daub huts of native homes.

After AD 410 Britannia ceased to be a province of the disintegrating Roman world and became prey to the incursions of illiterate barbarians. Towns were abandoned, roads neglected. A coin-using complex economy gave way to subsistence agriculture. During the next six centuries there were numerous waves of seaborne conquerors and settlers. First came the Angles and Saxons from north Germany. They divided what was soon called England into separate kingdoms such as Wessex, East Anglia, Mercia and Northumbria. Originally pagans, they were converted to Christianity during the seventh century thereby restoring a tenuous contact with Rome.

In 867 a Danish army captured York and for the next century Yorkshire was a Scandinavian kingdom. Monasteries, such as Whitby's, were destroyed. However, the Danes could not subdue Alfred's kingdom of Wessex and this left England divided in two until Alfred's son and grandson gradually asserted control over the north.

A second series of Danish invasions then culminated in 1016 in the coronation of Cnut, the first ruler of a truly united England. Finally, just 50 years later, when the English crown was again disputed, two foreign leaders, Harald, King of Norway, and William, Duke of Normandy, were preparing their invasion fleets.

First Summer Visitors

In the beginning there was the headland: the history of Scarborough starts with its most conspicuous natural feature - the massive coastal promontory, which separates and overlooks two wide-sweeping bays to the south and the north. *[plate 1]*. Except for a narrow spine of a land bridge from the west, this headland is surrounded and protected almost entirely by cliffs which at their highest rise vertically to 300 feet (92 metres) above the North Sea. Even after many centuries of erosion, there are still 16 acres (6.5 hectares) - equal to eight football pitches - of grassy, fairly level ground on top of the headland. Though water lies at a depth of about 180 feet (55 metres) under the rock on the western side, it collects close to the surface on the eastern seaward edge. Not surprisingly, this superb defensive and observation platform soon attracted its first human settlers.

What we know today of the earliest inhabitants of Scarborough's headland is due mostly to the excavations there between 1919 and 1927 of F.G. Simpson. Unfortunately, he published no complete account of his discoveries and therefore we must rely mainly on the first two chapters of Rowntree's *History of Scarborough* written by R.E. Mortimer-Wheeler, who later became a world-famous archæologist and R.G. Collingwood, the authority on Roman Britain. Both drew heavily on Simpson's notes.

On the most easterly edge of the sea cliff Simpson found remains of a late Bronze Age summer camp, a Roman signal station, a late Saxon Christian chapel, a Norman chapel and a fourteenth-century enlargement of it with a priest's house. They were all on nearly the same site at different levels. Some stones had been robbed and re-used. For example, the north wall of the Roman signal tower had become that of the nave and chancel of the pre-Conquest chapel. Simpson found human bones from all of these occupation periods except the Roman.

The earliest human residents of the headland belonged to the end of the Bronze and the beginning of the Iron Age between 700 and 500 BC. Most of their implements therefore were of wood, flint and bronze, and Simpson unearthed only one fragment of iron, a pin 2½ inches (6.6 centimetres) long. A more recent excavation on the headland

3

in 1984 produced a magnificent Bronze-Age sword, which is now in the British Museum. Since their pottery and other artefacts had many characteristics in common with those found in the lower Rhineland, it seems likely that these early visitors to Scarborough came there by sea.

Archaeologists are always delighted to find rubbish dumps and in 1923 Simpson discovered no fewer than 42 earth pits, which had been used first to store grain and then relegated to refuse holes. Since some of these pits contained household refuse in layers alternating with layers of rain-washed clay, Simpson concluded that occupancy was only temporary and summer-time, not continuous. He found no trace of dwelling huts.

On the other hand, Simpson did uncover the bones of horses, oxen, and, less often, sheep and pigs, and he found evidence that these people hunted wild animals such as deer, grew wheat, and herded domesticated animals with the aid of dogs. They cooked their meat on open fire hearths and by dropping red-hot stones, or pot-boilers, into water-filled pots set in the ground. Of the many fragments of bracelets, brooches, beads, necklaces and rings found on the site, some were made of local jet. Though Simpson did not find post-holes for the upright timbers of a loom, he did discover seven pottery spindle whorls, two of them edged with fingernail and fingertip impressions.

Human bones from this period were much scarcer than animal: almost all of them belonged to children. However, in Simpson's day little could be learned of the physique and health of Scarborough's earliest summer visitors.

Roman Signal Station

In the year 367 AD disaster struck Roman Britain. Barbarian Picts and Scots from the north and west and Saxons and Franks from across the North Sea shattered its shore and frontier defences. Like an irresistible tidal wave they swept over the whole province. Cities such as Eboracum (York) and Londinium (London) were plundered, towns and villas looted and burned. Though within three years the invaders were defeated and expelled, Roman Britain never completely recovered its prosperity and security.

The new Roman commander-in-chief in Britain, Theodosius, had to find a better way of protecting the province. Hadrian's Wall in the far north and the fortresses of the Saxon shore in the south and east

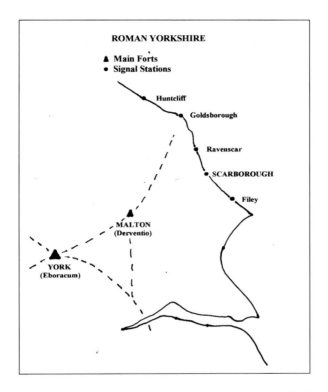

ROMAN YORKSHIRE

▲ Main Forts
● Signal Stations

Huntcliff
Goldsborough
Ravenscar
SCARBOROUGH
Filey
MALTON
(Derventio)
YORK
(Eboracum)

left between them a wide, defenceless gap along the North Sea coast, exposing Eboracum, capital of Lower Britain, and the farms on the Wolds which supplied it with grain and meat. Moreover, since the Romans were now outnumbered and outflanked by their seaborne barbarian enemies, Theodosius judged it wiser to concentrate his main military strength well inland at the legionary base of Eboracum, ready to respond quickly to any new threat of invasion. The success of this defensive strategy depended on the speed and accuracy of communication between frontier and interior zone: the Romans needed early-warning stations.

Consequently, Theodosius ordered the construction of a chain of signal towers along the length of the "Yorkshire" coast. Five of them – at Huntcliff near Saltburn, at Goldsborough, half a mile from the sea at Kettleness, at Ravenscar, Scarborough and Filey – are known to have existed. Two more, at Whitby and Flamborough, were probably the casualties of coastal erosion. Further south, beyond Bridlington Bay, the sea has long since washed away the Roman shore-line.

The siting of the towers at Huntcliff, Goldsborough and Ravenscar suggests that their purpose was to send warning smoke and fire signals up and down the coast, not inland. From Scarborough headland and Filey Brigg, however, the alert might also have been conveyed by intermediary hill beacons to the nearest permanent military garrison at Malton, the Roman Derventio. There, excavations have shown that, after the holocaust of 367, a military fort was rebuilt for a squadron of mounted militia. In the event of a large-scale invasion rather than a mere piratical raid, a whole legion might be summoned from Eboracum, another eighteen miles (twenty-nine kilometres) away. About this time, the Eboracum-Derventio road, now the A64, was widened to fifty-two feet, nearly sixteen metres.

In addition, the Romans probably operated scout ships attached to their fleet stationed in the Humber estuary. Vegetius, who dedicated his work to the Emperor Valentinian I (364-375), described a squadron of fast, light vessels with sails and twenty oarsmen. For camouflage their hulls and rigging were painted sea-green and even their crews all wore uniforms of the same colour. As with the signal towers, the purpose of these naval scouts was to pass on intelligence not engage enemies. Though claims have been made for a Roman harbour at Scarborough, they have not been proved by sufficient evidence.

All five surviving coastguard stations have suffered greatly from natural decay and deliberate destruction, but similarities in size and plan indicate that they were all built about the same time according to a standard design and as part of a common defensive system. The Latin inscription on Ravenscar's foundation stone, discovered in 1774 and now in Whitby museum, reads "turrem [et] castrum", tower [and] fort, and this provided Simpson with his only documentary clue to what he might find on the east cliff of Scarborough's headland.

Sure enough, Simpson unearthed evidence of a square stone tower, rising to perhaps one hundred feet (thirty metres) high, with a ground floor doorway, interior staircases, wooden floors and a battlemented parapet, set in the centre of a square courtyard. Tower and courtyard had been enclosed by a stone wall and beyond that a V-shaped earth ditch. Entrance by a bridge over the ditch and through double doors in the wall was on the landward western side. Turrets at the four rounded corners of the wall and above the gateway might have been used as catapult platforms, but the walls were too low and thin to withstand siege and the tower was too small to garrison more than about half a dozen defenders. Though the eastern ditch, berm and curtain wall had long since fallen away down the sea cliff, enough of the station remained for Simpson to make a full reconstruction on paper. *[plate 2].*

Roman coins found at Huntcliff, Goldsborough and Filey suggested that the watchtowers were manned for only about forty years. At Scarborough only one of the many surviving coins was of the reign of Emperor Honorius (395-423) who, in 410, told the British towns that they must henceforth provide their own security without the Roman legions. Soon afterwards probably all the signal stations were abandoned abruptly, permanently and, in two known cases at Huntcliff and Goldsborough, violently. At Huntcliff fourteen men, women and children had been slaughtered and their corpses thrown down the station well. At Goldsborough two men and guard dog had been killed in a fierce struggle and the tower had been burned to the ground. In contrast, Scarborough's coastguard fort seems to have been evacuated without a fight.

Skarthi's Burg?

Until the twentieth century it was generally assumed that Scarborough owed its name to the rock or scar of the headland under which the early town sheltered. However, during the 1920s several leading authorities argued that the name derived not from a natural feature but from a tenth-century Icelandic Viking, Thorgils, nicknamed Skarthi because he was disfigured with a cleft palate or hare-lip. So Scarborough, they suggested, was originally "Skarthi's stronghold". When this claim was re-examined more recently by an eminent scholar, Mr A L Binns of Hull University, his conclusion was that "the case for associating the name of Scarborough with Thorgils Skarthi" is "quite a strong one" and "the assertion" that Thorgils and his brother Kormak first built a stronghold at Scarborough is "by no means unlikely".

The "assertion" that the name of Scarborough springs originally from Skarthi's stronghold rests on a single reference in *Kormakssaga*, written down about 1220 but describing the exploits of Viking brothers more than two hundred and fifty years earlier.

7

'The brothers harried Ireland, Wales, England and Scotland and were thought very distinguished men. They first established the fort called Skardaburg. They raided Scotland, performed many great deeds and had a large band.'

They were born in Iceland during the 930s and served as mercenaries under Harald Greycloak, King of Norway from 961 to 965. After Harald's death they formed and led a roving band of sea pirates until Kormak died in 967, probably in Scotland. Their brief encampment at Scarborough must therefore have taken place sometime between 965 and 967, probably during the winter of 966-7.

Kormak and Thorgils might well have fortified their winter quarters at Scarborough with a stout fence and earth ditch, but it is not likely that they had founded a community there. Though archaeological evidence of a Scandinavian settlement at Scarborough remains undiscovered, by 966 east Yorkshire had been densely occupied by Norsemen and their families for nearly a century. In 876 a great Danish army had entered York unopposed and soon afterwards most of its members had become resident farmers in the area.

The richness of Danish place-names recorded in the Domesday Book indicates the density and extensiveness of their colonisation of east and north Yorkshire. After the Danes came the Norwegians, though in far fewer numbers and overland from Ireland in the west rather than by sea from the north. Of the 649 North Riding (Old Norse "thrithing" meaning a third part) settlements reported in the Domesday survey, 223 were of Scandinavian origin, and another 66 Anglo-Scandinavian hybrids. In many other cases Viking settlers left the old English names unchanged. If Scarborough was not itself a Scandinavian settlement before 966, it was adjacent to several that certainly were: Scalby, Newby, Throxenby, Falsgrave and Osgodby are now all suburbs of the modern borough. The abundance of becks, kelds, meres, carrs, fells, gills and fosses in the Scarborough locality betrays a strong Scandinavian presence.

In all probability, if Kormak and Thorgils Skarthi had beached their longships on the sands of Scarborough's South Bay in 966, they would have found there a shrinking settlement. Between 919, when it was seized by the Irish-Norwegian Ragnald, and 954, when Erik Bloodaxe, the last Norwegian king of York was killed in battle, Yorkshire had been a key link in a busy route between Dublin and Oslo.

8

However, after 954 Yorkshire had ceased to be an independent Norse kingdom and was reduced to the status of an English earldom; its language, culture and population remained strongly Scandinavian but politically it had become part of England. As a consequence, after flourishing briefly as a port of commercial importance, whatever Scarborough was then called, it returned to marginal obscurity.

If Scarborough was eventually called after Skarthi then clearly he did not deserve such an honour. He and his brother Kormak were no better than sea pirates. They came ashore at Scarborough only to repair their ships, replenish their stores with local plunder and wait for the winter weather to pass. They were not immigrants; they were neither farmers nor fishermen. Their fort could have been no more than a makeshift timber stockade built under the shelter of the headland cliff and close to their precious boats drawn up on the sands.

Nevertheless, the fame or infamy of Skarthi and the literary talents of his brother might have been sufficient to give a lasting name to a place that previously lacked one. If the Romans had a name for their signal station location on the headland we do not know what it was. Oliver Cromwell never set foot within forty miles of Scarborough yet by 1770, more than a century after his death, his deeds had become so legendary that a hill overlooking the town, which had always been called Weaponnness, had been re-named Oliver's Hill. Later still, Oliver's Mount was preferred. Skarthi's stay in Scarborough was short, but in name his "stronghold" is now more than a thousand years old.

Holocaust 1066

Nearly everyone knows that in the year 1066 the English king Harold lost his life in the battle of Hastings at the hands of the Norman invaders under their Duke William. Fewer are aware that three weeks earlier Harold had annihilated another invading army of Northmen at Stamford Bridge in Yorkshire; and fewer still appreciate that a fortnight before that battle these same Northmen had burned down Scarborough and wiped out its population.

The Northmen who destroyed Scarborough, just a century after Kormak and Thorgils wintered there, were led by the king of Norway, Harald Sigurdson, better remembered as Hardrada, the Ruthless; and among Harald's chief allies was Tostig Godwinsson, formerly the earl of

Northumbria and now banished by his elder brother, king Harold of England.

Harald Hardrada was the most feared warrior in Europe and the Near East. Before he was crowned sole king of Norway in 1047 he had established a reputation second to none as a merciless and cunning leader of an army in the service of the empress Zoe of Constantinople. According to Snorri Sturluson, his biographer, in ten years he captured eighty towns and cities, some by direct assault, others by deception and clever stratagem. He had a special talent for reducing defiant towns to ashes. Not content with his kingdom of Norway, which he taxed heavily, he waged war on the people of Denmark, killing, pillaging and burning without pity. When, in January 1066, news arrived of the death of the childless king Edward the Confessor, Harald's rapacious appetite was diverted to a new direction: he would make a bid for the English crown.

In 1053 Harold Godwinsson had succeeded his father as earl of Wessex, and two years later Tostig was made earl of Northumbria. The two brothers were rivals rather than allies; Tostig's appointment owed most to the favour of his sister Edith and to her husband, king Edward. Northumbria was notoriously lawless and riven by blood feuds and the rule of a Saxon outsider in a largely Scandinavian region was generally resented there.

Tostig tyrannised Northumbria with a savagery unusual even for those days. So severe and relentless were his punishments of law-breakers that it was said that a traveller could cross the earldom openly carrying a bag of gold in perfect safety. No doubt the story of how he murdered his brother Harold's servants, pickled their parts, and then invited Harold to dine on them is apocryphal, but it illustrates the notoriety for malice and cruelty Tostig acquired.

However, in 1064, Tostig went too far. Two Northumbrians who had come to his palace at York with assurances of safe conduct were treacherously murdered. The following summer while he was away in the south hunting with his brother-in-law, a revolt against him broke out in York. Tostig was declared outlaw, his house ransacked and two hundred of his guard and servants butchered. The rebels advanced as far as Northampton and plundered Tostig's estate in Huntingdon.

The revolt against Tostig brought England to the edge of civil war. The northerners had chosen Morcar, brother to Edwin, earl of Mercia, as the successor to Tostig, and they demanded the latter's expulsion from the kingdom. Edward and Harold had little choice:

Tostig had to go. Now angry and revengeful, Tostig took his wife Judith and their children to seek refuge with count Baldwin of Flanders, his father-in-law; but he would not accept the humiliation of permanent exile.

If Tostig had hoped that the death of the Confessor and the succession of his brother Harold as king of England might prompt an invitation for his return, he was soon disappointed. Morcar was confirmed as earl of Northumbria. Tostig was still banished from the kingdom. Consequently, when first count Baldwin and then king Sweyn of Denmark declined to help him, Tostig sought the assistance of Hardrada. Early in 1066, at Oslo, they agreed to combine forces and invade England.

Hardrada recruited half the fighting men in Norway. Together with Norse warriors from Iceland, Shetland, Orkney and the Hebrides they sailed southwards down the east coast of Scotland. After Tostig had joined them at the mouth of the Tyne they constituted one of the greatest armadas ever seen in northern Europe – 9,000 men in 300 longships. Pausing only to pillage the coast of Cleveland in north Yorkshire, Hardrada and Tostig led their fleet into Scarborough bay.

Their choice of Scarborough was no accident. Before his expulsion, for ten years Tostig had been lord of the manor and soke of Falsgrave, an extensive estate which included Scarborough. Like Scarborough, Falsgrave and its outlying farms were mainly Scandinavian settlements and no doubt Tostig assured Hardrada that he and his army might expect at least no resistance and perhaps even a welcome when they came ashore there. Tostig was mistaken. The farmers and fishermen in the area might have been descended from Northmen but several generations later they thought of themselves as natives and Norwegians as foreign enemies. Despite the odds, the men of Scarborough refused to submit.

Warning of Hardrada's progress down the coast of Yorkshire had given the local men time to swell their numbers and strengthen the town's defences. The Norwegian king was forced to resort to incendiary tactics. According to Snorri Sturluson's account:

He [Hardrada] climbed up on to the rock that stands there, and had a huge bonfire built on top of it and set it alight. When the pyre was blazing they used long pitchforks to hurl the burning faggots into the town below. One after another the houses caught fire until the town was

11

entirely destroyed. The Norwegians killed a great number of people there and seized all the booty they could lay their hands on. The English were given no choice but to submit: if they wanted to stay alive they had to give in to king Harald. In this way wherever he went he subdued the country. *[plate 3]*

Sturluson probably exaggerated the scale and drama of this event, yet given Hardrada's past record in such circumstances his treatment of Scarborough was all too characteristic; during the previous 35 years he had scorched a trail of terror and devastation from Palestine to the Faeroes. To defy Hardrada was always dangerous and usually fatal.

In this case, however, he who had lived and profited materially by bloodshed died on the battlefield, as no doubt he wished. After the invaders had routed the Northumbrians at Fulford Gate outside York, they in turn were massacred by king Harold only five days later at Stamford Bridge. Both Hardrada and Tostig were killed. In the end Hardrada got only the seven feet of English soil he was promised and allowed by Harold. Of the 300 longships that had carried the Norsemen to Yorkshire, 24 were sufficient to carry the survivors back to their homes.

The holocaust experienced by Scarborough in September 1066 probably explains its absence from the Domesday survey made twenty years later. Since the coastal region of north Yorkshire suffered further destruction by William's Normans in 1069, a Scottish raid in 1070 and a Danish one in 1075, the devaluation and depopulation recorded in 1086 are not surprising. Tostig's dispersed manor of Falsgrave, which consisted of 21 farmsteads as far north as Staintondale, as far south as Filey and as far west as Ruston, in 1066 had been home for more than a hundred families of free men. In contrast, Domesday clerks reported only half that number of men and most of them were poor cottagers. On the day of Edward the Confessor's death, the manor had been worth more than £56 a year; by 1086 the Conqueror's royal manor of Falsgrave was valued at no more than thirty shillings (£1.50p). Either Scarborough had been overlooked or it had become a waste and worthless. It would be another three generations before the reappearance of a community living under the shelter of the rocky headland with the name of Skarthi's burg.

2

GROWTH 1135 - 1307

When Henry I (1100-35) died his only legitimate daughter, Matilda, and Henry's nephew, Stephen, both claimed the throne. Stephen was crowned king, but Matilda and her son, Henry of Anjou, would not accept his title. The result was 19 years of civil war and intermittent anarchy. As the Peterborough chronicler wrote: 'Never did a country endure greater misery...for every great man built him castles and they filled the whole land with their castles'. One of these 'great men' was William le Gros, count of Aumale or Albemarle, and one of these castles was his at Scarborough.

In the long run, however, Albemarle backed the loser. When Stephen died his place was taken by Matilda's son, Henry, who at the age of 19 was already count of Anjou, duke of Normandy and, by his marriage to Eleanor, lord of Aquitaine. Henry II (1154-89) brought power and prosperity to England and it was this first Angevin ruler who gave Scarborough its mighty castle keep and its status of royal borough. Henry's bitter quarrel with the Church led to the murder of the archbishop of Canterbury and a new Christian martyr, Thomas Becket, whose name was taken by Scarborough's second church.

Henry's son and successor, Richard I (1189-99), known as the Lionheart, spent only five months of his ten-year reign in England. He pillaged the kingdom to pay for his Crusade and the £10,000 ransom demanded for his release from imprisonment was a further burden on his long-suffering subjects. For Scarborough, Lionheart's legacy was the doubtful privilege of having French monks drain off its fish tithe and monopolise its chapels and altars.

The soldier-crusader king was followed by his younger brother, John (1199-1216), arguably the most controversial ruler in English history. The black picture of John painted by contemporary chroniclers might have been unjustly dark: all the early Angevins were despotic, ruthless and immoral. However, John was more distrusted and hated than either his brother or his father and, worst of all, he lost Normandy and Anjou to the French for which he was never forgiven by his barons. Secondly, he lost his war with the Church. For seven years England was subjected to papal interdict: its churches were closed; no masses were sung, no marriages or funerals held; and only baptism and confession of the dying were permitted. Then John surrendered and the ban was lifted. It was a humiliating defeat. Finally, in 1215, faced by baronial revolt, John sealed Magna Carta, the Great Charter, which placed the king as well as all his subjects under the same laws.

Henry III (1216-72) was only nine when John, his father, died. Unlike his father he was pious and lavish, a builder of castles, palaces and churches. To him Scarborough owed its castle barbican and a series of charters granted between 1253 and 1256 which established and extended its exceptional rights as a royal borough, international market and seaport. Apart from a brief period of open civil war when Simon de Montfort led a baronial rebellion, these were prosperous times for the whole country as well as Scarborough. Since the Domesday survey of 1086 to the end of the thirteenth century, England's population had doubled from 1½ to 3 million. Henry renounced his family claims in Normandy and Anjou and the king of France acknowledged him as his vassal in Gascony. England and France enjoyed a period of peace. Henry's long reign coincided with a great age in the history of medieval Christianity: the ideals of St Francis and St Dominic were brought to England by the friars; universities at Oxford and Cambridge were founded; and churches were built and re-built in the Early English Gothic style.

Edward I (1272-1307) is best remembered for his conquests of the Welsh and Scots; but whereas the former were permanently subdued by his magnificent castles at Harlech, Caernarvon, Conway and Beaumaris, the latter, under William Wallace, were only temporarily beaten into submission. None the less, Edward was the first direct ruler of the whole of Britain; and he was also the first king to summon two knights from each shire and two burgesses from each of his leading towns to join his councillors, barons and clergy in a 'Model' Parliament.

14

Reconstruction of Albemarle's castle

Albemarle

Scarborough's first summer visitors had camped on the headland's grassy plain; a thousand years later the Romans had built a beacon tower near the edge of the sea cliff; more than 500 years after the tower was abandoned two Icelandic adventurers perhaps made their winter stronghold in its stone ruins; and finally from the cliff-top more Viking invaders had rolled down blazing logs into the wooden, thatched houses below. Three generations later still, Scarborough's promontory caught the eye of another visitor – this time a builder of castles.

When Henry I died in 1135 without leaving a legitimate son to succeed him, civil war broke out between supporters of the two claimants to the throne. Henry's nephew, Stephen, was crowned king but Henry's daughter, Matilda, mother of Henry, count of Anjou, refused to accept him as sovereign. One of the northern Norman barons who took Stephen's side was William le Gros, lord of Holderness, and count of Aumale or Albemarle.

Such was William's reputation for physical strength and size, loyalty and courage that Stephen made him guardian of all the royal lands in Yorkshire; and when Matilda's ally, king David of Scotland, came south across the Tees in August 1138 it was William who led out an army from York to confront the Scots. The battle of the Standard near Northallerton that followed was a great victory for the Anglo-Normans and a personal triumph for William. Stephen rewarded him with the new title of earl of York, though in the words of the contemporary chronicler, William of Newburgh, 'he ruled like a king' in Yorkshire.

The earth and timber, motte and bailey castle was characteristic of this time of exceptional insecurity. All the Yorkshire barons who fought under Albemarle at Northallerton – Walter Gant of Bridlington, Walter Espec of Helmsley, William Percy of Whitby, Robert Stuteville of Kirkbymoorside, Roger Mowbray of Thirsk – had at least one private fortress of this kind. By inheritance and wardship Albemarle had acquired several castles; chief of them was at Skipsea in Holderness with its huge mound nearly 50 feet high rising abruptly from the flat land around it; but the new castle at Scarborough was his own creation.

What we know of Albemarle's castle at Scarborough derives from a unique written source – William of Newburgh's chronicle, which he called 'Historia Rerum Anglicarum'. William was born at Bridlington about 1135 and lived all his adult life as a monk in Newburgh priory near Coxwold. Though well-informed by travellers' tales and his own rich reading, it is most unlikely that when Newburgh wrote his chronicle between 1197 and 1199 he had ever been to Scarborough. What follows is a modern translation of his Latin description of Scarborough and its castle, the earliest description to have survived.

A rock of wonderful height and extent, and inaccessible because of the steep cliffs on almost every side of it, stands into the sea, which nearly surrounds it except at one point on the west where it is joined to the mainland by a narrow isthmus. On top of this promontory is a broad grassy plateau, sixty acres or more, and a little well of water springing from the rock. At the entrance, which is difficult to reach, stands a stately tower. The town below the headland entrance spreads north and south of it and westwards where it is defended by a wall; on the east, however, it is protected by the castle rock and on both sides by the sea. William, nicknamed le Gros, earl of Albemarle and Holderness, observing this place to be well situated for a castle, increased its natural strength at great expense by enclosing the headland with a wall and building a tower at the entrance.

Clearly, Newburgh had been misled, in some respects, by exaggeration. The headland was never sixty acres in area and falls directly into the sea only on its eastern flank. Whatever the extent of the town in the twelfth century it would be many centuries yet before it spread out north of the castle hill. On the other hand, the 'little well of water springing from the rock' probably referred to what was later called the 'Well of Our Lady', a natural supply of surface water which explains the location of the Roman signal tower and its successor on the same site, a Christian chapel built about 1000 AD and destroyed by Hardrada's pagan warriors.

Albemarle might have been 'more truly a king than his master' Stephen but he did not possess the resources of a king. Nevertheless, on the basis of Newburgh's evidence, it has been assumed that the earl's entrance tower and perimeter walls were of stone even though the chronicle says nothing of a stone structure or a masonry wall and the only stone towers yet built in England, at London and Colchester, were the works of William the Conqueror. Even though Albemarle was saved the expense and labour of constructing a great artificial mound at Scarborough it is inconceivable that he needed or could have paid for a circumference stone wall to enclose a headland only sixteen acres in area. As for the earl's tower, Newburgh's final sentence disclosed its probable type:

> But this tower was so decayed and fallen through age that King Henry II ordered a great and noble castle to be raised on the same site.

Since Henry's construction of the keep at Scarborough began no later than 1158 and Albemarle's entrance tower could have been no earlier than 1138, the latter, in all probability, was built of wood not stone, and surrounded by a timber palisade fence inside a ring ditch.

There is no convincing evidence, documentary or archaeological, that Scarborough was re-founded as a settlement during Stephen's reign, though there is a strong possibility that, as at Skipsea, a cluster of houses was to be found sheltering under the protection of Albemarle's castle. All the five Yorkshire boroughs recorded in the

Domesday Book of 1086 – York, Pontefract, Tickhill, Pocklington and Bridlington – were closely related to adjacent castles, though as early as this date only York was a recognisable town; the others were mere villages with freemen burgesses permitted to hold weekly markets. At Scarborough the earliest domestic occupation was probably alongside a natural water course, later called the Damgeth or Damyot, which rose on what much later came to be called Albemarle Hill and ran out into the sea in South Bay.

Henry Plantagenet

The succession of Henry of Anjou as king of England in 1154 marked a defining moment in Scarborough's history. Soon after his coronation he came north to York where Albemarle reluctantly but wisely submitted to him and agreed to restore all his royal lands, including the manor of Falsgrave and his castle at Scarborough, to the crown. The earldom of York was allowed to lapse. William retired to his estate in Lincolnshire.

However, instead of demolishing and abandoning Albemarle's stronghold on Scarborough's headland, Henry now chose the same place for one of his principal castles. During the next thirty years the expenditure on the royal castle at Scarborough, altogether £682 15s. 3d., was exceeded only by the sums spent on those at Dover, Newcastle, Orford, Nottingham, Winchester and Windsor. Most of the money was paid for Henry's 'stately tower'.

Henry's investment proved sound and permanent. The 'great and noble keep', rising to a height of nearly 100 feet (30m.), has now survived nearly eight and a half centuries though fully exposed to wind, rain and frost. It took what was then the heaviest cannon in Europe firing repeatedly and at point blank range to bring down its west wall and roof in May 1645. *[plate 4]* Though never much used as lodging or even last refuge, Henry's donjon was a conspicuous reminder of royal power and wealth, visible at great distances from land and sea.

Just as the headland had drawn settlers and invaders, so now the royal castle attracted a community to service it and enjoy its protection. Henry II made Scarborough into a royal borough. Sometime between 1155 and 1163, both years when he visited York, the king favoured the burgesses of Scarborough with the same customs, liberties and immunities already granted to York. His new castle required labourers and carters to dig its ditches and embankments and to carry its timber and stone, food suppliers to feed its workforce and garrison, and a host of craftsmen, such as masons, carpenters, blacksmiths and plumbers, to build and maintain its fabric. By the end of Henry's reign there are references to Scarborough wool merchants trading overseas, to Scarborough weavers, to Roger the vintner, to Scarborough fishermen, and to town officials called reeves.

In return for their privileges Scarborough's householders had to pay an annual tax to the crown, which was called husgabel or gablage. Each house with its gable end on to the street was to pay fourpence and each lengthways to the street sixpence a year. From Michaelmas 1163 the sheriff of Yorkshire, the king's county representative, began to account for a new income to the crown of £20 a year described as 'the farm of Scarborough'. By 1169 the farm had risen to £30, and by 1172 to £33, indicating that as the castle building progressed on the hill above, below it the town grew rapidly in population and prosperity. After the holocaust of 1066, Scarborough's re-birth owed much to William of Albemarle but much more to Henry of Anjou.

St Mary's

The day before he set sail from Dover, 11 December 1189, Richard Lionheart sealed a charter granting the revenues of the parish church of Scarborough to the abbot of Citeaux to pay the expenses of the general chapter there. Richard's generous gift was made explicitly for the benefit of his soul and the souls of his dead father, Henry II, and his living mother, queen Eleanor, but in the light of Richard's record it seems more likely that his motives were material rather than spiritual. By 1189 the mother-house of Citeaux in Burgundy already had nearly 500 Cistercian offspring, most of them in France. As Richard led his army on the long land route to Marseilles, where he intended to take ship for Palestine, he wanted to be certain of favoured hospitality along the way. So in this curious accidental manner a link was made between Scarborough and a French monastic order which was to last for more than two hundred years.

For Scarborians the association with the Cistercians proved to be a mixed blessing. St Mary's might have been a new church but it was already a rich source of income: there were offerings and gifts made to its altars, rents received from tenants of its town properties and, above

19

all, tithes from the parish. Of these tithes, or one-tenth annual taxes on incomes and produce, only one in particular was mentioned in Richard's charter, that of 'Droguedrave', the codfish caught off the Dogger bank; but even more valuable must have been the tithe on herring which every late summer brought an enormous harvest into Scarborough. Even after 1251 when Robert Ughtred renegotiated a more favourable agreement with the Cistercians, Scarborough fishermen paid a tithe of every fortieth cod and every twentieth herring and other catches.

In 1198 Richard confirmed his original grant to Citeaux and extended its terms in two significant ways. At first St Mary's income had been earmarked to pay only the costs of the triennial general chapter at Citeaux, which lasted for three days; now Richard guaranteed that the Cistercians could keep any surplus after these expenses had been met. Secondly, the king now gave the White Monks a virtual monopoly of all the religious institutions in Scarborough. By this time three other churches – of the Holy Sepulchre, St Thomas and St Nicholas – had been built, but henceforth no new chapels or altars could be set up in the town without the approval of the Cistercians.

The unique presence of the Cistercians in medieval Scarborough brought some benefit. Though several other religious houses, notably Bridlington, Watton and Malton priories, and the hospitals of St Leonard's at York and St Giles's at Beverley, had substantial properties in the town, the Cistercians were exceptionally well represented there. Fountains abbey had land in Sandgate; Byland had houses on Sandside and in Baxtergate; and Rievaulx had a herring house and other buildings in Stainardgate and Cartergate. What is now King Street was originally called Rievaulx Lane.

On the other hand, money that might have stayed and been spent in Scarborough went abroad to France and the residue kept the proctor and his fellow monks in well-provisioned, comfortable quarters. One proctor tried to evade gablage on eight messuages by enclosing them and then claiming that they were only one property. Instead of a payment of 3s.10d. he offered only 6d. When the case came before the king's court it ruled that the proctor should in future pay four shillings a year in rent directly to the crown so that Scarborough was still the poorer for loss of gablage.

John

Lionheart had been a liability for Scarborough: he had alienated the income of its parish church and spent not a penny on its castle. To add penalty to neglect, in 1195 the town was assessed at £100 for its contribution to Richard's ransom. Scarborians must have been much relieved when he died prematurely and was succeeded by his brother John.

Though unintentionally, king John (1199-1216) was one of Scarborough's most important benefactors. By 1212 his expenditure on the castle had reached a total of £2,291 3s. 4d. Most of this enormous sum went to pay for a great curtain wall on the weakest south and west sides of the headland with solid half-round towers at intervals and a hall built against the outer bailey wall. In 1211-12 alone a staggering £780, three times more than was spent on any other royal fortress that year, paid for repairs to the keep, which included a new lead roof. From his first visit in February 1201 to his last just fifteen years later John came to Scarborough four times. No castle in his kingdom was better maintained, better garrisoned and better supplied with arms and food than Scarborough's, mainly because baronial opposition to John was most serious in Yorkshire. Significantly, when the 'northerner' rebel magnates compelled him to seal Magna Carta in the summer of 1215, Scarborough castle was one of the few royal fortresses to hold out for John.

Though the evidence is vague, it seems that Scarborough's population also remained loyal to king John: in 1215 the rebels were repulsed at the town's western wall. Driven by his insatiable need for ready cash John had taxed Scarborough's burgesses without mercy, but in return he had also been willing to sell to them a valuable enlargement of their privileges. After making Scarborough pay 40 marks (£26 13s. 4d.) for confirmation of its charter and 60 marks (£40) tallage – a tax on boroughs that were sited on former royal demesne – when he first came to the town in February 1201, John granted the borough 60 acres of his manor of Falsgrave and the common pasture rights attached to them. Previously, Scarborians had no arable fields of their own; for their supplies of wheat and barley they depended on the neighbouring farmers of Falsgrave and Scalby. From now on the burgesses could be self-sufficient in grain, grind their own flour in their own water mills in

Ramsdale, and graze their own cattle and sheep on the upland pastures of Weaponness (Oliver's Mount).

The Oldborough of Scarborough, originally laid out in a gridiron pattern of streets on the steep slope running down from St Mary's church to the Sandside seashore, was too confined to accommodate a rapidly growing population. John's grant now made possible a permanent expansion of the area of the town westwards into what was already called the Newborough. Always quick to exploit whatever new sources of revenue might be available, John took advantage of Scarborough's growth and prosperity by raising its farm rent from £33 to £76 a year.

Whatever others might have thought of him then and since, Scarborough's burgesses had reason to be grateful to king John. Thanks to his huge investment, the castle had become the most formidable stronghold on the east coast of England, permanently garrisoned and generously provisioned, and his successors were in effect obliged to maintain and strengthen this symbol and source of royal power in a remote corner of the kingdom. Secondly, the presence of a royal fleet of galleys in Scarborough is first recorded during John's reign, indicating that there was now an appreciation that Scarborough could be much more than a castle on a rocky promontory. And finally, whereas previously Scarborough had been merely a part of the royal manor of Falsgrave, in future Falsgrave would become part of the borough and liberty of Scarborough. The child had outgrown the parent and itself had become a parent.

Henry III

The dominating presence of a royal castle was not always a comfort and a benefit to Scarborough's burgesses: on occasions it could be the source of grievance and oppression. During the 1220s when John's son and successor, Henry III, was still only a boy, royal officials in the town supported by soldiers from the castle abused their powers at the expense of Scarborough's defenceless inhabitants. The surviving complaints of the burgesses against the castle governor, his garrison and his under sheriff, Simon de Hal, illustrate the insecurity of these times.

When corn, wine and salt entered the port the sheriff's deputies seized them and paid only half their market value. During the summer herring season the sheriff would come down to the harbour and insist on

The castle keep, drawbridges and barbican walls

taking the whole catch for himself at half price. If any fisherman or merchant protested he was threatened with imprisonment or even house-burning. Cattle passing through the countryside on their way to Scarborough market had been stolen by the sheriff's men, killed for their meat, or ransomed back to their rightful owners. Scarborough's burgesses claimed that they had lost up to £300 of 'bread, flesh, corn, salts, cloths and other chattels'; some had left Scarborough to seek a living elsewhere; and others had been reduced to poverty.

Though Simon de Hal would not be the last sheriff to behave in this way, it was clearly not in the royal interest for one of the king's boroughs to be so terrorized and impoverished. What happened to him is not known, but his malevolent regime was soon ended. During his long reign (1216-1272) Henry III never visited Scarborough; however, due mainly to the many special favours it received, the town prospered as never before.

As a result of a royal grant of 1225 the borough was permitted to levy murage and quayage tolls, the former on carts and carriers bringing goods into the town by land, the latter on vessels carrying cargoes into the port. Carts paid one penny, fishing boats twopence, larger ships sixpence, and the biggest merchantmen one shilling and sixpence. Murage was to pay for the upkeep of the town's defences, quayage for the repair of its harbour. To help the burgesses protect the town Henry granted them 40 oaks from his forest of Pickering. After 1225 royal grants of murage and quayage were regularly renewed for three, seven or ten years. In retrospect the charter of 1225 marked a key moment in Scarborough's history as a major market and a safe haven.

From this time onwards Scarborough harbour began to take shape. A new quay built at the foot of the steep slope and in front of the sandy shore along the line of what has become Quay Street provided a secure landing and mooring place. A new pier of timber frame and stone rubble core running southwards from the headland gave shelter from heavy seas driven by easterly winds. Since no other quay was allowed between it and Ravenser-Odd at Humber mouth, Scarborough came to be regarded by all mariners as an indispensable port of refuge on the North-East coast.

Further royal charters soon followed. One of the most valuable provisions of the charter of 1253 was the grant of an annual fair to be held for 45 days from 15 August (the Feast of the Assumption of the Blessed Virgin Mary) until 29 September (Michaelmas). Coinciding with the annual passage southwards of the gigantic shoals of herring, the fair soon became the busiest fish market in Western Europe.

And it was not only fish that sold in abundance in Scarborough. After one royal order forbade the loading of ships anywhere between Ravenscar and Flamborough except at Scarborough and another closed the hinterland markets at Brompton, Filey and Sherburn, Scarborough soon secured a virtual monopoly of commerce in the region. Farmers as well as fishermen, pedlars and merchants all had to come to Scarborough's weekly Thursday and Saturday markets.

Two more royal charters were both dated May 1256. The first confirmed the extension of the borough's boundaries to absorb the whole of the manor of Falsgrave. Scarborough's burgesses now had access not only to arable fields, summer pastures and the common grazing of Ramsdale and Weaponness but also to the freshwater lake of Byward Wath (Scarborough Mere) and the clean, abundant spring waters of Gilduscliff (Spring Hill).

The acquisition of Falsgrave brought other assets. Previously, Falsgrave manor had been part of the royal forest of Pickering; henceforth the king's foresters and verderers would be excluded and the burgesses hold rights to gather firewood, turf, bracken and whins and hunt the wild game in its woodlands and open spaces. In practice, however, there was no free warren for all: if conducted without a licence from the bailiffs, hunting, fishing and shooting within the liberty risked a penalty fine of £10. To pay for all these additional privileges the crown raised Scarborough's annual fee farm another £25 to £91.

Henry II's original charter had given Scarborough's merchants freedom from tolls throughout England, Normandy, Aquitaine and Anjou; his grandson added to these liberties by granting its burgesses free passage, or freedom from chiminage tolls, through the royal forests.

Scarborough's judicial privileges were also confirmed and extended at this time. The borough's own appointed coroners could try the pleas of the crown in the borough's own courts. Among the wide-ranging powers of Scarborough's magistrates were 'infangthief', jurisdiction over thieves caught in the act; 'gallows', the power to pass and carry out the death sentence by hanging convicted felons; 'pillory', the right to punish lawbreakers by exposing them to public condemnation and ridicule; and 'tumbril', the right to punish offenders by whipping them through the streets of the town. When the king's justices later examined the liberties of the 'men of Scarborough' they found that they also had 'pleas of Withernam', the right of their magistrates to recover unpaid debts by arrest or distraint of goods. Before long Scarborough's own justices had won a fearsome notoriety for carrying out summary penalties and the phrase 'Scarborough warning' had come to have a sinister meaning. As a Tudor ballad later explained: 'This terme, Scarborow warnyng grew (some say) / By hasty hanging for rank robbing there'. Thieves caught in Scarborough might find themselves at the end of a rope without the benefit of a fair trial. 'Scarborough warning' was no warning at all: a blow was delivered before a warning was given. Safeway supermarket now stands in what was once called Gallows Close.

Finally, one right claimed by 'the men of Scarborough' in 1274 and subsequently accepted by the royal justices was 'wreck of sea'. If there were no survivors, any ship or cargo cast ashore between Peasholm Beck and White Nab became the legitimate property of the borough. Such a 'liberty' was frequently abused and remained a source of dispute between Scarborough and central government for centuries to come.

Henry III did more for Scarborough than any monarch before or since. Like his father and grandfather he spent large sums of money on the castle, which suffered seriously during his reign from cliff erosion and storms. In the 1240s the barbican was converted into a formidable stone fortress and the gateway took the form that can be seen today. Many alarming defects in the fabric of the castle were reported in a survey of 1260 but it seems probable that they were the responsibility of neglectful and dishonest castellans. Since these men were neither salaried nor required to live in the castle they usually embezzled allowances earmarked for necessary repairs.

The condition of the castle and the relations between its garrison and the borough deteriorated further during the reign of Edward I (1272-1307). Edward spent his treasure building new, 'state-of-the-art' castles in North Wales. By 1278 repairs at Scarborough were said to be needed urgently at a colossal cost of £2,200. Though Edward held court there in 1275 and again in 1280, his main use for Scarborough castle was as a prison for Welsh hostages and Scottish captives. As for the borough, when William de Percy, Edward's constable, lodged a complaint against the 'excesses and trespasses' of Scarborough's burgesses, Edward refused to renew his father's charters and placed the town under Percy's direct rule. In fact, as a commission of inquiry discovered, the 'excesses and trespasses' were committed mainly by Percy, his family and their retainers. Roads out of Scarborough had been blocked and travelling goods stolen; town pigs had been lured by scattered oats into the castle dykes and then sold back to their rightful owners; townsmen had been forced to work without pay; and merchants had had their cloth stolen. This was a familiar catalogue of crime, reminiscent of the oppressions of Simon de Hal fifty years earlier.

William de Percy was deprived of his post and in 1276 the town was granted a royal pardon and given back its charters.

Edward I did make one substantial addition to Scarborough's many privileges. In 1283 Scarborough was named as one of the twenty 'cities and boroughs' in England invited to send two of their 'wiser and apter citizens' to a parliament at Shrewsbury. York was the only other place in Yorkshire to receive this royal writ. Though Scarborough did not always respond to such royal summons, few parliaments during the next 700 years have lacked a member or two representing the borough.

Friars

The Franciscans were the first friars to arrive in Scarborough. Early in 1240 Henry III ordered the sheriff of Yorkshire to provide them with food for one day a week and sixty yards of cloth for their grey habits. However, they were not welcomed by the town's resident Cistercians, who appealed to the Pope to have them excluded from Scarborough. Consequently, rather than offend the monks, the Franciscans retreated to the rural setting of Hatterboard, just outside the boundary of the liberty, where they remained for more than twenty years.

A generous donation of land on a favoured site astride the Damyot in the heart of Scarborough's Oldborough made by Reginald the Miller proved too tempting to refuse. By 1315, despite continued obstruction from the Cistercians, the Grey Friars were firmly planted back in Scarborough and enjoying a comfortable endowment there. Their church of the Holy Sepulchre, now rebuilt and enlarged, provided a permanent resting place for Reginald the Miller and presented a serious rival to St Mary's parish church. In payment of an outstanding debt to the Franciscans, the Cistercian monks of Meaux abbey in the East Riding removed the lead from the roof of their lay brothers' dormitory and gave it to cover St Sepulchre's roof.

By this time Scarborough had outgrown its original water supply; the borough well, fed mainly by the Damyot, was now both unclean and insufficient. An arrangement was reached therefore between the burgesses and the Franciscans to tap the springs of Falsgrave's Gilduscliff and convey their water by underground, stone conduit down more than a mile into the town. The burgesses and the friars shared both the costs of construction and the supply, though later the Franciscans built their own offshoot pipeline. For the next five hundred years Scarborough's underground aqueduct fed and filled three public troughs, known as upper, middle and lower conduit, with a plentiful flow of clean water.

Meanwhile, the Dominicans, or Friars Preachers, had settled in the town. As early as 1252 Sir Adam Sage had given them their first plot of land and the borough granted them freedom from its tolls. Though again the Cistercians complained that the presence of the friars had diverted alms that should rightly be theirs, the Dominicans soon found powerful patrons. During the following years, due largely to the special favour of Lady Isabel de Vescy, rich widow of John de Vescy, a former governor of the castle, the Black Friars acquired an extensive demesne of more than three acres in Newborough. In addition to grants of land, at her own expense Lady Isabel built the nave of their church, the cloister and the dormitory and in return thereby secured a burial place for herself next to the high altar. However, the Dominicans provided more than preferential graves for their wealthy benefactors; their most valuable service to the town was to pave a new wide road running north and south 214½ yards (195 metres) long giving access to their church. This highway from Haldane's Cross (St Helen's Square) to the northern end of Oldborough ditch was for centuries called Car(t)gate and is now known as Cross and Auborough Streets.

Last and least of Scarborough's friars were the Carmelites or White Friars. Founded in 1319 this severe order was always much poorer than either the Franciscans or the Dominicans. They seem to have suffered at Scarborough from the unwelcome behaviour of neighbours and disloyal servants. One brother was assaulted by three local priests 'so that he despaired of his life'; a carpenter failed to fulfil his promise to build a house for the prior and brethren; and a later prior complained that John Settrington had dumped so much 'manure and other filth so near to the walls of the Prior's house...that the walls became rotten'.

Still, however impoverished and austere the house of the order of the Blessed Mary of Mount Carmel of Scarborough, it did have one of the most distinguished priors in the whole country. First as 'poet-laureate and public orator at Oxford', then as official scribe of Edward I and Edward II for whom he wrote accounts of their sieges and battles, Robert Baston came to be regarded as the leading author of the day. In his youth he had become a Carmelite and when he died he was prior of the house at Scarborough.

There was one custom established by Scarborough's friars, which the Cistercians tried but failed to extinguish. When anyone was about to be buried in a local friary chapel or cemetery the friars would announce the event by 'traversing the town with a hand-bell' calling upon the people to pray 'for the soul of Edward II, chief founder of the Carmelite friars in that town', and for the souls of all the founders of the other friaries in Scarborough. The custom survived until the Reformation.

Long before the friars came to Scarborough the town had two hospitals: St Thomas the Martyr for the poor, and St Nicholas, for lepers. According to an inquisition held in 1298, more than a century earlier, St Thomas's had been richly endowed by the burgesses with a considerable estate of arable land, hall, garth and meadow in Burtondale. However, Roger Wasthouse had ejected the master, brethren and sisters, destroyed the hospital building and sold all its possessions. For many years the hospital lands in Burtondale lay uncultivated and the hospital itself was not re-built until 1296.

Even less is known of the church of St Thomas. Today only a street name survives to remind us of its existence. On the engineer's plat of about 1538 [plate 5] it was drawn only in conventional standard form with a long nave and tall tower, but located accurately just inside Newborough's gateway and wall. A few years later, Leland dismissed it in three words as 'a great chapelle'. A victim of Civil War vandalism, St Thomas's church was totally demolished in 1649. It seems that despite its greater convenience of site it was always overshadowed by Scarborough's only parish church, St Mary's. Newborough never became a separate parish from the old borough.

Though local witnesses claimed that the hospital of St Nicholas was founded by their ancestors, in fact it was the creation of William, abbot of Citeaux (1199-1203), who appointed Bernard as the first master and three brethren and three sisters to pray for the soul of Richard Lionheart and his successor. A century later, the hospital was said to have eight oxen, seven cows, six heifers, eight sheep, ten horses and five oxgangs of land in Scarborough's fields.

By this time the connection with Citeaux had gone and the warden or master of St Nicholas had become an appointee of the crown. Nevertheless, the hospital remained a refuge for lepers. In 1342, when John de Burgh, chaplain, was 'suddenly attacked by the disease of leprosy', had no means of livelihood, and was 'unable through shame to beg among Christians', he was granted 'maintenance for life' by the master and brethren of the hospital of St Nicholas. After the Reformation the hospital was abandoned and reduced to a pile of rubble, but the cliff on which it once stood and the street leading to it are still called after St Nicholas, guardian of children, sailors, merchants and pawnbrokers.

3

DECAY AND DECLINE 1307 - 1500

Many of the events from the death in 1307 of Edward I, hammer of the Scots and the Welsh, to the accession in 1485 of Henry VII, founder of the Tudor dynasty, are best remembered from Shakespeare's historical plays. In Richard II (1377-99), Henry IV (1399-1413), Henry V (1413-22), Henry VI (1422-61) and finally Richard III (1483-5), Shakespeare had more than a little to say about all the kings of late medieval England, except the Edwards, Edward II (1307-27), Edward III (1327-77) and Edward IV (1461-83). Kings and their queens are the central subjects of his plays; their character strengths and weaknesses his main concern: Richard II, ineffectual dreamer; Henry IV, scheming usurper; Henry V, hero of Harfleur and Agincourt; Henry VI, meek and pious; and Richard III, deformed and wicked. Yet all of these are dramatic inventions, not historical rulers, and there is much more to discover about this time than is to be found in the annals of monarchs and over-mighty barons.

One thread that runs through Shakespeare's historical plays is what became known as the Wars of the Roses. Richard II's failure to father a male heir and his deposition and murder in 1399 precipitated a contest for the crown between the royal houses of York and Lancaster which was not settled for nearly a century and wiped out a large number of feudal families in the process. Yet even bloody civil wars, executions and regicide were only some of the misfortunes suffered by the English during these dark years.

The Hundred Years War, which started in 1337 when Edward III claimed the French throne, and finally petered out in 1453, had profoundly damaging economic consequences for the English people. The dazzling victories over the French at Crecy (1346) and Poitiers

31

(1356) won the king and his son, the Black Prince, fame and booty, but their country had not the resources to hold on to their territorial gains and little was left of them when Edward died.

During the reign of his grandson, Richard II, the ruinous war with France went from bad to worse; excessive and inequitable poll taxes provoked the Peasants' Revolt in 1381. The battle of Agincourt was a victory even more spectacular than Crecy or Poitiers, but its benefits were brief. Henry V died before the hollowness of his arrogant claims was exposed by the weakness of the English and the growing strength of the French. When their former allies, the Burgundians, made peace with France, the total collapse of the English cause could not be long delayed. After French artillery annihilated the last English army in Gascony, except for Calais nothing was left of their continental empire.

To add to England's miseries, bubonic plague arrived by sea in 1348 and spread across the whole country during 1349. Initially, between a third and a half of the population died in the epidemic and there were several further serious outbreaks in the 1360s and subsequently in almost every decade. No place was spared: crowded communities, such as religious houses and towns, were the worst affected. Before the Black Death the population of England exceeded 4 million; by 1377, at the time of the infamous Poll Tax, it had fallen to 2½ million; and by 1500 it was still below 2¼ million.

Against this apocalyptic background of destructive civil and disastrous foreign wars, pestilence and death, Scarborough's decline and decay were all too typical of the times.

Riot and Rebellion

There is no truth in the often-repeated stories that Scarborough was burned to the ground by Robert Bruce in 1318 and again plundered by marauding Scots in 1322. However, there can be no doubt that the town did suffer from the revenge of Edward II for the capture and death of his beloved favourite Piers Gaveston.

Early in 1312, after the English earls had declared Gaveston an outlaw and the Archbishop of Canterbury had excommunicated him, Edward sought to ensure his lover's safety by giving him Scarborough castle for life and granting new favours to the burgesses of the town. The castle was one of the strongest in his kingdom and given support from town and harbour could be expected to withstand any assault.

However, Gaveston surrendered himself to the earls after a siege lasting only about ten days. His captors swore to preserve his life in a solemn ceremony that took place in Scarborough's Dominican friary, but a month later they executed him.

Edward was devastated by the loss of Gaveston but it was easier and safer for him to punish the people of Scarborough than to take revenge on his powerful murderers. Consequently, 'for certain causes' not specified in the royal edict, the borough was deprived of all its corporate privileges and brought under the direct authority of the king's appointees. During the next 15 years, for the remainder of Edward's reign, a succession of constables of the castle exploited their dictatorship over the town and on occasions the townsmen retaliated with extraordinary violence.

There is space here for only one example of the turbulence and distress of these years. Robert Wawayn had paid King Edward's new favourite, Hugh le Despenser, the younger, £120 a year for the custody of Scarborough town and castle. Nevertheless, he was soon protesting that the inhabitants refused to co-operate with him: they would not collect or pay his fines and customs duties; they had hired an assassin, William of Filey, to murder him; he had been physically attacked and on one occasion dragged by his hair from his house into the street. Early in 1319 Edward had to send an armed party into Scarborough to rescue Wawayn who was besieged in his own home.

The deposition of Edward in 1327 brought speedy relief to Scarborough. Within days the borough's charters and liberties were restored in full and the burgesses resumed control of their own affairs.

Not that Scarborough's own burgesses were necessarily less greedy, more responsible and more peace-loving than the king's sheriffs or constables. Indeed, what we know of the town's government during the 14th and early 15th centuries indicates that this was a time of insecurity, corruption and lawlessness, and that the principal culprits were Scarborough's own burgesses, not Frenchmen, Scots or royal officials.

The details of Scarborough's constitution before 1356 are unknown simply because six years earlier Adam Reginaldson Carter, then one of the chamberlains, had maliciously torn up the parchments and burned them. At the time, Carter was probably possessed by power-hunger and not the Black Death, which was raging in the town. As one of the small number of self-elected, self-perpetuating governing elite he particularly disliked that part of the old constitution that declared its object was to secure 'the peace and improvement ... chiefly of the middling and poor people of the town'.

Scarborough's new constitution of 1356 bears some resemblance to that of the Soviet Union of 1936: democratic in outward appearance but in practice thoroughly autocratic. On paper the annually-elected borough officers - two bailiffs, two coroners and four chamberlains - and the 36 other members of the Common Hall were to be chosen by 'the whole commonalty' and 'sworn by the consent of poor and middling people'. In fact the 44 members of the Common Hall, arranged and seated in a strict hierarchy of seniority, elected all the principal executive officers entirely from among their own number. Newcomers were allowed in only when old members died or left the town.

Oligarchy need not be oppressive but in Scarborough's case municipal office was often and seriously abused by the town's leading criminals. Principal among these 'malefactors' was Robert Acclom. Time and time again he and his son John were accused of extortion, bribery, robbery, assault and house burglary, but such was their local power they escaped punishment and continued in office. Robert was chosen by the Common Hall to be one of the borough's Members of Parliament in 1369 and elected bailiff by the same body in 1360, 1363, 1366, 1372 and 1380. John was bailiff no fewer than ten times and Member of Parliament in 1373.

The Accloms were outstanding lawbreakers but they were not the only criminal family. Other families at this time with deplorable records were the Sages, the Carters and the Scarborough Percys. Worst of all was a Robert Rillington, an accomplice and business partner of the Accloms, who committed treason in wartime as well as robbery. He bought goods and ships from the Scots, supplying them with victuals, and helped them to attack the harbour and town in a devastating raid known as Mercer's. For this treachery Rillington escaped with a fine of 100 marks (£66. 66p.).

Matters came to a head in the summer of 1381. Encouraged by news of the so-called Peasants' Revolt in the South and violent demonstrations in York and Beverley, a number of Scarborough men took to the streets and attacked the homes of several leading burgesses, in particular those of the Accloms, Carters, Sages and Percys. Robert Acclom fled to the sanctuary of the Franciscan friary; others sought the protection of St Mary's Church. The rising was planned, organised and disciplined. The insurgents wore conspicuous headgear of white hoods with red tails. There was no looting or arson as in London and elsewhere; lives were threatened but not taken. The leaders of the revolt were themselves men of substance driven to action by their perpetual exclusion from local government and the gross abuses of local office holders. No attempt was made to seize the castle.

Nevertheless, after only seven days, Scarborough's 'coup de ville' petered out. The death of Wat Tyler, the leader of the southern revolt, and the end of the disturbances in York and Beverley disheartened Scarborough's rebels. Robert Acclom's house was besieged but not entered. Ralph Standish, who had struck the fatal blow against Tyler, was rewarded by king Richard with a knighthood, 40 marks a year, and custody of Scarborough castle for life.

The ancien regime was fully restored in Scarborough. Though the ruling 40 were fined 500 marks and the rest of the community 400 marks, it seems unlikely that the former ever paid the penalty in full. Indeed, before long, the Accloms and their criminal associates were taking revenge. One of the leaders of the rebels, William Marche, had his home broken into and ransacked, 200 of his sheep and other goods stolen, and his servants beaten up. Two men who were known to have carried out these crimes were arrested but then released from gaol without charges being brought against them.

Robert Acclom's son John and John's two sons, Robert II and John II kept up the family tradition. John I was outlawed for murder in 1386 but soon received a royal pardon; in 1388 and again in 1399 fellow members of the Common Hall returned him as one of their two representatives in Parliament; and in 1397 he paid 40 shillings for yet another pardon, this one for misusing his office of bailiff to trade illegally in 'bread, wine, ale and other victuals'. He died in 1402 a very rich man.

Robert II sat in the Parliaments of 1401 and 1404. When accused of stealing two Hanse ships with cargoes valued at £300 he failed to appear before the justices and the sheriff of Yorkshire reported that he was not to be found! His brother John II sat in the Parliaments of 1421 and 1426 and was bailiff of Scarborough at least four times. Along with others called Sage, Percy and Carter, he was charged with robbing a Danzig merchantman of goods said to be worth £200.

It appears that North-Sea piracy had become the routine

practice of some of Scarborough's richest burgesses. When Robert Rillington died in 1391 his body was buried in a new chantry chapel before the altar of St Stephen on the south side of St Mary's church. He left two ships to pay for prayers for his soul. How he acquired the ships is not recorded. No one could have been in greater need of prayers for his soul than Robert Rillington, though that assumes generously that it had passed into purgatory and not gone directly to hell.

Falling Behind

In the reign of Henry II, when the Crown taxed English towns on the basis of their perceived wealth, Scarborough was placed 19th in value on the list. At that time only three other northern communities, at York, Newcastle and Doncaster, were considered richer. When England's provincial towns were assessed in 1334 for what was known as the Lay Subsidy, a tax levied on the valuations of personal property, Scarborough had slipped to 33rd place. York was then second after Bristol, Newcastle was third, Beverley 18th, and Hull, a relatively new town, already equal to Scarborough. Clearly, at this time, Scarborough was the home of many men of substance. In 1340, when the richest inhabitants of the town were taxed at one ninth of their movable goods, 105 were judged to own possessions of more than one pound in value.

Even by 1377, with 1,393 poll-taxpayers over the age of 14, Scarborough ranked 30th in the list of English towns. Outside London, York was the most populous with 7,248 taxpayers, Beverley 10th with 2,663, and Newcastle next with 2,647. On these figures, Scarborough was then a little smaller in population than Northampton, Nottingham and Winchester, but bigger than Southampton or Derby. When exempted children and clergy are added to the number of recorded taxpayers, Scarborough's total population might have reached about 2,500. However, already by 1377, with 1,557 taxpayers and 24th on the list, Hull had outgrown Scarborough, and other East-coast ports, King's Lynn (3,217), Boston (2,871) and the Great Yarmouth (1,941), all Scarborough's rivals, were now more populous.

During the 13th and well into the 14th century Scarborough had grown steadily in size and wealth, though not as rapidly as some towns, particularly Hull, its chief rival. However, Scarborough's decline in the 15th century was nothing less than catastrophic. When the subsidy rolls of 1523-7 are examined they show that Scarborough's contribution had become insignificant. Whereas all six of its main East-coast competitors, from Newcastle southwards to Ipswich, were still among the top 22 provincial towns, Scarborough had dropped out of the wealthiest hundred. York had slipped down to 14th, but Newcastle was third, King's Lynn 8th, Colchester 11th, Great Yarmouth 20th and Hull 21st. Of the major North Sea ports, only Boston, apart from Scarborough, showed any sign of relative decline: it now ranked 22nd. Assessed for a mere £9. 5s. in 1524-5, Scarborough was considered hardly much more affluent than Whitby, at £7 10s. 5d.

As well as the exceptional lawlessness and misgovernment which affected Scarborough in the late 14th and early 15th centuries, there are many other reasons to account for the town's decay. Like other urban communities, Scarborough was depopulated by the Black Death which first occurred there in 1349 and returned again and again with destructive results. Scarborians certainly benefited from downhill drainage and a plentiful supply of clean drinking water, but during the few years for which there are surviving records of burials and baptism, 1414 to 1418, 1434-5 and 1438-9, it seems that deaths in the parish far exceeded births. Apart from bubonic plague, other epidemics of malaria, tuberculosis, dysentery and typhoid took heavy tolls.

Scarborough's success as a medieval town had depended originally on the presence of a great royal castle; but the declining relevance and value of all castles in general and Scarborough's in particular deprived the town of one of its magnets and sources of revenue and employment. In 1361 Richard Tempest, then castle governor, reported that he had spent £79 19s. on repairs, yet it would require another £2,862 to put right all the damage and neglect of the past half-century. A similar estimate of the colossal cost of urgently needed repairs was made in 1393. Though John Mosdale made many improvements when he was constable from 1393 until 1423, most of them were intended to make the castle accommodation more comfortable not to strengthen its defences. Also, like most of his predecessors and successors, Mosdale was suspected of embezzling money intended for castle repairs.

Scarborough's second asset was it safe anchorage for shipping. However, the foundation of the king's town on the river Hull at the end of the 13th century and its spectacular growth as a principal port serving a wide, deep hinterland damaged Scarborough's maritime market role. Scarborough's own geographical hinterland - the bleak North York moors, the marshy Vale of Pickering and the chalk Wolds of the East

Riding - were never rich enough to make its Thursday and Saturday markets great concourses. Bristol had the textiles of the Cotswolds, Norwich flourished on the cloth trade of East Anglia, Hull had Yorkshire's wool and Derbyshire's lead. Moreover, other medieval towns had cathedrals, abbeys, universities or assize courts, whereas Scarborough had none of these. Nor did Scarborough have labour-intensive industries such as metal-working, textiles or leather making, which would have drawn immigrants from the countryside to replace its depleted population. Above all, Scarborough had poor communications with the interior. Unlike Hull, Newcastle or York, it had no navigable river to link it with potential suppliers or customers. Scarborough's destiny had to be seawards.

One economic development during these years which undoubtedly damaged Scarborough's export abroad was the drastic fall of the trade in wool and the enormous increase in the domestic manufacture of cloth. In 1300 the great Yorkshire abbeys of Rievaulx and Byland, Fountains and Jervaulx, had sent their wool overseas to Flanders and northern Italy; by 1500 their wool was being woven in the West Riding towns of Halifax, Leeds and Wakefield and sold for domestic use by the cloth merchants there.

Since fish was a staple of diet and Scarborough was well placed as a fishing port, the town might well have prospered as a major centre for landing catches and for treating and selling them. However, the fragmentary evidence available indicates that here too there was decline during the fifteenth century. There are repeated complaints from Scarborough's townsmen that 'strangers and aliens' were making most of the profits from fishing in the North Sea. Gigantic shoals of herring still passed down the coast in August and September and the harvest brought into Scarborough for drying and salting, but the fishermen were Flemings, Dutchmen, Danes and Scots. Scarborough fair still functioned but less successfully than formerly.

Scarborough's own fishing fleet was shrinking. In 1414-18 the town had about 40 fishing vessels of various sizes from one-ton cobles to 25-ton five-man boats; by 1440, this number had fallen to 30 and by 1546 there were only 17 altogether. Though Scarborough fishermen had been among the first English to catch cod in Iceland waters at the beginning of the fifteenth century, a hundred years later there were none paying tithes to St Mary's on the 'Iceland fare'. The abbot of Fountains grumbled that his income from Scarborough, derived mainly from the

The Three Mariners House

fish trade, was barely a third of its old value.

Finally, Scarborough was a victim of its earlier success. Though its population had shrunk and its community of once prosperous merchants had declined, it was still burdened with a farm of £91 a year and still subject to paying parliamentary subsidies. The only change made by the crown to the annual farm was that Edward III allotted £22 11s.of Falsgrave's share to the warden and scholars of King's Hall, Cambridge, and his grandson, Richard II, added another £20 a year of Scarborough's share to the same endowment. When Henry VIII refounded and renamed the college Trinity in 1546 it continued to claim £42 11s. a year from the borough.

There is only one, rather surprising, exception to this sad tale of fifteenth century malaise. About 1400, as a result of the continuing war with France, Henry IV transferred the custody of the church and revenues of St Mary's from the monks of Citeaux to the prior and convent of Bridlington. From then on, until the dissolution of Bridlington Priory in 1538, Scarborough's parish church was in the hands of the Augustinian or Black Canons. The building acquired by the canons - nave, west and middle towers and aisles - was almost entirely of the late twelfth and thirteenth century. The only recent additions were the four chantry chapels built against the south aisle between 1380 and 1397. Nevertheless, despite falling population and revenue and the acute insecurity of a country torn by civil war and demoralised by epidemic, the canons embarked on a most ambitious and expensive eastward extension of St Mary's. The new choir was 115 feet long and 53 feet wide with north and south aisles divided into five bays. Since this part of the Church was a casualty of the Civil Wars of the 1640s little is known about it, but in all probability the rich monks of Bridlington not the poor parishioners of Scarborough paid for it, and only they used it.

Richard the Good

If the third king Richard (1483-5) had won and not lost the Battle of Bosworth Field in August 1485 Scarborough might have made a miraculous recovery from chronic decay. No other king of England spent so much time in Scarborough or valued it more highly; his premature death was a calamity for the town. All his benefits were either aborted or withdrawn. His wall of squared stone which was made to enclose Newborough on its western and northern perimeter remained forever unfinished; the 'bulwark' he had built in the harbour with 300 oaks from the royal forest of Pickering was already ruined by the rage of

Richard III's house, Sandside

the sea when John Leland saw it 60 years later; and the charter of extraordinary privileges he gave to the borough was as dead as he was within five months of its confirmation.

Had Richard lived longer Scarborough would have become a

shire incorporate, a status hitherto enjoyed by only London, Norwich, Bristol and York; its port would have become independent of Hull; it would have acquired the staple or monopoly of the wool trade for the whole of north-east Yorkshire; and its new mayor would have exercised the powers of an admiral.

Richard's purpose in granting all these special privileges to an ailing community was to make Scarborough into his principal naval base for operations against his Scottish enemies on land and at sea. Newcastle was too far north and too vulnerable to Scottish raids; Scarborough was preferred to Hull because it was easier to control and closer to York, Richard's power base, and his many castles at Skipton, Richmond, Helmsley, Middleham and Sheriff Hutton. Moreover, Scarborough had a formidable royal castle of its own and was the home of one of Richard's wealthy merchant bankers, Thomas Sage.

In the event all Richard's plans came to nothing. After he and his Queen Ann had lived there in the summer of 1484 no English monarch has ever set foot in Scarborough castle. Whatever his reputation elsewhere, Richard III was the best royal friend Scarborough ever had.

4

REFORMATION AND RECOVERY 1500 - 1642

In the 1400s England was underpopulated and backward compared with its western European neighbours and the population, only about 2¼ million in 1500, did not begin to increase until the 1520s. From then on, despite repeated visitations of plague and the devastating influenza epidemic of 1555-9, population growth was almost continuous. By 1600 Queen Elizabeth had more than four million English subjects and on the eve of the Civil War, 40 years later, Charles I had one million more. However, there was a social price to pay in price inflation, unemployment, vagrancy, poverty and even famine. In the century and a half after 1500 food prices rose eightfold, but wages less than threefold.

In 1485 the battle of Bosworth had effectively ended the Wars of the Roses and allowed Henry VII (1485-1509) to tame the nobility and establish stable government. Henry VIII (1509-47) inherited a full treasury but lacked his father's industrious parsimony. He also lacked his father's good luck in fathering a male heir: 20 years of marriage to his brother's widow, Katherine of Aragon, produced only one surviving daughter, Mary. Henry's relentless pursuit of annulment, prompted by his infatuation with Anne Boleyn and frustrated by Katherine's nephew, Emperor Charles V, whose troops occupied Rome, led to a breach with the papacy. Parliament declared him Supreme Head of the Church in England. In three years 560 religious houses were closed and their lands, valuables and rights confiscated by the crown. A formidable rebellion in the north of England, the Pilgrimage of Grace, was crushed by Henry's deceit and brute force.

During the short reign of Edward VI (1547-1553), the sickly son of Henry's third wife, Jane Seymour, the English church became Protestant. Chantries where masses were sung for the souls of benefactors were swept away; purgatory was officially abolished; churches were cleared of statues and stained glass and their painted walls whitewashed; ornate altars became plain wooden tables; and Archbishop Cranmer's Book of Common Prayer in English displaced the Latin mass.

Though not without resistance, Edward's half sister, Mary (1553-8), carried through a counter-Reformation. England was remarried to Rome. Mary's mistake was to take Philip II of Spain, a deeply resented foreign match, as her husband, and her failure was to die childless.

Mary's successor, Elizabeth (1558-1603), daughter of Anne Boleyn, had better fortune and more sense. She took the title of Supreme Governor of the Church of England, but steered a judicious course between the extremes of her predecessors. She never married. The claims to the English throne of Catholic Mary, Queen of Scots, were ended by her execution; and the threat of foreign invasion blunted by the destruction of the Spanish Armada in 1588.

The succession of James VI of Scotland as James I of England (1603-25) was undisputed, and his reign was one of the most peaceful in English history. His union of the English and Scottish crowns ended centuries of warfare and brought permanent security to their borderlands. James made peace with Spain, survived the Gunpowder Plot, colonised Ulster with Scots and Virginia with English, and fended off the Presbyterians with his Authorized Bible.

His son, Charles I (1625-49), soon found himself at odds with Parliament but his resolve to rule without its financial assistance was undermined by his rash and futile attempt to impose an Anglican church on the Presbyterian Scots. After twice failing to subdue the Scots in the Bishops' Wars, Charles was compelled to re-call parliament. It was this Long Parliament's quarrels with Charles and his chief ministers that eventually led to the outbreak of Civil War in 1642.

Religious Reformation

When John Leland, royal antiquarian and intrepid traveller, came to Scarborough in the summer of 1544 Henry VIII's religious reformation had begun to take effect there. The Black Canons of Bridlington Priory no longer existed and their control of St Mary's parish church, along with its revenues, had passed to the crown; Scarborough's monastic properties, once possessed by great houses such as Rievaulx and Byland and small nunneries like Wykeham and Yedingham, had also been absorbed into the royal estate; and the three friaries in the heart of the borough, of Franciscans, Dominicans and Carmelites, occupying about seven acres of land there, had disappeared altogether.

Of these abrupt and revolutionary changes, the closure of the friaries was probably felt most keenly. Unlike the monks, the friars had lived close to and amongst the townspeople. Though their buildings had little value when they were surrendered in 1539, for nearly three centuries they had provided Scarborians with churches, confessors, burial places and preachers; they had brought its supply of clean water down from Falsgrave springs; they had paved some of its streets; and right up to their dissolution they were being paid by townspeople to sing dirges and say masses for the souls of the dead.

After Leland's visit the Reformation intensified. The abolition of purgatory and the official condemnation of prayers for the souls of the dead as 'superstitious' by Edward's Protestant parliament in 1547 allowed the crown to dissolve the chantries and confiscate their endowments. Chantry priests, who had once said prayers for the dead in St Mary's many chapels dedicated to St James, St Nicholas, St Stephen, St Crux, St Clement, St Christopher, St Catherine and Corpus Christi, were now dismissed and pensioned.

Some homeless monks, nuns, friars and priests were able to retire and lived sufficiently on their state pensions. Some had to find alternative employment. For instance, Richard Chapman, formerly the last warden of Scarborough's Grey Friars, after 1539 had become a chantry priest at the altar of St Mary. Seven years later he was described as 'of lviij [58] yeres, of good condicions and qualities, and well lerened, able to serve cure, having no other promocions but onelye the revennewe of his chauntery'. However, the following year, he lost his chantry, which had been worth 63s.8d. a year, for which Margaret Harwood's charitable gift to him of the new sheet 'that is not sewed' did not compensate.

Most of the chantry revenues were spent on the war with Scotland, but some did go to endow new schools. Across the road (then known as Market Gate and now as Castle Road) from St Mary's on the high ground overlooking North Bay was a mortuary chapel with two chantries dedicated to St Mary Magdalene. One chaplain there, presented by the crown, said prayers for the souls of Richard II and his family, another was responsible for the spiritual welfare of the deceased members of the Percehays of Ryton near Malton. When both of these chantries were dissolved in 1547 'le charnell' chapel as it was then called became the home of Scarborough's grammar or high school. Though William Percehay seems to have disendowed his family's chantry in 1533-4, it is possible that the royal chantry priest's income of six marks or four pounds a year, which had been paid out of Scarborough's farm to the Exchequer, subsequently became the schoolmaster's annual salary.

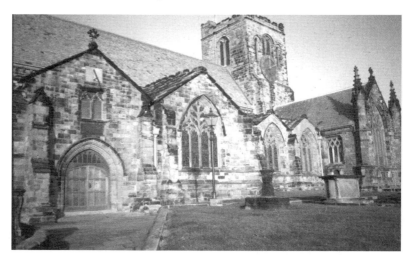

St Mary's medieval chantry chapels and south transept (Farrer's Aisle)

Scarborough's high school for boys only was to exist in one form or another and in several different places until secondary education in the town was reorganised on comprehensive lines in 1973. Its location in the charnel chapel lasted until the Civil Wars of the 1640s destroyed the building. How long the school had existed before 1547 is not known: the only evidence recorded is to be found in the will, dated 1457, of a Scarborough burgess, Robert Wardale, who asked to be buried in St Mary's near the font 'where Hugo Rasen [Rasyn], formerly grammar schoolmaster, was interred'.

Little is known of Hugo other than he had been a Scarborough bailiff in 1422, was elected member of parliament for the borough in the same year, and in 1444 the mayor of Hull tried to secure him for his town's grammar school. That Hugo was not a priest, unlike most

46

schoolmasters at that time, suggests that his office was a secular, municipal and not a church appointment. Even after the Reformation, when the schoolmaster was also the vicar of nearby St Mary's, he was licensed to teach by the Archbishop of York, but he owed his election and salary to the town's ruling Common Hall.

Though the Reformation deprived Scarborough of its three friaries, three of its almshouses, also known as beid or Godslove houses, survived at least for a time. As late as 1575, George Headley, a leading shipowner and master mariner, left 12d. to each of the three poor houses of St Thomas, St James and St Nicholas; but after this occasion only 'St Thomas House' appears in the corporation records. The hospitals of St James and St Nicholas had never been well endowed whereas St Thomas still had its arable and pasture fields and 20 acres in Burtondale. Their rents continued to supply the needs of the town's aged and orphaned children who were considered too young to be put out to apprenticeship.

From 1572 onwards, the bailiffs, as acting justices of the peace, were authorised by parliament to levy rates on the town for the maintenance of local paupers, and its seems that the decision was then taken to bring all of them under the one roof of St Thomas's. Finally, in 1598, the Common Hall decreed that 'Saynt Thomas howse shalbe the house of correction with all the revenues belonging to the same'. Four senior burgesses, William Conyers, Thomas Batty, John Farrer and Roland Marshall, were appointed to act as overseers. Since there are no further references in the corporation archive to this house of correction where vagrants, 'night walkers' and petty thieves would have been put to work, it appears that the project soon foundered. Nevertheless, Scarborough's 'aged, impotent and infirm' paupers continued to be cared for in what was still called St Thomas's hospital.

The church of St Thomas the Martyr survived the Reformation and was to be another casualty of the Civil Wars, but the Franciscan church of the Holy Sepulchre was a victim of Scarborough's poverty as much as religious revolution. In 1544 John Leland had observed at Scarborough that 'the peere wherby socour is made for shippes is now sore decayid, and that almost yn the midle of it'. Without the arm of the great pier to protect it Scarborough's harbour could no longer claim to be a safe haven for either fishing boats or merchantmen. Consequently, the town's governors drew up urgent petitions addressed to King Henry and his successor Edward. As a result, in 1551, Tristram Cooke, one of the borough's leading men who later became its member of parliament,

47

who was then one of the bailiffs, received a warrant from the crown to draw £200 from the treasury 'to be emploied about the reparation of the piere and haven' at Scarborough.

However, in some unexplained way, the warrant was lost and with it the hope of any crown subsidy. In desperation the burgesses ordered that the lead roofs of both churches of St Thomas and St Sepulchre should be stripped and sold to rebuild the pier now 'in ruyne'. One of the bailiffs who signed this order was Tristram Cooke.

The roof of the 'great chapelle by side by the Newborow gate', as a Leland described St Thomas's, was later recovered with slate, but there was to be no salvation for St Sepulchre's. During the next decade its contents were plundered and auctioned to the highest bidders. Bailiff Christopher Conyers was one: he paid £8. 9s. 8d. for the brass lectern 'with one pillican'. By 1564, except for its massive stone foundations, there was virtually nothing left to indicate where a church had once stood. Even its graveyard was let out as a pasture. Only the street name survived to remind residents of its former existence.

Though lectures or sermons continued to be given there on Thursday market days, St Thomas's church now had to concede primary place to 'the high church' of St Mary's on the hill. At the time of the Reformation, John Leland had described Scarborough's 'one paroche chirch ... of our Lady' as 'very faire'. Only five years after the canons of Bridlington had left, it was still in good repair. Leland also noted that St Mary's was a considerable size for such a relatively small community. There were full-length aisles on both north and south sides of the nave, a 'crosee isle and 3 auncient toures for belles with pyramides of them'. Two of these towers were at the western end of the church and the third rose above the middle of the 'crosse isle'.

Had Leland returned to Scarborough a few years later he would have been surprised to see that St Mary's had lost its western towers. In 1555 a violent storm had blown off their lead roofs and, without the money to repair them, the corporation sold the lead at eight shillings a hundredweight or three hundredweights for twenty shillings, and dismantled the towers. Some of the proceeds was spent by the churchwardens on repairs to other damaged parts of the church, in particular its glass windows, but most of it was used to pay for harbour maintenance. Once again, spiritual concerns had given way to commercial necessity: Scarborough needed a safe haven for ships more than it needed ecclesiastical architecture.

Reconstruction of St Mary's at its fullest extent

At the dissolution of Bridlington priory in 1538 the right to appoint St Mary's vicar passed to the crown. Until 1603 Scarborough's vicars, William Newton, Henry Langdale and William Ward, were presented by Tudor monarchs; after then, for reasons which remain uncertain, the advowson of St Mary's came into the possession of the earl of Bridgewater and his heirs. However, neither the crown nor the Bridgewaters were responsible for the fabric of the church; maintenance of the chancel rested with the lay impropriator, who was entitled to the great tithe of fish, whereas the remainder of the building had to be maintained by the parish, mainly out of rents on land leased out by the churchwardens. The churchwardens were chosen annually by the Common Hall from among their members.

During the century after the dissolution neither the lay rector nor the parish had the means to support the costs of maintaining a building which was as grand and as large as a cathedral. Visitation reports to a succession of archbishops of York complained of increasing neglect and dilapidation.

By 1633 St Mary's was said to be in a state of advanced decay. Timbers, glass and lead were all in need of immediate renewal. Stephen Thompson, who was then the rector and therefore responsible for the chancel, rather than re-glaze them had some of the windows there 'walled up'.

This official condemnation by the archbishop's visitors prompted a rapid and radical response. The following summer a programme of major alteration was begun. In effect the chancel was abandoned by the parishioners: its seats, altar and pulpit were removed and new ones erected west of the crossing. Modelled on those recently built at St Mary's, Beverley, new pews were made to fill the whole of the nave, north and south aisles, and the former chantry chapels. By Easter 1635, 155 seats had been finished, rated and allocated to 264 parishioners and their families. Finally, two years later, Stephen Thompson cleared the chancel of its lofts and galleries and sold their woodwork.

A century after it had begun Scarborough had eventually experienced the full impact of the Protestant Reformation. Formerly only the aged had been provided with free seating, now there were free pews only for the parents who had brought their children for baptism and for the boys of the grammar school; everyone else had to pay to sit down. Given that the parish population now exceeded 2,000 there were pews for about only half of them - the richer half. No attempt had been made to accommodate the whole community, even though every adult parishioner was now required by law to attend Sunday services. There was not even standing room at the back for those who could not afford pews. On the other hand, now that everyone of means had a fixed place it was easy for the churchwardens to check on attendance as well as keep order among the congregation now expected to endure lengthy sermons. Significantly, both altar and pulpit had been brought westwards into the nave: the physical separation of priest and people had ended.

Nevertheless, this was the established church of England, not one of the illegal chapels of nonconformist Protestants that were now springing up elsewhere. The seating plan inside St Mary's reflected the political, social and monied hierarchy outside. If Mr William Simpson, vicar since 1630, had his pulpit in the midst of his parishioners, these parishioners were exclusively members of the borough oligarchy: they were the Thompson, Batty, Fysh, Foord, and Headley families who ruled the town. The further away from Simpson the cheaper the pew and the lesser the people occupying it.

Unlike some other seaport towns Scarborough seems to have accepted the new religious order with only a few exceptions. During the Pilgrimage of Grace, John Borrowby, last prior of the Scarborough Carmelites, and Richard Chapman, last warden of the Franciscans there, dabbled in seditious prophecies and rebellious gossip, but neither took an active part in the open resistance to Henry VIII's closure of religious houses, otherwise they would not have escaped the terrible fate of those who did. In 1536 and 1537 the town was twice invaded by rebels from the countryside. However, the burgesses neither hindered nor helped them, though some did take refuge in the royal castle while their homes were looted. For his part in the Pilgrimage, John Wyvill of nearby Osgodby, 'a gentleman of £20 lands', was hanged in chains outside Newborough Bar, but the people of Scarborough hardly needed such a gruesome deterrent. When the chantries were dissolved a decade later, the only opposition to Edward's Protestant Reformation emanated from villages such as Seamer, East Heslerton and Hunmanby, from yeoman farmers and peasants, not from Scarborough's fishermen or merchants.

When Sir Thomas Stafford and about 30 followers used the cover of Scarborough's Thursday market to enter and seize the castle in April 1557, the townspeople seem to have been indifferent to this daring and surprising act of treason. Only two of the conspirators against Queen Mary are known to have had Scarborough connections. What the Privy Council described as 'the lewde traiterous doings of Thomas Stafforde at Skarburgh castell' were opportunistic rather than planned with local support: the royal castle had neither garrison nor guard. Afterwards the local population observed with detached curiosity as, within three days, the earl of Westmorland and his soldiers recovered the castle and sent Stafford and the other rebels off to London for their execution.

One lesson learned from Stafford's short-lived coup was the necessity of retaining a permanent, loyal garrison in Scarborough castle. Early in 1558 the Queen's Council ordered Sir Richard Cholmley, the governor of the castle, to reside there himself or put his son in there 'for the better garding of the same'. Queen Mary's sister and successor, Elizabeth, was less confident of Sir Richard's reliability. Though his attachment to the old faith was discreet, 'the great, black knight of the north' might be tempted to support the claims of Mary, Queen of Scots. At a time when Elizabeth feared a rebellion of northern Catholic lords she could not trust such a powerful man 'obstinant in his religion'. As a result, Sir Richard was effectively ousted from his custody of the castle and replaced there by Sir Henry Gates of Seamer, an utterly trustworthy Protestant; so when the northern earls did rise in 1569 Gates garrisoned the castle at Scarborough with his own men from the vale of Pickering and Scarborough town was identified as 'a very quiet place'.

However, Elizabeth would take no risks with Scarborough. Given the strategic importance of the castle and aware of what had happened there in 1557, it was a priority of her government's policy to keep a close watch on this east-coast port that might be used as entry for Catholic arms or Catholic priests. With these dangers in mind Queen Elizabeth's Privy Council had promoted the career and local influence of Sir Henry Gates of Seamer; he was to be informer and deterrent in an area already notorious for its stubborn recusancy.

From Elizabeth's succession in 1558 until his death in 1589 Sir Henry was the most influential figure in and around Scarborough. He represented the borough in the Parliaments of 1563-7 and 1572-81. As justice of the peace in the North and East Ridings and a member of the powerful council in the north at York, he made sure no Catholic exercised authority within his area. In 1584, when he was told by St Mary's curate, William Taylor, that Thomas Williamson, one of the town bailiffs, seldom went to church, avoided sermons or communion there, and was 'evillie affected in Religion', Gates had him removed from office and imprisoned in York castle on a charge of obstinate recusancy. As the war with Spain intensified and the execution of Mary, Queen of Scots in 1587 brought the danger of an English Catholic rebellion and a foreign invasion nearer, Sir Henry warned the Privy Council in London of the need to strengthen Scarborough castle's defences. In the same letter he reminded the councillors that for the past 17 years he had maintained a presence at the castle out of his own purse. To underline his warning he also referred to what he described as the 'unsettled affections of divers of the inhabitants' of the town without identifying any of them. In the event, the following year, the defeated Spanish Armada, running for home, passed by but made no attempt to land at Scarborough.

After the death of Sir Henry his eldest son Edward took his place at Seamer and elsewhere in the locality. For the previous ten years he had sat on the justices' benches of the East and North Ridings and for the previous five he had been constable of Scarborough castle. He sat for Scarborough in the House of Commons in 1571 and was again chosen as one of the borough's burgesses in 1589 and 1593. Like his father he saw to it that Scarborough, unlike Whitby, which had become a place of entry and refuge for Catholic priests, remained safely and overwhelmingly Protestant.

However, Edward was never able to wield the same authority in Scarborough as his father had done; and from 1596 he was eclipsed there by the new lord of the neighbouring manor of Hackness, Sir Thomas Posthumous Hoby. Like Sir Henry Gates, the third husband of Lady Margaret Hoby was a southern gentleman of the strongest Protestant persuasion who had been promoted by the highest in the land to keep an eye on Yorkshiremen with doubtful loyalties.

But there were few Catholics in Scarborough for Hoby to persecute, and he found no quarrel with the conscientious way the bailiffs and churchwardens there enforced the religious laws of the land. Scarborough was a model of conformity. Persistent absentees from St Mary's were fined; a few papists, who obstinately refused communion, such as William Lawson in the 1620s and John Wolfe in the 1630s, were punished according to the severe penalties against recusancy. Townspeople who failed to pay their penny Easter dues to the vicar were excommunicated; parents who allowed their noisy children to disturb church services were fined sixpence; and nobody above the age of seven could be educated anywhere in the town but at the grammar school whose headmaster was licensed by the archbishop of York and approved by Sir Thomas Hoby.

Scarborough's bailiffs could not punish every absentee from St Mary's Sunday services, particularly since many of them as fishermen and merchant mariners were legitimately at sea, but they came down heavily on residents who conspicuously flouted Sunday observance laws. During the 1620s and 1630s penalties were inflicted by the court for playing 'att coit[s]', 'playing at football', 'playing at knacks', and even just 'playinge on the sand' during 'sermon tyme'. Whether it was 'carying burdens of wood and coles', 'gathering roapes', 'traveling towards Semer fair' with a backpack, or just rowing a boat in the harbour, employment of any kind was forbidden on Sundays. Even in the privacy of your own home it was unwise to entertain friends with drink or games if it happened to be a Sunday.

Consequently, when the archbishop's visitors inspected the moral and spiritual behaviour of the town in 1633 they could find only one persistent recusant, John Wolfe, the tanner, only two habitual absentees from church, only three cases of fornication, and only three cases of ill conduct in St Mary's during the times of divine service. It seemed that Scarborians were not just outwardly conformist, they were also well disciplined and law-abiding.

Economic Revival

Scarborough had sacrificed the church of the Holy Sepulchre and the lead roof of the church of St Thomas the Martyr to save its harbour from ruin and its economy from bankruptcy; but the sacrifice proved only a temporary stop-gap to a chronic problem. There was a limit to the number of times a wooden pier could be patched and mended. As St Sepulchre's was being razed to the ground a lengthy petition for assistance was addressed by the bailiffs to Queen Elizabeth.

First, the Queen was informed that the harbour at Scarborough depended utterly for its security on the strength of its pier. The present pier, 800 feet long and 20 feet wide, was essential to protect ships from 'the raginge sea', particularly if the wind blew from the east or north-east; but the town was now too poor to maintain it. Not only was this pier vital for Scarborough's own seamen it provided the only safe haven between Tyne and Humber 'for all the fysheers and shyppes that passe from Scotland, Burwyke or Newcastle south warde and likewise for such as passe the contrarye waye'.

Next, Elizabeth was reminded, rather bluntly, that she had a personal interest in Scarborough's survival. Of the £91 her treasury expected annually from the borough as its fee-farm rent, all but £14 arose directly or indirectly from the profits of fishing. The Queen's income from Scarborough's parsonage of £40 a year was largely derived from the tithe on fish. Moreover, her rents of £50 a year from former religious houses in the town and the £33 6s.8d. she received when the borough paid a parliamentary subsidy would not be forthcoming if Scarborough's economic decline was not halted. Without the assurance of a secure anchorage there foreigners would no longer bring in their fish to be salted, dried and sold, and the Queen could no longer be guaranteed the 4,000 Scarborough fish she received every year at half the market price.

Rather than rebuild the existing wooden pier the bailiffs promised to construct an entirely new and much stronger stone structure at a cost of £1000. The new pier would be 60 feet wide at the base tapering to 15 feet broad at the top with blocks of stone on the outside and well - filled with stone rubble at its core. Such a gigantic mole, the bailiffs argued, would be so durable 'as it shulde be like to contynewe forever withowte muche more helpe'. However, for any future repairs to this pier that could 'never be moved' or 'much impaired by any rage of water', they asked the Queen to allow them the incomes of Scarborough and Filey parsonages!

Two years later, the Queen granted the town £500 in two equal instalments, 100 tons of timber from the royal forest, and six tons of iron. It was scarcely enough for what was planned and Scarborough desperately needed. Though the new stone pier was built it took 20 years to complete a length of just over 800 feet and £2000 to pay for it. Anchorage dues paid by users – a shilling for merchant ships, eight pence for the deep-sea fishing boats, and two shillings a year for every fishing boat - raised less than repairs cost. One section of the pier of 35 feet cost £92 10s. to rebuild after storm damage. The bailiffs had to employ a permanent workforce of 'keymen' to undertake maintenance.

In fact there never would be an end to such repair and maintenance work. The pier was built on clay not bedrock and could not withstand the prolonged effects of tide, gales and salt water without constant attention. Also, neither the town nor the crown had sufficient resources to bear the expense of permanent upkeep. The crown had other pressing priorities and the town was caught in a downward spiral; the poorer it became the greater its neglect of the pier, and if the harbour lost its reputation for safety Scarborough would become little more than a fishing village by the sea.

By the end of Elizabeth's reign Scarborough's decline had accelerated. Even when allowance is made for the exaggeration in the bailiffs' petitions - one claimed that the town was 'greatly depopulated, 3 parts thereof, to the number of 600 tenements being utterly ruinated' - other less partisan witnesses observed 'great povertie' in the town. At least king James was sufficiently convinced to excuse Scarborough from one of the two subsidies of £33 6s. 8d. authorised in 1601 but still unpaid in 1605. On the other hand, he was not sympathetic enough to discount any of Scarborough's fee-farm rent of £91 or to contribute to the upkeep of its harbour.

In the end it was coal that saved Scarborough harbour, not the town or the crown. On All Saints' day 1613, 'a sore and sudden storme and tempest' broke through the port's defences tearing a wide gap in its great pier. There was nothing extraordinary about such an event, but the reaction to the damage that had been done was unprecedented. During the next few weeks petitions poured in from the east-coast ports - from Newcastle, Hull, King's Lynn, Great Yarmouth, Ipswich, Harwich, Colchester, London and several others. In the words of the Hull petition, all of them pointed out that the 'peeres of Scarbrough lieth soe fytlie for shipps and vessells to come to or harboure their in any distresse ... their beinge noe other convenient or safe harboure for shipps betwixt Humber and Tynemouth'. Consequently, all of them argued that it was imperative to repair and strengthen the pier without delay; and some even suggested that Scarborough's harbour defences were so valuable that in future they should be paid for by a general levy on east-coast shipping.

What none of the petitioners mentioned was their great and ever-growing interest in the coal trade. As early as 1379, the crown had authorised a tax of sixpence on every ton of coal leaving Newcastle by sea, the proceeds to be used to pay for the defences of Scarborough 'contra inimicos Gallicos' [against the French enemies]. However, there is no evidence that this was anything more than a temporary wartime measure. Yet by 1613 the trade in sea-coal had become considerable and was growing rapidly. There were now as many as 400 English colliers engaged in bringing coal from the banks of the rivers Tyne and Wear down the coast to home ports and across the North Sea to continental customers. Exports of coal from Newcastle and Sunderland rose from nearly 200,000 tons in 1600 to nearly half a million tons by 1630. Coal had already replaced wood as the principal fuel in homes, factories, breweries, tanneries and many other industries such as alum and salt-making.

All this explains why Scarborough's own petition to the Privy Council received such a prompt and positive reply. In April 1614 Scarborough was granted a levy of 4d. on every voyage of ships under 50 tons and 8d. on every one made by ships over 50 tons burthen trading up and down the coast between Newcastle and London. Foreign vessels were not exempt. In practice Scarborough's 'pier money' was a duty on the coal trade gathered at Newcastle and Sunderland and then sent on to the borough's coroners who were the officers responsible for the quay and piers.

From now on, except during the Civil Wars, Scarborough harbour was never short of funds. As the coal-carrying trade grew year by year, the 'moneyes ariseing att Newcastle and Sunderland' provided more than was needed to keep the stone quay and piers in good condition. 'Mr coroners peare money' became a permanent reserve to be 'borrowed' for every conceivable use from mending St Mary's windows to providing the Common Hall with Christmas feasts.

In other ways too the beginning of the seventeenth century marks a recovery in Scarborough's fortunes: the long steep decline since the middle of the fourteenth century was halted. Though there are no demographic figures to compare with the poll tax records of 1377, 200 years later the little evidence that survives points to continued depopulation. The burgesses were now complaining that their impoverishment was the direct consequence of the reopening of Seamer's weekly Monday market in 1577, but as Sir Henry Gates argued convincingly Scarborough's decay had much deeper and older causes and had occurred long before 1577. In the 1520s the town had 700 households whereas during the next 30 or 40 years 'ther were decrease 400'. Where once there had been buildings now there were empty spaces. Sir Henry was too good a Protestant to refer to the damaging effects of the closure of Scarborough's religious houses and chantries, yet clearly the Reformation had created those waste areas in the old town.

Sir Henry's explanation for Scarborough's misfortunes is impossible to verify or disprove. According to his partisan claim the people of the town had caused their own downfall by forsaking profitable engagement in fishing, salting, net, rope and sail making, for such doubtful occupations as 'engrossing corn'. Both foreign and English traders had abandoned Scarborough except 'in tyme of distresse of wether' because they were denied there a free market and fair prices by the bailiffs and 'their consorts'. Even worse, the same corrupt and dishonest rulers of the borough had embezzled anchorage and pierage dues, neglected necessary repairs to the harbour and then had the effrontery to petition Her Majesty for pier money.

Whatever the truth of Sir Henry's allegations against them, Scarborough's burgesses reacted vigorously to his Monday market at Seamer. Only four miles inland from the coast, Seamer was better positioned than Scarborough to be an exchange market for the cattle and sheep of the moors and vale and the corn of the wolds. In winter especially the roads into Scarborough were often impassable and the artificial monopoly enjoyed by Scarborough's Thursday and Saturday markets for the past 300 years was at last being challenged. After Seamer market opened the sale of wheat in Scarborough collapsed and that of hides from Malton, Pickering and Whitby ceased altogether. The alarm bells had already begun to ring when William Fysh, one of Scarborough's richest merchants and landowners, had started a shop in Seamer. Scarborough's Common Council reacted by forbidding any townsman to attend, buy or sell in Seamer market on pain of imprisonment, a fine of ten shillings and the loss of all burgess rights in the borough.

The death of Sir Henry brought a lull: Scarborough's 44 elected Edward Gates and William Fysh to represent the borough in the parliament of 1589, and after the death of William in 1591, they chose Edward again in 1593. But it was only an armistice not a peace: Gates revived the market at Seamer and the controversy with Scarborough in 1594. The marathon dispute dragged on until 1602. Though it cost the borough up to £2000 in legal fees and costs, in the end Scarborough won and Seamer market was closed permanently.

The significance of this commercial warfare between Seamer and Scarborough was that it illustrated how weak and vulnerable the borough had become in the last years of Elizabeth's reign. The case had passed through almost every court in the land - the Exchequer, the Council in the North at York, the Queen's Bench, and the Queen's Privy Council - and the Gateses had come close to victory. If they had won the history of Seamer would have taken a different course: instead of remaining a village it would have grown into a market town comparable to Malton or Pickering. Scarborough, on the other hand, would have turned its back on the hinterland to become only an isolated seaport.

The Gateses lost because they had no allies to match Scarborough's. In 1597, instead of re-electing Edward Gates to the Commons, Scarborough's burgesses had chosen Sir Thomas Hoby of Hackness, a newcomer to the locality. Hoby was anxious to exert his authority and in particular to make Hackness, not Seamer, the seat of local power. In the same year Scarborough also benefited from the appointment of the Earl of Nottingham, lord high admiral and commander of the English fleet against the Spanish Armada, as the borough's high steward. As England's senior naval officer no one had a better appreciation of Scarborough's value as a harbour of refuge and a port of entry for seaborne enemies. When it came to a choice between Scarborough and Seamer the Admiral had no hesitation in favouring the interests of what he described as 'a place of good importance'.

Finally, as the bailiffs had already emphasized to the Queen in their petition for pier money in 1564, she had a vested financial interest in Scarborough's prosperity. For the rectories of Seamer, Cayton and Ayton, the Gateses paid only £34. 9s. a year into the treasury, a small contribution compared with Scarborough's farm, parsonage, subsidies and royal properties.

In the end the Gates family were silenced with money, or at least promises of compensation. In April 1602 the Common Hall voted to give £100 to Edward Gates and his heir Henry, £20 at Michaelmas, £20 at the next Annunciation (25 March 1603), and £10 on each of the following six Christmas days. However, there is no record that they received more than a small fraction of it. In the event, now sorely strapped for cash, Edward Gates first granted a 99-year lease on the Seamer estate to Sir John Thornburgh, and soon afterwards together they sold all their interest there for £200 to Thomas Mompesson, a land speculator and profiteer. It seems that the prolonged struggle with Scarborough had done more injury to the Gates family than to the borough.

However serious or superficial the challenge of Seamer's market had been to Scarborough's economy, there is no doubt that the latter's fortunes improved slowly but steadily after 1602. In the past Scarborough's maritime commerce had suffered severely from repeated wars with the Scots, the French and the Spanish; but now the union of the two crowns under James I and VI and the peace treaty of 1604, which ended the 20-year war with Spain, brought welcome freedom and safety to North Sea trade and fishing.

Without the assistance of any original parish registers before 1682 and depending almost entirely on fragments of bishops' transcripts, any estimate of Scarborough's population is necessarily approximate; however, during the years 1602 to 1642 it seems that there was a gradual and significant increase in the number of residents. Between 1602 and 1606 the average number of annual baptisms at St Mary's was 54; during the years 1626 to 1629 inclusive it was 73; and for the years 1632 to 1639 this figure had risen to 87. From 1602 to 1639 the average number of marriages performed annually at the parish church trebled. During these years the people of Scarborough suffered from at least three epidemics of plague but only during the worst visitation in 1635-6 did recorded burials exceed the number of recorded baptisms. On the basis of these figures, the population of the parish might have grown from less than 2,000 at the beginning of the century to nearly 3,000 on the eve of the Civil War four decades later.

Scarborough's growth in population reflected a gradual restoration of commercial activity during these years. The spectacular rise of the national coal trade did more than rescue Scarborough's harbour: it also brought new business to Scarborough's own shipping. In 1600 no Scarborough ship was employed in the coal-carrying trade; in 1625, 75 cargoes were transported by Scarborough colliers; and by 1639, of the 154 cargoes of coal imported into Scarborough harbour, 138 were in home vessels. Though coal was by far the most valuable commodity conveyed in Scarborough ships, during the same years there was also a recorded increase in other cargoes: cloth, malt, beer and barley went out abroad, mainly to Scotland, deals and tar came in from Norway, raisins, prunes and iron from Rotterdam and apples from Ostend and Dunkirk.

Finally, though Scarborough, unlike Whitby, had no alum industry on its doorstep, ready supplies of cheap coal stimulated new productive enterprises in the town. Whale and seal blubbers were boiled down to make 'train oil', which was used as fuel for lamps and to make candles and soap. Scarborough's 'oyle house' was at the southern end of St Nicholas Gate where the present Town Hall is situated. Coal was also used as fuel to boil sea water to produce salt, a commodity much in domestic demand as well as in the town's flesh and fish shambles.

Oligarchy

From the time of Henry VII's confirmation of Scarborough's medieval charters to the outbreak of Civil War 150 years later there was remarkably little change in the town's form of government. Scarborough remained a closed oligarchy where only the names of leading families changed: Percy, Bedome, Lacy, Langdale, Cooke and Shilbottle gave way to Fysh, Batty, Headley, Peacock, Conyers and Harrison, but they occupied the same offices and exercised the same powers. Occasionally and briefly some representative of the families, such as Tristram Cooke in 1554-5, William Fysh in 1589, and John Harrison in 1628-9, sat as burgesses in the House of Commons. These were exceptions, however: normally Scarborough's two parliamentary seats were occupied by east Yorkshire landed gentlemen with names such as Strickland, Eure, Gates, Hoby, Hotham and Cholmley. The only outstanding break in this routine was the extraordinary dominance in Scarborough's affairs achieved by the Thompsons in the first four decades of the 17th century and the vain attempt by Sir Thomas Posthumous Hoby of Hackness to destroy it. In the end Scarborough's constitution remained unchanged and its oligarchy survived intact

The earlier Thompsons were gentlemen farmers with principal estates at Humbleton in Holderness and at Kilham on the Wolds. The first to make his mark in Scarborough was Christopher. Altogether he was elected bailiff six times between 1588 and 1617. He had the status and the means to take Isabel Hutchinson as his wife. She was the eldest daughter of Edward Hutchinson of Wykeham Abbey (1543-91), who was granted arms in 1581, and sister of Stephen Hutchinson (1573-1648), who sat for Scarborough in the parliament of 1626, and of Thomasin Hutchinson. Thomasin was wife to John Farrer and is better known as Mrs Farrer, who discovered the medicinal qualities of Scarborough's spa waters in the 1620s.

After the death of Christopher Thompson the elder, his brother William became pater familias. William served as town bailiff eight times between 1586 and 1630 and sat for Scarborough in the first parliament of Charles I. William's two sons, Francis and Richard, and Francis's two sons, Stephen and Christopher, were all members of Scarborough's elite, the First Twelve, when William died in 1637. For the next four years in succession one of the Thompsons was Scarborough's senior bailiff.

By then the Thompsons also owned Scarborough castle, which had passed from the crown first to John Ramsay, the earl of Holderness, and afterwards had been bought from him in 1630 by Francis. Once an impregnable fortress, after decades of neglect Scarborough castle had become derelict, valued only as a cow pasture and playground for the more adventurous boys of the town. Along with the castle grounds, which included dykes and holms, the Thompsons had also bought a major leasehold interest in the royal manor of Northstead. In 1609 William had paid £670 for half the manor of 200 acres and three years later his son Francis acquired a lease on another quarter. Though members of the royal family continued to hold the lordship of Northstead - Charles I gave it to his wife Henrietta Maria and their son Charles II did the same favour for his queen, Catherine of Braganza - the Thompsons held on to the lease until the 1780s

Not satisfied with the extent of their control of Scarborough's business, property and politics, the Thompsons had tried to carry out a complete family takeover of the town on the accession of Charles I. In 1626 a new royal charter reduced the borough's ruling body from 44 to 14. Instead of two bailiffs, two coroners, four chamberlains and three benches of twelve each, there were to be only a mayor, a coroner and twelve aldermen. Stephen Hutchinson was named in the charter as the first mayor, John Farrer, his brother-in-law, was to be coroner, and five of the aldermen were Thompsons. Since all the aldermen were chosen for life, and future mayors and coroners were to be chosen annually by the aldermen and only from among their number, the new charter would have put Scarborough under the rule of one extended family.

However, the Thompson tribe had underestimated or ignored Sir Thomas Hoby. His intervention effectively killed the charter and, encouraged by his success, he then attempted to discredit the Thompsons by claiming that they had broken the old rules of election by excluding non-residents from the body of the corporation. If Hoby's action in Star Chamber was meant to drive a wedge between the Thompsons and the other members of the oligarchy, then it failed. The Common Hall stood unanimously behind the Thompsons. Secretly, they even agreed to pay their legal costs. Hoby had to drop his suit. When he persisted with his vendetta against the Thompsons, Sir Thomas Wentworth, then lord president of the council in the north, intervened to reprimand Hoby and call a halt to his campaign.

Hoby's final gesture was conciliatory. In 1636, four years before his death, he presented the corporation with a magnificent silver mace. A year later, when William Thompson, his enemy, died, he left only three rather commonplace silver bowls to the same corporation. In one sense at least Hoby had beaten the Thompson godfather: more than three and a half centuries later, his silver mace is still carried proudly before Scarborough's mayors, whereas Thompson's tumblers are almost hidden away in one of the Town Hall's dusty cabinets.

5

CIVIL WARS 1642 - 1660

The first Civil War lasted from 1642 until 1646. The opening campaigns were indecisive: King Charles failed to secure the military arsenal and port at Hull, and the only battle between the two sides at Edgehill in Warwickshire settled nothing. The Royalists retired to winter quarters at Oxford. Parliament held London, East Anglia and the south-east of the country; generally speaking, the further away from the capital the greater the loyalty to Charles. Given the capital's manpower, wealth and credit, the King's failure to retake London made almost certain his eventual defeat. Parliament's control of the navy allowed them to supply their outposts by sea yet denied the Royalists uninterrupted supplies and reinforcements from the continent. The battles of 1643 still left the two fairly evenly matched, but the crushing defeat of the King's nephew, Prince Rupert, in the biggest battle of the whole war on Marston Moor near York in July 1644 turned the balance in Parliament's favour. In 1645 Charles lost the last major engagement at Naseby and the following year was taken prisoner.

However, there was a heavy price to pay for Parliament's victory: to win the alliance of the Scots, Parliament had promised to dismantle the English church and substitute a Scottish Presbyterian form of government and worship, a prospect that was greatly resented and resisted in England especially by Parliament's New Model army. When the King made a secret pact with the Scots they invaded England in 1648. The second Civil War was soon over. General Oliver Cromwell routed the Scots at Preston and isolated risings in Kent, East Anglia and Yorkshire were quickly suppressed by the army. In January 1649 Charles was put on trial for his life, found guilty of betraying his people and beheaded at Whitehall, much to the dismay of most of his subjects.

From 1649 to 1660 England was a republic for the first and last time. Monarchy, House of Lords and Church of England were all abolished; Scotland was fully integrated into Britain; and the Irish Catholics crushed by an army paid for out of the sale of Crown and church lands and led by its commander since 1649, Oliver Cromwell.

Between 1653 and his death in 1658 Britain was effectively ruled by Cromwell as Lord Protector and head of state. During the Protectorate Cromwell's unbeaten army and superb navy were admired and feared throughout the world. The mighty Dutch were beaten at sea; and a war against Spain yielded much American silver, Jamaica and Dunkirk. At home, however, the Lord Protector had little success: none of his religious or constitutional ideals found popular support and a 'reformation of manners' could not be imposed by the military rule of 'Major-Generals'. Yet, when offered the crown, Cromwell refused it. After his death the republic soon collapsed in chaos and bankruptcy. His successor son, 'Tumbledown Dick', lacked Oliver's authority and experience and lasted less than 12 months. In 1660 one part of the army under General Monck marched on London, and a new parliament invited Charles II to return from exile. The revolution had ended.

Parliament's Outpost

Though by 1642 Scarborough had begun to recover some of its former prosperity, in relative terms it was still little more than a quiet backwater. The great stone harbour pier was now in good condition, but as a commercial port Scarborough had been outgrown by neighbouring Whitby, and even Bridlington had as much foreign trade. Both these rivals had profited from the removal of monastic control which Scarborough's port had never experienced.

In population and buildings Scarborough was still no bigger in 1642 than it had been in 1377 when 1,393 adults had paid the poll tax. From Newborough and Oldborough Bars, the town's main landward entrances and exits, down to Sandside on the seashore the distance was less than 300 yards, yet within even this small area there were gardens, orchards, wastes and pastures. Where the three friaries had once stood a century earlier, there were still open spaces. What the Franciscans had called Paradise was still pasture and garden. The site of the church of the Holy Sepulchre was now leased out for animal grazing by St Mary's churchwardens, and in the shelter of Richard III's unfinished rampart and stone wall there was now a bowling green.

Beyond Newborough Bar were open arable fields and enclosed pastures. Falsgrave was half a mile away on the road to York. What much later were to become residential districts - Wheatcroft, Holbeck, Garlands, Burtondale and North Leas - were then distant farmlands. With annually-appointed officers called pasture masters, warrener, and netherd, and the chief governors still known as bailiffs, Scarborough retained many features of a village by the sea. Its status as a royal borough seemed anachronistic.

When ship money was first levied on the whole country in 1636 Newcastle, King's Lynn and Hull were assessed for £700, £300 and £140 respectively, whereas Scarborough was required to raise only £30. Of the eight other Yorkshire towns separately charged, York was assessed at £520, Leeds at £200, Doncaster at £100, Pontefract at £60, Beverley at £57, Richmond at £50 and Ripon at £40. Only Hedon, expected to pay £20, was judged poorer than Scarborough. Perhaps the assessment under-estimated Scarborough's wealth, but by 1642 there were at least fifty English towns with populations greater than Scarborough's.

Scarborough still had two members in the House of Commons. However, whereas these two seats had once been a quarter of Yorkshire's total representation, when the Long Parliament opened in 1640 the county's representation had grown to thirty. Since the reign of Henry VIII parliamentary representation had been conferred on Hedon, Thirsk, Ripon, Knaresborough, Boroughbridge, Aldborough, Beverley, Richmond, Pontefract, Malton and Northallerton and the whole House had swollen from the 341 to 507. In short, Scarborough's parliamentary status had been devalued in relative terms.

Furthermore, the once formidable royal fortress on which Henry II, John and Henry III had lavished so much treasure was now little more than a ruin on the skyline above the town, a private pasture belonging to the Thompsons. There had been no garrison in the castle since 1603; in 1608 it was described as 'very ruinous and in great decay'; in 1619 minimal repairs were estimated to cost £4,000. James I had rid himself of an irksome liability, and there is no evidence that the Thompsons did more than plunder its fabric for building stone. In 1632 the bailiffs reported that there was only one piece of ordnance 'fitt for service' remaining in the castle, yet on inspection even this sole survivor was dismissed as 'of very lyttle or no use'.

Three years later Scarborough's defencelessness was exposed and underlined by two incidents during the naval war between Dutch and Spanish ships operating out of Dunkirk. In the first 'insolence' committed by foreigners, the *Post* of Amsterdam seized a Dunkirker sheltering in Scarborough harbour and towed out its prize into the open sea. In the second, the *Prince Henry* of Amsterdam chased a Spanish frigate into the harbour and then landed 60 or 80 armed men to make sure none of the Spaniards escaped ashore. As bailiff Atmar complained in his letter to the council at York: 'The harbour is of great importance to his Majesty, being the refuge of the Newcastle ships in their way to London, and for all the fishers upon the coast.' However, he continued, since 'the ordnance in the castle [is] old, dismounted and of no use', there was nothing that could be done to deter foreign warships from entering the port and terrorizing the town.

Though the Privy Council in London reacted with speed to the alarming news from Scarborough, there is no evidence that the harbour's defences were significantly strengthened as a result. Events at Scarborough were used, however, to give further justification to the imposition of ship money and its extension to cover the whole country, not just coastal communities. When ship money had been first collected in 1634-5 on seaports only, Scarborough was assessed at £100, whereas the second writ, dated only a few days after the two 'insolencies', was addressed to the entire country and assessed Scarborough at only £30. The tax was paid quickly and willingly in Scarborough, if not elsewhere: no place in the kingdom had greater need of English ships to protect it.

If Scarborough by 1642 was little more than a harbour of refuge for colliers; if it had long since lost the protection of a great royal castle and its reputation as an international market and fair; if it was by then overshadowed by many East-coast ports such as Newcastle, Hull, Boston, King's Lynn, Great Yarmouth and Ipswich and more recently by its adjacent rival Whitby; why was it a place of such crucial importance throughout the English Civil Wars of 1642-6 and 1648? Why did Roundheads and Royalist spill so much blood and spend so much printers' ink over it? Why did the town change hands five times in as many years? Why were town and castle subjected to two prolonged and costly sieges in 1645 and 1648? And how do we explain that when all of Yorkshire's castles, apart from Clifford's Tower at York, were ordered to be demolished in 1649, Scarborough's was exempted from the order?

Sir Hugh Cholmley 1600-57

For other reasons Scarborough would seem to have lacked military or strategic value. As Sir Hugh Cholmley so accurately described it, Scarborough stood at 'an outangle' - it was both remote and inaccessible. From London it was easier to reach by sea than by road. Unlike most major inland towns such as Bristol, York, Leicester, Newark, Skipton, Pontefract and Gloucester, it did not lie on or across key routes; and unlike others, such as Northampton, Sheffield, Birmingham or Bradford, it produced no vital war supplies such as shoes, metals or textiles. Neither Roundheads nor Royalists would fight over Scarborough's fish. Nor, it seemed, were they likely to fight over a derelict, disarmed and obsolete medieval castle by the sea.

Soon after the outbreak of hostilities, in September 1642, Parliament had sent Sir Hugh Cholmley, one of Scarborough's two Members, to assume military command in the town. His commission was to hold Scarborough, its harbour and castle, with the trained bands or local militia of the town and those of Whitby Strand and Pickering Lythe. At that time Parliament also had forces in Yorkshire at Hull and in the West Riding, the latter under General Lord Fairfax. However, when Cholmley was commanded by Fairfax and his superiors in London to bring his troops to Tadcaster to protect the West Riding from a Royalist invasion, he deliberately disobeyed the order and withdrew all his men to Scarborough. A four-point justification of his conduct, which he and his officers signed and sent to London, is the best contemporary explanation of the military and strategic value of Scarborough.

First, they wrote that 'he who is master of the Castle hath a great power over the adjacent parts of the country'. Although much decayed as a result of prolonged neglect and coastal erosion, the castle's natural defensive position behind sea cliff and land dykes overlooking town and port still gave it a considerable military potential. Even in an age of cannon and musket its high stone walls and towers provided adequate protection for a garrison if they were reinforced with earth and timber buttresses. One of the signatories of the letter was Captain Browne Bushell, a veteran of warfare in the Low Countries, and he was already busy modernising the castle's defensive works. Eventually, two outer artillery platforms were constructed: the first, soon to be called Bushell's battery, would dominate the only entrance to the castle, the second, South Steel battery, overlooked the harbour and the great pier. With these improvements and if garrisoned and provisioned, the castle, they claimed, might withstand an army of a thousand soldiers.

Secondly, the officers argued, Scarborough was the only convenient port available to the king through which he could receive reinforcements and munitions from Holland or Denmark. They were right. Even before the first battles were fought, it was clear that overall advantage lay with Parliament. Most of his warships had deserted the king; he had lost London with its Tower magazine, trained bands and mercantile credit. Parliament controlled the richest and most populous south and south-east of the kingdom whereas Charles found ready support only in the far north of England, Wales and Cornwall. His only hope of victory rested on continental assistance. This is why Henrietta Maria had sailed to Holland to secure a marriage alliance with the House of Orange and to raise money and men there by pawning the crown jewels. Charles also expected help from his wife's French and his mother's Danish royal family connections.

However, Stuart strategy depended critically on securing a safe North Sea port. With the king at York, Hull was obviously the most desirable and suitable point of entry: it was accessible, well defended and had a store of military equipment to rival that in the Tower of London. Bridlington Quay had no defences at all and Whitby was too difficult to reach by land and vulnerable to Parliament blockade by sea. Consequently, when Charles failed to persuade Parliament's governor there, Sir John Hotham, to open Hull's gates either by verbal threats or physical force, he was left with only Scarborough. All this explains why Parliament sent Cholmley to Scarborough: the purpose was to deny its port to the king.

In their third point Cholmley's officers contended that, though the king could count on the loyalty of Newcastle, the road between it and York was too long and hazardous, particularly in winter. In contrast, from Scarborough 'ordnance or carriages may passe in the depth of winter to Yorke without difficulty'. Compared with Scarborough, Newcastle suffered from two other disadvantages: it was too vulnerable to Scottish invasion by land and the mouth of the Tyne was too easily blockaded by sea. Scarborough had more than a castle overlooking a safe haven: in the open sea Parliament's warships would never be able to keep station there in all weathers.

Finally, the officers pointed out that from a secure and defensible anchorage at Scarborough 'pinnaces...may upon every occasion make out and hinder the bringing of arms from Holland'. Scarborough was perfectly located for such a purpose: any ship running between the continent and Newcastle would have to pass within a mile or two of its harbour. In peacetime Scarborough was a place of refuge for coastal traffic; in wartime it might become a privateers' port.

Royalist Port

If Scarborough had remained Parliament's most northerly outpost its role in the Civil War would have been negative and insignificant. Parliament had no use for Scarborough when it held Hull through which its army in Yorkshire could be supplied. Cholmley's aim had been to prevent the Royalists from using Scarborough and his unqualified success there was sufficient to satisfy his masters in London. On the other hand, the king managed well enough without Scarborough. More than one convoy of arms and soldiers had reached him via Newcastle, despite the presence of Parliament's warships at Tynemouth. The queen's landing at Bridlington Quay in February 1643 with the largest supply of all - £20,000 in money, arms for 4,000 soldiers, and a thousand mercenaries - was unintended but fortunate. Her destination had been Newcastle but contrary winds forced her fleet to find shelter in Bridlington Bay. The Quay was bombarded by Parliament's warships and Henrietta Maria was lucky to escape with her life and her precious cargo. How she must have cursed Sir Hugh for making her homecoming so unnecessarily perilous.

Cholmley's reasons for changing sides a month later were complex and remain controversial; nevertheless, his decision undoubtedly had momentous consequences for the people of Scarborough. By going over to the king Sir Hugh certainly saved Scarborough from the terrible fate of other towns which suffered a Royalist siege and assault. At Leicester, for instance, more than 700 civilians were butchered after Prince Rupert's Welshmen took the town by storm. Moreover, because the Royalists then held such a dominant influence in the area, for the next year and a half the people of Scarborough were spared the worst horrors of civil war: all they had to endure was crushing taxation, guard duties, unpaid labour and a gradual loss of personal and commercial freedom.

As a Royalist port Scarborough's role became positive and potentially crucial. Throughout 1643 there was a steady flow of arms across the North Sea to York via Scarborough. However, as Royalist resources dried up and the king's victories were followed by defeats in

Yorkshire and elsewhere, it gradually became evident that Cholmley had gone over to the losing side. In 1644 when the Scots joined Parliament, crossed into England and blockaded Newcastle and Sunderland, Scarborough became the only useful Royalist port on the North Sea coast. Then when the Royalists were decisively defeated at Marston Moor and York fell to Parliament, it seemed that Scarborough's only remaining value was as an exit for Royalist runaways to the continent. There was no longer a Royalist army in the north to supply. Even now Cholmley might have saved Scarborough from further distress if he had accompanied the Royalist officers into exile; but his gallant yet stubborn decision to hold Scarborough to 'the last extremity' doomed its people. Just as they had accepted him as Parliament's governor in September 1642 and as the king's colonel in March 1643, so now nearly all of them stood by him as Parliament's victorious army moved inexorably towards the coast.

Cholmley's control of Scarborough was an extraordinary feat. Not one drop of blood had been spilt in March 1643 when he had suddenly defected. This was mainly because Sir Hugh had allowed every soldier and every civilian who could not live under a Royalist regime to leave the town in peace. Several senior officers and some burgesses departed to Hull. Cholmley's successful coup also owed much to the overwhelming Royalist predominance in Yorkshire at that time and the Royalist preferences of the Thompsons. More surprising was Sir Hugh's continued control of the town throughout 1644 as the Royalists lost battle after battle, culminating in the catastrophe on Marston Moor. As Cholmley was compelled to make yet heavier demands on Scarborians his majorities in the Common Hall dwindled and the number of absentees increased. Aware that he could no longer count entirely on the oligarchy, Sir Hugh called an unprecedented meeting of the whole community early one morning in November. Though no account of this assembly has survived, in the light of what happened during the next three months, Cholmley probably assured the townspeople that he would not inflict a close siege on them but would withdraw his soldiers to the castle. Civilians who sought sanctuary in the castle would be admitted. There would be no bombardment of property, no street fighting, and no plunder and rapine in the town.

After the fall of Newcastle to the Scots in October 1644, Scarborough remained the only Royalist North Sea port. Yet Parliament was reluctant to make a direct attack on the town partly because it was thought to be strongly held and also because there were several castles in Yorkshire - at Skipton, Bolton, Sandal, Knaresborough, Pontefract and Helmsley - still in Royalist hands. However, the damaging activities of Scarborough's sea pirates forced the Committee of Both Kingdoms to give priority to the capture of its harbour.

During the winters of 1642-43 and 1643-4 the king's control of the north-eastern coalfields had deprived Londoners of their sea-coal and put the colliers of the East coast ports out of work. In the summer of 1644 the Venetian ambassador predicted riots in the streets of the capital if Londoners were again denied their precious winter fuel. The price of firewood there was prohibitive. In the past two years exports of coal from Newcastle and Sunderland had fallen from half a million to three thousand tons, but once the rivers Tyne and Wear were reopened it was assumed that the huge stockpiles on the banks would soon find their way southwards. Such an optimistic assumption reckoned, however, without Scarborough.

The coastal traffic in coal had rescued the port of Scarborough from terminal decline; now that harbour had become 'a den of thieves' and Scarborough captains preyed on that traffic with impunity. Browne Bushell, Francis Fawether, William Cooper, John Denton and Browne Thomas had all become such successful privateers that the masters of colliers dare not put to sea.

In these alarming circumstances Parliament had no choice but to order an assault on Scarborough by land and sea. That such a target was regarded as vital is indicated by the choice of Sir John Meldrum to command the ground forces. Meldrum was a highly valued, greatly experienced and fearless general, one of the best available to Parliament. He was given 2,000 infantry and 600 cavalry to fulfil his urgent and important task.

London rejoiced when Scarborough fell on Shrove Tuesday, 18 February 1645. The messenger who brought the good news received £20; Meldrum was rewarded with a promise of £1000; one of Parliament's newspapers, *Mercurius Britanicus*, declared that 'god was visible at Scarborough'; the victory was celebrated on 12 March as a day of national thanksgiving; and the London Committee congratulated Meldrum for having secured a 'place of very great concernment and future influence'. Of the 120 ships captured in the harbour, many of them were stolen prizes.

Castle siege

The bad news for Parliament was that Cholmley and his men had retreated to the castle in good order and intended to withstand siege there. The harbour was now Parliament's but without the castle above it was not yet a safe haven for Parliament's ships. Meldrum knew that it would be sometime before he had the ordnance to reduce the castle to rubble. In the meantime, desperately short of money to pay his troops and buy provisions for them, Sir John appealed to the leaders of the East coast ports who valued Scarborough as a place of refuge for their colliers. For example, he warned the burgesses of Ipswich that without their help he would be compelled to lift the siege and allow Scarborough to become 'a Receptacle for the Enemyes of the Kingdome, and obstruction to the Northerne Trade'. Meldrum's pleas were well directed: altogether Hull, Boston, King's Lynn, Yarmouth and Ipswich sent him well over £1000 in money and goods.

Not that Meldrum's masters in London were unaware of the essential value to 'the Northerne Trade' of Scarborough's harbour. Though the Scots general soon lost his cavalry, he and his successor, Sir Matthew Boynton, got infantry reinforcements, a blockading squadron of 16 warships under Vice-Admiral Zachary and several pieces of heavy artillery. 'Sweet Lips', a brass demi-cannon, and a cannon-royal, the biggest in the country, firing a ball weighing 65 pounds, were especially welcome to the besiegers. On 1 May 1645, with no progress reported from Scarborough, Lord Fairfax was ordered 'to send a sufficient force' to take the castle. The London Committee explained to him that they considered 'the taking in of that castle to be of greater consequence than any inland fort whatsoever can be...'.

The king's press in Oxford and Parliament's newsheets in London showed the same appreciation of what was happening at Scarborough. During the spring and summer of 1645 reports of the siege of the castle were printed every week, though usually they were flawed both by ignorance of the topography and blatant bias. However, for the only detailed, though far from impartial, account of the five-month siege of Scarborough castle, there is only one surviving source - Sir Hugh Cholmley's reminiscences, which he wrote two years later as an exile in Rouen and called 'Memorialls Tuching Scarbrough'.

After an angry exchange of letters in which Sir Hugh refused haughtily to surrender and Meldrum lost his temper, there was a lull in the siege until Parliament brought up its heaviest cannon. Under cover of darkness, the huge cannon-royal was dragged through the west door of St Mary's, down the length of the nave and mounted at the east end of the chancel. From there it was fired through the great east window at point-blank range at the castle keep. After three days of this treatment, in Cholmley's words, 'the great Tower splitt in two'. The south-western side, 15 feet thick, with newel staircase and mural chambers, came crashing down on to the entrance road below, bringing with it corner turrets, parapet and two men who was standing on it at the time. Meldrum's assumption that Cholmley's capitulation was now certain and imminent could not have been more mistaken. The fall of the keep actually prolonged the siege because it provided the defenders with a ready arsenal of deadly stone missiles and a barricade which gave them cover and effectively blocked the only entrance on to the headland. When the surrender did finally come eleven weeks later the approaches to the castle was so 'barracadoed' that to allow Cholmley's garrison to come out a new passage had to be cut through the curtain wall into the ditch.

During the next few days there were bloody encounters in hand-to-hand battle for possession of the barbican and the drawbridges over the dykes. Both sides suffered heavy casualties, but the greatest blow was the death of Meldrum after he had taken a musket ball 'in at the bellie and out of the backe'. The old general had been the bravest example to his soldiers and his replacement, a local Yorkshiremen, Sir Matthew Boynton, was much more cautious and patient. Also, the prospect of summer weather meant that coal supply to London was less of a priority. Infantry assault gave way to attrition by long-range artillery. The defenders were gradually worn down by cannon fire from land and sea.

On his 45th birthday Sir Hugh Cholmley signed terms of surrender. His original garrison of 500 had been reduced to half that number and most of the survivors were dying slowly of scurvy, hunger and thirst. There was no hope of relief. The utter defeat of the king's army at Naseby on 14 June in effect meant that the war was lost. To prolong resistance to Boynton would have been futile and suicidal. Moreover, considering the costs and tribulations Sir Hugh had inflicted by his defection to the king and his obstinate defiance since, the terms offered to him by fellow Yorkshiremen were magnanimous. Cholmley and his officers could not afford to reject them. The garrison was allowed to go freely either to the Royalist defenders of Newark or abroad to Holland. Lady Cholmley could return to her home at Whitby.

According to 'An Exact Relation of the Surrender of Scarbrough Castle', written at Hull on 26 July, the day after, 'the women in Scarbrough could hardly be kept from stoning of Sir Hugh Cholmley'. Perhaps this was yet another example of Parliament's propaganda, but all the same the inhabitants of the town had sufficient reason to seek revenge for their sufferings of the past five months.

St Mary's church was reduced to ruins. The chancel, north transept and north aisle were without windows, roofs or complete walls. The central tower was so undermined by vibration and shattered by direct cannon shot that it collapsed during a gale in 1659. All the new pews had been broken up and used for firewood. The parish registers of baptism, marriage and burials were also casualties of the siege; all that now remain are very incomplete bishops' transcripts dating from 1602. When Sir Hugh had paid his garrison their '12 pence a weeke besides dyett' and 'sixpence for everie dayes labour' he had to cut up church plate to make crude silver coins. The only surviving pre-war silver belonging to St Mary's is a chalice given to the church by William Thompson's heirs after his death in 1637.

St Mary's had been used by the Roundheads as a forward bastion and artillery battery and had taken the worst punishment. Other buildings, in particular the schoolhouse in the charnel chapel and the church of St Thomas, were badly damaged but survived until they were mercifully demolished during and after the second siege of 1648. Though the town's official claim for compensation was much exaggerated, some of it was certainly factual. The lead pipes, conveying water into the town from Falsgrave springs, had been pulled up and presumably converted into ammunition. The three water mills in Ramsdale were damaged but reparable whereas the windmill, which Meldrum had used as an observation post overlooking Newborough, had 'quite gone'. The town's pinfold had also disappeared. On the other hand, though the burgesses alleged that 'spoile of the ground 3 years & more' had robbed them of £600 in rents and herbage, the only pasture to be seriously devalued was the town Common, through which soldiers, horses and wagons had passed en route to and from the castle. It took 20 years for the Common rent to return to its pre-war level.

Yet in other ways the townspeople had been lucky. Material damage from cannon fire had been restricted to St Mary's Quarter, the most thinly inhabited area, still mainly garden, pasture, paddock and graveyard. The siege of the town lasted barely three weeks and took place before Meldrum received his 'great ordnance'. Civilian deaths and injuries were the result of misdirected shots from both sides: there was no deliberate bombardment of the town. During the siege of the castle Scarborough's street markets were closed, but residents were given ration tokens to ensure that in the safety of Peasholm they all had 'a bare subsistence' of food. Where soldiers were billeted in the town the tickets they gave to their hosts were usually redeemed.

For a full year, from October 1644 until October 1645, there is almost a total blank in the records of the Corporation. First Cholmley, then Meldrum, and finally Boynton ruled the town like a military camp. The Common Hall did not meet on Sandside. The borough courts were suspended. There is only one fragment of information, now available only at second hand, to indicate that perhaps the most deadly consequence of civil war in the town was bubonic plague. A note, dated 21 June 1645, stated that 547 men were to be employed each week at a shilling a day 'for washing the infected houses'. Since the Black Death is known at this time to have visited other east coast ports such as Boston and King's Lynn and inland places such as Leeds, it would be surprising if Scarborough escaped the epidemic. Moreover, the absence of normal municipal government and the presence of so many itinerant troops in the locality probably made this visitation even more costly in human lives than previous ones in 1598, 1624-6 and 1635-8. In 1626 a pest house for victims had been built on the north side in Tintinholmes; in 1645 another was put up at the opposite end of the town at Driple Cotes on South Cliff.

Other losses were less evident yet still material. The serious disruption of the sea-coal trade deprived the harbour of its maintenance revenue from Newcastle and Sunderland; so many of the town's richest residents, such as the Thompsons, were Royalist 'delinquents' who now that their estates were sequestered or taxed could no longer contribute to the borough's income; and Parliament had already confiscated Stephen Thompson's share of the rectory of St Mary's so that the parish not only lacked a vicar but also the means to pay his stipend.

Worst of all, whatever the extent of Scarborough's sufferings, no compensation could be expected from an unsympathetic Parliament. If Scarborians had not so passively accepted Cholmley's defection and not so actively assisted him for nearly two years they would have saved themselves from Parliament's siege and occupation by force. For what had happened they had only themselves to blame. The only relief permitted to the town by the London government was remission of the king's fee-farm rent of £91 a year for the three years 1643, 1644 and 1645.

The events of 1642 to 1645 had once more drawn attention to the crucial military importance of Scarborough's castle and harbour. The House of Commons decreed that all Yorkshire's castles - Tickhill, Sheffield, Knaresborough, Cawood, Sandal, Bolton, Middleham, Helmsley, Mulgrave, Crayke, Wressle, Skipton and Pontefract - should be 'made untenable and no garrison kept or maintained in them'. There was some dispute about whether Pontefract should be garrisoned permanently, but none about Scarborough. In addition to the 100 men assigned to the castle guard, Parliament ordered that 'the forts which command the harbour at Scarborough be kept up, with three score men in them'. Barbican and gateway were repaired, the castle was replenished with gunpowder, match and ammunition, and Parliament's most northerly outpost was granted £540 a month for its 'present relief'.

Second War

Mindful of how Scarborough had been betrayed to the enemy by Sir Hugh Cholmley, the castle garrison was to be commanded by Captain John Lawson and the new town governor was Colonel Matthew Boynton - both thought to be utterly trustworthy.

Lawson was a native of Scarborough, a master mariner and shipowner, who had refused to live under Cholmley's Royalist regime and taken his family into exile in Hull. During the next two years he had given brave and distinguished service to Parliament as captain of an armed merchantman. After Cholmley's surrender Lawson returned home with his family. He was promptly elected into the Common Hall's First Twelve and represented the borough in London in its attempts to win compensation for war damages.

Matthew Boynton's credentials were almost as sound as Lawson's: he was the second son of Sir Matthew Boynton of Barmston, near Bridlington, who had received Cholmley's surrender and then been elected along with Luke Robinson to sit in the House of Commons for Scarborough. . Both father and son had outstanding records of loyalty to Parliament.

It therefore came as a stunning surprise in July 1648 when Colonel Boynton hoisted a red flag over the castle walls and declared for the imprisoned king Charles and the Prince of Wales. Boynton's attachment to Parliament had been eroded by chronic shortage of money to pay his soldiers their wages and lodging and by a lengthy secret correspondence with the Prince, who had promised to sail north from Yarmouth to Scarborough with a squadron of warships. For several months Boynton had had to beg the Common Hall to allow his soldiers free accommodation in the town. When he asked General Fairfax at Hull for money to billet his men he was told bluntly that they could sleep out of doors it 'being summer time'.

Boynton's sudden coup was as bloodless as Cholmley's had been five years earlier: there was no resistance to it and once again Lawson took himself and his family off to Hull. However, this second defection at Scarborough gave Parliament even greater anxiety than the first. Scarborough was to be a key link in a far-reaching Royalist strategy: while Sir Marmaduke Langdale raised his men from the far northern English counties to join the Duke of Hamilton's Scots, the Marquess of Newcastle would return from Holland, land at Scarborough, and raise another Royalist army in Yorkshire. To protect Newcastle's crossing and line of supply from the continent, the Prince of Wales would bring his ships northwards and take station off Scarborough or come ashore there. Also, the news from Scarborough was more alarming this time because Parliament's power in the North Sea had been jeopardised by a Royalist revolt in the fleet and it had no troops to spare until first the Scottish invasion had been repulsed.

Having failed to suborn Boynton with a bribe of £4,000 and his garrison of 80 soldiers with another of £1000, Parliament sent inadequate forces under Colonel Hugh Bethell to subdue them and recover Scarborough. Since Bethell had not the strength to take and hold even the town, after a series of bloody clashes with Boynton along what is now called Castle Road, he had to withdraw his battered regiment to Falsgrave.

Meanwhile Scarborough's oligarchy had either fled or abdicated to Boynton. After a succession of almost daily meetings on Sandside, the survivors of the Common Hall reluctantly agreed to raise a company of 80 armed men and pay the colonel £20 a week for their maintenance. By 2 August there were present only 25 of the 44 to vote in favour of a 'loan' of £70 to Boynton. In view of his superior power and threats to use it there was nothing else they could do: if they had voted 'no', he would have closed the Hall and ruled the by martial law.

Neither the Prince of Wales nor the Marquess of Newcastle ever came to Scarborough and Cromwell's victories over the Scots at Preston and Winwick in the third week of August dashed any remaining Royalist hopes and plans. Nevertheless, reinforcement was slow to reach Bethell and before it did Boynton's numbers were swelled by a motley collection of about 300 Welsh, Irish, Scottish and English mercenaries who arrived by sea from Deal and Colchester. Parliament's press chose to describe all of these refugees as 'Walloons', French-speaking Catholics from the Spanish Netherlands, presumably because this name denigrated the Royalist cause by association with foreign papists and justified any ill-treatment of them.

Terrorized by these 'Walloons' and increasingly impoverished by Boynton's financial demands, on 11 September the 19 surviving members of the Common Hall refused to pay a penny more. No doubt their courageous defiance was bolstered by the news from Lancashire and that Bethell had been lately reinforced with another regiment of infantry and a company of musketeers. In reply Boynton locked the doors of the chamber which henceforth was to be used only 'to keepe provisions'.

For the second time in three and a half years Scarborough town was taken by storm on the morning of 15 September 1648. But now there was no orderly withdrawal to the castle by the Royalist defenders: instead, Bethell's soldiers had to fight their way through street by street. Parliamentary estimates of Royalist dead varied between 25 and 40; Roundhead losses were said to be no more than half a dozen. Among the 156 prisoners taken some such as James Headley, John Foord, William Woodall and Thomas Wolfe were probably Scarborians. That some of the 300 'Walloons' were butchered after they had surrendered was not just the propaganda of *Mercurius Melancholicus*, it was also admitted by Parliament's *Moderate Intelligencer*: 'prisoners, some Walloons, whom the soldiers took for Irishmen [were] put to the sword, countreymen not knowing the difference of languages'. Since they were Catholic and spoke a foreign tongue they must be Irish, and since Parliament's ordinance of October 1644 any Irishman in arms could be legitimately executed.

The second Civil War siege of Scarborough castle lasted just three months. Compared with the first siege it was almost uneventful:

unlike Meldrum, Bethell had no heavy artillery, whereas Boynton, unlike Cholmley, had an abundance of cannon, powder and match. Boynton's cannon did further injury to St Mary's. Unlike Cholmley's, Boynton's garrison did not suffer from scurvy or lack of water. However, as temperatures dropped, the Royalists soon began to complain of the shortage of warm clothes, shoes and firewood; and it was probably the prospect of spending months on the exposed headland in mid-winter without adequate cover that caused a seepage of desertion and Boynton's eventual capitulation.

Boynton's resistance was hopeless: he had no realistic expectation of rescue either by land or by sea. However, Bethell was misinformed that southerly winds were bringing a Dunkirk ship to Scarborough with 'men, money and store of provisions for relief of the castle'. Since Parliament had failed to station warships off the harbour, the Roundhead colonel made haste to offer terms so generous that Boynton and his officers could not refuse them. Consequently, on 19 December 1648, 260 soldiers were allowed to march out of the castle gates down to the town Common, 'colours flying, drums beating, muskets loaded, bandileers filled, matches lighted and bullet in mouth'. The officers could keep their side arms, horses were available for hire, and all the defenders were free to go home, go abroad or anywhere else 'except besieged places'.

The messenger who brought the news of the surrender to London was voted a reward of £40. Colonel Bethell was appointed governor of the town and castle. Captain John Lawson resumed command of the castle garrison. Scarborough's civil wars were over at last, or so it seemed.

Aftermath

In fact, Scarborians were now faced with the bill for damages. St Mary's was more ruined than ever: again its pews had to be rebuilt. St Thomas the Martyr was beyond repair: what was left of it went up the hill to patch up St Mary's. Boynton had pulled down the school house in the charnel chapel: its stones were reused to convert Farrer's aisle, the south transept of St Mary's, into what was intended to be only a temporary home for the boys and Mr Penston. In the event, there was never enough money to build a new school: Farrer's aisle remained Scarborough's makeshift grammar school until the Victorian

Capt Browne Bushell 1609-51
[reproduced by kind permission of Pannett Park Museum, Whitby]

reconstruction began just two hundred years later. Perhaps more burdensome than these repair costs was the charge to the town of giving free quarter to Bethell's soldiers, who were months behind with their pay. Some of the credit vouchers given to Scarborough's householders in 1648 and 1649 are still unredeemed in the Corporation archive. To add to the town's miseries, the North Sea was still infested with Royalist privateers, some of them, such as John Denton, themselves Scarborians. Only Browne Bushell had been captured and he was a prisoner in Windsor Castle awaiting trial.

Still, there was no question now of demilitarising Scarborough. The Council of State in London considered and even ordered the demolition of the castle because it was too attractive to the enemy landing from the sea and because the people of Scarborough had twice shown themselves to be disloyal. The Council soon thought better of it, however: the order was rescinded and instead troop reinforcements were sent from Hull to Scarborough 'in regard that place is of so great importance'. Soon afterwards approval was given for a permanent artillery battery at South Steel. When the first Dutch war began in 1652, General Fairfax was instructed to bring his Yorkshire forces 'towards Scarborough'.

Civil War had taken its toll of Scarborough's population as well as its architecture. Different kinds of demographic evidence point in the same direction. In the 1630s, according to the bishops' transcripts, the average number of annual baptisms at St Mary's was 87; in the 1660s, it had fallen to 48; during the 1670s it was still only 57; and even by the early 1680s no more than 77. Even allowing for the presence of a Nonconformist community, who from the 1650s refused to have their children christened by the Church of England, the fall seems catastrophic. As late as 1673 Scarborough had only 497 households recorded in the Hearth Tax assessment - in other words, probably no more than 2,000 inhabitants - and this total figure is confirmed by a list of inhabitants of *circa* 1675 for Newborough (502) and Undercliff Quarters (689). Scarborough escaped the bubonic plague when it returned for the last time in 1665, but clearly it took several decades for the town to recover from the demographic disasters of the 1640s.

Parliament's victory in the Civil Wars brought about a political revolution in Scarborough's hierarchy. The Thompsons were ousted: not one of them kept his place in the Common Hall. Richard, Francis, Stephen and Christopher all had to pay composition fines as Royalist

Admiral Sir John Lawson c. 1615-65
[reproduced by kind permission of the National Maritime Museum, Greenwich]

'delinquents'. Stephen lost Scarborough castle, his lease on Northstead manor and his rectory of St Mary's. Out too went Tristram Fysh, now head of that family, who was later said to have 'beene in armes against the Parliament'. In came the radicals and the republicans - the two John Harrisons, father and son, and master mariners, such as Thomas Gill,

William Nesfield, Peter Hodgson and Captain John Lawson. Scarborough's two new MPs, Luke Robinson and John Anlaby (Sir Matthew Boynton had died in 1647), were also newcomers of a very different political and religious persuasion from their predecessors, Sir Hugh Cholmley and Captain John Hotham.

Out too went St Mary's vicar, William Simpson, who had condemned himself by acting as Cholmley's domestic chaplain and denouncing from the pulpit those who fought against the king as 'caterpillers' and 'canker wormes'. Both of Simpson's sons had been with Cholmley in the castle and one of them had later gone to sea as a pirate. Now the vicar found himself without post, income or home. After a sequence of temporary preachers St Mary's finally got a resident vicar - a severe, humourless puritan called Edward Carleton. The change could hardly have been more radical; Simpson had kept the town's vintners happy with his regular demand for canary wine and claret whereas Carleton had informed against his own parish clerk when he saw him 'stagger in the street'.

Nevertheless, there were also continuities: names such as Foord, Batty, Chapman and Conyers were still there in the First Twelve. William Penston, the schoolmaster, who had sworn allegiance to Charles I and the Commonwealth, would later do the same for the Protectorate and Charles II. Richard Dighton held the post of town clerk for 20 years under four different regimes.

The Scarborian who profited most from Parliament's success was John Lawson. In 1642 he had been no more than a young master mariner and part owner of a collier carrying coals from Sunderland. In 1643 and again in 1648 he had been forced by Royalist coups to leave his home; but his loyalty to Parliament, his navigational skills and experience, his deep religious faith, and his good luck, accelerated his promotion in Parliament's service. In the first Civil War he commanded his own armed merchantman, the 'Covenant'; during the second, he was captain of infantry in the siege of Scarborough castle. In 1650 he was given his own warship in the Commonwealth's navy. When the Dutch war ended in 1654 he was Vice-Admiral of the Fleet, the fourth highest ranking officer in the Republic's navy. Unlike most admirals of the day, Lawson was a 'tarpaulin', a seaman by trade and profession, of lowly social origins, who had graduated in the demanding school of North Sea seamanship. No senior officer of the day had closer affinity with the lower deck and none was more respected by ordinary seamen.

6

RESTORATION AND REVOLUTION 1660 - 1699

The reign of Charles II (1660-85) was judged to have begun at the moment of his father's execution; and all Acts since 1642 to which Charles I had not assented were nullified. The Anglican church was fully restored and a fifth of its Puritan clergy expelled from their livings. Despite Charles's commitment to religious toleration, his Cavalier parliament passed a series of Acts persecuting all kinds of non-Anglicans by excluding them from offices and commissions and outlawing their religious services.

After the national turmoils of the 1640s and the 1650s, only Londoners suffered the consequences of bubonic plague and the Great Fire (1665, 1666). Abroad, English fortunes were mixed: of the Portuguese Queen's dowry, Bombay was kept but Tangier eventually abandoned; New Amsterdam, subsequently renamed New York, was taken from the Dutch but two years later they took revenge by burning the best of the Royal Navy's warships at Chatham. An attempt by the country's first political party, the Whigs, to prevent James, the Catholic Duke of York, from succeeding his brother, failed; and during his last years, Charles and his Tory supporters tightened their hold on central and local government.

Charles had been a deathbed Catholic but James II (1685-88) made no secret of his bigotry. To undermine the Anglican establishment he made advances to the Dissenters by offering them religious liberty in a Declaration of Indulgence, which was to be read by all clergy to their congregations. Even then there would have been no Tory revolt until totally unexpected news that James's Catholic wife had given birth to a son and heir opened up the appalling prospect of a dynasty of Romanist rulers. Both Tories and Whigs now invited the Protestant Dutch Prince, William of Orange, husband of James's Protestant daughter, Mary, to come over to England. Support for James evaporated when he lost his nerve and fled to the arms of his French ally, Louis XIV. The throne was declared vacant and offered to William and Mary.

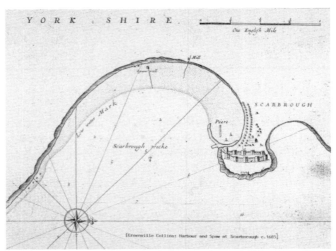

Scarborough harbour and Spaw about 1685 according to the coastal survey of Captain Greenville Collins.

The only serious challenge to William's rule was met and routed by the defeat of James's Irish Catholic army at the battle of the Boyne in July 1690. William's reign (1689-1702) was significant in a number of ways: from now on Parliament became a permanent and vital agent in the constitution; a Toleration Act legalised 5,000 non-Anglican chapels, though it failed to remove the civil disabilities of nonconformists; a Bill of Rights excluded Catholics from the throne and an Act of Settlement determined that the Protestant House of Hanover would inherit the British crown; and finally, the foundation of the Bank of England and the National Debt led to London becoming the world's financial centre.

Restoration

The restoration of the monarchy and with it the established Church of England in 1660 eventually reversed most of the revolutionary changes of the late 1640s. The royalists came back in strength and the republicans and religious radicals were routed. Luke Robinson, one of

Scarborough's MPs, 'all bathed in tears', saved his neck by delivering a pathetic speech in the House of Commons, but soon lost his seat there to John Legard of Ganton. The other seat went to William Thompson, son of Stephen, and the head of the next generation of that family. From now on, with only brief intervals of Tory dominance, until 1744 one or both of Scarborough's representatives at Westminster were the Whig Thompsons, William 1660-81 and 1689-91, Francis, his son, 1679-93, and William, son of Francis, 1701-22 and 1730-44. From 1661 until his death in 1670, Sir Jordan Crosland, royalist colonel, Roman Catholic and the governor of Scarborough Castle at a salary of £16 a year, also sat in the Commons for the borough.

Though Francis was junior bailiff in 1663-4 and senior in 1668-9, he was the last Thompson to sit in the Common Hall. The Thompsons still had the grandest mansion in the town but were now too grand to appear on Sandside. After an absence of 20 years, Tristram Fysh re-entered the First Twelve. He was elected senior bailiff in 1664, 1670 and 1678. Another Scarborian who had fought for the king in both wars, Francis Sollitt, was admitted to the ruling body and finally reached the heights of bailiff in 1670. Six years later, his son, Christopher, gained a licence to teach in the grammar school.

Only Anglicans were permitted to become schoolmasters; only they were allowed to occupy municipal offices and take commissions of peace and in the armed forces. The official toleration of nonconformity which had characterised Cromwell's Protectorate came to an abrupt end. William Simpson returned triumphantly to St Mary's and remained vicar until his death in 1668. After 1662, the radicals - the Harrisons, the Nesfields and the Fowlers - were ejected from local government, though some of their descendants later returned as penitent Anglicans.

Quakers

One Scarborian who did not forsake his faith was Peter Hodgson, unofficial leader of the town's Quakers. He was one of the earliest converts to an extreme religious sect which called themselves Friends of Truth, or just Friends, but were soon better known and feared as Quakers. When George Fox first visited Scarborough in 1651 he stayed as a guest in Hodgson's house in Cargate and was said to have preached there from an upper floor gallery. Peter was a successful corn merchant and master mariner. Scarborough's records of indentures show that between 1645 and 1653 he and his wife, Eleanor or Ellen, took in at least five apprentice boys to learn 'the art and mystery of mariners'. That the first Quakers were at that time tolerated is illustrated by the fact that Peter Hodgson was chosen junior bailiff by the Common Hall at Michaelmas 1653, along with his senior and business partner, William Foord. A year later, according to traditional practice, the two became coroners, and the following year, 1655-6, they were numbered among the First Twelve.

George Fox

However, the spectacular success of George Fox and other preaching missionaries, particularly in the north of England, and the uncompromising militancy of the Quakers aroused the fear and antagonism of all the other Protestant groups - Presbyterian, Baptist,

Independent, as well as Anglican. As a result, Peter Hodgson's name disappeared altogether from the list of Common Hall members when the new elections were held at Michaelmas 1656. Whether he was expelled or withdrew under pressure is not known. Whatever the particular circumstances in Scarborough, a general persecution of Quakers in England had begun. After 1660, even though by then Friends had abandoned physical violence and adopted pacifism, persecution of them became official and vindictive.

Peter Hodgson's house remained the principal meeting place of Scarborough Friends. Though such meetings, 'upon pretence of joynge in a religious worshipp', were now illegal and those attending them were subject to fines and even imprisonment, they were held regularly in Cargate. When Fox returned to Scarborough in 1663, thanks to Hodgson's faith and fortitude, he found there a well established congregation of about 30 Quakers. Soon afterwards Peter was imprisoned and spent the next 5½ years in York castle. While he was there George Fox paid a third visit to Scarborough, this time as prisoner, not preacher.

Fox was shut up in Scarborough castle for 16 months, from May 1665 until September 1666. Though his first cell had hearth and chimney, he had to pay 50 shillings to have the flue unblocked. When he protested to the resident governor, Sir Jordan Crosland, whom he knew was a Catholic, that his quarters were like purgatory, Crosland was not amused. Fox was moved to a worse place, more like hell. Charles's or Cockhill tower at the extreme eastern end of the curtain wall was entirely exposed to weather from all directions, yet lacked either window shutters or fireplace. The rain drenched him and his bed; he had to bail out the water with a plate. He was numb with cold and damp. The soldiers of the garrison stole his bread and beer. No Quaker was permitted to see him. He was treated like some exotic, caged animal for hostile visitors to revile and mock.

Nevertheless, Fox withstood every discomfort and indignity. Catholics, Anglicans and different kinds of nonconformists argued with him and then departed defeated or just angry. No one knew the Bible better than Fox. The deputy governor threatened to hang him over the castle walls, but he remained 'as stiffe as a tree & as pure as a bell'. Dr Robert Wittie, Scarborough's spa physician, rebuked him for refusing to swear allegiance to the king. In reply, Fox said it was easy to swear oaths of loyalty, as Wittie had done first to the Covenant and then to

Charles; true faith, however, was expressed in deeds, not false promises. Wittie returned a few days later to be told that Christ had died for all, sinners included. Wittie, 'the great presbyterian', left in a rage and never visited Fox again.

Even Sir Jordan was favourably impressed by Fox's courage and endurance When the release order arrived from London the governor was glad to carry it out in person, and when Fox came back to Scarborough for the last time in 1669, Crosland invited him up to the castle as an honoured guest for refreshment and conversation. Though he died a Catholic, after his experience of Fox and Hodgson, Sir Jordan refused to persecute Scarborough's Friends.

Not so some of the town's own bailiffs. Soon after Peter Hodgson came home from York, Sir John Legard and William Lawson distrained his goods to the value of £26 14s. for allowing his house to be used as a meeting-place. However, Hodgson was as obstinate as Fox, and also had the money as well as the determination to protect the interests and ensure the survival of his fellow Quakers. As early as 1658 he bought a plot of land 14 yards square on the south side of Bull Lane (now Westover Road) and put it in the care of a group of local trustees. From then on the Friends of Scarborough had their own burial ground. In 1675 for £40 he bought from William Thompson a piece of land in Cook's Row formerly occupied by two tenements and a garth. This he intended to be the site of a new meeting house. Consequently, within little more than a year, a new building 'for the publique meetings of the Lord's people' was finished at a cost of £150 13s. 4d. The money was raised by voluntary subscription. Peter Hodgson gave £20, the largest single contribution. The list of subscribers included 25 men and 12 women of Scarborough, 17 men and women from Staintondale and other places, Thomasin Smailes of Bridlington Quay, and Richard Sellers of Holderness.

Sellers, an in-shore fisherman from Kilnsea, was another Quaker who suffered extraordinary pain for his faith, yet still kept it. In 1665, on the outbreak of the second Dutch war, he was press-ganged for service in the Royal Navy. Taken by force onto the *Royal Prince*, he refused to work the capstan or even eat 'the king's victuals'. The boatswain flogged him, the captain struck him, and the Admiral put him in irons below deck in the 'bilboes'. Only a last-minute intervention by Admiral Sir Edward Spragge saved Sellers from a hanging from the mizzen yard-arm. Even then the most that Sellers would agree to was to stand watch for the pilot; he would neither work nor fight. When the *Royal Prince* went into battle, Sellers saved the warship first by warning the pilot of a sandbank and then by directing it away from a Dutch fireship. Spragge was so impressed by the courage of Sellers, 'the Quakerly dog', that he subsequently signed a certificate granting him release from further service. Sellers came home and resumed his life as a fisherman. As late as 1684, he and his wife, 'Prisseley', appear on a list of Friends charged with attending a meeting in Scarborough.

Persecution of Scarborough's Quakers depended much on the views of the current magistrates, the town's bailiffs; it was left to them to interpret and enforce the law. When Timothy Foord and Nicholas Saunders were bailiffs in 1682-3 the Friends were locked out of their meeting house and then violently dispersed by the constables when they congregated outside. The following year six Quakers were brought before the Quarter Sessions for opening their shops on Christmas day. Nevertheless, by 1689, the year when the Toleration Act was passed to allow freedom of worship to all nonconformists, there were still 40 signatures to a certificate of marriage conducted in Scarborough's Friends' house between William Stonehouse and Sarah Breckan. One of the signatories was Peter Hodgson, senior.

Whigs versus Tories

By the time of the Act of Toleration Scarborough's government had experienced its own version of the Glorious Revolution that overthrew the Stuart monarchy. Anxious to raise money without recourse to Parliament and 'purge' corporations of Whig supporters of the movement to exclude his Catholic brother, James, Duke of York, from the succession, Charles II made a direct attack on municipal autonomy. After he had forced London to concede that its charters were entirely within the gift of the crown, the king made similar inroads on the privileges of other cities and boroughs. Between 1683 and his death two years later Charles sold 37 new charters: one of these concerned Scarborough.

According to the new charter Scarborough still had 44 councillors, but instead of two bailiffs, two coroners, four chamberlains and 36 burgesses there were to be a mayor, twelve alderman and 31 burgesses in the Common Hall. These apparently superficial differences concealed fundamental changes. The first mayor, John Knowsley, and the 12 aldermen were all crown appointees. Furthermore, the majority of the aldermen, seven of the 12, were country squires, not townsmen: John Legard of Ganton, William and Arthur Cayley of Brompton, Richard and William Osbaldeston of Hunmanby, John Wyvill of Osgodby and Cayton, and Matthew Anlaby of Etton. Even among the remaining 31 members there were new names of outside gentlemen such as Hugh Cholmley of Whitby, Thomas Slingsby of Scriven, Henry Crosland of Helmsley and Edward Hutchinson of Wykeham Abbey. Unable to trust the majority of Whig townsmen, Charles had drafted in the Tory squires. Many familiar Scarborough names were missing: there were no Robinsons, Fowlers or Porrets, and not a single Thompson to be seen. Ominously, mayors were to be sworn into office by the constable of Scarborough castle.

Scarborough had to pay a high price for its new charter. To raise the necessary £300 to meet the demand of the Treasury the borough had to mortgage its 50-acre farm of Wheatcroft and two pastures on the north side, Great and Little Northstead closes.

King Charles's strategy seemed to have worked perfectly. After his death, James, his openly Catholic brother, succeeded to the throne, and to his first parliament of 1685 Scarborough obediently sent two Tory gentlemen, Sir Thomas Slingsby and William Osbaldeston. When it was confirmed in January 1688 that the Queen was with child, Scarborough corporation 'thanked the Almighty on their knees for so gracious a king', prayed that God would grant him 'an heir masculine of his body', and promised it would elect two members of the House of Commons who would vote as the king wished 'against the test and penal laws in matters of religion'.

In April 1688 James issued his Declaration of Indulgence, granting freedom of worship to Catholics as well as Protestant nonconformists and ordering it to be read from every pulpit in every parish church in the land. However, Scarborough's vicar, Noel Boteler, 'being no friend to Popery', refused to obey this royal command, whereupon mayor Thomas Aislabie caned the unfortunate cleric in his own reading desk during Sunday service on 11 August 1688. Aislabie was the fifth mayor under the new constitution and a Catholic.

One of the officers in the castle garrison, William Wolseley, took exception to the mayor's behaviour and summoned him to the old bowling green. When Aislabie ignored the invitation, the captain sent a number of musketeers to change his mind. So there at the bowling green mayor Aislabie was publicly disciplined by captains Carvil, Fitzherbert, Hanmer and Rodney, who tossed him in a blanket.

Naturally, mayor Aislabie took his complaint to London and captain Wolseley also went up to the capital to defend his action. In the event neither plaintive nor defendant won his case. Within little more than a month, Protestant William of Orange had landed at Torbay and Catholic James had fled from England. Contrary winds had driven the Dutch Prince south and west; his original intention had been to land at Bridlington. Yet it is clear from the military treatment of Aislabie that William would have been welcomed at Scarborough. Not only was Aislabie the last mayor of Scarborough for the next 150 years, but from 1689 borough charters like Scarborough's were to be free of royal interference. In William III's first Parliament William Thompson and Francis Thompson, Whig father and Whig son, represented the borough. By that time John Wyvill and James Cockerill were serving as the town's bailiffs. Things were back to normal. On 30 July 1689, Wolseley achieved fame by his overwhelming defeat of the Irish Jacobites at Newtown Butler.

The 'Spaw'

Scarborough's history had begun to turn in a new direction sometime during the late 1620s when Mrs Thomasin Farrer took a stroll along the sands of South Bay under the cliffs of Driple Cotes. She noticed that the spring waters bubbling up from the base of the cliffs had stained the stones there a reddish-brown colour, and to her experimental tongue they tasted sharp and bitter. Even if Thomasin had not recently read *Spadacrene Anglica, or the English Spaw Fountaine*, written by 'the father of Harrogate', Dr Edmund Deane and published in 1626, she was sufficiently knowledgeable to appreciate that such natural waters might well have medicinal properties.

Mrs Farrer was later described as 'a gentlewoman of good repute', yet this understated her local status and influence. Thomasin was one of the ten children of Edward Hutchinson, who had inherited the manor of Wykeham, ten miles inland from Scarborough, at the age of 17 and been granted arms in 1581. Edward was chosen one of Scarborough's MPs in 1586 and his eldest son, Stephen, followed in his father's footsteps in 1626. Thomasin's elder sister, Isabel, had married Christopher Thompson, the Scarborough merchant, and Thomasin herself became the wife of another, John Farrer, in 1600. In the year of her marriage Thomasin's husband and her sister's husband were Scarborough's bailiffs

By 1600 John Farrer was already well established in Scarborough and probably some years older than his bride. He had land in West Sandgate, Newborough and Scarborough's fields. He was one of eight foremost businessmen in the town who shared a local monopoly to make salt from evaporated seawater. With the Thompsons he also shared a lease on Scarborough's only windmill. Of the 35 original shipowners who founded Scarborough's Society of Owners and Master Mariners in 1602, John Farrer was third on the list. After his year as bailiff 1599-1600, he was re-elected to that office in 1602, 1607, 1613, 1619 and 1625. The new, abortive royal charter of 1626 granted by Charles I named John Farrer as Scarborough's coroner. In short, when Thomasin walked along the shore of South Bay she was the town's leading lady by birth, wealth and prestige.

According to the first account of her discovery by Dr Wittie, Mrs Farrer was 'physically addicted' to the waters which she found 'did both loose the belly, and also amend the stomach, and cure some distempers'. Her recommendation and the therapeutic qualities of the spring proved irresistible: some people living as far away as York and Hull came to Scarborough to drink it. If we are to believe Dr William Simpson, whose *History of Scarborough-Spaw* was published in 1679, survivors of the siege of 1645 who had 'fallen into scurvy' were 'perfectly and speedily cured' when they 'drank of the spaw water'.

It is also clear that even before Dr Wittie's first published advertisement of Scarborough spa appeared in 1660, the fame of the spring waters there had already begun to identify the town as a place of summer resort and relaxation. Dr Wittie himself was resident at Scarborough in July 1648 when Colonel Matthew Boynton raised his rebellious red flag above the castle battlements. Whether he was there as physician or government spy or both cannot be determined, but according to his own statement he was accustomed 'to step to Scarborough' during the summers of the 1650s and send his patients there from Hull, York and other places in the neighbourhood. Another Hull correspondent, its military governor at the time, Colonel Charles Fairfax, writing in May 1660, might be credited with the earliest reference to 'the season' at Scarborough spa.

However, during the 1640s and 1650s, Scarborough was not the best choice of invalids or geriatrics seeking peace, pleasure or better health. After the physical battering the town received in two civil wars, it was then bombarded by the puritan strictures of men such as Luke Robinson, its Member of Parliament, and Edward Carleton, its killjoy vicar. Mrs Farrer went on living in Scarborough throughout its troubles until 1654, by which time she had been a widow for nearly 30 years. But she did not live long enough to witness the fruits of her curiosity and observation. Though we might agree with Thomas Gent, who in 1735 wrote that her 'memory ought to be for ever precious', it was not Thomasin Farrer who launched Scarborough as Britain's first seaside resort: the credit for that must go to the Restoration and Dr Robert Wittie.

Some of the years of Robert Wittie's early life are shrouded in mystery probably because after the Restoration he was concerned to conceal his earlier political and military activities and attachments. He was the son of George Wittie, sometime mayor of Beverley, and baptised there in the church of St Mary in 1613. Like Sir Hugh Cholmley, he was a pupil of Beverley Grammar School. From there he went up to King's College, Cambridge where he took a BA degree in 1632. Later he claimed to hold doctorates in medicine from both Cambridge and Oxford, but it was only after serving as deputy headmaster at Hull Grammar School that he took out a licence to practise medicine in 1641.

Though there are no surviving records of his civil war service, Wittie was probably commissioned in Parliament's army and served under Sir John Hotham, Hull's governor, when that town was twice besieged by Royalists in 1642 and 1643. In July 1648 Captain Robert Wittie was at Scarborough, no doubt attending his patients who were there for 'the spa season' as well as keeping a watchful eye on Parliament's disgruntled governor of the town and castle, Colonel Matthew Boynton. According to Wittie's own unique account, he was summoned up to the castle by Boynton who told him that he had just received a letter from the Prince of Wales at Yarmouth. The Prince had 12 warships there under his command and intended to bring them north to Scarborough. Two days later Boynton declared for the king and Wittie left Scarborough hurriedly. He rode to Beverley and from there wrote two letters, one to Colonel Overton, Parliament's governor at Hull, the other to William Dobson, then Hull's mayor. These two letters were Parliament's first warning of Boynton's defection and the threat posed by the Prince of Wales.

If, at that time, Wittie was indeed 'a great Presbyterian', as George Fox later sarcastically described him, then this might explain why Boynton confided in him after King Charles had made an 'Engagement' with the Scots. It might also explain why 'the great doctor of physic', another of Fox's sarcasms, was subsequently anxious to steer clear of politics and concentrate on winning patients. Sometime during the 1650s he moved from radical Hull to conservative York, but continued to visit Scarborough every summer and recommend its waters for a variety of ailments. Mrs Alice Thornton first referred to him in her autobiography about the year 1651. On that occasion the doctor attended her husband, William, at their home at East Newton in Ryedale, and from then on he was her physician as well as his. Apart from rickets, for which he prescribed frequent immersions at St Mungo's well at Knaresborough, all other ailments were in Wittie's opinion curable either by bleeding or drinking Scarborough's spa waters. According to Alice's memory, the Thorntons took the coach to Scarborough in 1659, 1666, 1667 and 1668, and Wittie also came to see them at East Newton when they called him. When William died of the palsy, 'good Dr Wittie' wrote 'a most comfortable letter' to his widow.

By that time, as the author of two books advertising the virtues of Scarborough water and the attractions of the town as a health resort for 'persons of quality', Wittie's fame had spread beyond Yorkshire. *Scarbrough Spaw, or A Description of the Nature and Vertues of the Spaw at Scarbrough in Yorkshire* was completed, by fortunate coincidence, on 29 May 1660, the same day of 'His Majesties most happy restoration', so it gave its author an opportunity to express his loyalty as a subject as well as his science as a physician. The book was printed in London and York and advertised in two of the capital's weeklies, *Parliamentary Intelligencer* and *Mercurius Publicus*. In retrospect, Dr Wittie's pioneer first edition marked a new and significant stage in Scarborough's rich and eventful history.

Surprisingly, Wittie's *Scarbrough Spaw* of 1660 revealed little about the subject of its title. Praising the benefits of water and condemning the vices of alcohol, he opened his book with a temperance lecture. Before Noah discovered wine men had often lived a thousand years; afterwards life expectancy had plunged to no more than three score and ten. The doctor then thought it necessary to explain to his readers his own unscientific analysis of the different kinds of water to be found in rain, hail, snow, sea, rivers, lakes and springs. When finally he arrived at Scarborough's waters his appreciation of them knew no medical limits. In his professional opinion, there was no known disease or disability that would not benefit from liberal doses of this particular 'spaw'; but he had to confess that it was especially effective as an antidote to chronic constipation, excessive windiness and 'frequent fluxes of the belly'. In this respect Wittie had nothing favourable to say about fresh fruit, vegetables, herbs or 'sallets' (salads). Gentlemen and ladies who suffered from the effects of a surfeit of meat and a lack of exercise would find no speedier purge than that on offer at Scarborough's well.

Visitors in search of a cure should come to Scarborough between May and September, not because these were the warmest months, but because during the winter and spring the spa waters were diluted by rainfall. After his journey to Scarborough the visitor ought to rest and relax for several days before starting treatment. At the beginning he should drink only two or three half-pints a day and gradually increase consumption until it reached an optimum of four or five pints daily. It was essential that these waters were taken during the early hours of the morning, say between six and nine o'clock, so that they passed through the body before dinner at midday. If meat was eaten on a stomach still full of water it would be 'washed down into the bowells unconcocted'.

In 1660 Wittie claimed that Scarborough's spa was already famed in Hull, York and other parts of Yorkshire; that some visitors to it had travelled 'above an hundred miles'; and that they preferred it to 'Italian, French and German Spawes ... for its speedy passage and innocent working both by siege and urine'. Seven years later, the doctor was able to address his second edition of *Scarbrough Spaw* to two noble and notable witnesses to the efficacy of his prescriptions - Lord John Roos, heir of the earl of Rutland, and the earl of Suffolk. Many physicians had been unable to cure Roos of chronic 'Hypochondriack wind'. However, after three visits in three years to Scarborough from his home in Leicestershire, Lord John now enjoyed 'a constant state of health' and had become 'much more lively and fleshly than formerly'.

Wittie cited many other cases of almost instant and permanent remedy. Sir John Anderson had been cured of scurvy and gout. He had drunk eight pints of spa water and then urinated eleven, thereby relieving himself of three pints of harmful 'humours of the body'. Christopher Keld from nearby Newby had been tortured with the most painful gall-bladder stones, yet within less than half an hour after consuming two or three quarts of bottled Scarborough waters he had passed 'several stones besides much gravel'. Not that Scarborough waters travelled well: Dr Wittie recommended that if at all possible they should be taken straight from the well rather than out of bottles.

After seven more years of trial and treatment, Wittie was now able to extend the number of ailments for which Scarborough waters were beneficial. With confidence he prescribed them for 'diseases of the head', such as 'Apoplexy, Epilepse, Catalepsie and Vertigo'; diseases of the nerves, lungs and stomach; asthma, scurvy, yellow and black jaundice and leprosy; and of course they were a proved, sovereign remedy for 'Hypochondriack Melancholly and Windiness'.

Wittie's second edition also added something more that was to be of the greatest future value to Scarborough as a resort: from his own experience he recommended that sufferers from gout should bathe in the sea. By 1667 England already had nearly a dozen major spa resorts, such as Bath, Bristol, Tunbridge, Epsom, Buxton and Harrogate, where the well-to-do and fashionable drank the waters and took their pleasures. Bath and Buxton also drew visitors to their hot, mineral bathing springs. However, all of these places were inland and nowhere in the whole of Britain, or perhaps even yet in Europe, was bathing in cold sea water practised either as a medical cure or as physical exercise. Nevertheless, Wittie had convinced himself, and sought to convince others, that plunging naked into salty, turbulent, frigid sea water followed by 'a sweat in a warm bed' had been a certain therapy for his gout. Whatever doubts might exist about Wittie's qualifications as a doctor of medicine, as far as sea bathing is concerned he was a revolutionary pioneer.

In his *Anatomy of Melancholy*, published first in 1621, Robert Burton had broken through long-standing custom by suggesting that gentlemen might learn how to swim. Hitherto, bathing in rivers and lakes was thought to be a vulgar, immoral practice, best left to peasants and labourers. Burton's book was widely read, much admired by the gentry and aristocracy, and could claim to have successfully promoted therapeutic bathing or hydrotherapy. Yet Burton did not recommend sea bathing: he wrote that sea air was purer and more invigorating and coastal views provided prospects to 'relieve melancholy', but the sea should be left to common sailors and such gentlemen who chose to join the Royal Navy.

In fact, as late as the 17th-century, there was still a general fear of the sea, even for those who lived on an island surrounded by it. In an age when perceptions and values were strongly influenced by the Bible, the ocean was regarded by most as awesome, malevolent and devilish. There was no sea in the Garden of Eden; Noah's flood was God's punishment of a disobedient people; and the oceans remained as reminders of this terrible calamity. In Shakespeare's plays the sea is associated with disaster, chaos and death. Little wonder therefore that in these times people were reluctant to travel by sea and terrified of drowning in it.

There is no evidence that sea-bathing became a common exercise at Scarborough as an immediate result of Wittie's recommendation. However, there can be no doubt that at least a generation before this new form of hydrotherapy was introduced at southern resorts such as Brighton, Weymouth and Margate, it was already well established at Scarborough. Besides Wittie's initial advertisement, Scarborough possessed all the natural advantages soon to be endorsed by other physicians elsewhere. High cliffs behind the beach sheltered it from cold winds; the wide sweep of South Bay offered magnificent views of coast and open sea and at the same time fresh, bracing breezes. Above all, an extensive, flat, firm, clean, sandy beach allowed bathers to walk, ride in carriages or even gallop their horses in safety to the edge of the water. Scarborough sands were free of hills, shingle and rocks. As William Hutton enthused over South Bay beach in 1804: 'a space of pure sand, two hundred yards wide [at low tide], and eleven hundred long; the most pleasing, safe and useful I ever saw; perfectly adapted for the foot, the horse and the carriage'. Moreover, since there was no easy direct access to the spa well from the cliff top, and both drinkers and bathers had to come from the town from as far away as West Sandgate, they had no choice but to cross this superb strand on the edge of the sea.

As later physicians testified, the sea at Scarborough was perfect. Because it was cold, salty and rough, it had the most invigorating affect on bathers. Unlike those off the west and south coasts of Britain, these waters did not suffer from the enervating influence of the Gulf Stream. They were the coldest around the country, and they were particularly salty because they were not diluted by a freshwater river running into them. Finally, nature had contrived to provide mineral spring waters at the foot of the cliffs adjacent to this ideal shore and salubrious sea - a unique combination that was to make Scarborough into Britain's earliest seaside resort. Only one disadvantage prevented Scarborough from becoming a spa to rival Bath or a resort to equal Brighton - its distance from London.

Wittie's reign as king physician at Scarborough was short-lived. Scarborough's growing success as a resort for the nobility and gentry made certain an influx of ambitious doctors. In 1669 only two years after Wittie's second edition, there appeared *Hydrologia Chymica*, a spiteful, mocking attack on him and it by Dr William Simpson. After lavishing scorn on Wittie's ignorance of chemistry and his infantile analysis of Scarborough's spa waters, Simpson went on to consider their therapeutic claims. He accepted that they were a cure for 'scurvy, dropsie, stone or strangury [painful, difficult urination], jaundise, hypochondriack melancholy, cachexia's [chronic mental or physical disability] and women's diseases', but rejected them as remedies for an even longer list – 'pestilential diseases, pleurisies, prunella's [inflammation of the tonsils or abscessed throat], poysons taken in or inbred... leprosie, French disease [venereal syphilis], morphew [leprous or scurfy skin eruptions], cancer, falling sickness...apoplexie, palsie or asthma'.

Furthermore, with remarkable good sense, Simpson observed that physical exercise, fresh, sea air, wholesome food and abstinence from excesses of any kind were more likely to cure Wittie's sick and over-indulged patients than any amount of Scarborough's waters, taken internally or externally. He agreed that the optimum time to visit the resort was during the summer months, but he contended that, if they were boiled down, 'the essence' of Scarborough spa waters could be taken at any time in any place, and that mixed with any fluid would still act as a gentle and effective laxative. In one final broadside, aimed at Wittie and Scarborough, Simpson concluded that the air of Knaresborough, 'being upon high heathy common', was superior to that of the sea coast.

It soon emerged that Wittie and Simpson were old enemies, personal and professional. Within weeks of the publication of *Hydrologia Chymica*, there came the blasting reply from Wittie, *Pyrologia Mimica*, a continuous torrent of insult and anger. Wittie's competence had already been questioned some years earlier by Simpson when they both practised in York. Now Wittie's position as unofficial champion of Scarborough was being challenged by a fellow physician, and his reaction was predictably aggressive. 'Sir Simpson', as Wittie sarcastically addressed him, was 30 years his junior, a cockerel newly-hatched from the shell, and merely a Bachelor of Arts. In contrast, Wittie described himself as a doctor in physic in both universities, who had been curing diseases before Simpson had learned their Latin names. Stung by accusations of being out of date and unscientific, Wittie recalled that Simpson had advertised 'his Amulet' for sale to the plague-stricken people of York.

Simpson's attempt to undermine Wittie's authority and the reputation of Scarborough's spa proved counter-productive: he succeeded only in attracting the attention of other physicians and extending the fame of the waters to many more 'persons of quality'. In 1670, in *Scarborough Spaw Spagyrically Anatomised*, Dr George Tunstall, of Newcastle upon Tyne, joined the literary and professional fray. He claimed that after taking Scarborough waters he had been struck down by 'a fit of the stone' within a fortnight and gout in his big toe after a month. Moreover, he went on to allege that Lord Irwin of Temple Newsam had been seized by jaundice after a visit to Scarborough and had died of it. Tunstall's devastating opinion was that Scarborough's spring waters contained 'stone powder' which damaged the kidneys of the imbibers.

Wittie was outraged. Tunstall had betrayed him. Two years earlier, Tunstall had brought his wife to consult Wittie at Scarborough. After childbirth her belly had remained swollen and her husband 'with all his art' had not been able to 'take it down'. Wittie had prescribed one of his 'preparations' and within a few days Mrs Tunstall was able to close her bodice for the first time. Not a word of this had appeared in Tunstall's ungrateful and ungracious book. Wittie dismissed Tunstall's explanation of Lord Irwin's death and attributed it instead to excessive drinking of wine. Tunstall, he concluded, had condemned Scarborough's mineral springs only because he had lately become a resident physician at Harrogate.

Further attacks on Wittie were delivered by Simpson in his *Hydrological Essays* published in 1670, and by Tunstall in his *New-Year's Gift for Dr Witty*, which came out two years later. Wittie responded with his customary vulgarity: if his book was not superior to theirs, it was 'fit only for bum-fother'. No doubt Wittie was particularly hurt by Tunstall's description of him as 'the crackfart of Scarbrough Spaw'.

In the end it was Simpson who had the last, best word. In his old age Wittie retired first to York and finally to London and his departure allowed Simpson to become the chief propagandist of Scarborough. Now that Wittie had gone for good, Simpson could afford to be more objective: his *History of Scarbrough Spaw*, published in 1679, was by far the most lucid, literate and informative account up to that date.

The greater part of Simpson's *History* consisted of more than 70 case studies of successful treatments of patient visitors to Scarborough, many of them prescribed and supervised by Dr Wittie. The most distinguished beneficiary named was the Marquess of Winchester, who required only one visit 'at the latest season of the year' to receive a complete cure for his chronic 'hypochondriacal wind'. Other invalids were of a lower social rank but had more serious afflictions. Lady Legard of Ganton had been relieved of jaundice; Mr Watson, of nearby Throxenby, voided his worms at the daily rate of 30 or 40 and soon found a 'perfect cure'; Mr Woodyear of York discovered that Scarborough water was a remedy for diarrhoea; and Mr Roger's daughter, a local girl, got rid of 'a scorbutick elephantiasis'.

Even more miraculous was the way that Scarborough spa provided remedies for different kinds of sexual problems. For instance, Mr and Mrs Thomas St Quintin of Flamborough had been married for seven years but remained childless until they came to Scarborough for the season. Within a month there she had conceived and subsequently gave birth to a son. Four years later, they visited Scarborough again with the same purpose and the same happy result, a daughter this time. On the other hand, for those who had need of it, the spa also worked its wonders with venereal disease. Simpson knew two anonymous gentlemen who were pleased to be relieved of 'the reliques of a clap' after taking generous quantities of Scarborough waters. Of course he did not say where the two had contracted gonorrhoea, perhaps because Scarborough was already notorious for the number of its seasonal prostitutes.

Even mental illnesses succumbed to the healing powers of Scarborough spa. Mrs Granville, daughter of a bishop and wife of the dean of Durham, had for long suffered from bouts of over-excitement. However, after a succession of annual excursions to Scarborough in the

LADY CHOLMLEY,

1670s she found herself much more tranquil and content. Whether drinking at the spa well had anything to do with her improvement was not questioned by Simpson, or by a German doctor there who was said to have been 'exceedingly civil'. Dr Simpson later removed himself to Leeds and transferred his favour to Knaresborough, but by that time Scarborough was already deeply in his debt.

THE CONDITION OF THE PEOPLE

Public Health

By contemporary standards Scarborough during the seventeenth century was a very healthy town: this had much more to do with its regular supply of fresh, clean water from Falsgrave's springs than anything discovered by Mrs Farrer or publicised by Drs Wittie and Simpson. During the next century the demands of a growing population gradually exceeded the Falsgrave flow, but in the 1600s the public conduit was sufficient, reliable and usually well managed. Though after the dissolution of the friaries in 1539 the stone-lined aqueduct running through the Franciscan precinct was blocked, the main public pipeline which was leaded remained the responsibility of the borough.

By 1630 there were three places where Scarborians without private wells could draw their water – at St Thomas's Cross in Newborough, at the lower end of the Dumple where it met St Sepulchre's Gate, and near the Butter Cross, at the top of West Sandgate. These cisterns were known locally as the upper, middle and lower conduit.

To maintain the lead pipes the Common Hall made a contract with the town's plumber, usually for a term of seven years. If the conduit ran dry for ten consecutive days, the plumber forfeited his bond. However, in 1628 after George Fletcher had failed in his duties, 'for his badd usadge and carriadge', the town broke its covenant with him and refused to pay any of the £7 a year previously promised. Soon afterwards every household was required to provide 'a sufficient laboring man' to dig up and re-lay the conduit pipes running from Falsgrave to Newborough, or pay sixpence 'for the sayd worke'. When this order failed to raise enough money for the new pipes, the chamberlains borrowed £43 4s. from Mr Paul Peacock 'for the maykyng

& amending the conduitt' with lead and repaid him with a loan from the 44 members of the Common Hall.

Once the new pipes had been laid the town made an agreement with Christopher Gilson, the plumber, to maintain them and the cisterns. He was to have 20 shillings a year for his responsibility and 3s. 4d. more for the school and church windows. Gilson proved to be much better than Fletcher: 12 years later he was awarded a seven-year contract, this time with a salary of 40 shillings per annum plus 10 shillings for his 'entry penny'. However, the chamberlains were still responsible for the cleanliness and security of the water supply: there was a fine of one shilling on any townsman who allowed his horse or beast to drink at the conduits; and the same penalty on anyone who washed clothes or cleaned vessels within six yards of them. After brewers and malsters took too much water from the middle conduit it was covered with a locked trapdoor between six in the evening and six in the morning by the town bellman.

There were other reasons why Scarborough's mortality rate was lower than that in most other urban communities of the time. Just as fresh water came down to the town by gravity, so the same slopes down to the sea washed away its debris and sewage waste. William Hutton, a frequent visitor to Scarborough early in the nineteenth century, was much impressed by the steepness of the hillside on which the old town stood. He counted 94 steps from the foreshore sands to the top of Merchant's Row, another rise from there to St Mary's churchyard of twice that altitude, and then a further climb to the castle - in all a rise from sea level to 250 feet in a distance of 1,500, or an average gradient of one in six. As a result, in the words of a visitor to Scarborough in 1804: 'filth cannot lodge from the great descent of the streets and the power of the rain'. Animal dung was dumped in heaps outside Newborough and Oldborough Bars, but most street and shambles refuse probably found its way into the sea. The town employed 'sand dressers' to clean the foreshore after the fish market was held there, yet the twice-daily high tide must have done more to cleanse the beach that any human activity.

Nevertheless, the borough was small enough and the bailiffs powerful enough to make sure that the comprehensive bye-laws on street and open, surface sewer cleanliness were usually respected and enforced. The so-called sheriff's tourn, a court that met twice a year, at the end of March and beginning of October, was responsible for punishing infringements of the town's bye-laws or 'pains' which concerned matters of public hygiene.

All residents were required to 'dress' the street in front of and behind their houses and to ensure that the gutters there were scoured out regularly. During this period charges were brought against townspeople corrupting the pavement or highway with offal, dung, dirt, manure, carrion, waste, trash and rubbish. The bailiffs themselves were held responsible for the street in front of the Common Hall on Sandside, and they were also obliged to keep clean the other public places such as the sands, markets, fish and flesh shambles, Common and pinfold.

Wandering pigs were a particularly persistent problem. Though the town employed a swineherd to keep pigs off the streets and out of the market places, he seems to have found the job impossible. In seventeenth-century Scarborough pigs were everywhere they were not supposed to be: on the sands, in St Thomas's churchyard, in the Thursday and Saturday markets and even in the corn fields of Falsgrave. Owners of such trespassing swine were fined fourpence a foot, but the penalty was nearly doubled to 2s. 6d. per beast in an effort to deter this most common of offences.

Though the town might be run by a handful of rich merchants and shipowners, even the highest burgesses were brought before the sheriff's tourn for breaches of these bye-laws. In 1620, Francis, Richard and William Thompson were all presented for not dressing the streets before their houses and shops. In 1657 even 'vice-admarall Lawson' was in trouble for 'his doore not being drist'.

Scarborians were also less likely than other town dwellers to be poisoned by negligent or unscrupulous bakers and brewers. The borough still employed breadweighers and alefiners whose important duties were to guard consumers against short measures, excessive prices and inferior quality. The two breadweighers were given accurate scales to make sure that Scarborough's standard penny loaf was sold at the correct weight as determined by the current price of local flour. Depending on the success or otherwise of harvests and the balance between supply and demand, the penny loaf might weigh as much as two pounds or as little as six ounces. As for quality and content, no bread could be sold legally in Scarborough's markets until it had first been approved by the breadweighers.

The same strict regulations and control applied to brewing and beer sales in the town. Only licensed brewsters were allowed to retail their beer; brewhouses were inspected regularly; publicans had to submit their quart and pint pots for examination at least once a year; and none was permitted to charge more than a penny a quart.

The town was allowed only two vintners and their licences were renewed annually. Oliver Digle was heavily fined £10 in 1564 'for kepyng of a victulyng house' without the bailiffs' permit, and selling 'claret wine with honey unlawfully which were unwholesome for the queens people', at a price, fourpence a quart, which was 'contrary to the statute'. That Oliver had also sold herrings, 'kept certain Flemings in his house', and wounded a constable who called at his home probably accounts for the severity of his penalty.

Bread, beer and wine were not the only victuals tested before sale in Scarborough: all foodstuffs offered in the town markets were subject to inspection. In October 1639 a butcher from Seamer was brought before the sheriff's tourn for selling meat 'nott holesume for mans bodye and beinge forbidden by the trayde'.

Control of food marketing was made easier at a time when markets were still specialised. The butter and corn crosses were still the sites of produce stalls; what is now called King Street was then Apple Market; the flesh and fish shambles were then in the heart of the town where the present Market Hall stands; live cattle were offered for sale in what had been Blackfriargate, was now more commonly called Beast Market, and one day would become Queen Street; and pigs were bought and sold in St Thomas Gate. The only general markets, held weekly on Thursdays and Saturdays were held in Newborough Gate and what became Princess Street in the Oldborough Quarter. By this time, what is now the upper end of Castle Road but for centuries was known as Market Gate seems to have lost its market.

Even the poorest Scarborians benefited from what would have been by contemporary standards a healthy and nutritious diet. They ate great amounts of fish, especially herring the most nutritious of all. Fish is a rich source of protein, vitamins and minerals, but oily fishes such as mackerel and herrings also have a high content of polyunsaturated fatty acids. Fresh herring were brought into Scarborough at any time between April and October, and during the other winter months they were eaten dried, salted or smoked. Though less rich in calories, fats and vitamins, cod, haddock, ling and skate were taken by Scarborough and neighbouring fishermen throughout the year. Such was Scarborough's fame as a fishing port and market and so plentiful was the fish in its adjacent waters that the large cod caught on the Dogger Bank was sometimes called Scarborough Fare and the waters Scarborough Seas.

But Scarborough was much more than a fishing port and market. The four Quarters of the built-up town, Oldborough, Newborough, Undercliff and St Mary's, constituted only a small part of the extensive area of the Liberty, which ran from the Ingrift (Peasholm Beck) in the north to White Nab in the south, a distance of more than three miles, and inland for about the same distance.

Ever since the beginning of the thirteenth century when King John had granted the burgesses the fields and pastures of Falsgrave manor they had been largely self-sufficient in meat and grain. In this respect, 400 years later, little had changed: the town had not outgrown its medieval limits or its highest medieval population. The Long Furlongs of the North Leas, the Short Furlongs on the north side of Ramsdale, and the Elriggs of South Cliff still provided Scarborians with the raw materials of their bread and beer. The windmill on Bracken Hill and the three water-mills driven by Ramsdale Beck still turned Scarborough's corn into Scarborough's flour. Moreover, the Liberty contained grazing land of every kind and quality, from the rich water meadows of St Thomas's Fields and Marr Closes in Burtondale and the horse pasture of South Field to the poorer scrub and bracken of Falsgrave moor and Weaponness. Weaponness alone covered more than 400 acres. Wheatcroft (formerly Whitecroft) in the far south-east corner of the Liberty, described in 1651 as 'messuage, farmhold, tenements and closes' when it raised a mortgage of £450, was a 50-acre tenancy of the corporation.

So Scarborians not only kept pigs and poultry in their backyards: many of them owned or leased pastures for cattle, sheep and horses in the Liberty. A few examples from contemporary wills illustrate the mixed character of the town's economy. When one of Scarborough's richest merchants, William Fysh, died in 1591 he left a mansion house and a shop, stable and barns in Cargate, several tenements with garths and orchards in different parts of the town, and dozens of closes of meadow and pasture scattered far and wide across the length and breadth of the Liberty, many of them on lease 'from the burgesses of the town'. Men of more modest means might have a close or two of grazing land for their animals: Nicholas Wolffe, the tanner, had a little close on Pillory Hill; Christopher Coverdale, the tailor, had half an acre on the High Leas; Stephen Dickinson, shoemaker, an acre on the Elriggs; Robert Stowsley, butcher, a close of meadow at Northstead Lane; and William Powell, skinner, an oxgang in Falsgrave's fields. The majority of Scarborough's men might win their livings from the sea or trade, but they still valued possession of land within or beyond the Liberty. Edward Hickson, master mariner, lived in Shilbottle Lane (Whitehead Hill) but had a close of pasture in Holbeck; George Pearson, stringlayer, had part shares in three ships and two closes; and Thomas Sedman, fishmonger, owned a farm at Rillington.

Not just the shrinking town Common but most of the Liberty's pastures belonged to the corporation and were leased out as closes or, in the case of extensive areas such as South Field and Weaponness, as 'horse gates' or 'beast gates'. In 1649 a horse gate cost three shillings a year and a cow or beast gate half as much. The town employed two pasture masters for Weaponness and a netherd whose duty from May Day to Michaelmas was to take cattle from Ramsdale up to Weaponness at six in the morning and return them there by six in the evening. The netherd was also responsible for the town bull which he kept on the Common.

Even within the confines of the built-up town there were still many open spaces, described variously as closes, orchards, gardens and wastes. St Mary's Quarter had Paradise Close, Paradise Gardens, the Vicarage Garden and the burial ground surrounding the parish church. The sites once occupied by the three friaries remained mostly empty until well into the eighteenth century. In Newborough, the northern end of St Thomas Gate, the New Dyke Bank, and the southern end of St Nicholas Gate towards King's Cliff were not yet residential areas. Of the four Quarters, only Undercliff, overlooking the harbour, might be described as densely populated.

So most seventeenth-century Scarborians enjoyed space, light and greenery; they drank clean water and wholesome beer; they ate good bread, oily fish and were able to buy or grow vegetables and fresh fruit. According to a surviving customs book of 1642-3 and a list of incoming cargo of November 1643, chief imports from Ostend, Dunkirk and Rotterdam were apples, raisins and prunes.

Scarborians were also fortunate to have access to relatively cheap winter fuel. There was never any shortage of coal arriving by sea from Newcastle and Sunderland and the bailiffs licensed authorised coal porters and fixed the prices they were allowed to charge for the carrying distances from the quayside. Clearly, it was cheapest to keep warm and bake your bread and brew your beer in a house on Sandside where the coal carriage rate was 12d. a chalder; and most expensive to burn the same coal if you had lived or had your workshop in St Thomas or St Nicholas Gate, where the premium was 2s.4d. a chalder. However, carriage charges remained unchanged not just for years but for generations during the seventeenth century.

Homes and Households

Only during the years of plague, 1626-7 and 1635-6, is it certain that burials at St Mary's outnumbered baptisms there. If the parish register of 1645 had survived the Civil War it would probably have recorded a third year of deficit. It seems, therefore, that except during exceptional epidemics Scarborough was able to maintain and usually increase its population, even though the principal occupation of its menfolk, seafaring, was then, and still is, the most dangerous of all. Also, it was only during times of plague that some Scarborians were so hungry that they were driven to steal for food.

Other towns at this time renewed and expanded their resident population only by immigration, but this seems unlikely in Scarborough's case. In the first place, the town's magistrates consistently tried to exclude newcomers, known as undersettlers, on the grounds that they might become a burden on the poor rate or bring in infection. Severe penalties were imposed on Falsgrave and Scarborough householders who took in 'strangers' without permission from the bailiffs. Constables who failed to report such illegal settlement were also heavily fined.

Not until after 1660, when Scarborough began to accommodate and entertain an increasing number of well-to-do visitors, was the persecution of 'new lodgers' relaxed and then abandoned. Until that time the only legitimate incomers were potential apprentices. During the years 1643 to 1654, when it appears that a fairly full record of indentures has survived, 23 apprentices taken on by Scarborough men and women were from outside the borough. They came from as far north as Lythe, as far south as Patrington, and as far inland as Malton. Not surprisingly, nearly all of these 23 young men and boys were to be trained either in 'the art and mystery of a mariner', 'the art or faculty' of a shipwright, or 'the art and trade' of a fisherman. The one exception, who was not apprenticed to a sailor or a ship- builder, was to learn 'the trade or faculty' of a joiner.

By far the great majority of indentured servants in Scarborough for which records remain were boys and girls of about ten years of age whose parents had died or abandoned them and who had been maintained by the parish until considered old enough to learn a trade. Invariably, the girls were indentured either to a widow or to a gentleman's household to be taught 'the art and mystery of housewifery'; whereas the boys went into the families of fishermen, masons, blacksmiths, shoemakers, tailors or porters. Apprenticeships were usually for a term of six years, though orphans were bound to their masters and mistresses until they were married or became 21, or even 24. All apprentices were expected to receive food, drink, clothing, and free lodging; masters and mistresses were authorised to 'chastise' them when they found it necessary; but only some were allowed spending money and free time during their terms of lengthy apprenticeship. The presence of apprentices and adult domestic servants in many households swelled the average size of Scarborough's families.

Much has been written and argued about mean family sizes in seventeenth-century England, but in Scarborough's own case the surviving evidence is too fragmentary to allow better than approximate assessment. The so-called 'List of Inhabitants' is incomplete: it contains only the households of Newborough and Undercliff and not those of St Mary's and Oldborough Quarters. Though undated, the list must have been drawn up sometime between the Hearth Tax return of Michaelmas 1673 and the death of Francis Sollitt in 1680. Nevertheless, in the absence of other kinds of records, it provides welcome information.

For each household the 'List of Inhabitants' gives the names of master and/or mistress, the number of their children living at home, the number of their servants and apprentices, and their annual wages. In Newborough Quarter there were 118 masters, 124 mistresses (16 of them widows), 171 children (82 of them under the age of 16), 47 servants, 36 apprentices and seven journeymen, a total of 503 living in 131 households, an average of 3.8 per family. Undercliff was a little more populous but otherwise very similar: it had 689 people in 171 households, an average of just over four under each roof. By contemporary standards of other pre-industrial urban communities where mean household size has been found to range from four to seven, Scarborough's extended families seem to have been smaller than most; and since household size usually varied according to family wealth, Scarborough's relatively low figure suggests below average income.

On the other hand, the most complete Hearth Tax return for Scarborough, that of Michaelmas 1673, along with other taxation documents of the 1640s, indicate that, in contrast to other towns, the segregation of rich and poor had not yet begun. Whereas York, Norwich, Newcastle and others had affluent central parishes and poorer suburbs, Scarborough's wealth was fairly evenly spread across all four Quarters. Fifteen of the 109 homes in Undercliff had four or more hearths; in St Mary's, the number was 17 out of a total of 75; in Oldborough, 21 out of 182; and in Newborough, 21 out of 131.

Clearly, St Mary's was the most favoured: much of it was still grassland and garden, open to the south with commanding views of sea and harbour. In 1673 its principal residents were Mr William Lawson, one of the town's two vintners, and soon to be elected for the fourth time as bailiff, two of the Thompsons, Richard and Francis, and John Knowsley, the future Tory mayor. Yet much less favoured Undercliff was the home of Mr William Saunders, the other vintner, who had 11 chimneys, and of the Harrisons, the Tindalls and the Cockerills, all well-to-do shipbuilders and shipowners.

The most populous Quarter, Oldborough, was still not shunned by the rich and privileged. Here was Scarborough's grandest private house with 12 hearths, at the lower end of St Sepulchre Gate, and now occupied by William Thompson, one of the borough's two MPs. Nearby lived William Robinson, soon to be chosen bailiff for the third time, and Daniel Foord, who was to be his junior in that office in 1673-4. Finally, Newborough, the home of the Fysh, Hickson, Sedman, Sollitt and Key families, as well as Timothy Foord, Daniel's elder brother, also had its share of poorer residents.

Under the terms of the Act of 1662 householders whose poverty already excused them from paying poor and church rates or whose premises were worth less than 20 shillings per annum were exempted from the new hearth tax. In practice, anyone with fewer than three hearths lived on or below the poverty line, whereas possession of ten or more chimneys indicated considerable affluence. In 1673 Scarborough had only four residents assessed at ten or more hearths; two of these were vintners who owned inns, and the other two were William Thompson and Mrs Harrison, widow of Mr John Harrison. Just as prosperity seems to have been fairly evenly distributed across the four Quarters, so too was poverty. The percentages of exempted households

113

were Newborough 27%, Oldborough 26%, St Mary's 23% and Undercliff 26%.

If Scarborough had a poor suburb it was the detached community of Falsgrave. Of the 44 households in the village, 13 or 32 per cent were exempt, and only five of them were taxed on three hearths. It would be some time yet before sea captains and shipowners chose to retire to the rural setting of Falsgrave. A constables' list of 1665, giving the names of Scarborough's master mariners, seamen and apprentices, showed that only nine of the 189 had homes in Falsgrave.

The same constables' list also confirms a fairly even spread of sea-going men and boys across the town's four districts. Nine master mariners and 44 seamen lived in Newborough, 14 masters and 31 seamen in Oldborough, eight masters and 24 seamen in St Mary's, and eleven masters and 39 seamen in Undercliff - altogether a total of 189, 45 masters and 144 seamen and boys. There were three 15 year-old boys, seven 16-year-olds; only a few seamen were 60, and the eldest was 65. Henry Nicholson, the 70 year-old master mariner, was unique; only four other masters were aged 55 or over.

Information about the houses of Scarborians at this time is hard to find: only fragments of dwellings that predate 1700 are described and contemporary records on the subject are disappointingly thin. However, we know that as early as 1636 William Saunderson, the brickburner, formerly of York, had become a Scarborough resident and that year was contracted to produce 52,500 bricks and 31,500 tiles. Members of the First Twelve agreed to buy 1,500 bricks and 900 tiles, the Second, 1000 bricks and 600 tiles, and the Third, 500 bricks and 300 tiles. Saunderson was to have ten shillings for every thousand bricks and eighteen shillings for every thousand tiles. Extensive pits and trenches where clay was dug out for brick-making at this time have been discovered in the Paradise area.

Most dwellings were probably still thatched and built of timber, wattle and daub, but during the course of the 17th-century more and more were converted to brick, pantile or slate. When the market-place shambles were repaired at the charge of the town in 1627 they were covered with pantiles. Sometimes only part of a roof was modernised: in 1628 when a house in Newborough was disputed it was said to be 'half slated & thother half thatched'. By mid-century, pantiles had become commonplace. When George Wynd, described as a yeoman, died in 1647, in his will he left a thousand pantiles.

Probably the most conspicuous and important change in domestic architecture during the century was the addition of chimneys for coal fires. The availability to Scarborians of cheap sea-coal for their home fires meant that even the poorest had at least one hearth. No doubt some of the 52,000 bricks 'burned' by William Saunderson were used to build new chimneys on to wooden-framed houses. Even the town gaol was fitted with a 'chimley', as well as 'a house of ease', by order of the Common Hall in 1637. There are no pictures of seventeenth-century Scarborough, but if any were drawn they would have shown a forest of chimneys belching forth coal smoke, especially in winter. That chimneys had become so numerous explains why Parliament decided to tax them in 1662.

Only one comprehensive description of a Scarborough house and its contents, dated 1631, has survived, but this was certainly a superior dwelling. The ground floor was divided into five areas: a central hall, with table, benches and fireplace was flanked by kitchen and buttery on one side, and parlour and study on the other. Above them, on the first floor, were four chambers or bedrooms, each with a single bed and bed linen. The chamber over the hall had a spinning wheel and the kitchen had a brewing vessel among its utensils.

Household sizes were usually greater than today's because it was then the custom for several generations of the same family or different families to live under the same roof. Men of quite modest means would commonly leave part of their home to their widows and other parts to sons and daughters. In Scarborough widows received a variety of part properties ranging from the 'backside of a house in Conduit Row' and 'a little low room' to the more generous 'forehouse and kitchen' or 'forehouse and parlour'. William Harrison, the panyerman, left his house to his son 'except the chambers and kiln to his wife for life'. Substantial houses, usually called mansions, might be split between sons: William Fysh left the west part of his mansion in Cargate to his son Robert and the east part to his son Thomas.

Crime and Punishment

So seventeenth-century Scarborough had a relatively homogeneous resident population. There were no great extremes of wealth and poverty. Scarborough had no householder or house to compare with the Cholmleys in their Abbey House at Whitby with its 39 chimneys. Rich and poor lived side-by-side. There were no ghettos and no socially exclusive places. This was a small, closely-knit, face-to-face society, largely self-sufficient economically and unwelcoming to outsiders, at least until after 1660.

Modern research into urban societies reveals a clear correlation between social inequality and crime. Poverty of itself does not cause crime, but gross, perceived inequalities of income and lifestyle produce high rates of criminal behaviour. Social cooperation and cohesion are the keys to a law-abiding community. In the seventeenth-century, Scarborough might still be ruled by a privileged, self-perpetuating oligarchy, but the members of it were just as vulnerable to illness and epidemic as the poor and equally subject to law enforcement. Above all, all these people lived closely together and even in an age of civil war and revolution they reacted as a community and retained their social cohesion.

Of course there were other reasons why Scarborough was so relatively free of crime and disorder. The borough's magistrates were even more severe on breaches of the criminal law than they were on infringements of the town's 'pains'. The harshness and certainty of punishment might well have been sufficient to explain why the clerk of the quarter sessions was often able to write 'omne bene' (all's well) in the court book.

Though Scarborough still called one of its fields beyond Newborough Bar 'Gallas Close', there is no evidence that by the seventeenth-century the hangman had employment there. Capital offences, from murder down to theft of property worth more than a shilling, were now referred to the assizes at York for trial and sentence. Scarborough's magistrates were concerned mainly with petty larceny, bastardy, scolding, assault, drunkenness, poaching and breaches of the sabbath.

If found guilty, male thieves were locked in the stocks for an hour or two, and female thieves were whipped in public. Since the town stocks were in Newborough Gate, victims hoped that their sentence did not coincide with Thursday market. In any case, constables were put on duty to protect them from being pelted with anything worse than insults. In fact, even the pettiest of larceny was rare or rarely reported perhaps because its victims often settled the score without recourse to the constables or the court, and punishment was so barbarous. For example, in 1649, William Sheppard had been caught attempting to steal clothes from a hedge, but he was put in the stocks for two hours and 'a paper [pinned] on his brest expressing his fait'. Ann Harwood confessed to milking Michael Dickinson's cows in the night and was whipped from the doors of the Common Hall on Sandside all the road up the hill to Newborough Bar. For taking 'two gowpen fulls of coales' from the cellar of Francis Sollitt, on the night of 2 January 1661, Elizabeth Stonehouse was whipped by the bellman on her naked shoulders all the way from West Sandgate 'to the cellar under the castle' where the coal had been stored. No allowance was made for the season of the year or Elizabeth's desperate need. Public humiliation as well as physical suffering must have been strong deterrents.

Women were also stripped to the waist and flogged through the streets for bearing bastard children. For example, Ann Barry was whipped by the constables along the whole length of Longwestgate 'until her bodie be bloodie'. For 'her wicked acte & for the better detteringe of others from the same', Margaret Merryale received similar punishment, only she was drawn in a cart on a circular route of the town starting and ending on Sandside.

The fathers of illegitimate children got off comparatively lightly: they were required to pay the mother a weekly allowance, usually about a shilling, and after seven years a lump sum of 40 shillings for binding the child to an apprenticeship. There was also a requirement on the father, if he could be identified and located, to pay 10 shillings compensation to the mother's 'lying in the child bedd one month at the least'.

Women were also ill-treated for an offence known as 'scolding', that is verbal public abuse. Though there is no evidence that Scarborough, unlike some towns, punished convicted scolds by padlocking their heads into iron cages, there is a reference in the corporation records that in 1616 members of the First Twelve contributed to the cost of making a ducking stool. This high-backed, wooden chair with iron bands to tie the victim's hands and feet was fastened to one end of a beam which stood on the old great pier. Repeated, full immersion in cold sea water was not yet considered a cure for any bodily ailment; but in Scarborough it was used to cure 'scolding'. Parliament did not ban the employment of punishment 'cuck stools' until as late as 1837. Scarborough's last ducking chair is now a museum exhibit in the Rotunda.

When men abused each other verbally in public the result was usually a brawl, but in Scarborough it was particularly inadvisable to slander any of the borough's officers, especially the bailiffs and coroners. For calling coroner William Foord 'a snotty foole', William Robinson, the butcher, was fined 3s 4d. Unfortunately, it is not recorded what happened to William Slee, the mariner, after he had described the jury as 'shitbucketts', but John Potter was fined the colossal sum of five pounds for complaining loudly that the bailiff was a 'knave'. Potter was a panyerman from York so this might explain the indignation of bailiff Nesfield.

Physical assault or affray causing bloodshed was the most common charge heard in the quarter sessions, though not all the cases concerned men. Sometimes men were the victims of female aggression. Widow Margery Fysh drew blood from Robert Deeton in 1646, and it was not for his health. After Christopher Clarke, a town constable, had assaulted Thomas Carr twice on the same day, Clarke's wife, Ann, joined in the action and gave Carr a third beating. Wife-beating with hands or feet was perfectly permissible as long as it was your own wife, not someone else's. The borough's own officers were natural targets and there were many cases reported when they had to defend themselves physically from attack. On the other hand, at least two bailiffs, John Farrer and Robert Harthropp, had short tempers and ready fists. On more than one occasion, Farrer was obliged by the court to pay bonds of recognizance to keep the peace, and Harthropp was frequently involved in fracas. Nevertheless, soon after striking George Weare's wife, Harthropp was elected senior bailiff, an office he had already held once before. Clearly, even magistrates were not expected to be always law-abiding and peaceful.

Fornication, adultery and incest remained the exclusive concern of the church courts until they were abolished during the Civil War and not revived afterwards. For the sexual morals of Scarborians there are few sources of reference other than the infrequent archbishops' visitation reports. For example, according to the report drawn up for archbishop Grindal in 1575, Scarborough had no more than half a dozen adulterers and one incestuous pair of brother and sister; whereas in 1633, a similar survey recorded only three cases of fornication and one of them was between a couple who were about to be married. There are surviving references to prostitution in the town, but these are very rare. In 1564 John Robinson was brought before the court 'for kepynge Elizabeth

Walmsley as a harlott', and at the same sessions another townsman was presented for keeping a bawdy house. Nearly a century later, the widow Robinson, who lived in Falsgrave, was accommodating several violent men in her house.

Only a single case of alleged witchcraft has survived in the records of Scarborough's quarter sessions. When the four-year-old daughter of John and Anne Allen suffered frightening fits, the finger of accusation was pointed at Anne Hunman. Sure enough when Hunman was examined on the orders of bailiff Luke Robinson, she was found to have the mark of a witch - a blue spot on her left buttock, the devil's own sign. Though the spot was pricked with a pin, the accused never flinched and the mark grew 'out of her flesh as a wart of a greate bigness'. However, when Robinson questioned Hunman she vehemently denied 'practising any conjuracions witchcraft or evil intents', and accused another one of 'the vocation...of evill and wicked spiritts'. Unfortunately, the outcome of this inquiry is unknown since the reports of subsequent proceedings at Michaelmas 1652 have now been lost.

Drunkenness in public was commonplace and not in itself usually sufficient to bring a man or woman before Scarborough's magistrates. Brewing, selling and drinking beer were principal activities in the town: at any one time during the seventeenth century there were up to 60 licensed brewers, any number of unlicensed, illegal brewers, about 30 licensed ale-house keepers and two taverns, licensed to sell wine and spirits as well as beer. Beer was as essential as bread. Workmen were paid wages in drink; children drank small or diluted beer; bargains and contracts were sealed with beer; ale houses were open throughout the day; and alehouse keepers were forbidden to sell beer at more than a penny a quart.

During the 1650s, particularly in the year 1651-2, when Luke Robinson, the Presbyterian, was senior bailiff, attempts were made to keep Scarborians more sober. Eighteen men, including three with the title of 'Mister', were each fined 3s. 4d merely for 'tipling in alehouses', and ten publicans ten shillings each for 'entertaining people in their houses'. The proceeds were sent to the overseers of the poor. However, after Robinson's term of office, there were no more magisterial purges of habitual drinkers and their hosts. Two of the fined tipplers, Matthew Fowler and William Saunders, were elected junior bailiffs in 1652 and 1654 respectively. The number of brewster's licences granted by the bailiffs every April had fallen steadily between 1652 and 1658, but by

1660 it was rising again. After the puritan regime at St Mary's of vicar Edward Carleton, the Restoration brought the return of the bibulous Edward Simpson. If Scarborough had been more temperant it was only temporary.

What Scarborians did during their limited leisure time apart from consuming beer, is revealed by the many examples of Sabbath-breaking brought before the quarter sessions. The law required all his Majesty's subjects to attend Sunday and holy day services; in practice, however, only those who obstinately refused communion, such as Catholics and Quakers, or the far greater number of those who blatantly flouted the rules by enjoying themselves or working on Sundays, were reported by the churchwardens.

If you did not attend St Mary's on Sunday the wisest alternative was to stay at home on your own. It was unsafe to work out of doors. The town magistrates frequently fined men for driving cattle, carrying goods, 'gathering roapes in sermon time', rowing boats in the harbour, and, on one occasion, 'for traveling towards Semer fair with a pack'. All kinds of games, even indoor ones, were forbidden on Sundays. There were several cases of young men presented 'for playing at football, upon the Sabbath day', for playing 'att coit[s] in sermon tyme', and for 'playing at knacks'. Other forbidden Sunday sports are harder to identify. What exactly was 'the joyling ball' that nine youths were condemned for playing one Sabbath day in 1656, or 'pene pricke', which had occupied two others? A year later, six young men were caught at 'swechpoynt'; whatever that might have been, it was illegal on a Sunday. Even the playing of 'a Jews harpe' aroused the indignation of the magistrates in 1659. If it coincided with 'sermon time', just strolling on the sands at Scarborough was considered an affront to the Sabbath. Indeed, strolling on the sands of anywhere on a Sunday could get you into trouble. In an extraordinary presentment before the sessions in July 1656, seven Scarborough fishermen were accused of 'walking the streettes & sand upon the lordes day the time of prayers & sermon - att Yarmouth'!

Even inside your own home there was no certain safety from the churchwardens or the constables. Playing at cards, dice or shovelboard, drinking, or merely entertaining guests at home on Sunday might bring you up before the bailiffs. Child-beating was limited to six days a week. In October 1660 Will Wret, the mason, was summoned to the sheriff's tourn 'for beattin of Raf Richson boy of the Saboth day'.

120

Whether the boy was an apprentice or a servant was not explained, but presumably Will's error was to beat him on a Sunday. More puzzling is the case of Bartholomew Duesbery who was presented in July 1650 'for abusing the saboth ... with casting stones amongest children contrarey to the statute'. Bartholomew was later condemned as an alehouse tippler so perhaps he was the worse for drink, but was he throwing stones at the children or showing off his skill at skimming pebbles over the sea?

Scarborough's magistrates heard only a few cases of poaching perhaps because Scarborians were rarely driven by hunger and also they were confined to their homes from dusk to dawn by the town watch. Anyone discovered abroad in the darkness of the night was assumed to have evil intentions. So daytime poaching was restricted to shooting passing pigeons with firearm or bow and arrow or hunting hares and rabbits with dogs. Guard dogs had to be muzzled when they were taken out into the streets. There were repeated public warnings of a shilling fine for breach of this bye-law and several incidents of vicious mastiffs biting innocent victims. Foxes and foumarts (polecats) were regarded as predatory vermin and therefore fair game for anyone. The churchwardens paid a shilling each for fox heads and fourpence for foumart heads, whoever brought them in; but other ground game was the preserve of the town's official warrener. The fishing rights in Scarborough Mere, or Byward Wath as it was then called, were on long-term lease for an annual rent of twenty shillings, though the two bailiffs also had access to them during their year in office.

Work and Trade

Scarborians spent most of their waking lives working, and Scarborough's bailiffs spent much of their time enforcing statutory and local laws concerning conditions of employment. No man was allowed to practise a trade in the town unless he had first completed an apprenticeship. Wages were regulated by law. Masters were forbidden to pay below, and workmen to take wages above, the recognised daily rate for the job. Even rates of interest on debt were controlled. William Sedman, master mariner, was said to have taken more than that permitted - eight per cent on a private loan of twelve pounds.

To prevent fraud and exploitation all Scarborough's markets were strictly supervised. Of the three trading offences - forestalling (buying goods before they reached the public market), regrating (buying in order to resell at a profit in the same market), and engrossing (buying up large quantities of the same goods to achieve a monopoly for re-sale) - forestalling was the most commonly recorded in the proceedings of the borough courts. All sales had to be made in public in the open market. Quality and condition were just as important as price. For instance, the Common Hall appointed leather searchers and sealers who inspected, passed or rejected all the leather offered for sale locally. There was a fine for anyone who tried to sell 'untanned' leather which had not received the borough's seal of approval.

Since fishing went on night and day throughout the year, and fish had to be sold or treated within hours of landing, control of its marketing was the most difficult to achieve. From time to time the bailiffs had to be content to hand down exemplary punishments on fishwives who tried to cheat the authorised market in the fish shambles. In the case of herring, where most landings were made by 'strangers', the bailiffs resorted to taxes on fish porters and fines on illegal traders.

After completing an apprenticeship it was still necessary to join a company in order to qualify and practise a trade as a journeyman or master. By the seventeenth century Scarborough's craft companies had declined in number and membership since their medieval apogee. According to Baker there had been as many as 20 such companies or guilds in the fifteenth century, but by his time (1882) only the coopers and joiners remained. Corporation records of the 1600s refer only to the companies of tailors, butchers, bakers, glovers, masons, smiths, carpenters, shoemakers or cordwainers, skinners, weavers and porters, and some of their compositions or rules have survived from these years. The purpose of these companies was to protect the interests of the masters and journeymen by restricting competition; they were closed shops. However, the compositions had to secure the approval of the corporation and there were occasions when the bailiffs modified the rules if they believed them to be too rigid and punitive. Of nearly all fines imposed by the guilds on their members half went to the Common Hall. Yet the companies were more than trade unions operating restrictive commercial practices: they also acted as friendly societies. When any member died his company 'in decente maner accompanyed the dead corps to the place of buriall' and cared for his widow and any other dependants.

Of all the 'trades unions' in Scarborough by far the newest yet most powerful was the Society of Shipowners, Masters and Mariners.

The Society was founded on 21 December 1602, the feast day of St Thomas the Apostle, and annually on this day, after a service in St Mary's at nine in the morning, its members solemnly walked down through the streets of the town to the Common Hall on Sandside. It was there that they elected their four wardens for the following year.

For every successful return coastal voyage and every successful voyage abroad owners were obliged to pay fourpence and eightpence, and their master mariners one and twopence respectively. Only fragments of the wardens' accounts have survived from the seventeenth century but they show that 'the seamens charity' was dispensed widely and generously. For example, in 1635, at the height of the Spanish-Dutch war in the North Sea, shipwrecked sailors of all kinds were aided: six 'shipp broaken men of Dunage (Dunwich)' received 3s. 4d.; six 'Frenchmen that had lost their ship' the same sum; four Flemings got one shilling and sixpence; two Sunderland men two shillings; and six Yarmouth seamen, 'lost at Whittbie', a shilling each. Of course most of the charity went to Scarborough men and their families. In 1638, Ambrose Gilbert, 'being a poor man and taken with the Spainyerds', was given sixpence; 'a broken seafareingman' one shilling and sixpence; and Ann Bowland, probably a widowed woman, received four shillings. Moneys left over were distributed at Christmas to the poor, sometimes as much as 30 shillings, more often only 20.

However, since the wardens and the principal shipowners were invariably senior members of the Common Hall, it became customary for the corporation to borrow from the 'sailors' money'. By 1660 the corporation owed the Society a hundred pounds and was persuaded to hand over the two Northstead Lane closes of meadow as security for the outstanding debt. By 1689 the Society held seven closes of corporation meadow on the north side of Weaponness at a peppercorn rent and the 'loan' had increased to £200. However, by that date, the Society had, at last, acquired a house of its own and was no longer obliged to use the Common Hall for its meetings.

Aware of the corporation's reputation for 'borrowing' from charitable funds, Lady Lawson, the Admiral's widow, was reluctant to hand over the £100 her husband had bequeathed to the poor people of the town in 1665. After two years she accepted a promise that six per cent would be paid out on the sum and doled out every Christmas, and that a search would be made for 'a convenient piece of ground' on which the Society of Owners and Masters might build almshouses. Lady

Lawson's suspicions were well founded: the corporation spent her husband's legacy on rebuilding St Mary's church tower which had fallen down in 1659, and it was not until 1682 that the first Trinity House in St Sepulchre Gate was finally opened. From then on the Society provided free accommodation for 27 aged seamen and the widows of seamen.

Seafaring of one kind or another occupied the largest number of Scarborough men. Apart from the 189 masters and seamen and boys recorded in the constables' list of 1665, there were at least as many more engaged in off-shore and deep-sea fishing. Queen Elizabeth had been informed in the petition of 1564 that 'the towne hathe bene maynteyned heretofore onelie by ffishyng' - an exaggeration, but not an excessive one. As long as the herring migrated in enormous numbers down the east coast every summer, Scarborough would continue to act as a major centre for their landing, sale, and preservation by salting, smoking or drying. From April off the Shetlands to October when the herring reached the Channel waters, Scarborough men fished the great shoals which might be six miles long and four miles wide and so dense that 'the water before them curls up as if forced out of its bed'.

It was mainly for the herring that Scarborough's fishermen went to sea in their so-called five-man boats. These boats were 50 feet long, 15 feet broad, decked at each end with a hatchway in the middle and carried two sails. Though they had a crew of six men and a boy, who was cook, only five of the men were shareholders, the sixth man and boy were paid wages. When they were not following the shoals of herring, Scarborough's fishermen went as far as the Dogger Bank in search of cod, haddock, ling and skate. They used lines up to three miles long each with more than 2,500 baited hooks. For inshore fishing they used the smaller cobles, only half the size of the five-man boats. The cobles were clinker-built with a single sail and two or three pairs of oars. Since they were almost flat-bottomed and only about one ton burthen, the cobles could be beached and launched from the sands with relative ease.

However, far more fish, especially herring, were landed at Scarborough by foreigners than by natives. Scotsmen followed the shoals southwards; men from Boston, King's Lynn, Great Yarmouth, Lowestoft and Harwich came northwards to meet them; and Dutchmen, Flemings and Danes crossed the North Sea to intercept them on their southward journey. Scarborough was still an important place for marketing fish, even though Scarborough Fair was much diminished in size since its medieval zenith. In 1661 John Ray could still write: 'The town hath a great trade in fish taken thereabouts'.

If fewer Scarborough men were fishing, more and more of them were engaged in ship building and the carrying trade; and the carrying trade was overwhelmingly in coal. After the interruptions caused by the Civil War in the years 1642-5, the volume of coal transported out of the Tyne and Wear and down the east coast increased year by year. A succession of naval wars, first with the Dutch, 1652-4, 1664-7 and 1672-4, and then with the French, 1689-97 and 1702-13, made Scarborough all the more valuable as a port of refuge for the collier fleets.

The importance of Scarborough's harbour was emphatically illustrated as early as April 1653 in the first year of the First Dutch War. A great fleet of 300 colliers had put to sea from Newcastle escorted by nine English warships. The price of coal had trebled in London during a winter of shortages there and the government was afraid of popular disturbances if supplies were not soon replenished. Aware of the value of this collier fleet, Admiral de Witt lay in wait for it with 20 Dutch men-of-war off Flamborough Head. Fortunately for the colliers the bailiffs of Scarborough were informed of de Witt's presence and plan, and so the fleet was advised to come into the protection of their harbour, pier and castle.

About half of the smaller colliers crowded into the harbour behind the great pier while the other 150 anchored outside under the castle headland amongst the Navy's warships. Some cannon were unloaded from the ships onto the pier while the castle guns of the South Steel Battery were made ready to repel the Dutch. Though de Witt closed in and fired a few cannon shots, after two days he decided not to risk his ships and sailed away. Not a single collier had been lost. Thanks to Scarborough's location, safe anchorage and artillery defences, the whole fleet of precious colliers resumed its voyage southwards.

Perhaps a fleet of 300 colliers was exceptional in size but it remained Admiralty practice for a long time to come to escort convoys down the east coast. In case of enemy attack they always passed close to Scarborough. For example, in 1697 during King William's war with the French, when Celia Fiennes visited Scarborough she observed '70 saile of shipps pass the point (castle headland)...supposed to be colliers, and their convoys'.

If the coastal coal trade had greatly enhanced the value of Scarborough as a harbour of refuge particularly in wartime, during the course of the seventeenth century it also made it into a leading shipbuilding and ship-owning port. In 1600 no Scarborough vessel was recorded as a collier. In the year ending Christmas 1612, of the two and a half thousand cargoes of coal shipped from Newcastle down the North Sea coast mostly to London, Ipswich provided ships for 363, King's Lynn 299, Yarmouth 258, Newcastle 206, Hull 167, London 136, Harwich 136, York 55, Bridlington 46, Selby 26 and Scarborough 25. Ninety years later, on a comparable list, Scarborough had jumped from 21st to 7th place. By the beginning of the eighteenth century Scarborough was one of only seven English ports with more than 100 ships, and only London, Bristol, Liverpool, Exeter and Yarmouth had significantly more of their men than Scarborough who were employed on their ships. In Scarborough's case, 606 men were recorded as engaged on that port's ships in 1702.

And by that time most of Scarborough's merchant and collier vessels had been built in Scarborough's own shipyards. According to one authority on the subject, Scarborough already had a 'flourishing shipbuilding industry' as early as 1640, but evidence for it is hard to find. The key event in Scarborough's shipbuilding history seems to have occurred towards the end of the century in 1691 when William Tindall set up his yard on Smithy Hill, Sandside. During the next century and a half several generations of the Tindall family built hundreds of ships on the site.

The Tindalls were not the first family of Scarborough shipbuilders, even though they became the most successful and productive. Before their arrival on Sandside there were already shipwrights and boatbuilders with names such as Breckon, Porrett, Allatson, Sollitt, Bilborough and Cockerill. The Cockerill shipyard had been so profitable that James of that name had moved up physically as well as socially from Undercliff to St Mary's by the 1670s. When the Hearth Tax assessment was made at Michaelmas 1673 James Cockerill and his wife were already occupants of Paradise House, second only to the Thompson mansion as the finest dwelling in the town. When he died in 1719 James left a considerable estate which included three houses in Newborough Gate, a tenement and warehouse in East Sandgate, a raff yard on Long Greece, as well as his tools, ships and Paradise House with its gardens, meadows and maltkilns. His daughter, Anna, was to have £500 for her marriage portion and his mother-in-law four guineas for 'a suite of mourning'. In William Porrett's will of 1706 James was described as 'a gentleman'.

There is still a lane from Quay Street on to Sandside called Porritt's Lane, but Bilborough Hill has long since disappeared from the inner harbour. Richard Bilborough had fought for the king during the Civil Wars; after the Restoration he gradually climbed Scarborough corporation's greasy pole of preferment up through the three Twelves and via the usual offices of churchwarden and chamberlain. Richard never reached the exalted place of bailiff, but he and his descendants built boats long enough for a sandhill where they were launched, to be named after his family. Bilborough Hill appears on John's Cossins 'New and Exact Plan' of Scarborough drawn in 1725. *(back end paper)*

These sandhills in the inner harbour - Smithy Hill, Bilborough Hill and Tindall Hill - were in fact the sloping launchways of shipyards. Each vessel was constructed on a gradient ramp with its stern to the sea and then run out into the harbour at high tide usually with masts and rigging already fitted. The earliest shipyards were at the northern end of Sandside but as their number increased they spread southwards along the whole length of the shore.

The shipbuilding community was small and closely-knit: William Tindall married a Cockerill: each of his three daughters had shipwright husbands. Mary married George Cockerill, Ann's husband was Anthony More, and Thomasin became Mrs Joshua Sollitt. Until a Shipwright's Society was founded in 1775, all the shipbuilding menfolk belonged to the Society of Owners, Masters and Mariners and many of them had foremost places in the Common Hall.

However, party politics and local government were rarely priorities for this shipbuilding fraternity. It was the custom for the sons of Scarborough's shipbuilding families to go to sea as apprentices and serve their time before becoming master mariners. Experience at sea was considered essential: shipbuilders had first to learn the art and mystery of the mariner and then practise it for several years before coming ashore to design and make new vessels. Then, only when they had merited status, did they offer themselves for places in the Common Hall. Maritime men were prominent but not predominant in Scarborough's oligarchy.

Oligarchy

Even after all the political upheavals of civil war, republic, restoration and revolution, Scarborough's government remained persistently a privileged closed shop. Lord Presidents of the Council in the North had once exercised influence from outside, but that council had been abolished in 1641 and had not been restored. The office of lord high admiral had been revived on the return of the monarchy in 1660, but its new holder, James, Duke of York, failed to get his candidate, Sir Hugh Cholmley, elected to represent Scarborough in the Cavalier Parliament. As governor of the castle from 1661 until his death in 1670, Sir Jordan Crosland was also one of the First Twelve and the borough's senior member in the House of Commons, yet even he seems to have had little involvement in the affairs of the Common Hall.

After 1670 several attempts were made to open parliamentary elections in Scarborough to a 'free vote', that is to all the freemen, who numbered between 80 and 100, instead of merely to the 44 members of the Common Hall. However, such attempts were no more than party political manoeuvres in the contest between Whigs and Tories, not genuine efforts to make the government of the corporation more fairly and fully representative. When Francis Thompson, Whig, fought the election of 1685 by trying to poll the town's freemen, the Tory mayor had him arrested on the grounds that he was trying to provoke a civil riot! Once the Thompsons were back again in their Commons seats after Tory rout of 1689, there was no more talk from them of widening the franchise. In January of that year, William Thompson gave one of the town's innkeepers two guineas and told him to 'make the freemen merry'. Presumably, he hoped that they would be happier with beer than with votes. Further attempts were made in 1693 and 1705 to extend the franchise to freemen, but to no avail.

Meanwhile the exclusive 44 continued to enjoy their own hospitality. Mr William Lawson, vintner and member of the First Twelve, found the Common Hall a ready and profitable customer. Between January and August 1668 bailiffs Hickson and Key ran up a colossal bill of £14 15s. 8d. on food, wine and tobacco for their quarter sessions dinners and entertainment for their guests. Apart from these magistrates' sessions there were many other occasions during the year - Christmas, Easter, Lammas, and the perambulation of the Liberty's boundaries every June - when the wine, beer and punch flowed freely.

The Common Cryer

17ᵗʰ Century Street Scenes

For example, on 1 June 1736 the corporation ran up a debt of £19 13s. 9d. for what was called 'the perambulation dinner'. Every year the bailiffs and councillors rode and the 'common folk' walked the lengthy boundaries of the borough and afterwards rewarded themselves with a feast. On this occasion in 1736 the mountains of food were washed down with 20 quarts of brandy in punch, three quarts and eight bottles of wine, and many barrels of ale and porter. The 'common folk' were given bread and beer; no doubt bailiffs John Huntriss and Allatson Bell preferred the brandy and wine punch with their dinners. As in Rome when the college of cardinals elected a new Pope so in Scarborough when the Common Hall every St Jerome's day, 30 September, met to choose its officers for the forthcoming year, the doors were closed until agreement had been reached. That some elections on Sandside took all of three days and nights when the 44 were provided with free food, alcohol and tobacco might suggest to some cynics that proceedings were deliberately prolonged.

8

FIRST SEASIDE RESORT

The Long Eighteenth Century 1700 -1835

The 'long' century that began with the death of the last reigning Stuart, Queen Anne, in 1714, and ended with the accession of Queen Victoria in 1837, is described as 'Georgian' because for most of these years four Hanoverian Georges – George I (1714-27), George II (1727-60), George III (1760-1820) and George IV (1820-30) – ruled in succession in Great Britain and Ireland. However, by this time, royal had given way largely to parliamentary power; who occupied the throne mattered less and less. Anne was the last monarch to veto legislation; George II was the last to appear on the battlefield at Dettingen in 1743.

Throughout the century the British were frequently at war with their French neighbours – on the European continent, at sea, and in North America and India. Whatever the issue fought over, Britain and France always took opposing sides – in the War of the Austrian Succession, 1740-8, the Seven Years' War, 1756-63, the War of American Independence, 1776-83, and the prolonged conflicts known as the French Revolutionary, 1793-1802, and Napoleonic Wars, 1803-15. The net result of all these Anglo-French wars was that the Royal Navy became supreme in all the world's oceans and seas; and, though Britain lost the 13 American colonies, it conquered another empire that included Canada, much of coastal Africa, India, Australasia, and a string of vital naval bases such as Gibraltar, Malta and Cape Town. By 1815 Britain was the strongest and richest state on the planet. 'Rule Britannia', 'Heart of Oak' and 'God Save the King' were all written and sung lustily during this century.

At home this was an era of revolutionary economic and social change. Other than Holland, England became the most urbanised country in Europe. Between 1714 and 1811 the population of England doubled from five to ten million. Nowhere was this transformation more evident than in the Midlands and the North where industrialisation created new concentrations of workers and their families.

By 1831, 1.3 million people lived in Yorkshire, now England's most populous county, but nearly one million of them were inhabitants of the West Riding, where Leeds, Bradford, Sheffield, Halifax, Huddersfield and other 'new' towns had broken out of their old parish boundaries. The factory system gradually displaced the old domestic textile industry. Apart from Hull, Yorkshire's older towns, such as York, Beverley, Ripon and Richmond, kept their two Members of Parliament but were losing their former prominence.

This was also an age of radical improvements in transport by way of navigable rivers, canals and turnpike roads, and finally railways and steam locomotives. It was the new Iron Age. The problem of smelting iron with coal instead of charcoal was successfully overcome and by the end of the century railroads, bridges and ships were all being made of iron. England had become Europe's leading iron-producer and Yorkshire one of its main sources of coal.

There were also profound changes in agriculture. Though the enclosure of open arable and common pasture had been going on since the fifteenth century, between 1760 and 1810 Parliament passed well over 2000 Acts of enclosure. The familiar English landscape of small, cultivated fields and closes bound by fences, stone walls and hawthorn hedges became almost universal. At the same time, scientific breeding of cattle and sheep improved their health and increased their weight; and new grass and root crops kept them fed during the winters. English diet was liberated from salted meat. Finally, new soil and rotation techniques increased cereal yields and made it possible to grow wheat almost everywhere. All but the very poorest could now eat fresh beef and white bread throughout the year. England was largely self-sufficient in food yet only 40 per cent of its labour force were employed in farming.

Politically, however, the changes were minimal. In contrast to the fate of many of their continental equivalents, particularly the French, the British ruling class, a small oligarchy of the landed aristocracy and gentry, remained firmly in control. By 1821, the electorate was still less than three per cent of the population, lower than at any time since the Civil Wars. Representation in the House of Commons was antiquated: Cornwall had 42 parliamentary borough seats and Lancashire had 12. Of Yorkshire's 14 enfranchised boroughs only two, Hull and York, had electorates numerous enough to have a choice. The other 12 were either 'pocket' boroughs, like Beverley, Knaresborough, Malton, Pontefract, Ripon, Scarborough and Thirsk, controlled by local landlords, or 'rotten' boroughs like Hedon, whose 300 electors sold their votes to the highest bidder. Leeds, Sheffield, Bradford, Halifax and Wakefield had no Members of their own. With only minor concessions, though in the face of mounting protest, this grossly unrepresentative situation remained unaltered until the Great Reform Act of 1832.

If anti-French chauvinism was one factor that saved Britain from the revolutions that ravaged and liberated the European continent, the revival of religious enthusiasm was another. At the beginning of the 18th century perhaps no more than four per cent of the nation were Nonconformist Protestants, yet according to the church attendance census of 1851 almost half preferred chapels to Anglican churches. Congregationalists and Baptists had greatly increased their numbers, but Methodism had won over by far the largest Dissenter group. Responding to the challenge, the erstwhile dormant and complacent Anglicans took on a new evangelical lease of vitality and at last began to build new churches, usually with parliamentary subsidy. In 1828 Parliament repealed the Test and Corporation Acts which excluded non-Anglicans from public office, and the following year freed Roman Catholics from similar discrimination.

In this national context, Scarborough's experience was mostly untypical. Apart from shipbuilding and its allied trades, the town had no industry of its own; it benefited from the new turnpike roads but lacked river communication and never gained a canal. On the other hand, the Puritan aversion to pleasure-seeking dissolved in the permissive environment of the times. Drinking, feasting, gambling, dancing, theatre-going, coffee-house gossiping and other pleasures became the accepted indulgences of those few who had the leisure and the money to afford them. And Scarborough specialised in providing them. Though still a vital harbour of refuge for the coal-carrying trade and an important shipping mart, the town had also become the North's leading coastal and sea-bathing resort for the well-to-do.

Dicky Dickinson

Predictably, Scarborough's rulers were very slow to appreciate the commercial potential of the spring waters bubbling from the base of the South Cliff, or Driple Cotes, as it was then called. Even twenty years after Mrs Farrer's famous discovery, the corporation chose the site for a pesthouse during the plague epidemic of 1645. Whether the inhabitants of the pesthouse were expected to drink the waters for their cure is not known, but their presence in the vicinity was not calculated to attract summer visitors.

The first reference in the corporation records to the spa spring betrays a lack of understanding and interest. In 1684 the Common Hall agreed that the water was to be sold at sixpence an 'anker' (approximately 64 pints or 41 litres), but any measure less than half an anker was to be granted free of charge. The same minute reveals that the spa water was by then being drawn off by women, later known as 'dippers' or 'servers', and profits from the sale were being put to the use of the town's poor. Though these charges were doubled seven years later, the water was still offered free of cost to sick persons who could prove their condition and need with certificates signed by churchwardens or clergyman. As yet, there was no evident motive that Scarborough might derive material profit from the diseased and distressed who came there to find relief and comfort. The springs of Driple Cotes were still regarded as 'a gift from heaven', and therefore freely available to all who sought their miraculous therapy.

Consequently, when Celia Fiennes rode into Scarborough in 1697, she discovered only 'a very pretty sea-port town' that had not yet become a busy health and leisure resort for those rich enough to afford it. As the War Office survey of 1686 had already shown, Scarborough was only fifteenth in a list of Yorkshire towns offering guest beds. With sleeping accommodation for only 74 visitors, Scarborough's resources fell well short of the 483 guest beds at York, 294 at Leeds, 205 at Malton, 182 at Beverley, 110 at Thirsk and 82 at Northallerton. It seems that the inland market towns and settlements on old major roads still provided much more for travellers than Scarborough, or even Harrogate, its main rival, could yet offer. And this applied also to accommodation for horses as well as people: Scarborough was said to have stabling for only 114 horses compared with York's 800, Malton's 543, Beverley's 460 and Richmond's 228.

Nevertheless, Miss Fiennes found advantages in a place not yet fashionable. She wrote that in Scarborough there was 'good accommodation and on very reasonable terms', whereas in more popular Buxton she had had to sleep in a room with four beds with sometimes three to a bed. Since there was always someone making a night-time visit to the toilet, no peaceful sleep could be had in such public dormitories. Celia noted that Scarborough's best lodgings were in the private houses of Quakers, who kept meticulously clean rooms and offered set meals at fixed prices for their guests.

Disappointingly to Miss Fiennes and other visitors at this time, Scarborough provided no accommodation whatsoever at its spa well. Visitors were expected to descend the perilous slope of St Nicholas Cliff or negotiate 400 yards of sands at low tide to reach the spring. There was no shelter from wind or rain at the 'spaw'. Worst of all, having taken gallons of brackish water to purge their sluggish bowels, 'spawers' would then have to relieve themselves publicly in the open.

Two years after Celia Fiennes rode away from Scarborough, the corporation finally stirred itself into action; but its purpose was to preserve the precious spa waters, not to save drinkers from discomfort or embarrassment. Though Dr Wittie had referred to a 'cistern' as early as 1667, this was probably no more than a natural hollow in the rocks at the foot of the cliff. The earliest reference to an artificial catchment and storage facility comes in a Common Hall minute of 15 May 1699 ordering that 'a large seasteron be made for keeping the spaw water'. As the note went on to explain, such a cistern would bring several benefits and improvements. The well could now be covered and locked to prevent unauthorised users from polluting it or drawing it without payment. The bailiffs only were to be trusted with keys and they were to appoint night-watchmen to guard the cistern and its supply pipe. Secondly, instead of running wastefully into the sea or out on the sands, the spa waters would now be safely stored. And finally, the well head would be covered from high tides which made the water too salty. At the same time, the corporation forecast optimistically that proceeds from the well would be sufficient to maintain all Scarborough's paupers in St Thomas's hospital.

Mrs Thomasin Farrer had first discovered the mineral and medicinal properties of Scarborough's seaside springs; Dr Robert Wittie had first publicised their therapeutic claims; and it was Richard Dickinson who first grasped and exploited their commercial potential. Entrepreneur, eccentric and showman, first self-styled 'governor of the spaw', Dicky Dickinson was to Scarborough what Beau Nash was to become to Brighton.

Though the original lease seems not to have survived in the corporation records, there is an undocumented tradition that about 1700 Richard Dickinson became a tenant-at-will for the parcel of Driple Cotes which contained the spa cistern. Dicky's rent was probably fixed at a pound a year. Scarborough's ruling body had at last woken up to the realisation that its mineral waters needed a full-time guardian; what it did not foresee was the enterprise of the new tenant.

Dicky calculated that he could attract a growing number of well-to-do customers to the spa and persuade them to return regularly only if they were offered more than drinking salty water on a windswept, open beach. Within a short time he had transformed the site at Driple Cotes.

What Dicky had done there is fully revealed by a drawing made of the 'Spaw' by Francis Place in 1715. By that time there were three buildings at the foot of the cliff immediately behind the well head. Set back from the other two was a simple, single-storey structure which Place labelled 'the Ladeys House'. A similar building, further forward towards the sea, at the top of a flight of wooden steps leading up from the sands, he described as 'Another house for the Gent[s]'. The third building, between the other two, of a more substantial kind with a chimney, he labelled 'Dickies House'. All three stood on a natural shelf in the rock face, buttressed by a staith of stones and upright timbers. Below them, on the sands, Place showed the well to be covered by a stone table which served as a counter for the women dippers.

Dickinson's 'conveniences' for gentlemen and lady visitors to his spa ought to have been welcome improvements, but they were far from satisfactory for the clientele he favoured most. In 1732, Sarah, duchess of Marlborough, widow of the great general and confidant of the late queen Anne, spent six weeks in Scarborough for her gout, rheumatism and scurvy. Her description of the town was almost entirely derogatory and her reaction to Dicky's 'Ladyes House' one of disgust. In a letter from Scarborough to her granddaughter, the duchess of Bedford, she wrote:

There is a room for the ladies' assembly, which you go up a steep pair of steps into, on the outside of the house, like a ladder. And in that room there is nothing but hard narrow benches, which is rather a punishment to sit upon than an ease. When the waters begin to operate, there is a room within it where there is above twenty holes with drawers under them to take out and all the ladies go in together and see one another round the room, when they are in that agreeable posture, and at the door there is a great heap of leaves which the ladies take in with them ... I came home as fast as I could for fear of being forced into that assembly.

From then on the duchess usually took her water bottled with oil on the top of the fluid and wax on the cork to seal it.

In short, here was one grand lady who would not demean herself to defecate in public, however genteel the company. Sarah conceded that the waters had rid her of scurvy, which had caused the itching that had so tormented her, and they were 'the best in the whole world for those that purging is good for'. However, she was disappointed that the spa had done nothing beneficial for her gout.

Furthermore, the duchess was less than pleased with Scarborough as a resort. Not only was the place where they drank the waters 'horrid', but the town itself was 'very dirty' compared with Bath or Tunbridge Wells, and with 'vast poverty in every part of it'. The food was worse than that at Hanover. The company was 'as dismal as a funeral' so that she deliberately avoided 'the public drawing room'. In another letter to her granddaughter she complained: 'There is no company here that one would not choose rather to be deaf and dumb than to be with them.' To add to her trials, she was kept awake every night by 'the barkings and howlings of dogs and hounds which is [sic] kept all round me for the entertainment of fine gentlemen in this place'. To deaden the noise of passing carts she had straw laid in the street outside her apartments.

Finally, Sarah was not the only 'spawer' who had cause to complain of the inaccessibility of the well which, she wrote, was 'so extremely steep and disagreeable to get to either in a coach or chair'. Mr Hanbury had nearly broken his neck trying to descend 'the precipice' to the well. Not surprisingly, the duchess vowed never to return to Scarborough. Indeed, in view of her many and strong objections to the place, it seems odd that she should have chosen to spend as long as six weeks in Scarborough. Her own explanation was that at the end of July, after three weeks there, she could not leave for York until the races were over, since there would be no suitable accommodation in the neighbourhood. An alternative explanation is that having endured a six-day journey from St Albans which she found 'very long and tiresome', she was most reluctant to face the return passage. That unlike the duchess of Manchester she did not try Dr Wittie's cold sea-bathing therapy for her gout is not surprising for a rather feeble lady of 72 years.

Another illustration of the failure of Scarborough's oligarchy to encourage visitors to come to the town is that it was left to private initiative to improve public access to the spa well. After a severe storm had damaged properties along the foreshore in 1720, John Bland, a local Quaker and shopkeeper, offered to build a new staith and a coach road running down to the sands from Carr Street, on condition that he received an adequate subsidy from the corporation. Hitherto the only approach to the spa from the town for horseback riders or coach and chair occupants was from West Sandgate, nearly half a mile distant. By 1723, at a cost to the Common Hall of £85, Bland's 'horse-way' was finished. Though to the duchess of Marlborough and her like who must have descended it, Bland's Cliff was still frighteningly steep and dangerous, it was still a shorter and better route than its predecessors. John Cossins's 'New and Exact Plan' of Scarborough, drawn two years later, shows 'Dickey's House', the 'Spaw Well' and the new 'Coach Road to the Spaw', zigzagging its way down to the foreshore sands from Carr Street and Newborough.

A more direct way for pedestrians to the spa from St Nicholas Cliff down into Ramsdale and then on to the sands by Mill Beck was not made into a proper footpath until as late as 1735 – too late for the unfortunate Mr Hanbury. In May of that year the Common Hall at last approved the work 'for commodiousness of the spawers', but only on condition that the costs were entirely covered by receipts from spa subscriptions. 'Spawers' could not expect subsidies from Scarborians: they would have to pay for their own amenities.

Meanwhile, Richard Dickinson had made Scarborough spa into a commercial success. Only in his renewed lease of 1727 is it made clear that Dicky, and not the corporation, had been responsible for the staith and the houses behind it, and this would explain why his rent remained at one pound a year for the next seven years. The corporation retained ownership of the land and the well, received the subscriptions from users, and paid the water servers. There was no question of surrendering freehold rights to the unofficially-styled 'governor'.

In the terms of Dicky's new lease of April 1727 he is described as 'a yeoman'. Here there is no hint of that extraordinary appearance and eccentric behaviour that attracted visitors to 'his' spa. Indeed, very few facts are known about Scarborough spa's first and most famous governor. Two daughters of a Richard Dickinson were baptized at St Mary's in 1690 and 1699, but there is no certainty that this Richard was the governor-to-be. A Mrs Anne Dickinson referred to in corporation accounts of 1738 might have been his widow. All that we know for certain is that Dicky lived in his spa house with 'Peggy', who was not his legal wife.

What can be discovered about Dicky Dickinson is to be found almost entirely in observations made by visitors in the season of 1733. From his lodgings in Scarborough in July of that year, Edmund Withers wrote to his brother, William, the vicar of Tunstall, that 'a remarkable creature, known by the name of Dicky' was 'perhaps the most singular deformity in the king's dominions'. A few months later, the anonymous author of 'A Journey from London to Scarborough' provided more descriptive details of the governor's looks and character. Dicky was 'one of the most deformed pieces of mortality' he had ever seen; his speech was 'uncouth'; but like Aesop, who was also physically handicapped, he was very sharp-witted.

After explaining that Dicky rented the spa well at a small rent from Scarborough corporation, had built two houses near there for the convenience of ladies and gentlemen, and that he charged five shillings for a season's use of these 'retirements', the author then descended into doggerel:

> Behold the Governor of Scarborough Spaw,
> The strangest phiz[1] and form you ever saw.
> Yet, when you view the beauties of his mind,
> In him a second Aesop you may find.
> Samos[2] unenvy'd boasts her Aesop gone,
> And France may glory in her late Scaron[3]
> While England has a living Dickinson.

---

[1] 'phiz' means face, a colloquial archaism derived form 'physiognomy' and abbreviated from 'phizog'.
[2] 'Samos' is the Aegean island where Aesop was born.
[3] Paul Scarron (1610 – 1660) was the French author crippled by rheumatism at the age of thirty.

In an even longer and vulgar verse, Dicky 'sovereign of the Spa', was compared with the shape of the letter Z; and because he could not straighten either his back or his legs his posture was 'fit to shite'.

Drawings of Dickinson made at this time and later depict various kinds of physical deformity. His left arm is shown to be permanently bent at the elbow and left hand misshapen and paralysed. His legs are crooked and stiff and feet splay outwards at 'a quarter-to-three'. Usually he has a mischievous grin on his ugly face. A portrait of him [see opposite] dated 1725 shows him accompanied by a monkey and a fox, both animals chained to a chest where he kept his subscription takings.

In the background to George Vertue's engraving of this portrait of 1725, Dicky's own house features as a splendid mansion of two storeys with roof turrets. Ten years later, depictions of the same dwelling by John Setterington and John Haynes indicate that Dicky must have made several additions and improvements to the simple house first sketched by Francis Place. Whether any improvements had also been made to the ladies' conveniences which so disgusted the duchess of Marlborough is not known.

However, there is no doubt that by the late 1720s Dicky and his spa were doing extraordinarily well, whatever the duchess might think of them. A corporation order of 1729 maintained the price of waters at the well at a shilling an anker, and now added that when bottled and sold locally they were to cost sixpence a dozen, most of the profit going to the bailiffs. Income from the spa was now considered sufficient to pay for a new correction house, workhouse and prison in the town. When Dickinson's seven-year lease again came up for renewal in 1734 his annual rent was raised from one to forty pounds!

Evidence of Scarborough's increasing success as a fashionable resort is plentiful by the 1720s. In 1724-6 when John Cossins appealed for subscribers to his town plans, he received 190 for York, 192 for Leeds, 60 for Beverley, 5 for Whitby and 168 for Scarborough. His maps of Whitby and Beverley were never published, but the list of subscribers for that of Scarborough makes impressive reading. Though the majority were residents of Scarborough - shipowners, tradesmen and professional men - there was a considerable number living in York, Hull, Malton, Pickering and Whitby, and some from as far away as London. Altogether, of Scarborough's subscribers, ten were clergymen,

Dicky Dickinson first 'Governor' of Scarborough Spa

four were doctors, five lawyers, thirty described as 'esquires', three lords, three baronets and a knight.

By 1733, the year after the duchess of Marlborough's uncomfortable stay, with the exception of Bath, Scarborough had become the most attractive of all fashionable resorts in England. Since visitors who arrived for the season paid subscriptions for the Long Room (five shillings), the coffee house (two shillings and sixpence), and for Dicky's spa (five shillings for men and two shillings for the ladies' convenience), all their names were then recorded in their subscription books which were open to public view. During the season of 1733, 695 gentlemen and 360 ladies paid one or more of these subscriptions. The gentlemen included two dukes, Argyle and Rutland; the marquess of Lothian; seven earls, Anglesey, Carlisle, Chesterfield, Cholmondley, Huntingdon, Marchmont and Stair; three barons, Carmichael, Coleraine and Langdale; and five Yorkshire knights, Francis Boynton, George Cayley, Charles Hotham, Henry Slingsby and William Strickland. That summer the town was favoured with the presence of Colley Cibber, the poet laureate, and Nicholas Hawksmoor, already the architect of Castle Howard, Blenheim Palace and All Souls' College, Oxford, and soon to start work on the western towers of Westminster Abbey.

The ladies were less numerous but not less distinguished. The duchess of Argyle was there and so were the marchioness of Anandale and the countesses of Huntingdon, Hyndford and Kinnel. Apart from the prominence of aristocratic Scottish ladies with names such as Campbell, Hay and Carmichael, there was a strong gathering of the wives and daughters of Yorkshire's gentry, with names such as Howard, St Quintin, Wentworth, Savile and Irwin. Not all gentlemen were accompanied by their wives; not all the married ladies brought their husbands. Sexual and social informality was not the least of Scarborough's attractions.

In the words of Edmund Withers, who was clearly in awe of this company: 'Starrs, Blue ribbons & red ribbons glitter in abundance … The number of strangers resorting to the Spaw was never known to be so great at any time as the present, most of them from remote corners, especially crouds of Scotch gentry. The money spent, and wared, in a season by strangers is not computed at less than £14,000.'

Such a dazzling constellation of stars and garters did not come to Scarborough's season merely to drink its distasteful waters or to laugh at Dicky Dickinson: as John Setterington's 'Perspective Draught' of the town in 1735 clearly illustrates, sea-bathing had by then become an organised, normal exercise in the waters of South Bay. Some bathers simply walked into the sea, others dived into it from hired rowing boats; but a growing number of the less robust and more cautious preferred to

South-west view of Scarborough
engraved by John Haynes for Thomas Gent in 1735

enter the icy salt water from Scarborough's new invention – the purpose-built bathing machine.

Significantly, the world's first wheeled, horse-drawn bathing hut was depicted by Setterington on the edge of the sea close to the spa well and Dicky's houses. As the anonymous spectator of 1733 explained, gentlemen went into the sea in hired coble boats and from them jumped naked directly into the water, whereas the ladies, stepping out from the bathing machines, had 'the conveniency of gowns and guides'. However, both sexes had the use of 'two little houses on the shore to return to for dressing in'. Whether Dicky owned the mobile bathing huts as well as the 'two little houses' is not known.

Besides Dicky's spa water and the doubtful pleasures of an invigorating plunge into the North Sea, the aristocracy and gentry came to Scarborough for 'the company'. In 1700 a visitor to the town had complained: 'I can yet see nothing but close stools and drying fish … the company there was but few, most Scotch and no diversion at all.' Five years later, another visitor, Joseph Taylor, gave a different view; according to him, 'most of the gentry of the north of England and Scotland resort hither in the season of the year'. Both verdicts were

143

exaggerations in opposite directions, yet a generation later Taylor's would have been much closer to the truth. By the 1730s Scarborough's amenities and company had so improved that it rivalled Tunbridge Wells or even Bath as a resort. Indeed, as another observer at this time wrote: 'amusements and the pleasure of seeing company induces many to come [to Scarborough] who are not really in want of water'.

In fact, the success of Scarborough as an 'up-market' place of resort owed at least as much to the town's new amenities as to its spa or sea waters. In 1722 John Macky reported in his *Journey Through England* that Scarborough had no public assemblies only private balls. Three years later, however, the town had at least two assembly rooms, one in Low Westgate (now numbers 11 and 11A Princess Street) and a second, which was destined to become the Royal Hotel, in St Nicholas Gate. The latter eventually became so important and famous that St Nicholas Gate was renamed Long Room Street.

Even though the building has survived as two private houses, little is known about the smaller assembly room in Low Westgate, whereas that in St Nicholas Gate was described in detail by the author of *A Journey from London to Scarborough*, published in 1734. He wrote that it was 'a spacious and noble' building, 52 feet long, 30 feet wide and 16 feet high. Here there were balls every night and the gentlemen paid only one shilling each to dance. At one end of the room there was a gallery for the musicians, and at the lower end a pharo bank, a hazard table and fair chance. Side rooms contained card tables for the gamblers and below stairs there were billiard tables. There was no sleeping accommodation here, but Mr Vipont, who was also master of the Long Room at Hampstead, provided sumptuous dinners at 2pm every day. From London Mr Vipont had brought his own cooks and a poulterer. Subscriptions to the Long Room were five shillings each for gentlemen and ladies. Dinners, which consisted of ten or a dozen courses, cost one shilling. Diners usually took a glass of spa water mixed with their wine. The charge for extra wine was another shilling. Formerly, it had been the custom for the gentlemen only to pay for the wine, but now the ladies paid 'an equal share of the whole reckoning'.

In the afternoon the company enjoyed watching one of Mr Keregan's plays. From the early 1730s Thomas Keregan's theatrical group had been granted a monopoly of performances in the city by York corporation. Only Norwich and Bath then had similar permanent companies of players. In May 1733 Keregan was permitted by

Scarborough's bailiffs to set up 'a large booth for his comedians' with 'scenes and decorations' by the sign of the Crown and Sceptre in the Horse Fair, 'very convenient for coaches'. After the end of the play, it was the custom to go back to the Long Room for dancing, gambling and playing before supper at about nine o'clock.

The Long Room was the social centre of what has been described as 'an egalitarian commonwealth' of the rich, titled and leisured. However, it was not the only place or source of entertainment in Scarborough. Private apartments and houses were still favoured by the most affluent visitors, but now the town had acquired several new 'ordinaries' where guests could find stabling, bedrooms and meals. The author of *A Journey from London to Scarborough* named the principal 'ordinaries' as the New Inn, the New Globe, the Crown and Sceptre, the Blacksmith's Arms and the Old Globe.

For visitors as well as residents there were two outdoor bowling greens in Scarborough, an old one on New Dyke Bank and a newer one on the site of St Sepulchre's church. Evidently, both were flat greens, since crown bowling greens were not yet known in the area. Later, a third flat green was laid out behind the Long Room.

For those with less energy, Scarborough had a coffee house on the corner of Newborough and St Thomas Street. For a season's subscription of half a crown gentlemen could pass the time of day there and have the free use of pen, ink and paper for their correspondence.

Finally, on Long Room Street, there was a bookshop where subscribers of five shillings could buy or hire books and newspapers. The post office was down the hill on Sandside, 'a considerable distance from ... the polite parts of the town', so that gentlemen could arrange to have their mail delivered to the bookseller's shop or sent from there to their lodgings.

To ensure that 'the quality' kept their boots and skirts clean and dry, the streets of the so-called 'polite parts' of Scarborough were paved with flagstones. By 1733 Long Room Street was covered with 'broad stones' for a pedestrian way and posts set up there for tethering horses. One correspondent of the time described the street as 'the Pall Mall of Scarborough'. Two years later, a donation to the corporation of £100 by the duke of Leeds and £50 by John Hill, commissioner of customs, paid for the paving of Newborough, and the whole town contributed to expensive repairs to the footpaths and carriageways of Merchants Row, King Street, Castlegate, and Longwestgate. And for those who were too lazy or too invalid to walk Scarborough's streets or climb its hills, there was now a sedan-chair service to and from 'the principal parts of town' – another import, like Mr Vipont and his cooks and poulterer, from London.

Clearly, by the 1730s, spending the season at Scarborough was no longer a purgatory imposed on the sick and elderly: the quality who came to the seaside between June and September were more likely to be looking for pleasures than remedies. Despite the presence of Royal Navy frigates at the mouth of the harbour and the vigilance of local customs officers, by this time smuggling, especially of spirits, wine, coffee and tea, had become an important and profitable occupation of some of Scarborough's seafarers. As Edmund Withers noted, brandy and tea were very cheap in Scarborough, and so were many 'other sorts [of] clandestine wares'. Other visitors commented favourably on the comparatively low costs of accommodation, food and drink to be found in the town.

Even for visitors like Withers, of modest means and simple tastes, hospitality at Scarborough's inns was both inexpensive and more than adequate: 'We have bread and broth every morning, after the Spaw, for nothing. We sit down at noon to a twel[ve]penny ordinary, when we have eight or ten dishes handsomely served up, of things best in season – extraordinaries may amount to fourpence. Dayly charge of my horse sixpence. Civil usage and as good accommodation for lodging as I have at home.'

For many pleasure-seekers it was the relaxed informality and intimacy of the company, where social conventions and moral constraints were less strict than at home, that attracted them to Scarborough. As one visitor explained: 'Gentlemen appear in all places naked (that is without their swords) not through any apprehension of danger from the intoxicating nature of the spa water, but from a polite declaration that in places of public resort all distinctions ought to be lost in a general complaisance.' In other words, therapy had become in many cases an alibi rather than an honest motive for risking the discomforts and hazards of the long journey to Scarborough: 'spawers' really came for a good time they could not have at home. What John Byng wrote about Cheltenham's company applied with equal truth to Scarborough's: 'widows wanting husbands, old men wanting health, and misses wanting partners'. Scarborough marketed husbands and wives, as well as fish.

**Scarborough town and South Bay
from castle dykes by T Ramsey 1770**

Only one insuperable handicap now prevented Scarborough from surpassing Bath or Tunbridge Wells as the favourite resort of English upper class society – its distance from London and the south. It took four nights and five days to reach Scarborough from the capital. Coaches left London three times a week, Mondays, Wednesdays and Fridays, stopping overnight at Biggleswade, Stamford, and Barmby Moor before arriving at York. Altogether the road distance was 239 miles. A shorter route of 217 miles, by way of Cambridge, Lincoln and Hull, using part of Ermine Street, required a ferry crossing of the Humber at Winteringham, and took just as long to reach Scarborough. The coach from London to York cost forty shillings – a sum far beyond the means of all but the richest travellers.

Alternatively, the sea journey from London in one of the colliers returning to Newcastle, Whitby or Scarborough itself, might take only three or four days and cost as little as a guinea, 'if you diet with the master, and half a guinea or fifteen shillings for a servant.' However, there was no regular passenger service; sea voyages were at the mercy of the treacherous North Sea conditions; and a general, natural fear of the sea meant that nearly all the 'spawers' preferred to endure the more predictable and smaller hazards of the road. One gentleman who had gambled away all his money on Scarborough's tables had to sell his horse and buy a return passage by collier to London with the money. It must have been a humiliating experience for him to sail home with a cargo of sea-coal.

As a consequence, except in the matter of sea-bathing, Scarborough always lagged behind rival resorts. Epsom had two Long Rooms as early as 1710; Bristol's Long Room was built in 1722. The earliest horse-race meeting recorded at Scarborough took place in 1736, whereas there had been regular meetings at York since 1530, at Kiplingcotes since 1555, at Hambleton since 1613, and even at Hunmanby since 1730. Indeed, it became the custom to leave Scarborough for York when the races started there in September. Even in its heyday Scarborough was never able to attract more than a few intrepid customers from the South and Midlands: it depended overwhelmingly on visitors from Yorkshire and Scotland.

On the morning of 28 December 1737 a crack opened up in the cellar of Dicky's spa house. During the next 24 hours Driple Cotes was utterly and permanently transformed. About an acre of land at the top of the cliff, over 200 yards long and more than 30 broad, slowly subsided along with the five cows grazing on it, until it had fallen about 17 yards. As this upper ground sank, that at the foot of the cliff, for about 100 yards in length, rose in some places as much as seven yards to form another new terrace.

Dicky's house, the two houses of convenience, the wooden staith and the spa well head were all entirely buried beneath thousands of tons of earth and sand. Dicky and Peggy were lucky to escape with their lives; they lost everything in the house and the wine in their cellar. Though at the time and since this spectacular and potentially disastrous event was described as an 'earthquake', it was probably similar to the massive earth movement of June 1993 which swept away the Holbeck Hall hotel on South Cliff. However, whatever its causes, the cliff fall had fatal consequences: within six weeks, on 8 February 1738, Dicky Dickinson was dead, and the first era in the history of Scarborough spa ended with him.

Now fully alive to the indispensable value of the spa to the town, the corporation took direct responsibility for it. No time was lost. Two days after Dicky's demise, John Haynes's 'South View' shows men with horse-drawn carts digging out the foot of Driple Cotes where soon they found not the old spring but two new ones. One of Scarborough's surgeons, Charles Cotterill, declared that the new waters were even superior to the old; and this unbelievable verdict was soon endorsed by Dr Peter Shaw, 'the residentiary physician' of the town. *The Daily Gazetteer* of 1 May contained assurances from Scarborough's bailiffs, James Hebden and Francis Goland, that for the forthcoming season there would be no shortage of spa water and that 'proper accommodation' for visitors would be 'finished'.

Surprisingly, the bailiffs' promise was delivered promptly. By 17 May the *London Daily Post* reported the completion of a new ladies' room, 53 feet 6 inches long, 26 feet wide and 13 feet high, built of brick with a chimney at each end. Inside, the walls were 'wainscotted throughout' and the ceiling lined with wood to keep out the damp. This single storey 'walking room' had four windows to the outside and double doors at the entrance. A 'gentleman's room' would be 'finished exactly according to the same dimensions in ten days time'.

Richard Dickinson was the first and last of his kind: his successor as governor of the spa, Captain William Tymperton, formerly master of Wills coffee house in London, lived on the site but only as a salaried employee of the corporation, not as its tenant. Though the Common Hall recognised the importance of the post by granting Tymperton a salary of twenty guineas a year, they did not build a house for him at the spa. The *London Daily Post* of 16 February 1738 described Tymperton as 'a man well known and respected for his comical facetious disposition'. Hoever, if the corporation hoped to replace Dicky with another showman eccentric they were soon disappointed.

Before the 'earthquake' of 1737 the spa well and the spa buildings had been in greater danger from the sea than from the cliffs. More than once severe storms had swept away the well head and damaged the staith behind it. As late as August 1736 bailiffs John Huntriss senior and Allatson Bell authorised the payment of £20 to William Vincent, the corporation's construction engineer, for his recent work on the spa staith. After two new springs were dug out in 1738, Vincent set to work enclosing them with a stout, stone wall so that they were no longer washed over by high tide or endangered by gales. The drawing of South Bay by Samuel and Nathaniel Buck, published in 1745, shows a single-storey building labelled 'the gentlemen's and ladies' walking rooms' set high up on a two-tiered platform buttressed by stone walls. The wells were now inside the staith and no longer on the open sands. Not that a final solution to the security of the spa had been found: the sea continued to imperil the staith which had still to be repaired frequently. Vincent also had to be employed 'lighting the Spaw Cliff', which meant removing overhanging rocks and clay threatening the buildings and spawers below.

The Great Schism

The landslide that engulfed the spa in 1737 had consequences far less damaging than might have been expected: it alerted the corporation to its responsibilities, led to the discovery of new mineral springs, and raised new spa buildings and the wells on to an enclosed platform where they were safer from the sea. Dicky's death was premature, but he was not immortal and could never have been adequately replaced. In contrast, the schism which split the corporation from 1736 until 1743 into two warring parties had serious, long-term results.

The quarrel that fractured the Common Hall arose from a parliamentary bye-election following the death of Sir William Strickland in September 1735. William Osbaldeston of Hunmanby, grandson of a former Member for Scarborough, was supported by a powerful relative, John Hill, commissioner of customs, and had the backing of Walpole's Whig government. However, the duke of Leeds, who did not support the government, put up his own cousin, Thomas Hay, Lord Duplin, to contest the seat.

Unlike most parliamentary elections at Scarborough, which were predetermined and uncontested, this bye-election was fiercely fought and deeply divisive, for reasons which are far from evident. Since the town's economy now depended heavily on Admiralty orders for new ships and hiring of merchant vessels for government service, Scarborough's shipowners, ship-builders, sail and rope makers, timber merchants and master mariners naturally favoured government candidates to represent them in the House of Commons. However, though Osbaldeston was the official ministerial candidate, his opponent, Lord Duplin, was also a Whig, a government supporter, and had the backing of the locality's most influential peer.

The contest had the effect of revealing and exacerbating existing rivalries between and even within Scarborough's ruling families. The Cockerills sided solidly with Osbaldeston, but whereas John Harrison backed Osbaldeston his son Christopher, the town clerk, favoured Duplin. The two Melborne Botterills, father and son, took opposite sides. When the Common Hall was polled on 26 January 1736, 26 voted for Osbaldeston and 18 for Duplin. John Huntriss and Allatson Bell, bailiffs and returning officers, voted for Duplin and refused to accept defeat. Instead, they called in the freemen, of whom 154 backed Duplin and only one Osbaldeston! Duplin was then declared Scarborough's duly elected Member of Parliament.

When these extraordinary events were brought to the notice of the House of Commons committee on elections by Osbaldeston's petition, it ruled that by ancient custom and right the franchise of Scarborough belonged exclusively to the 44 members of the Common Hall. Therefore, the verdict of the committee was that Osbaldeston and not Duplin had been legally returned to sit for the borough.

Here the matter might have ended, but unfortunately it did not, despite the pleas of Duplin who accepted his defeat. Too many insults and threats had been exchanged, too much pride injured, and too much resentment caused within the Common Hall for a peace settlement to be reached. The post boy who brought the news from London of Osbaldeston's triumph was stoned in the streets of Scarborough: as so often happens, the messenger was punished for his unwelcome message.

The rift finally opened on St Jerome's day, 30 September 1736 when the Common Hall met to choose its officers for the forthcoming year. When the town clerk, Christopher Harrison, announced that according to ancient custom the sitting bailiffs, Huntriss and Bell, were elected to be the next coroners, the majority of members refused to accept the poll. Instead they chose their own alternative coroners. As a result, by the end of that day, Scarborough had two sets of bailiffs, coroners, chamberlains, serjeants-at-mace and other officers and burgesses forming the two corporations. Though there was some overlap between the two bodies, their meetings were to be held separately and in effect the twofold division was complete. For the next three years Scarborough had two rival corporations.

The former bailiffs, Huntriss and Bell, now coroners, and their successors, William Batty and Matthew Armstrong, though the original minority leaders, retained the borough seal, the mace, the town records and occupied the Town Hall, while the original majority bombarded the Court of King's Bench in repeated attempts to force them out. The minority replied with their own suits against majority officers. In December 1738, Thomas Skelton, senior bailiff of the minority, fought with Melborne Botterill, senior bailiff of the majority, for occupation of the senior bailiff's pew in St Mary's church. Skelton got the place, but by then the legal battle was running in favour of the majority. However, as the legal costs mounted and both sides anticipated that they would have to be paid by the corporation, it became increasingly prudent not to be responsible for the final bill: to win might be financially ruinous!

In November 1739 an accommodation was agreed between the two parties: all lawsuits would be withdrawn and all legal costs would be met out of corporation revenue. However, the truce was almost immediately broken by 'Mr Cockerill's Faction' in the majority party which refused to drop charges against minority officers. A year later Thomas Cockerill was elected senior bailiff and Thomas Vickerman his junior by the majority, but though they both acted as magistrates at the borough sessions they were excluded from the Town Hall and denied the regalia of their offices. Vickerman had a constable of the minority interest arrested and sent to York castle; he retaliated by prosecuting Vickerman for misuse of office; and a minority serjeant-at-mace was compelled by Vickerman to appear at York assizes for an alleged assault on Cockerill!

In the parliamentary election of May 1741 Cockerill and Vickerman had no trouble securing the return of William Osbaldeston and William Thompson: all they did was to poll their own party members in the Common Hall: Duplin was bottom of the poll but consoled by his success at Cambridge. Neither he nor the duke of Leeds showed any further interest in Scarborough: in future, the minority party looked to Lord Carlisle for aristocratic patronage.

A single corporate body was finally restored to Scarborough in April 1743. John Huntriss senior and Valentine Fowler, leaders of the minority and majority respectively, were chosen as coroners, and two minority members, James Hebden and Francis Goland, elected bailiffs for the remainder of that year. Even so, Scarborough's internal quarrels were far from finished.

The death of William Thompson in 1744 provoked another crisis in the Town Hall as that of Sir William Strickland had done nine years earlier. This time, however, an impasse was reached before the bye-election, not after it. Since the bailiffs were returning officers, no agreement could be found on who they should be on St Jerome's day 1744. Twelve electors were locked in the Town Hall from 30 September until 8 November, supplied by their friends with food, drink and bedding, but still unable, or unwilling, to come to a decision. Finally, the coroners chose a new set of twelve electors, sacked Christopher Harrison from his post as town clerk, and forcibly expelled five of the old electors, including the former bailiff, James Hebden. When the bye-election at last took place a month later, 8 December, Edwin Lascelles was returned with 24 votes defeating Lord Carlisle's candidate, Savage Mostyn, who polled 18.

Harrison's rebellious 18 had lost the parliamentary contest and when new officers had to be elected on St Jerome's day 1745 they refused to cooperate with the other councillors. By failing to attend the Town Hall on that day they prevented the remaining 21 members from providing the borough with a government during the critical months of the Jacobite rising.

Nevertheless, whatever damage was done to Scarborough by these unpleasant events, at least the business at the spa seems to have been little affected. After the disaster of the previous December, it was the minority's officers and servants who dug out and rebuilt the wells and houses in record time for the 1738 season. Fortunately, the majority decided not to interfere when Tymperton was chosen to take the place of Dickinson and not to send their own collectors of subscriptions to the spa. Duplin's wish that 'your Grace's [the duke of Leeds] diversion at the spa' should not be interrupted 'by their idle squabbles' was granted.

Moreover, since the bailiffs of both parties were allowed to exercise their authority as magistrates and there was double the number of constables, Scarborough's laws were protected and local justice functioned almost normally. Also, since central government now appeared indifferent to corruption or incompetence in local government, no attempt was made to deprive Scarborough of its ancient privileges. Only interpretation of, not the legality of Scarborough's charters was at issue in the law courts.

The worst consequences of the great schism were financial: during the many years of trouble and strife the corporation incurred huge debts which it found impossible to pay off. For example, the borough failed to collect and hand over to the collector the tax on windows; and by 1743 the fee-farm rent was six years overdue. As a result, Trinity College, Cambridge, to whom the rent was payable, sued the corporation for arrears of £255, and bailiffs Hebden and Goland were arrested for this debt.

The heaviest liability incurred by the corporation was for legal costs. In the recent past the Town Hall had borrowed sums to pay off exceptional debts, but now its revenue was quite inadequate to cover the £3,000 owed for the lawsuits of 1736-43. Ever since 1732 an Act of Parliament had granted additional duties on Newcastle and Sunderland coal for a new outer pier at Scarborough. Though work on this pier had been halted by the death of engineer Lelam, the corporation continued to receive these duties and use them for other purposes. In March 1743 it was decided to borrow £3,600 from Walter Crompton on the security of the new pier dues. Subsequently, though money which should have been spent on the construction of the new pier was finding its way to Crompton, in 1746 he brought a case against the corporation for failure to pay the interest on this loan, and in 1747 he took over the entire revenues for the pier.

The diversion of money into the pocket of Crompton and the slow progress being made in the construction of the outer pier eventually provoked a petition of protest from the owners and masters engaged in the coal trade and the 'freemen, landowners and inhabitants of the borough of Scarborough'. Consequently, a new Pier Act of 1752 implicitly recognised the failure of the corporation to fulfil the terms of the Act of 1732 and transferred responsibility for the new pier to an independent body of commissioners. According to the terms of the Act, the bailiffs and burgesses had been guilty of 'great frauds and abuses' and could not be trusted to carry out their duties under the Act of 1732 any longer. More than a hundred new commissioners with country gentry names such as Strickland, St Quintin, Cayley, Legard, Cholmley, Hill and Osbaldeston, were summoned to meet in Scarborough at the Old Globe, now run by Mrs Stockdale, to take up their responsibility. The only qualification required of each of them was a minimum rental income of £100 and capital of £3,000. From now on, Scarborough's harbour had two authorities – the corporation retained control of the old piers and the commissioners took over the work on the new outer pier.

However, the corporation still owed more than £3,000 on the new pier tolls to Crompton and its revenues were still insufficient to meet such a debt. By 1752 'the College rent', as it was called, was again in arrears, this time for three years. As late as 1754 Edwin Lascelles agreed to pay £3,000 'towards discharging the Pier debt' if the corporation returned him and Sir Ralph Milbanke to the House of Commons. However, though Milbanke got one seat, the other went to William Osbaldeston, and Lascelles's money went begging. Five years later, the corporation was still pressing both its MPs in vain for the £1,500 each had promised if elected but had still not delivered. When the financial records of the borough end in 1760 the corporation was heavily in debt.

Invasion Scare 1745 - 6

If there was one common danger certain to unite a bitterly divided town it was the threat of a Jacobite invasion. In 1745-6 Scarborough had only a makeshift, incomplete and disputed government, but the public response to Bonnie Prince Charles was prompt and impressive.

In a letter to Sir Conyers Darcy, deputy lieutenant of the North Riding, dated 10 October 1745, his 'lordship's most devoted obedient servants, the inhabitants of Scarborough' reported that they had already raised £300 by voluntary subscription which they proposed to use to defend the town and port. Without 'soldiers of proper persons' and with only eight cannon planted on the pier, Scarborough was then in 'a very defenceless condition both by sea and land'. They asked Darcy for his permission to raise 50 armed men to man the guns and choose their own officers 'to enlist, train and instruct' them.

As a later plan of the town, castle and harbour, drawn in 1747 by William Vincent, 'engineer for building the new pier', shows, Scarborough's defences had far exceeded the modest proposals of 1745. No fewer than 99 guns were eventually deployed to defend approaches to the town. There were 16 at High Tollergate on the North Cliff, six at Oldborough Bar, 24 along the New Dyke Bank, ten by the workhouse, six at Newborough Bar, 16 along the Bar moat, seven on St Nicholas Cliff, six overlooking the mouth of Mill Beck and eight on the foreshore commanding the approach to the New Coach Way up Bland's Cliff. The Newborough moat was cleaned out, probably the first time for nearly a century. On a stone preserved in the Rotunda museum an inscription reads: 'This mote was cleansed out and 99 guns mounted on account of the Rebellion by subscription of the Inhabitants in 1745.' There were also batteries of cannon positioned on the old pier and at South Steel overlooking the harbour. According to Vincent's plan, these guns were manned by 400 seamen and another 400 men from the town were armed to guard them.

The names or the thirteen-man committee appointed to organise the defences and of the captains of batteries, nearly all of them local, suggest that personal animosities were suspended if not forgotten when it was reported that 'the rebels were in full march to Scarborough'. Happily, the report was incorrect. The Young Pretender chose to lead his Highlanders down the west side of the Pennines and no attempt was made by his French allies at a seaborne landing at Scarborough. Nevertheless, though the guns were soon returned to the Royal Navy's warships and the moat was soon refilled with debris and litter, the events of 1745-6 brought some permanent changes to Scarborough.

The exposure of Scarborough's defensive weakness and the continued strategic importance of its harbour of refuge and castle, especially at the time of yet another war with France (1740-48), prompted the government in London to restore the castle's military garrison. The battery works at South Steel originally dated from Cholmley's time there in 1643-5, but long-term neglect and rapid cliff erosion had rendered them unsafe. It was decided to enclose the site with stone walls, keep cannon there, and build store-houses, guard room and magazine to serve them. Directly above and behind South Steel, Charles's Tower, where Fox had been imprisoned so uncomfortably, was now much decayed and perilously close to the cliff edge. Therefore the military demolished it entirely and re-used the stone for the new works below.

At the same time, work began on constructing a new brick barracks on the site of the medieval Mosdale Hall along the curtain wall. Accommodation for the 120 soldiers was provided in 12 apartments with additional space for their officers. No attempt was made to repair the ruined keep, but in its basement the army stored 900 barrels of gunpowder. Overlooking the castle holms on the north side the army had built a new stone house on two floors, part of it to be occupied by the master gunner. Finally, to guarantee a reliable water supply for this enlarged garrison, the soldiers constructed a brick reservoir inside the ruins of the chapel.

9

MARITIME RESORT

Spa Waters

Despite fears of personal injury after the landslip of 1737, despite the corporation schism of 1736-43, and despite the war with France in 1740-48 and the Jacobite rebellion of 1745-6, the best financial years for Scarborough's spa were precisely during this most troubled period.

Corporation receipts for bottled waters reached a peak in 1738-9, when well over 6,000 dozen were sold for more than £130. Thereafter, sales declined steadily and irreversibly. By 1778-9 corporation income from this source was less than £10; by 1800 it had become insignificant. Fortunately, the drop in the numbers of subscribers and visitors to the wells was not so catastrophic. The highest number who signed Tymperton's book and handed over 7s.6d for the season was 766 in 1748. From then on, however, the decline was gradual and almost continuous, from 581 in 1762-3, to 328 in 1779-80, then levelling out in the 300s during the 1780s and 1790s but falling again in some years, 1818-19, 1820-1 and 1822-3, to below 200.

As a result, the corporation found itself running the spa at a loss. The largest annual income from this source was recorded at £320 in 1738-9 and until the 1760s the bailiffs spent less money on repairs and improvements to the site and its approaches than they received from subscriptions and sales of bottled waters. However, from then on the spa became a financial liability to the corporation. From 1778-9 total receipts fell below £100, whereas not until 1809-10 did expenditure on the spa fall well below that figure.

At its apogee the trade in bottled Scarborough spa water was big business, even though all the physicians agreed that the water at the wells was far superior to the same taken elsewhere: it did not travel well.

Nevertheless, during the 1730s, when drinking bottled mineral water was all the fashion, John Fiddes seems to have made a profitable living from the trade. As well as a house and shop in Scarborough he also traded in London from the Golden Wheatsheaf warehouse in Tavistock Street, Covent Garden. By 1733 he was advertising that he had a guarantee from senior bailiff, Culmer Cockerill, and resident physician at Scarborough, Dr Peter Shaw, that his bottled water was drawn directly from the well 'at the most proper seasons and cemented down in the bottles with a well-adapted cement', according to their directions. From London, Fiddes offered German spaw water at 14 shilling a dozen flasks, and Bristol waters at 6 shillings a dozen bottles, whereas Scarborough and Bath waters, at 7s.6d. a dozen, were equally priced. Meanwhile, at Scarborough, a dozen bottles of native water could be bought from Fiddes at 5 shillings, most of which went to him. The serjeants-at-mace who sealed the bottles got only a penny a dozen, the women who filled them the same, and the bailiffs only five pence 'for the town's use'. According to Scarborough's customs Port Book for 1734, the town imported 2,797½ dozen glass bottles in that year from Newcastle and Sunderland.

Meanwhile, literature on Scarborough's spa waters was pouring out of the presses. In 1734 there appeared Dr Thomas Short's *Natural History of the Mineral Waters of Scarborough etc.*. After summarising the Wittie, Simpson and Tunstall controversies of the 1660 and 1670s, Short condemned the self-indulgence of many 'spawers' whose 'improper diet' countered or even nullified the therapy of the mineral waters. He also warned imbibers to 'use conjugal pleasures with great caution and discretion, for ... the use of this water give some a pretty brisk priapism'. Not only was the water an aphrodisiac, it could also be intoxicating: like champagne, it was volatile, sparkling and gaseous.

A year later, John Atkins, a naval surgeon and author of travel books, published *Mineral Springs in General, Particularly the Celebrated Waters of Scarborough*. No doubt Scarborians were pleased that he recommended a course of 'three or four months' for invalids whose 'distemper' was either 'chronical or stubborn'. For weak stomachs Atkins prescribed 'the Scarborough Whey', 'a posset' of water and boiled milk, which as early as 1661 John Ray on his visit to Scarborough had found 'not unpleasant to drink'.

By 1734 Dr Peter Shaw had written his *An Enquiry into the Contents, Virtues, and Uses of the Scarborough Spaw-waters*. Later

158

Shaw was to achieve fame and fortune as physician to kings George II and his grandson, George III, but at the time of his *Enquiry* he was merely 'Physician at Scarborough'. Shaw was already a party to the lucrative business in bottled waters and now he also recommended what

A plan of Scarborough 1811

he called 'Scarborough Salt'. This concoction, which never displaced Epsom salts, was distilled from the spa waters and prepared, surprisingly, by 'Mr Culmer Cockerill, a judicious surgeon and apothecary at Scarborough', who had been prevailed upon to offer it for sale. Shaw forgot to mention that he and Cockerill were partners.

Neither 'Scarborough Whey', nor 'Scarborough Salts' were ever so successful commercially as the town's trade in bottled waters, though even as late as 1932 the Spa Company was still selling its waters in the form of salt tablets.

What were the reasons for Scarborough's failure to capitalise on its early success in the 1730s and 1740s as a fashionable maritime resort?

First of all, Scarborians were too slow to adapt to and cater for their wealthy visitors. It had taken a natural landslide to demolish the primitive accommodation at the spa provided by the private initiative of Dicky Dickinson. Access to the waters remained difficult, dangerous and distant, even after John Bland's enterprise had resulted in the first

159

carriageway to the sands. Not until 1735 did the corporation agree to cut steps into the steep side of St Nicholas Cliff for pedestrian access to the spa, and it was not until three years later that the coach way from the Assembly Room in Long Room Street down to Ramsdale was made into a turnpike road. Even so this route was so steep and winding that carts and wagons had to be banned from using it. Dr Falconer's coach road down into Ramsdale from Vernon Road was not finished until as late as 1793.

Apart from providing seats for the panting St Nicholas Cliff climbers, no improvements were made in access to the spa for half a century. In 1744 the drinking room of the spa and the area around it were described as 'miserably mean and dirty'. There were still no public walks or gardens in the vicinity where visitors could stroll and relax outdoors. A visitor in 1768 thought Scarborough a 'dirty, ill-built, and very badly paved town'. Soon afterwards, Mark Hildesley, bishop of Sodor and Man, had the same complaint as Sarah, duchess of Marlborough, had expressed forty years earlier – that the way to and from the spa was intolerably steep and perilous. For this reason alone, the bishop preferred Harrogate. Even as late as 1793, Anna Seward grumbled about 'the long fatiguing walk' and the 'toil-some cliff to be descended to the sands', adding ominously that such inconvenience was not to be endured at Bridlington! Not least of the 'inconveniences' suffered by spawers was an inconsiderate tide which every twelve hours prevented all access to the wells either on foot or by vehicle.

As already noted, public subscription and private donation rather than corporate enterprise were responsible for the earliest improvements to the surfaces of Long Room Street and Newborough. However, after the innovations of the 1730s there was a long delay before further street renovations. Not until 1776 did the town's principal thoroughfare and market place, Newborough, gain an 'excellent flagged footway', nine feet broad on either side of the road which was 50 feet wide. The expenses were shared between adjacent property owners and the corporation, and the latter condescended to carry the costs of maintenance of the pavements.

Long Room Street, St Sepulchre Street and the Dumple had to wait until 1773 before the chamberlains paid for repairs to their badly-worn surfaces. On the other hand, the corporation repeatedly refused to help the desperate residents and traders of Helperby Lane (later King

Street) until eventually they were forced to pay entirely for their own paving.

Many 'polite' visitors to Scarborough had reason to complain of the prevailing and pervasive smell of fish and worse. In 1700 one of them had written that he had seen and smelled nothing in the town but excrement and fish. Almost a century later, Anna Seward referred to 'the long, steep, dirty streets ... with their tainted gales of fishy fumes'. Most of these offensive odours emanated from the fish shambles, an untidy, ugly jumble of wooden stalls in the very heart of Scarborough. Yet despite many demands, from residents as well as visitors, for its removal, the medieval shambles and the old market cross nearby were not demolished until 1802, and even then only at the expense of local property owners and shopkeepers.

Not only were Scarborough's streets steep, dirty and smelly, they were also dark at night time. James Schofield, writing at the end of the century, had much to say in praise of the town, but even he regretted its lack of street lighting. In 1805 a local Improvement Act set up a commission to cleanse, pave, watch and illuminate Scarborough's thoroughfares, but the commissioners seem to have preferred status to activity. When the lamps were finally put up in 1810 in Long Room Street and Newborough, the corporation refused to pay for all but six and the others had to be maintained by private subscription. Then, when the Improvement commissioners assumed responsibility for these gas lamps, at first they decided not to have them lit. If local residents wished they could fuel and light the lamps at their own expense and risk! Fortunately, thanks to the intervention of other commissioners and the borough bailiffs, this order was rescinded almost immediately.

Scarborough might have had a surplus of mineral waters yet it suffered from a serious shortage of fresh water for cooking, washing, cleansing and brewing. As early as 1729 the corporation had set up a committee to look into the town's water supply from Falsgrave. The flow from Gildhouse Cliff was increasingly insufficient to meet the basic needs of the resident population, let alone the additional ones of visitors during the summer months. The following year councillors agreed to ask Mr Peacock 'the Miner' to dig twelve yards deeper into Falsgrave's springs to find more water. There was clearly a reluctance to extend exploration to other potential sources, or to incur expenses that might not be absolutely necessary. Mr Peacock's endeavours gave only temporary relief. There was a limit to Falsgrave's supply however deeply it might be tapped.

By 1802, with three major breweries in the town and a resident population of nearly 6,500, the situation had become desperate and deplorable. There were long queues to draw water from the public conduits, described by William Hutton as 'two miserable springs' or 'two dirty wells in the street, from which is drawn a miserable supply with a string and bucket'. His conclusion was that Scarborough must have had the worst as well as the best water in the country.

As so often the case, the initiative and the money required to meet the problem came from outside the corporation. Lord Mulgrave offered the town £500 to build a reservoir which would guarantee a constant and ample supply, and the duke of Rutland doubled it. However, it was not until three years later, in 1805, that the corporation finally acquired an additional source of water when they leased Stoney Haggs spring from Joseph Denison at an annual rent of five guineas; and it was not until 1828 that the Improvement commissioners built a large reservoir in what had once been St Thomas's churchyard.

Law and Order

In one respect at least Scarborough's unreformed corporation succeeded in carrying out its duties: its two magistrate bailiffs, two serjeants-at-mace, eight constables (two more for Falsgrave), bellman, gaoler and keeper of the house of correction policed the borough efficiently and effectively. In the words of the final report on the old corporation, published in 1834, there were 'few places so quiet and orderly' as Scarborough.

Whether described as 'vagabond beggars', 'vagrants', 'counterfeit vagrant beggars', or 'counterfeit wandering rogues', such unwelcome visitors to Scarborough could expect no mercy from the bellman and his constables. Usually they were stripped to the waist, females as well as males, whipped through the streets until they were bloody, and returned to where they had originated.

Petty thieves and prostitutes were certain to receive similar harsh treatment. A few examples from surviving constables' records offer factual illustration of the severity of punishments meted out during the eighteenth century. In 1715 Richard Lazenby, Mary, his wife, Peter Evans and James Dodgson were found by the justices to be 'vagrants using crafty games or plays in the highways thereby to allure people to play and lose their money'. All but Dodgson were to be whipped on their naked bodies from the house of Mr George Porrett, a former bailiff, all the way up the town to Newborough Gates. In 1780 Ann Edward was found guilty of stealing a piece of linen cloth, value unspecified. She was whipped on her naked back by the bellman from the Market Cross to the gaol at Newborough Bar and from there 'escorted by two constables to the extremities of the Liberty'. Scarborough not only punished criminals, it also exported them. Nine years later, a pregnant woman called Jane Pratt was convicted of keeping a disorderly house in the town. She was kept in prison until the delivery of her child and then, when passed by 'a skilful surgeon', she was sentenced to be bound to a cart at the Saturday market cross and whipped up St Sepulchre and Newborough Streets back to the gaol.

In 1788 a beadle had been appointed by the Common Hall to 'parade the streets and the Spaw ... to prevent strollers and other persons presenting themselves as objects of charity from begging at the lodging houses...' Clearly, the presence in the town during the summer months of many well-to-do visitors acted like a magnet to potential beggars and prostitutes as well as cheats and pickpockets. Nevertheless, there is no further reference to the office of beadle, so it seems that bellman and constables were considered sufficient to clear Scarborough of vagrants and rogues. During his stay of 18 days in the summer of 1803 William Hutton 'did not observe one beggar in the streets'.

The old corporation continued to operate medieval controls on marketing in the town throughout the century. The principal Thursday market in Newborough and the subsidiary Saturday market in lower St Sepulchre Street were policed by the sergeants-at-mace and their constables. Market tolls were leased to the highest bidder annually. Though there were now far many more bakers and brewers, the bailiffs still appointed breadweighers and ale tasters to test the quantities and qualities of the two staples of consumption. The borough also still employed leather searchers and sealers to examine and give official approval to the products of Scarborough's tanneries. Butchers caught selling bad meat were not just fined: they were compelled to witness their wares being burnt in public at the market cross. As late as 1831 the sergeants seized a cargo of rotten mutton and set fire to it in Newborough near the cross with a shilling's worth of straw.

Forestalling and regrating the market remained punishable offences. Fishermen were obliged to sell their catches in the open market. It was illegal to sell straight off the boats or at night time. On the other hand, the bailiffs still expected to have first refusal on all goods coming into Scarborough for sale. The old regulations regarding coal sales also remained in force. Coal meters were appointed by the Common Hall to measure the hundredweight sacks when the colliers unloaded their cargoes at the harbour and coal haulage charges within the borough were strictly controlled.

Only at exceptional times of dire emergency did this orderly system break down. For instance, during the appalling winter of 1799 after another disastrous harvest and in a time of acute distress, the bailiffs bought 200 quarters of wheat and distributed them to the poorest in the town.

No doubt visitors to Scarborough, as well as residents, benefited in some ways from these controls. Market regulations kept down prices, maintained quality and prevented fraud. The presence of constables deterred thieves who otherwise might have prospered among the crowds of buyers and sellers. Since the markets were confined to the older parts of the town – live cattle were sold in Queen Street, vegetables and fruit in King Street, meat and fish from the stalls in the shambles – the 'polite' quarters of Long Room Street and St Nicholas Cliff were free of the noise, congestion and smell they caused. Open to the sea breezes, the air on St Nicholas Cliff was certainly cleaner and fresher than elsewhere in the town.

Moreover, the judicial authority exercised by the bailiffs within the Liberty allowed them to ignore inconvenient legislation regarding gambling while enforcing the laws on vagrancy. The Act of 1745 prohibited gaming tables of the kind that were so popular in Scarborough's assembly rooms, but there is no evidence that they were removed at that time or later. Illegal gambling remained one of the resort's attractions. Not until as late as 1761 do the constables' accounts record payments made to them for arresting gamblers.

Similarly, since cheap tea, coffee, wines and spirits smuggled into Scarborough by sea were another of the town's appreciated attractions, bailiffs, sergeants and constables were content to turn a blind eye on such illegal activities. Clearly, it was impossible for customs officers at the harbour to control this profitable traffic, which also came into Scarborough by land from other nearby coastal receiving points.

There is no evidence that any of the town's law officers were engaged in the suppression of smuggling.

Lodgings, Gardens and Roads

If Scarborough had continued success as a seaside resort it owed that success mainly to the enterprise and business acumen of a few of its more imaginative and active leaders and to the increasing popularity of sea-bathing.

Dicky Dickinson and John Bland in the early part of the eighteenth century were followed by Robert Harding, John Huntriss, John Bean and the Reverend Dr James Falconer as men who substantially improved Scarborough's facilities for visitors.

Even as late as 1760 Scarborough town was still physically confined within the medieval dykes, walls and gateways, yet by that date there was a pressing need for expansion westwards and upwards into the pastures and fields beyond. The first major breakout from these limits occurred during the 1760s with the construction of the so-called New Buildings on the west side of St Nicholas Cliff. The New Buildings, described as 'handsome and stately', were perhaps the earliest purpose-built lodging houses for guests in Britain. They consisted of a terrace of seven houses in all, built 'for the purpose of letting as lodging to the company resorting to [Scarborough] in the summer season'. Each house was spacious enough to accommodate several families and their servants since it contained two parlours, two dining rooms, six bedchambers, five attic rooms, and a kitchen. At the back of each house were stables for eight horses and garaging for three coaches. The New Buildings commanded superb frontal views northwards to the harbour and castle headland, and they were closer to the spa and the sea-bathing shore than any other lodgings in the town.

The New Buildings on St Nicholas Cliff remained a detached, isolated development outside the town until Harding's Walk was built. Thomas Jeffrey's map of Scarborough, published in 1775 but drawn as early as 1771, shows a straight road from Newborough Bar running southwards towards the New Buildings but not quite reaching them. This is probably the earliest evidence of what was to become Harding's Walk. In 1773 the *York Chronicle* advertised the lease of the Pied Bull Inn, just outside the Bar, along with land 'adjoining to and in virtue of the tenure thereof, [which] may be used as a new and very convenient road from the front thereof by the new building down to the Spaw'. However, though Harding's Walk was finished by 1776 it remained a private route even after the corporation in that year had offered him 50 guineas to open it to the public. It appears that Harding took the money and reneged on the agreement. Not until January 1779 was the town clerk able to report that 'after much altercation' the private walk had become a common street.

Even so there was local opposition to the new thoroughfare. A petition to the bailiffs, signed by 42 residents, argued unconvincingly that the new road would be 'a great detriment to the Town, by reason it will be a hindrance to many of the nobility &c coming into the town, and thereby be a loss to those in trade'. For this and many other 'obvious reasons' they hoped that the bailiffs would 'cut off the communication'. How a public road could be a 'hindrance' was far from 'obvious' unless the objection was that the area of St Nicholas would be less exclusive than formerly and that therefore the socially superior visitor would be deterred from using it.

Harding built only two houses along his Walk and then sold the remainder of the land to a speculative builder and bricklayer called John Huntriss. It was he who eventually gave his name to what became and remains Huntriss Row. During the 1790s the east side of the street was gradually filled with houses. When some of these buildings encroached on the town ditch behind them the corporation ordered the encroachments to be demolished. Eventually, the tenants of the east side of Huntriss Row were permitted to occupy the town dyke on the sensible condition that they did not build over it. This condition has been observed ever since and is still active. In 1805 the corporation finally agreed to pay for the paving of the street. By that date there were two boarding houses and eight lodging houses there, though it was still called Harding's Walk for some years to come.

The area to the south and west of Huntriss Row, that in the future would become Vernon Place, Brunswick Terrace and York Place, was laid out as Mr Bean's gardens. Though other genteel resorts had long since acquired formal, enclosed, pleasure gardens where paying visitors might take fresh air and exercise and mix socially, Scarborough was late to benefit from these amenities. For what Scarborough's first historian, Thomas Hinderwell, described in 1798 as 'a trifling annual subscription', those who had the means could escape the lower town's fetid odours. However, Mr Bean's gardens also had a more mundane and more useful purpose. As the author of Scarborough's earliest guide, James Schofield, had already reported as early as 1787, Bean's gardens provided both residents and visitors with fresh fruit and vegetables during the season. Indeed, such was the skill and special care devoted to a sheltered part of Mr Bean's gardens that he was able to grow there grapes, figs, peaches and other exotic fruits. Of course, his success was also a tribute to Scarborough's mild climate!

Finally, in 1791, the Reverend Dr James Falconer of Lichfield petitioned the Common Hall for permission to build 'a new way to the sands', which would run down from Bean's gardens to Ramsdale, thereby providing a less precipitous link than the old coach road between Newborough and the spa. In the same petition Dr Falconer signalled his intention to build a new Anglican chapel in White Bread or Great St Nicholas Close, an area destined to become the Crescent half a century later. The limited space inside St Mary's, its notorious inaccessibility, especially for visitors at the other end of the town, and the growth of Scarborough's Anglican community, all pointed to the need for a chapel of ease in the western outskirts. In 1757 the corporation had offered 100 guineas towards the cost of building such a chapel, but there was no response from the established church. In 1772 the corporation agreed to raise 100 guineas by buying out the pews around the pulpit in St Mary's, and even offered a site for a new chapel in lower Queen Street, but again nothing happened.

Falconer was the first to bring forward what seemed a practical plan. His chapel would have 2,000 places, each rented out at between two and seven shillings and sixpence each. He would have a road built from Huntriss Row and St Nicholas Cliff to the chapel and charge tolls for its use – seven shillings and sixpence a year for a carriage and five shillings for a horse. On no account would he allow 'waggons, carts or timber trucks' to use his road. From the chapel a coach road would wind its way down a natural ravine to Ramsdale and the sands.

The coach road, which became the New Road or Falconer's, was finished by 1793. However, the start of the war with France that year ended hopes of a chapel. Dr Falconer offered Great St Nicholas Close for sale at 3,000 guineas, or a shilling a square yard, but it and the coach road were not bought by James Tindall until 1806. Finally, the corporation purchased the New Road from Tindall in 1819.

Falconer's chapel of ease, which eventually took form as Christ Church, was not to be built until 1826-8, and then not in Great St

Nicholas Close, but in part of Bean's gardens. However, despite the demands and privations of the protracted war with France, the corporation did effect some improvements to the town's appearance and facilities. The paving of the Beast Market, at the lower end of Queen Street, '2 flags broad', was carried out by the corporation in 1799 though at the expense largely of adjacent residents.

The following year, the corporation finally abandoned its old town hall on Sandside, which had served its purpose with decreasing convenience for two hundred years. The old building, single-storied with a flight of wooden steps at the entrance, was bought by the Tindalls and became the Bethel for seamen. The 44 members of the Common Hall came up the hill to Long Room Street where they leased one of the two Assembly Rooms for 31 years at an annual rent of £42. Their move from harbourside to Scarborough's 'Pall Mall' might be interpreted as a significant shift in gravity from seaport to resort. Alternatively, that Scarborough no longer had use for two assembly rooms suggests a decline in the number of visitors during the French war.

At the same time changes were made on the northern and southern perimeters of the town. In 1800, the road from Auborough Bar to Greengate Lane, the start of the route northwards to Whitby, was turned into a horse and pedestrian way. Shortly afterwards, what was to become a stretch of Castle Road, passing along the top of Queen and Auborough Streets was widened and stabilised. The remains of Auborough Bar were destroyed and part of the New Dyke filled in to make this work possible.

Now lodged comfortably in its new spacious quarters in Long Room Street, the council seems to have acquired a taste for landscaping and tree-planting. The waste land between Tanner (formerly St Thomas) and Queen Streets, next to the old bowling green, and the slopes of lower Ramsdale were planted with a variety of trees and bushes and the latter provided with public seats. As a result, the former was for a time known as Mount Pleasant. Soon afterwards, the corporation planted trees and put up seats 'for the accommodation of the public' in the lower part of Ramsdale Valley, which became known simply as the Plantation.

For centuries Ramsdale had marked the furthest boundary of development and acted as a barrier to any southern access to or from the town. The old road across it was narrow and steep on both sides and the crossing of Millbeck bridge so close to the sea that it was endangered by storm-driven high tides. Between 1810 and 1814 a new road was built across the valley, further west than its predecessor and on an easier gradient. It linked Falconer's with South Cliff and the road to Bridlington. To protect this new thoroughfare from the sea a huge mound of earth and rubble was thrown across the mouth of the valley and a tunnel dug through it to allow the passage of Mill Beck out into South Bay. The corporation contributed £100 towards the costs of digging out and building the water tunnels; the bailiffs ordered an assessment on the town's householders of up to a maximum of sixpence in the pound in 1813 and 1814; and the Common Council decided that neighbouring landowners who would benefit from the road improvement should be asked to subscribe to its bill. Though it would be some years before building began on South Cliff, none of that would have been possible without the new road across Ramsdale and up Ramshill.

Meanwhile, what had always previously been known as Weaponness was gradually becoming Oliver's Mount. A survey map of Yorkshire drawn by Thomas Jeffrey and dated 1770 was the earliest attempt to change the name of Weaponness which appears on it as 'Oliver's Hill'. A clue to the origin of this mystery is to be found on Scalby's enclosure award map of 1777 which labels the hexagonal Civil War earthwork above Peasholm Gap, not Peasholm Fort but 'Oliver's Battery'. It seems that more than a century after Cromwell's death and the Civil Wars of the 1640s the Lord Protector's reputation and the extent of his activities were much exaggerated; he had become a legendary figure. So, though Oliver Cromwell never came within 40 miles of Scarborough, he was credited with artillery emplacements to the north and south of the town. Peasholm Fort was almost certainly a Civil War earthwork, whereas no one, and definitely not General Cromwell, had ever climbed Weaponness to plant artillery there during the two sieges of 1645 and 1648. Nevertheless, such is the power of myth and wishful thinking, Oliver's Hill and later Oliver's Mount displaced Weaponness.

When this 435-acre site entirely owned by the corporation was finally enclosed and leased in lots in 1797 it was still described as Weaponness. By 1806, when Broadrick's new Guide appeared, 'a driving road' had been built a mile long around the top of what was now called 'Weaponness Hill or Mount Oliver'. Thomas Hinderwell was well aware that Cromwell was never present at Scarborough's Civil War sieges, yet concluded that 'the modern name' of Mount Oliver derived from 'a mistaken opinion' that he had erected cannon batteries there 'against the castle'. Subsequently, it seemed that 'Olive Mount' might be preferred, but finally sentimentality and historical ignorance prevailed and Scarborough was stuck with Oliver's Mount. Still, as Hinderwell had rightly pointed out in 1811, the enclosures of Seamer and Falsgrave Moors together with that of Weaponness had soon converted areas of rough grazing into cultivated fields and recreational playgrounds.

Sea-Bathing

If it had depended entirely upon the spa Scarborough might not have survived as a resort into the nineteenth century. During the second half of the previous century visitors came to take the waters externally rather than internally. As early as 1778, in his *A Tour Through Parts of England, Scotland and Wales*, Richard Joseph Sullivan had remarked on the decline of drinking spa waters at Scarborough whereas 'the bathing is the chief inducement for company to resort hither'. Later, as William Hutton put the matter, with some characteristic exaggeration, in his *Tour to Scarborough in 1803*: 'Drinking the waters [here] is an ancient custom; bathing is a modern but growing fashion'.

Robert Wittie's recommendation of cold, salt water bathing at Scarborough, especially for sufferers from gout, made few converts at the time. Even as late as 1732 the duchess of Marlborough spent six weeks in Scarborough for her gout but she did not once venture into the sea. On the other hand, she did report that the duchess of Manchester went into the sea every day and that Lord Chesterfield had warned that so many 'spawers' were now bathing regularly that the corporation was considering taxing them for the use of its sea water! A year later, naked men were jumping into the sea from hired coble boats and ladies were undressing in 'two little houses on the shore' before they were led into the sea by guides. The first wheeled bathing machine seen on any British beach was drawn by John Setterington on Scarborough's south sands in 1735. Setterington's 'Perspective Draught' also depicted naked men swimming in the sea from nearby rowing boats. Sea-bathing might have begun at Brighton, or Brighthelmstone as it was then called, as early as 1736, but the Reverend William Clarke was a solitary pioneer there in that year, as Dr Wittie had been at Scarborough seventy years earlier.

The 'growing fashion' of sea-bathing can be measured by the number of bathing machines shown on contemporary drawings *[plate 6]* and in the town's early guide books. Originally mobile changing rooms merely saved bathers from a long walk across the sands to the edge of the sea at low tide, but these machines were soon taken by horses directly into deep water. On 'The South Prospect of Scarborough', drawn in 1745, Samuel and Nathaniel Buck showed five of these 'bathing houses' in the water and several more on the sands. When Schofield came to write his first guide to the resort in 1787 he claimed that there were 26 such machines in South Bay. Bathers then paid as much as a shilling for the vehicle and horse and another shilling for attendants, two females for ladies and a male for gentlemen. The ladies took to the water in 'flannels'; gentlemen bathed in the nude. Ten years later, the author of another guide, John Hatfield, wrote that Scarborough then had between 30 and 40 'large, roomy and commodious bathing-machines' parked on its shore. By 1804 the charge for the hire of one had fallen to sixpence 'exclusive of perquisites'.

In the year 1798, when Thomas Hinderwell published his first history of the town, he was able to record that there were now two new warm and cold sea-bathing bath houses opened on the cliffs, one run by Wilson and Travis, surgeons and apothecaries, the other by Willis of the same profession. Also, a general sea-bathing infirmary for the diseased poor was promised but not yet built. By the time the third edition of Hinderwell's history appeared posthumously in 1832, Scarborough had no fewer than five 'neat and commodious structures for warm, sea-water bathing': Travis's, at the entrance to St Nicholas Cliff, which had been modernised in 1822 and now had rooms for steam and vapour baths; Weddell's, built in 1812, overlooking the harbour at the end of the old pier; Harland's, at the bottom of Vernon Place; Champley's, opposite Harland's, which boasted separate suites for ladies and gentlemen; and Vickerman's, the newest, erected in 1829, on the foreshore.

Perhaps the best description of sea-bathing at Scarborough is to be found in Tobias Smollett's *Humphry Clinker*, a novel written in the form of letters and published in 1771. The bather ascended by wooden steps into 'a small, snug, wooden chamber, fixed upon a wheel-carriage, having a door at each end, and on each side a little window above, and a bench below'. As the bather undressed inside, an attendant yoked a horse to the carriage which pulled it forward into the sea until the water was on a level with the floor. The horse was then unyoked and tied to the other end and the bather emerged and plunged headlong into the sea. 'After having bathed he reascends into the apartment by the steps which had been shifted for that purpose, and puts on his clothes at his leisure, while the carriage is drawn back again upon the dry land, so that he hasnothing further to do but reopen the door and come down as he went up.' If the bather needed help to undress and dress there were servants on hand to assist. The carriage was spacious enough for half a dozen people. Ladies and children were invariably accompanied by guides. Some machines were fitted with 'tilts', or hoards that could be lowered over the seaward end to sea level to screen shy bathers from the eyes of prying spectators.

Female attendants on ladies and children, nicknamed 'Mother Duckers', had a reputation for physical strength and merciless impatience. They insisted on 'three dips', or three full immersions, and were known to force nervous or unwilling customers if they failed or refused to do as they were told. An annual visitor to Scarborough with his family, John Courtney of Beverley, ordered his son to bathe in the sea and employed 'two or three men for the purpose'. The colder the water the more effective its therapy, according to physicians. A sure sign of cure was a ringing in the ears. As Smollett's fictitious correspondent noted, 'for health as well as pleasure', the sea was more satisfying and exhilarating than fresh water because it 'braced every sinew of the human frame'.

Of course, the elderly, children, invalids and delicate females were advised to take care. They should not bathe until at least three hours after breakfast, and even then only on alternate days. On the other hand, healthy males could bathe before breakfast every morning, unless their nerves and muscles had been weakened by a night of debauchery or excessive consumption of alcohol and food. If any of the bather's extremities turned blue in the sea he or she should come out immediately. Cold sea water bathing was a 'powerful stimulant' and left the bather with a feel-good body glow, but it might prove too much of a physical shock for the weak-hearted. Hinderwell was honest enough to concede that cold sea water immersion was far from efficacious in many cases of illness: whereas gout, rheumatism, scrofula, nervous complaints and ague usually succumbed to regular deluges of cold salt water, it might do more harm than good when the patient was debilitated by age or other diseases. As for pubescent boys and girls who suffered from 'obstructions', an ill-managed course of cold sea bathing could 'produce great mischief'; they would benefit most from all the other natural advantages and exercises Scarborough had to offer the visitor – its fresh, clean, bracing air, its mineral drinking waters, and its walks, rides and boat excursions.

Amusements

After taking the waters, externally, internally or both, during the mornings, what entertainment could visitors to Scarborough expect during the rest of the day? Should they survive the journey to the resort, the daily dunkings, the stench of rotting fish and the perilous passage to and from the spa wells, Scarborough's seasonal 'spawers' might be rewarded in the afternoon or the evenings at the theatre in Tanner Street.

By 1777 Mr Keregan's 'large booth' had been replaced by Mr James Cadwell's 'fine theatre'. Built in 1767 and opened the following year, the theatre was near the same site as its predecessor on the east side of Tanner Street. Since 'the edifices consecrated to the service of Almighty God' had greater claim on his attention than Scarborough's 'elegant' Assembly Room or its 'neat Theatre', Hinderwell neglected to describe the last two. However, if the architecture of Scarborough's first theatre is elusive, there are more than a hundred surviving play bills dating from 1777 to 1798 to record what happened inside it. Plays were performed there on alternate nights from June through to October. A box cost three shillings; a seat in the pit stalls two shillings; and one in the gallery only one shilling. The whole theatre was lit by candles. Most performances included one, radically reduced, Shakespearian play with songs and recitations between the acts. Also performed were all the new plays by Sheridan – *The Rivals*, 1775, *The School for Scandal*, 1777, *She Stoops to Conquer* and *The Critic*, 1779. Sheridan's *A Trip to Scarborough* was first played at Drury Lane in 1777. It had nothing to do with Scarborough, but the author knew that his customers were well acquainted with the place as a summer resort.

Thanks to Hinderwell's Spartan tastes and Hutton's lack of means, we also know less than we would like about what the former disparagingly called 'the refined amusements of polished life'. Even by 1800 there was still only one coffee house, the same as that depicted in 1725 at the corner of Tanner Street and Newborough. The house was now kept by Mrs Park who charged her subscribers five shillings for the season. For this they could read the London and provincial newspapers at their leisure. Moreover, and rather surprisingly for a coffee shop, dinners and suppers were also provided, and some of them were sent out to families in lodging houses nearby.

For those who wanted to read something less ephemeral than newspapers, James Schofield, author of the town's earliest guide of 1787, had a bookseller's and stationery shop in Newborough and a summer book store on St Nicholas Cliff. It was said that he had 4,000 volumes for hire. For five shillings a season a subscriber could take two books at a time; for seven shillings and sixpence, four; and for half a guinea, six. Books could be changed every day except Sundays. When visiting the spa in 1803, William Hutton had been so impressed by the list of subscribers to Hinderwell's first edition published five years earlier that he paid a shilling for a two-hour loan of the volume before deciding to buy it outright.

Next to another newsroom at the south end of King Street, which charged a season's subscription of ten shillings and sixpence, was the Agricultural and General Library. Founded in 1801, this library was also designed to meet the needs and the pockets of visiting gentry. As one of the illustrations in the *Poetical Sketches of Scarborough*, published in 1813, shows, 'The Library' was frequented only by well-dressed and well-to-do ladies and gentlemen. Initial membership fee and annual subscription charge were well beyond the resources of the ordinary people of the town even if they were literate. And so were the fines for overdue books: threepence a week for a volume of quarto size, and twopence a week for one of smaller octavo size.

Meanwhile the Assembly Rooms, which had once been the focus of interest and the main source of entertainment, were losing their appeal by the end of the century. Scarborough's first Long Room on the south side of Low Westgate, or Princess Street as it had now become, was now occupied as a private dwelling. Later still, it was divided into two separate houses, numbers 11 and 11A.

A second Long Room on Sandside experienced a worse fate. Even less is known about this building than the one in Princess Street, chiefly because it was seriously damaged by fire in the middle of the nineteenth century and then utterly wrecked by conversion into an amusement arcade in the twentieth. It was said to have been used as a military barracks at the time of the Jacobite rising of 1745-6 before Mosdale Hall at the castle was rebuilt to house troops. The rear of the premises backing on to the Bolts was once called the house of the dead when it was used as a mortuary for corpses washed ashore. All that remains today of Scarborough's second Assembly Room is the recently named Long Room Passage running alongside the site connecting the Bolts with Sandside.

Like so many of the amenities in Scarborough catering for visitors, by the end of the eighteenth century, the Assembly Rooms had moved up hill. The Long Room which had given its name to the street by 1783 was joined by another a little to the north of it on the same west side. The old Long Room was owned by Edward Donner and the new one by William Newstead, but they worked in tandem, not in competition. They shared the same master of ceremonies, Robinson Farside, and the same rules and charges. Subscription for the whole season cost a guinea. Once a week there was a dress ball night and twice a week two undress nights. On these occasions tea, cakes and hot sweet wine were served to the company.

Yet clearly there were now fewer 'stars and garters'. Arthur Young was enchanted by Scarborough's location and dramatic scenery, but profoundly unimpressed by its public buildings: 'even the rendez-vous of pleasure, the long-rooms', he wrote, 'are paltry holes'. John Courtney had been coming to Scarborough annually since 1759, but in July 1790 he recorded in his diary that there were only a few people in Donner's Long Room and after 'taking a turn or two we all came away'. Something of a snob, Courtney deplored the lack of persons of quality now coming to Scarborough.

Scarborough no longer had the custom sufficient to support two assembly rooms. When the second edition of Schofield's guide appeared in 1796, Newstead was dead and his room had closed. Mr Donner now had a monopoly. The only surviving Long Room had dress nights, Mondays and Fridays, for which non-subscribers paid five shillings, and an informal dance on Wednesday nights, which would cost them three shillings. In addition, a gentleman wishing to dance with a lady was required to pay two shillings for the music and a shilling extra if he wanted tea.

The days of the assembly room were numbered: by 1800 visitors to the town had many other kinds and places of amusement and recreation. A century earlier, Celia Fiennes had gone out to sea 'in a little boate', but she had found it 'very rough even in the harbour'. By Schofield's time, 'sea parties' particularly during settled weather in August, had become the common experience of visitors. For half a guinea a day you could hire a coble, and for twice that figure you could have one of the three bigger boats which had cabins below deck 'with bed spaces', in case bad weather or contrary winds kept the company at sea all night. Mr William Henderson, who kept a lodging house at St Nicholas Cliff, also had one of these vessels of 30 tons.

Most of the 32 cobles counted by William Hutton were available for hire on Sundays when each took as many as a dozen passengers on pleasure trips. For those who fancied their skill and chances as fishermen, there were cobles to be hired during the week to catch haddock, whiting, codling and mackerel. Less adventurous and less affluent anglers could try their luck from the East Pier at high tide. Schofield reported day cruises up the coast to Cloughton Wyke as early as 1787.

Whereas earlier all the riding was up and down the sands of South Bay to and from the spa, by the time of Schofield and Hinderwell visitors had extended their range to include local places such as Hackness, Forge Valley and Scalby Mills. Significantly, visitors' guides now gave detailed attention to the hinterland of Scarborough. Schofield's guide started with a description of the last stages of the road to Scarborough from Malton referring to the grand houses and their owners along the route – the St Quintins at Scampston Hall, the Thompsons at Ebberston Hall, the Cayleys at Brompton and the Langleys at Wykeham Abbey. Ten years later, Hatfield recommended excursions from Scarborough to Castle Howard and Duncombe Park at Helmsley, both about 30 miles distant. Whether the owners of such stately properties would have welcomed uninvited parties long before they were opened to the paying public seems unlikely. Nevertheless, some 150 pages, more than a third of Hinderwell's *History*, was devoted to the vicinity of Scarborough, from Bridlington to the south as far north as Mulgrave castle, and inland to Rievaulx and Sheriff Hutton.

Part of the explanation for this territorial extension of Scarborough as a resort was the great improvement of local roads in the second half of the eighteenth century. Though the journey to Scarborough by sea was still cheaper than by road, it was still less fashionable and, especially during the French wars, much more dangerous. Even as late as 1808, the steam packet from London was only fortnightly and cost £1. 6s. The overwhelming majority of visitors, from the north as well as the south, came by coach. In 1736 the ferry service across the Humber between Wintringham and Brough had been improved, but most visitors to Scarborough came from York. The

Turnpike Act of 1752 greatly improved the 43 miles from Monk Bridge to Newborough Bar, via New Malton, Rillington and Scampston, from where the road crossed the Vale of Pickering through Yedingham to Snainton, and then reached Scarborough through Ayton and Falsgrave. By 1754 coaches were using this route daily from Leeds, and four years later there were two running every day during the season. At the same time, the final stretch of the southern approach to Scarborough from Beverley and Hull, the six miles from Spital House via Hertford Bridge and Seamer, was also made into a tolled turnpike.

By the time that Schofield's second edition was published, the coach from London arrived in Scarborough four times a week and the fare of £2 14s. was more than twice that of the sea passage by steamer. There were two coaches a day from Leeds arriving at the George and the Blue Bell inns, and one diligence each from Hull and Whitby, running to and from the New Inn and the Blue Bell. The journey from Leeds cost a pound, from York and Hull, twelve shillings, and from Whitby, seven shillings. The road from Hull via Beverley and Bridlington was now almost as good as that from Leeds and York, but the coach ride over the moors from Whitby must have been testing for both horses and passengers.

If the road journey to Scarborough had become more convenient and comfortable, accommodation there had much increased and improved since the days of Dicky Dickinson. Celia Fiennes had been fortunate to find 'good accommodation and on very reasonable terms' in 1697, probably because she was happy to lodge with the Quakers. Other visitors, who were perhaps less lucky and more fastidious, had experience of Scarborough's houses and rooms that was far from pleasant. Joseph Taylor discovered only 'indifferent entertainment' in his lodgings and chose to move to others nearby. Sarah, duchess of Marlborough, had higher standards of comfort and service than Scarborough could then supply: she told her granddaughter that the town was noisy, dirty, poverty-stricken and overcrowded with dismal and disagreeable people. She complained about almost everything, including the food. In contrast, Edmund Withers – no doubt more easily satisfied than the duchess – had only praise for the wholesome, cheap fare he had 'at one of the best inns in the towne'. Of these inns or 'ordinaries' there were five advertised in 1733: the New Globe, the Old Globe, the New Inn, the Crown and Sceptre and the Blacksmith's Arms.

For some time yet there were no boarding houses in Scarborough. In 1759 and again in 1762, John Courtney and his family rented three rooms, each at ninepence a week. They had to find their meals elsewhere – at one of the inns, the Long Room or at the coffee house. Even as late as 1756, according to official War Office figures, Scarborough had still only 151 beds for guests and stabling for 358 horses.

The construction of the terrace of New Buildings on the west side of St Nicholas Cliff during the late 1760s marked a new step forward in providing visitor accommodation. These purpose-built lodging houses were designed to furnish everything a family needed for the season. Rooms were ten shillings a week; sheets, towels and table-linen were included; a fully-stocked kitchen cost twenty shillings a week and a cook to go with it half a guinea extra. Visitors might bring their own servants or hire them on arrival. Alternatively, families could have their meals brought in from nearby inns or Long Rooms. Thanks to 'the extraordinary nimbleness and care of those who convey dinners to the respective lodgings', wrote Schofield, 'the provisions are always served hot and well'. Hot dinners brought in were eighteen pence per head.

The New Buildings were clearly intended for well-to-do 'spawers' and even as late as the 1790s there were still too few boarding houses catering for visitors of more limited means. The first guide to include a list of accommodation street by street was not available until 1797. It was written by John Hatfield, a notorious charlatan, debtor and deceiver of rich ladies, who compiled it during a seven-year sojourn in Newborough Bar prison. After his release he was later hanged at Carlisle in 1803 for forgery. After naming the dozen proprietors of houses on St Nicholas Cliff, most of them with 'a full sea prospect', Hatfield's guide named eight in Harding's Walk, which fronted Bean's gardens and had attics at the back with sea views; 34 in Newborough; 13 in Long Room Street; two in Tanner Street; and seven in Queen Street.

Clearly, Hatfield's list of lodging houses was far from complete. However, a so-called 'second edition', printed by and for George Broadrick of Scarborough in 1806, filled some of Hatfield's original gaps. Four more places 'Below the Cross', two in King Street, four on Bland's Cliff, and 20 on Merchant's Row were added. Even so it seems highly unlikely that other locations, such as Longwestgate, Princess Street, St Sepulchre Street, Tuthill and Palace Hill, were also not offering guest rooms at this time. Broadrick distinguished between

178

'lodging' and 'boarding' houses, the former providing only rooms without meals were usually also commercial or business premises. So Mrs Hodgson on Merchant's Row had a grocer's shop on the ground floor and let rooms above it, and in the same street Mr Crathorne took guests on the floors above his toy shop. Indeed, apart from the purpose-built large houses on St Nicholas Cliff and in Huntriss Row, nearly all boarding and lodging dwellings had retail or workshops on the ground floor at street level.

Broadrick's incomplete guide to lodging and boarding houses in Scarborough listed fewer than 120 in 1806 and a similar number in the next edition of 1810. However, he did not attempt to calculate the number of visitors who might have occupied them. If the experience of the Huttons, father William and daughter Catherine, was not untypical then there might have been upwards of two thousand visitors in Scarborough in August 1804, when the town's resident population, according to the census of 1801, was only six and a half thousand. Along with the Huttons, there were 23 others dining at Crathorne's on Merchant's Row, and as many as 60 crammed into the Bell on Bland's Cliff. Though prices had risen sharply since Hatfield's first edition, Catherine Hutton complained of overcrowded conditions in 1804 and again in 1806, and she was not happy with many in her company of 'cloth-makers and merchants from the West Riding'. These men might be 'honest' and 'hearty', but she disapproved of their gluttony and heavy drinking. Since the stars and garters of Dicky's days, Scarborough was going down-market.

For descriptions of the accommodation offered by Scarborough to 'the company' such as the Huttons, we have to turn to property advertisements in the only local newspaper then available – the *York Courant*. Here again the mixture of all-year-round trade and seasonal tourism is to be found in the many three-storeyed houses offered for sale. In June 1790 a property on the south side of Newborough was said to have a large front shop, dining and drawing rooms, five lodging rooms, three garrets, a kitchen, two cellars, a well, warehouse, two workshops and two yards. In other words these premises, offering a fine prospect of sea, spa and harbour piers, had much more than seasonal value: they could provide an income throughout the whole year.

Some houses were so spacious and self-sufficient that today they would be called hotels. One such property in Queen Street, put up for sale early in 1759, had drawing, dining and breakfast rooms as well

179

as library on the ground floor, four large lodging rooms on the first floor, five smaller lodging rooms in the attic, and a kitchen, scullery, brewhouse, coachhouse and stabling for eight horses. With houses like this it is no wonder that James Schofield was able to write that Queen Street 'would not discredit a metropolis'.

On a smaller scale, lower down in the older part of town, some homes had been divided into several tenements. In 1800 one such property in East Sandgate was advertised as consisting of four tenements; whereas ten years later, another with the same address, had a shop at the street level, a common room above it, and lodgings on the top floor.

10

TRADE AND INDUSTRY: THE OTHER SCARBOROUGH

Ship Market

Only a passing visitor who probably saw little more than the spa and St Nicholas Cliff could have written, as T. Pennant did in 1771, that Scarborough was 'a place entirely without trade'. In fact, the evidence, if not the opinion, is overwhelming that even during the best attended summer seasons most of the town's resident population derived its livelihood from sources other than 'the company'. Moreover, since the season lasted only from June at the earliest to September at the latest, during the remaining eight months of the year Scarborough's lodging houses and inns were unoccupied. Shipping was more important to Scarborough than spawers.

On evidence derived mainly from St Mary's parish register of baptisms and burials, enrolments of apprenticeship indentures, and the first published directory of the town dated 1823, between 1773 and 1823, Scarborians were engaged in between 70 and more than 100 occupations. Of these occupations, seafaring was the one that employed most. During the years 1773 to 1787, of the 366 men whose occupations can be identified, 115, or more than 30%, were mariners of one kind or another. Between 1813 and 1820, the percentage was still as high as 26, and not until Baines' directory of 1823 are their numbers (115) exceeded by those of innkeepers and lodging landlords (158).

However, numbers of men who went to sea for a living as fishermen or merchant mariners represented only a lesser fraction of all those in Scarborough who were engaged in one way or another in ship-building. 'Shipping and its dependencies are the principal branches in which the inhabitants are most generally interested', was Hinderwell's informed conclusion; and as a master mariner with 20 years experience

181

of the sea, a part owner of several vessels, and for 40 years one of Scarborough's ruling 44, he was as well placed as any to know.

Hinderwell conceded that extreme fluctuations in the market made ship-building and ship-owning precarious businesses, yet even so they were 'an important object of employment' and 'a great source of emolument' in Scarborough. According to the figures in the third edition of his history published in 1832, between 1785 and 1831, 301 ships were built at Scarborough. However, this number is almost certainly an underestimate, since no launchings between 1811 and 1817 are included. During a slightly longer but similar period, from 1771 to 1820, the author of *The Outport of Scarborough* gave the number of launches in the harbour as 320. From both sets of statistics of ship-building the truth of Hinderwell's reference to 'sudden fluctuations' in demand is evident enough. For example, during the three years 1784-6, nearly 40 ships were built at Scarborough, more than the number finished in the seven years 1804-10. The highest figure given by Hinderwell for launchings in one year was 15 in 1801, and the lowest three in 1805. Fluctuations in the demand for ships and shipping space were particularly great in wartimes and Britain was at war almost continuously from 1776 to 1783 and from 1793 until 1815.

In the half century from 1770 to 1820, 155, or nearly half of the total of ships built at Scarborough were brigantines. These two-masted, merchant vessels varied enormously in size from as much as 230 to as little as 80 tons. The biggest vessels launched at Scarborough, registered simply as 'ships', had an average tonnage of about 300. The largest of them during this half century, weighing in at 444 tons, was the *Fortitude*, built in 1811 and registered under the mastership of William Batty.

The *Fortitude* of 1811 was only one of the 155 ships launched from the Tindall yards between 1771 and 1820. Of the seven owners of the company named at that time, five were called Tindall – James, senior and junior, Robert, senior and junior and William. The family had by then prospered so greatly that it had bought out and taken over most of the other shipbuilders' yards along the Sandside frontage. For instance, in 1806, the Tindalls had absorbed the Whartons, their only serious competitor at Scarborough. A few years earlier, John Tindall had purchased the 3,000-acre estate of Knapton Hall in the Vale of Pickering, which became the source of fresh vegetables and fruit for the crews of his ships, so that Tindall mariners as well as Tindall vessels won a deserved reputation for reliability and strength. There was no dry dock at Scarborough but Tindall ships were coppered and well finished in Millwall dock on the Thames. By 1820 the Tindalls and their partners owned 47 vessels.

Not all the ships registered at Scarborough were built there. Of the 106 registered as Scarborough vessels in 1786, 39 had been launched elsewhere, seven at Hull, four at Whitby, four at Stockton, and the others even further away. Indeed, Scarborough was much more than a ship-building port of refuge: as Hutton wrote in 1804, it was also a 'ship market', where carriers of all kinds were hired for service all over the world. Between 1709 and 1751 Scarborough was first of all the English provincial ports in terms of shipping tonnage registered there; by 1782 it was still in that position, just ahead of Liverpool; and by 1830, ninth behind Newcastle, Liverpool, Sunderland, Whitehaven, Hull, Bristol, Yarmouth and Whitby. A high proportion of Scarborough's ships were in government service, particularly as transports in time of war. Pennant was told in 1769 that a quarter of Scarborough's 300 vessels had been employed in the Seven Years War of 1756-63.

The whole fleet of Tindall ships took part in the War of American Independence, transporting troops across the Atlantic and then ferrying them up and down the coasts of the rebellious colonies. The *Emerald*, under Robert Tindall, was scuttled during the disastrous defence of Yorktown in 1781. Other Tindall vessels known to have served in North America during that war were the *Ocean*, the *Diana*, the *Symmetry* and the *Harmony*.

The resumption of war with France in 1793 again stimulated government demand for sea transports. In the next four years 44 ships were launched at Scarborough, most of them from Tindall yards. However, the war also inflated the prices of every commodity and the Tindalls and other owners were soon petitioning the Treasury on the grounds that hiring allowances no longer covered the increasing costs of provisions and maintenance. The war also caused a great number of losses. In 1807, for example, John Tindall lost *Alfred the Great*, a ship of 383 tons valued at £10,000, to a French privateer. Moreover, the Napoleonic war had a catastrophic affect on commerce with the Continent: the Milan and Berlin decrees effectively denied British trade with Europe and closed the Baltic to British ships. From 1804 until 1812 there was a prolonged, deep depression in shipping and foreign trade. John Tindall was the only builder who refused to close his yards and lay off his workmen. When he died in 1809 he had been responsible for building 110 ships.

The Tindalls survived partly because their fleet operated out of the Thames, whereas other builders were over dependent on the Baltic trade. Also, plentiful supplies of local timber and the low cost of skilled labour in north Yorkshire meant that building expenses at Scarborough were about half those in London. Thirdly, Tindall success was based on the high standard of their design and construction of ships. Their brigantines or snows could expect an active life of half a century: first employed in long-distance service in the Far East, North America or the West Indies, they were then used in the Baltic trade, and finally, as they aged, ended their usefulness as North Sea colliers.

Coal and Piers

Whatever the state of marine commerce elsewhere, in peace time or in war time, the coal trade out of Newcastle, Sunderland and Blyth remained the most important of all the mercantile carriers. For collier construction Scarborough gave precedence to Whitby, which had a more spacious and sheltered harbour, but Scarborough was still regarded as the most convenient refuge for colliers between Tyne and Humber. In 1697 Celia Fiennes had seen a convoy of 70 coal-carrying ships pass the headland on their way south. Just over a century later, William Hutton observed 'two hundred sail from Newcastle passing towards the south'. Shipments of coal down the east coast increased from less than half a million in 1700 to well over two million tons by the end of the century.

By 1800 Scarborough harbour had benefited from substantial improvement and enlargement. Ever since 1614 Scarborough's two coroners had been receiving toll money from Newcastle and Sunderland explicitly for the purpose of maintaining a pier and secure haven. However, a century later, this considerable revenue was being spent indiscriminately and improperly. When a storm made a great breach in the pier in 1711 and there was no pier money in hand, the Common Hall had to raise the necessary funds by borrowing £200 on the security of the Wheatcroft farm. Though the coroners afterwards decided to use toll money exclusively for pier repairs, the Common Hall continued to make raids on it for other pressing purposes. A hundred pounds were taken to mend the town windmill during the 1720s and £76 12s misused, this time to pay a two-year debt of 'College rent' owed to Trinity College, Cambridge. By 1726, a total of £227 17s had been robbed from the coroners' pier account.

In response to the complaints of collier masters and pleas from Scarborough burgesses, Parliament passed an Act in 1732 levying an additional duty of a half penny on every chaldron of coal leaving the north-east ports. There were also to be new duties on timber and spirits entering and fish, pork, skins and tallow leaving Scarborough's port. All this extra revenue was to pay for a new pier, estimated to cost £12,000, which would increase the capacity and the safety of Scarborough's harbour.

At first the outcome was both unintended and unsatisfactory. A new pier to run from Ramsdale Scar in South Bay to a point on the shore where Millbeck entered the sea was begun in 1733 and then dismantled when it proved to be a dangerous obstacle to sea-bathing and access to the spa. The corporation stopped the work and ordered the stone to be re-used for a pier in the harbour.

Work on a branch of the old pier to extend it southwards was halted almost immediately by the death of Lelam, the civil engineer in charge, and there was some delay before a replacement, William Vincent, could restart building. Nevertheless, Setterington's drawing of 1735 shows Vincent's branch or spur running southwards to form a 'V' neck between it and the end of the old pier. By 1747, when Vincent's own plan of the town and harbour was drawn to illustrate their anti-Jacobite defences, his new extension and the old pier had parted company. Afterwards the gap between them was widened to allow first cobles and then bigger vessels to pass through what was known as the Pet Hole. The detached end of the old pier came to be called the outer island pier to distinguish it from the longer inner island pier to the north of it.

One of the provisions of the Act of 1732 was the appointment of 15 commissioners to act as watchdogs and examine the coroners' pier accounts every year. By 1750 they were so dissatisfied with the administration of the harbour that they decided to take legal action against the corporation. Nothing came of this action but it did focus the attention and concern of Parliament. The preamble to the Scarborough Harbour Act of 1752 opened with the damning words: 'Whereas great frauds and abuses have of late years been committed in the execution of the several trusts reposed in the said bailiffs and burgesses' and accused them of wilfully misapplying more than £3,000, which had been raised by mortgaging the new pier duties.

The Act of 1752 took the new pier duties and responsibility for a new east pier out of the hands of the corporation of Scarborough and placed them in the care of a body of commissioners from which members of the Common Hall were excluded. From then on Scarborough's harbour piers were maintained by two quite separate authorities, the new east pier begun in 1753, by the independent commissioners answerable directly to Parliament, and the old pier, which remained the responsibility of the corporation. In 1778 the two bailiffs were allowed to join the ranks of the commission, and surprisingly the two bodies seem to have worked well in tandem. When friction did occur in 1806 because the commissioners had secured a new Act of Parliament without even consulting the corporation, the bailiffs were placated by being allowed to appoint the harbour master. Even at the end of the life of the old corporation there were still complaints recorded that pier money was not kept separate from other Town Hall revenues, but the old pier seems to have been properly maintained.

Vincent's pier gave greater protection against easterly gales, but the sea still broke over the old pier so that vessels could discharge or load on its western side only in fine weather or in off-shore winds. During two heavy storms in 1763 and 1767 the waves tore right through and over the old pier, drove ships in the harbour from their moorings, and scattered them along the sands of the foreshore as far as Millbeck. Many vessels were wrecked. The roof of the old Assembly Room on Sandside was damaged by the yard arm of a ship beating against it. A new ship was washed off its stocks.

In these circumstances, the construction of a new pier to the east of the old one would provide not only more anchorage room; it would save the old pier from more harm or even destruction. However, progress on this outer mole was painfully slow – about 18 feet or 5 metres a year. Local stone was quarried from White Nab down the coast and the north side of the castle headland, and conveyed to the site on flat-bottomed 'floats'.

Scarborough's East Pier is one of the greatest achievements of marine civil engineering. From the foot of Castle cliff running in a shallow crescent line to its original terminus, subsequently called Donkin's Bight, the pier is 1,380 feet or more than 400 metres long. Its first design and construction owed much to John Smeaton (1742-92), who built the third Eddystone Lighthouse, the first of stone. Smeaton concluded that the mole would have to be flexible to withstand the enormous impact of wind and tide-driven sea. The lower courses of quarried stones, weighing between 20 and 30 tons each, rest on the solid rock scar of the sea bed, but they and the upper interlocking blocks are not tightly knit together; slight gaps were deliberately left between them to allow the passage of air and water and thereby lessen their impact. The outer face of the pier is battered, again to minimise the force of the sea. Finally, the inner side of the pier was also angled outwards so that when the highest seas passed over the parapet they did not damage the ships tied up alongside it.

Each of the three editions of Hinderwell's *History* marked stages in the lengthy construction of the East Pier. By 1798, when the first edition came out, Hinderwell wrote that 760 feet, more than 200 metres, had then been built. In 1811, when the second was published, he reported the completion of 'upward of one thousand feet', nearly 300 metres. Finally, it was left to his successors responsible for the third edition of 1832 to announce that 'the new or outer pier is now completed', though that event had taken place some six years earlier.

Whatever the total costs of this gigantic project, they had been met entirely by the coal trade. The half-penny levy per chaldron on north-eastern coal shipments originally granted in the Act of 1732 had been renewed in 1763 and again in 1801. It was only proper, therefore, that Scarborough's outer harbour between the old and new east piers should be officially designated a haven of refuge for all small craft up to 500 tons. What pages of the books of the harbour master have survived show clearly how the colliers were still dependent on finding shelter at Scarborough. Between 1 January 1796 and 10 October 1805, no fewer than 744 vessels belonging to coal ports took refuge there, but because the outer harbour was still unfinished at this time 61 of them were damaged at anchor.

During an easterly storm in 1800 much of Vincent's pier broke away and collapsed into the sea. The structure of the East Pier gave protection to the old one but it diverted the full force of waves southwards at Vincent's spur. Fortunately, the destruction of Vincent's extension coincided with the appointment of a new harbour engineer from Newcastle, William Chapman, who during the next 31 years until his death was principally responsible for converting Scarborough harbour into its modern form. Vincent's pier was rebuilt and a lighthouse, Scarborough's first, erected on it; the harbour floor was excavated and levelled, deepening the water by an average of a metre; the inner island pier was removed in 1819; a western jetty of timber and stone was built to protect the harbour from silting; the East Pier was finished; and a new quay was constructed on the north side of the inner harbour at Sandside.

Chapman did not live long enough to see all his plans fulfilled, but he alone was their original architect.

Lighthouse and Lifeboat

Scarborough's first lighthouse was ordered to be built by the harbour commissioners at a meeting they held at the Bull Inn in September 1806. As a result, a round tower of brick with railings around its flat top was raised near the end of Vincent's rebuilt pier. During daylight a flag was hoisted to indicate that there were at least 12 feet of water at the pier end; at night it was replaced by a coal brazier burning on the top platform. The coal fire was soon found to be impractical: in its place six tallow candles were set in a circular tin behind a window below the roof. A watchman stood by to renew or relight the candles, and it was not until 12 years later that a copper reflector was installed to enhance the light. On more than one occasion a ship's master was misdirected by house lights on the shore.

As late as 1809 vessels were expected to enter or leave the harbour without communication with, or even approval of, the harbour master. In that year, however, Chapman devised a code of signals to control movements in and out of the port.

After Vincent's spur was built silting had become a major problem, and the construction of the East Pier worsened it. Unlike the old pier the East Pier had no gully hole to sweep the sand at high tide out of the harbour. Even after Chapman had recommended and cut a second corridor through the outer pier the inner harbour became shallower and shallower. Consequently, as a result of complaints from owners and masters, the inner harbour was deepened by as much as a metre. During the winter of 1816-17, in the aftermath of the Napoleonic wars, Scarborough's unemployed ex-seamen and former soldiers were put to work at nine shillings a week excavating and dredging the harbour bottom.

To safeguard the advantages of deeper water and to provide safer and more mooring, a new western jetty was first begun in 1817

188

along a line from West Sandgate towards Vincent's pier. At the outset this jetty was a makeshift construction of timber carcasses filled with stone, but the success of the new structure convinced the harbour authorities that it should be made more permanent. Two-thirds of the costs were met by the corporation. By 1822 it was finished. The inner island pier was removed, leaving only the outer island pier between the ends of the west and Vincent's pier.

Scarborough's lifeboat heading off in a rough sea, 1801

One of the most enduring and beneficial achievements of Thomas Hinderwell was his successful campaign to secure a lifeboat for Scarborough. It was he who first launched a public appeal for a lifeboat fund in 1800 and was chairman of the lifeboat committee. However, only £212 1s. 6d. was raised by the first appeal whereas the bill for building the boat on Sandside alone came to £129 5s. After further necessary expenses had been paid the fund soon went into debt. Henry Greathead of South Shields, who designed the vessel, was paid five guineas for his plan and each of the eleven-man crew was given half a guinea every time he was called out. A shed was built for the lifeboat at the east end of the old pier.

Of the fishermen originally appointed to man the lifeboat, there were four Hodgsons, two Potters, two Robinsons, two Peeks, two Waughs, and several others with names such as Normandale, Nightingale and Daniel for long associated with Scarborough's seafaring community. John Harwood was first master of the boat. After Tynemouth, Scarborough became the second lifeboat station in England.

Despite initial financial difficulties, Scarborough's lifeboat very soon justified it existence. Within the first year of its operation the lives of the crews of the brig *Aurora* and sloop *Isabella* and the brigs *Assistance* and *Experiment* had been saved in storms which would have swamped any ordinary rescue boat. At the end of 1801 the London *Sun* printed a graphic account by Hinderwell of the rescue of the seven men on board the *Aurora*. When the House of Commons Committee examined Greathead's reward claims for his invention it was Hinderwell again who appeared before it and spoke on his behalf. Scarborough acquired a second lifeboat in 1822, and what became the Royal National Lifeboat Institution was founded in 1824, a year before Hinderwell's death. Thanks to him, Greathead and Scarborough's brave fishermen, Scarborough had become a haven of refuge in a sense never previously imagined.

Commerce and Fishing

Though Scarborough was a place of national importance as far as ship-building, ship-hiring and ship refuge were concerned, it could never become a major commercial port without access to the interior by river or canal. Even most of the fish landed there was re-exported by sea. As Hinderwell made the point in 1811: 'The vicinity of sterile moors and a thinly peopled neighbourhood, without any water-communication with the interior country, are formidable impediments to trade, and essentially operate to check the spirit of enterprise'. Accordingly, in the absence of a navigable river and before steam locomotives and railways were thought of, the idea of linking Scarborough to the hinterland by canal was raised on many occasions.

As early as 1752, the Act of Parliament which allowed the canalisation of the river Derwent permitted the undertakers to make it navigable 'from Scarborough Mills down to the river Ouse'. However, no attempt was made to improve the Derwent above Malton, thirty miles down river from its course inland from Scarborough. In the 1790s a proposal to link Malton and Scarborough by a canalised Derwent costing up to £80,000 again came to nothing. It would have had no fewer than 24 locks. Finally, when the channels of the Derwent and its tributary the Hertford were straightened at the beginning of the nineteenth century, the purpose of the project was to drain the waterlogged carrs for cereal cultivation and not to make them navigable.

Consequently, Scarborough harbour's commerce remained relatively small and static. Exports were mainly agricultural – corn, butter, hams, and bacon, and imports included coal, iron and glass from Newcastle, Sunderland and Blyth, timber, hemp, flax and iron from the Baltic, and brandy and gin from France and Holland. Some wine came in from Portugal, stationery and groceries from London, and textiles from the West Riding via Hull. Exports of grain increased considerably after Flixton and Seamer carrs were drained and became arable fields. Nevertheless, Hinderwell's table of duties collected at Scarborough port between 1786 and 1810 shows little change overall. Scarborough was said to have been badly affected by Napoleon's blockade of British trade with the continent. After 1815 the port failed to recover. Post-war unemployment and distress in Scarborough were especially acute.

Hinderwell deplored the failure of Scarborough men to exploit the rich fishing grounds of the North Sea and beyond. He argued that lack of their enterprise not lack of fish explained the sad decline in the industry during his lifetime. In 1769 John Travis, the local surgeon, had written that there were then only 105 fishermen in the town. In 1803 Hutton had counted 32 cobles, each with two or three fishermen, but made no reference to the number of five-man boats at Scarborough. By 1811 Hinderwell was claiming that the number of active fishermen had fallen to 60, and a footnote in the third edition of 1832 changed this figure to 'no more than fifty or sixty'.

Here again, apart from the lack of enterprise, there was the handicap of poor internal communications. As a fish market Scarborough could not compete with Hull or Grimsby. With these and other ports in mind, in 1823 Baines concluded that Scarborough's 'fisheries' were 'not on a large scale'. Not until the railway came to Scarborough was there any chance that it might supply the fish markets of the populous West Riding.

Victorian housing. Artisan dwellings in Victoria Street (above) and Patrician villas in Westwood (below).

11

POPULATION, CHURCHES, CHARITIES & NEW BUILDINGS

Inhabitants

By eighteenth-century Anglican standards Thomas Herring was an unusual clergyman. Fortunately for subsequent historians, as well as contemporaries, he did not follow the bad example of his predecessor as archbishop of York, Blackburn, who was both scandalously immoral and notoriously idle. As soon as he entered the see in 1743 Herring instigated a thorough investigation of all the parishes in his care; and not content to leave this to subordinates, during the next months he travelled hundreds of miles and gathered a mass of evidence of unique value to future historians.

Without the assistance of official census returns before 1801, and dependent on parish registers of doubtful accuracy, demographic historians are hard pressed to measure population numbers and trends in an age of rapid industrialisation. The figures produced by archbishop Herring's visitation, however approximate, fill a serious gap. The first question every vicar was asked concerned the number of families then resident in his parish. Though their answers were only in round figures and expressed in families, not individuals, they provide an additional measure to baptisms and burials. Furthermore, in Scarborough's case, these figures serve as a corrective to the several wild guesses of contemporary authors.

Estimates of Scarborough's resident population during the eighteenth century were invariably exaggerated. In 1725 John Cossins accompanied his New and Exact Plan of the town *[see back endpaper]* with the statement: 'This place by moderate computation appears to contain ab[ou]t 2000 familys'. If the average size of Scarborough's families had remained at four, as it had been two generations earlier, and was still at the time of the 1801 census, then this estimate would have given the town a population of 8,000 inhabitants.

Writing more than 60 years later, James Schofield's guesses were just as fanciful. According to his Guide, in 1745 Scarborough had had upwards of 10,000 residents, and by 1787, this total had increased by another thousand. Even Thomas Hinderwell, who was not prone to hyperbole, estimated than in 1798 Scarborough then had 1753 families and a total population of 7,350, when three years later the census officials could find only 6,409 inhabitants in the town.

In 1743 archbishop Herring was informed by Theophilus Garencières, then vicar of St Mary's, that his parish, which covered the whole communities of Scarborough and Falsgrave, was home to 1,500 families. Even this suspiciously rounded figure, when set against St Mary's parish register entries, looks inflated, though nothing like as much as those of Cossins and Schofield.

Both the baptism and burial entries in St Mary's parish register suggest that the Anglican population of Scarborough and Falsgrave had passed 5,000 by the time of Herring's visitation. However, from then on this number remained almost static until the 1790s, when it broke through the 6,000 ceiling. Epidemics of smallpox and measles in 1730, 1742 and, worst of all, in 1796, seem to have had less permanent impact than trade cycles and foreign wars, though in the last year 185 of the 301 burials were of infants.

No credence can be given to Scarborough's earliest surviving parish register, which for baptisms begins in 1687, and for burials in 1689. Noel Boteler, who was vicar for 20 years from 1676, failed badly to keep a full record of both events. By his own confession, he was frequently absent from the parish 'occasioned by my attendance on the Regiment'. And such absences 'causd these fatal chasms in the Registers'. However, the death of Boteler and the induction of his successor, John North, in July 1696 mark the start of a much more reliable record.

Using ten-year averages of baptisms and a multiple of 33, it seems that by 1700 the parish had a population of about 3,700, a considerable increase on the 2,541 produced by the same calculation on the bishop's transcript of baptisms in 1683, which is probably incomplete. Though these certainly indicate an exaggerated increase, there is no doubt that during these years at the end of the seventeenth and beginning of the eighteenth century the number of residents in Scarborough grew rapidly. In the decade from 1696 to 1705 baptisms far exceeded burials in every year except 1704. During the ten years from 1719 to 1728, the difference was not so marked, and burials outnumbered baptisms in 1722 and 1727. In the decade 1739 to 1748 there were four years when baptisms were outnumbered by burials, and during the decade 1759 to 1768 this occurred in six of the ten years.

In short, Scarborough's population had probably reached 5,000 as early as 1745, but from there on it levelled out on to a plateau. Theophilus Garencières, vicar from 1721 to 1750, baptised more than two hundred babies in at least four of his years in that office, whereas John Morfitt, vicar from 1750 until 1782, never conducted that number of baptisms in any of his thirty-two years. In five of the ten years between 1779 and 1788 there were more burials than baptisms. However, during the 1790s there was a significant change in the balance from negative to positive: in the decade 1799 to 1808 there was a surplus of baptisms over burials in every year, and from the census of 1801 onwards there were steady rises in the total number of inhabitants.

Even official census returns can be misleading. The 1801 census, for example, did not include mariners at sea – a large number of Scarborough men in peacetime and even more in times of war. Muster rolls of Scarborough seamen who were charged sixpence a month for the relief of widows and orphans recorded 665 names in 1786, 587 in 1804, and 445 in 1811.

None of the four censuses taken before 1841 included the permanent military garrison at the castle which during the French and Napoleonic wars was considerable. According to Hinderwell, in 1798, there were 650 soldiers billeted at the castle, a troop of horse and six corps of militia. The addition of both of these groups, naval and military, perhaps explains why Hinderwell's estimate in 1798 of the population of Scarborough and Falsgrave of 7,350 exceeded that of the 1801 census by many hundreds. After 1815, the castle garrison was much reduced, but men serving abroad in the armed forces and the mercantile marine returned home, so that the balance between the sexes was nearly restored. In 1801 women outnumbered men by 18%, in 1811 by 16%, but in 1821 by only 10%.

St Mary's marriage registers and enrolments of apprentice indentures show that Scarborough's population was swelled by a steady stream of immigrants. Between 1760 and 1820 up to a fifth of the weddings at St Mary's involved at least one partner born outside the borough. Most of these outsiders were originally young male apprentices drawn into Scarborough's maritime trades, particularly shipbuilding and its supporting crafts and industries. Yet this immigration in an era of explosive population growth was marginal compared with what was happening in the new industrial towns of the West Riding and Lancashire, or to immediate competitors, Hull and Grimsby. Scarborough's demographic history is entirely untypical of the period.

During the fifty years from 1681 to 1731 while Scarborough's population was growing quickly, England's increased hardly at all, from 4.9 million to 5.2 million. In the 1680s and 1720s the national figure actually declined. Then from the 1730s England's population increased every year from 5.5 million in 1741 to 9.8 million in 1811. While Scarborough's population stagnated, Hull, Leeds, Sheffield, Halifax and a dozen other Yorkshire towns were mushrooming. As far as the industrial revolution was concerned, it did not happen in Scarborough: here there were no coal mines, no textile mills, no factories using water and later steam power, no forges or furnaces, and not even a canal to link the town and port with them. Scarborough's only important industry was building ships, by methods and with a skilled labour force that scarcely changed in a century.

Scarborough's eighteenth-century demographic record therefore seems to match its political and social experience. After the collapse of South Cliff and the death of Dicky Dickinson coinciding with the great schism in the town's oligarchy, Scarborough's spectacular and unique growth as Britain's first seaside resort and fashionable spa came to an abrupt halt. In the 1730s Scarborough's seasonal clientele compared in wealth and social rank with that of any of the country's spas, including Bath. By the 1750s the contest had been lost. Scarborough stood still while Bath went from strength to strength. In 1700 the resident population of Bath was only 2,000; by 1800 it was 34,000, more than five times that of Scarborough, and twice that of York. Scarborough pioneered sea bathing, but it was Brighton which attracted more bathers and was favoured by the Prince Regent. George III favoured the sea at Weymouth. Londoners ventured no further than Margate, which had nearly 5,000 inhabitants by 1801. And as far as shipbuilding and shipowning were concerned, Scarborough now lagged behind Whitby, which had a thousand more residents in 1801.

Anglicans

Most Scarborians never passed through the porch of St Mary's church between their baptism and their burial. Of the parish's 5,000 inhabitants in 1743, only 1,000 were recorded as Anglican communicants and of these only 120 took communion regularly and only 220 had taken communion the previous Easter. Not that Scarborough was a hotbed of religious dissent: on the contrary, the vicar, Theophilus Garencières, said that there were only 27 Presbyterian, 29 Quaker and three Roman Catholic families living in his parish. In other words, of Scarborough's 5,000 residents, as many as 3,750 had no religious affiliation at all.

St Mary's, therefore, remained remote in a spiritual as well as a physical sense for nearly four out of five of the people of Scarborough; and even for those who managed the climb up to it only the town's hierarchy had access to its limited number of private pews. As when they were first built and occupied in 1635, these pews were reserved for those who could afford their rates, but a century later they had become even more expensive and exclusive. The best seats, nearest the vicar's pulpit in the great alley of the nave, had originally cost £2 13s. 4d.; in 1752, ten poorly-placed pews in the south aisle next to the porch cost as much as £11 15s. and averaged £4 8s. each. Though the parish population had doubled in size since the pews were first installed, accommodation in St Mary's had not expanded to meet it. The south transept or Farrer's Aisle was still occupied by the grammar school; the chancel, north transept and north aisle, all casualties of the Civil War and the town's post-war impoverishment, had not been rebuilt.

The only concession made to the increasing number of potential churchgoers was to build upper lofts and galleries with flights of wooden steps leading up to them. A north gallery dated from 1694, a south-west loft from 1710, and a west gallery from 1719. Yet none of these provided more than a few extra places. The west gallery was put up 'for the use of the boys and girls of the charity school' and paid for by Timothy Fysh. The south-west loft supported only seven pews, each costing four or five pounds. Several projects later in the century to build a chapel of ease in the town foundered on lack of funds or lack of enthusiasm. St Mary's remained Scarborough's only place of Anglican worship until Christ Church was opened in 1828.

If living Scarborians had limited hopes of a seat in one of St Mary's box pews, after death their chances of a burial plot in church land had improved. In 1779 the land adjacent to the west side of St Mary's was acquired by the corporation as a cemetery; a year later, the land on the east side of the church, known as Paradise Close, was bought for the same purpose; and finally, in 1809, the field called Vicarage Close, on the south-west slope below the church was added to the parish graveyard area. All these lands were sold or exchanged by Sir Charles Hotham, hereditary patron and impropriator of St Mary's. Like their predecessors, the Thompsons, the Hothams seem to have done much less for Scarborough's living Anglicans than they did for the dead ones. One of the few references to William Thompson in the parish register records that in 1720, when he was governor of Scarborough castle and MP for the borough, 'he gave an Engine to the Corporation to quench fire'. Whether this fire was for the exclusive use of St Mary's or for general use in the town is not made clear; but it is certain that it was intended to put our terrestrial fires, not those in hell.

The vicars of St Mary's – Noel Boteler (1676-96), John North (1696-1708), Henry Docker (1708-21), Theophilus Garencières (1721-50), John Morfitt (1750-82) and John Kirk (1782-1828) – were all long-lived clergymen of learning and distinction. Since all of them remained vicar until their deaths they must have been content with the benefice, even though it was a far from lucrative living. St Mary's vicars were entitled only to a salary of £28 a year, paid in quarterly instalments by the patron, and to the vicarage house on the north side of Longwestgate.

The vicar's house was less than palatial. Not until 1713 was his parlour floored with deal boards and only gradually during the following century were its seven rooms – two on the ground level, three bedrooms above, a garret and a back kitchen – plastered and ceilinged. By 1825 another smaller tenement, on the east side of the vicarage, with parlour, kitchen, two bedrooms and an attic, was provided for a curate.

St Mary's was not generously endowed with properties. As long ago as 1640 Gregory Fysh had left it half an acre of land on the north side of the vicarage; but another piece of land on the north side of Market Gate (now Castle Road) also bequeathed by him and formerly an acre in size 'owing to the encroachment of the sea' had shrunk to a quarter of its former extent by 1825.

The same terrier (a survey of church lands and property) of 1825 which recorded these details also noted that by this date the vicar's salary, though still only £28 a year, formerly paid by Lord Hotham was now paid by the corporation. When the main roof of the church had urgent need of repair in 1820, money to pay for it had been raised by sale of old materials and a parish rate. However, since then, a parliamentary grant of £1,800, yielding interest at 4%, had rescued St Mary's from penury and further decay.

However, as Garencières's replies to Herring's questions revealed, there were other sources of income besides his annual stipend available to Scarborough's vicar. In addition to St Mary's, he also had the vicarage of Staintondale, and there was nearly always the salary for his headmastership of Scarborough's grammar school. Eighteenth-century vicars could afford to keep a curate to teach in the school and deliver weekly lectures on Wednesdays. Garencières's family was too big for the vicarage, which he used only as a study and occasional bedroom, and he rented a spacious house only four hundred yards from the church.

Meanwhile, St Mary's still housed the grammar school. What was originally intended as only temporary accommodation for the boys, after the charnel building was demolished in 1648, became a permanent situation for the next two centuries. Farrer's Aisle, the south transept, was blocked off from the nave, divided into two floors for upper and lower classes, and given a new doorway in its west wall to give access from the outside.

After the fifty-year rule as headmaster of William Penston (1627-77), which ended only when the Scots grammarian went blind as well as deaf, the town found it difficult to secure a suitable replacement. Christopher Sollitt, initially the most promising candidate for the post of headmaster, proved negligent; the Latin school of between 30 and 40 scholars was soon reduced to eight or ten. After Bryan Bales, there came John Phillips, but 'poore Mr Phillips' could not raise the number to more than a dozen. Part of the problem was the existence in the town of a petty or English school which attracted as many as 50 boys. Furthermore, a certain Mr Urquhart, who might have kept a Latin school, had ruled himself out in the eyes of vicar Boteler by continuing 'his state of concubinage with Mrs Adrian'.

In 1692 Francis Thompson (1653-93) undertook to the then bailiffs, Thomas Sedman and Paul Batty, that he would pay £6 annually, the interest on the principal sum of £100, 'for and towards the use of a schoolmaster', on condition he was approved by Francis and his heirs.

This arrangement continued until 1743 when William Thompson, son of Francis, handed over £142 to bailiffs Hebden and Goland, the principal sum and seven years' unpaid interest.

During the 1690s it seemed that a new grammar school would be built, or at least found. Collections were made for 'a free school'; the trustees, the two bailiffs and the two coroners, viewed a suitable site; and Henry Docker, clerk, was appointed master of the new school and authorised to employ an usher or deputy teacher. Docker became headmaster and later succeeded John North as vicar of St Mary's, but there was no new school. The association between Scarborough's parish church and Scarborough's grammar school grew even closer since from Docker onwards every vicar or his curate was also headmaster.

Apart from Thompson's bequest, the grammar school had only one other well-documented endowment. As early as 1640, Gregory Fysh had given a piece of land in Falsgrave, called Worlington Grove or Grave, to pay the fees of four scholars. The four were to be kindred of the testator or four others, two selected by the bailiffs and two by the vicar. For more than two hundred years, and long after the Fysh family had become extinct in Scarborough, Worlington Grove or Grammar School Field in upper Ramsdale provided a rental income intended for the school but often misappropriated by the town council. Finally, when the railway came to Scarborough in 1845, the York and North Midland railway company paid the corporation £150 for the freehold of Grammar School Field, though it was not until 1851 that the money was handed over to the school trustees.

By default, ignorance or indifference, Scarborough's rulers allowed St Mary's vicar to regard the grammar school as his own, a misunderstanding reinforced by the continued presence of the boys in Farrer's Aisle. This misunderstanding about the status of the school was not known publicly until 1824 when the Charity Commissioners revealed it. John Kirk had then been vicar for more than 40 years and during that time, on his own authority, he had appointed four curates to be schoolmasters. When questioned by the commissioners he denied that the town had any say in such matters, and his curate, Thomas Irvin, who had been master for the past 28 years, claimed that he had not received a penny from the Town Hall and knew nothing of an obligation to teach four free scholars.

The confusion exposed by the Charity Commissioners was ended when Irvin conceded the right of Scarborough corporation to appoint the schoolmaster, accepted £5 as his annual salary for the post, and agreed to give tuition in English and arithmetic to four poor scholars from the town. It seems that his employers considered such subjects more appropriate than the Latin and Greek Gregory Fysh had intended they should learn. From 1825 onwards the borough seal was affixed to the headmaster's document of appointment.

Otherwise the commissioners approved of the teaching of the Reverend Thomas Irvin. He had broadened the curriculum so that it satisfied those who had university and professional aspirations as well as the many more local farmers and traders who wanted their sons to have 'a useful liberal education'. By 1824 Scarborough's grammar school had about 40 boys, all paid fees, and some boarded with Irvin in his house in Queen Street. After 40 years service Irvin retired in 1833; his successor as master was the Reverend Joseph Skelton (1833-8), the last clergyman to hold the post, though the school was not ousted from St Mary's until 1848.

Anglicans in Scarborough were not concerned only to see Latin taught to the sons of fee-paying fathers: in 1729 they founded the Amicable Society to clothe and educate the daughters as well as the sons of the poor. In the words of one of the town's later historians: 'no charity in Scarborough [had] been so liberally supported' as this one. Though for many years classes were held in the rooms of Trinity House in St Sepulchre Street, by 1817 a grant of land from the corporation and a series of generous bequests from local benefactors allowed the Society to build a new school between Duesbery's Walk (now North Terrace) and what became Castle Road. The building contained apartments for the master and mistress and cost £1,200. In 1817 sixty children were being clothed and taught the four Rs – reading, writing, arithmetic and religion – and the Society that supported them had 250 members. By 1825 the number of Amicable pupils had risen to seventy.

Among the Society's trustees was Thomas Hinderwell, who had served as its president in 1784-5 and who left £50 to it in his will when he died in 1825. No better description of the purposes and successes of the Amicable school can be found than in his words:

> Experience has confirmed the utility of this establishment, in preserving the children from the contagion of vicious examples, and leading them into the paths of holiness and social duty. Instead of falling victims to profligacy, many of them have filled useful occupations in life with credit and advantage.

Himself a master mariner, Hinderwell was pleased and proud to recall that many of the boys had later gone to sea to qualify as mates and masters, and some had served gallantly in the Royal Navy during the French wars. It was Hinderwell who re-wrote the rules of the Amicable Society in 1804 and on leaving the school every child received a copy of 'a judicious tract' also written by him.

Nonconformists

In his answers to archbishop Herring's searching questions, the Reverend Theophilus Garencières had to concede that St Mary's was not the only place of worship in his parish. According to his own figures, there were 27 Presbyterian families with 120 members and 29 Quaker families with about the same number of members, and both had their licensed chapels. The Presbyterians had two services every Sunday and one every two months and the Friends assembled in their meeting house twice on Sundays and once every week.

By 1743 Scarborough's Presbyterian community gathered in their place of worship in lower St Sepulchre Street or Gate, as it was still called. Their house had been built about 1704. From about 1725, thanks to its purchase by its first minister, William Hannay, the building stood in a surrounding and substantial plot running down to Palace Hill. After Hannay retired to his native Scotland, taking his famous Covenanter bible with him, the Presbyterians enlarged their chapel in 1744. However, it was during the long ministry of Samuel Bottomley (1773-1830) that a new much larger and grander building to seat 450 was erected on this site. Though Bottomley himself deplored this 'sectarian' description, henceforth on maps and in guide books his Presbyterian meeting house was called the Independent Chapel. The unusual strength of the Presbyterian community in Scarborough was probably the result of the town's long-standing Scottish seafaring connections.

Practising Presbyterians, in defiance of the Test and Corporation Acts, were sometimes selected to Scarborough's governing body, but Quakers were still excluded and regarded with the greatest suspicion, even though they had become politically inactive. Consequently, there are few references to the town's Friends in Scarborough's corporation records.

The Friends' Meeting House in Low Conduit Street or Cook's Row, opened as early as 1676 and built at a cost to the Society of more than £150, seems to have been of greater interest to visitors than to residents. In 1697 Celia Fiennes noted that the town had an 'abundance of Quakers', but she pitied their 'delusion and ignorance' when she observed one of their meetings 'where 4 men and 2 women spoke'. Other visitors found the Meeting House more convenient than the parish church. In 1733 it was recorded that 'one Sunday afternoon several stars and garters' were seen 'at the Friends' meeting-house, which is easy of access' – certainly easier than the steep hill climb up to St Mary's church.

Though no longer the victims of the most cruel and harassing persecution, Scarborough's Quaker community probably declined in number during the eighteenth century. St Mary's parish register records several 'conversions' of former Quakers who brought their children to be baptised by the vicar. For example, John Bland, the Quaker merchant after whom Bland's Cliff road was named, had his son William christened by vicar Garencières. Fourteen years later, Jacob Swales, another former Friend, did the same for his daughter Mercy. One of the most affluent members of the local Society was the shipbuilding and shipowning Tindall family. However, during the American war they were forced to choose between pacifism and the demands of their crews for firearms. St Mary's register shows that in 1788 John and Isabella Tindall had their son James baptised there.

If some of the Tindalls left the Friends, their places were taken by Rowntrees. A release and conveyance document dated 1 December 1782 records that John Rowntree of Scarborough, mercer, was one of the twelve trustees who bought the meeting house and courtyard in Cook's Row and their burial ground in Bull Lane (now Westover Road) for £100 from John Bland of Ilford and Jeremiah Henderson of Stockton-on-Tees. John Rowntree was the first head of that family to live in Scarborough and the founder of the grocery business there.

By 1810 Scarborough's Society of Friends numbered only about 74, with 16 resident families, but what they had lost in numbers they had gained in affluence. Whereas a century earlier nearly all the town's Quakers were seafaring folk, now they included grocers, tanners and merchants, and at least one gentleman, Joseph Taylor. In 1800 for their old meeting house and yard in Cook's Row they had exchanged half an acre of land belonging to Sir Charles Hotham on the north side of

St Sepulchre Street. On this ground they built a new meeting house the following year, described by Hinderwell as 'a neat building, characteristic of the simplicity and decency of that orderly society'. Their first meeting house was afterwards used as a joiner's shop and ultimately destroyed in a fire. Finally, in 1803, the trustees of the Society, led by Taylor and Rowntree, were able to buy an extensive plot of former Friary land adjacent to their new meeting house for £153. After demolishing the three dwelling houses that stood on the site the Friends converted the frontage on St Sepulchre Street into a burial yard and the rest they kept as a garden.

Unlike Whitby and several rural areas in North Yorkshire such as Eskdale, in Scarborough few Catholics survived the Reformation. Only three Catholic families were identified in 1743 compared with the 25, 'all pretty numerous ones', at Whitby. Catholic gentry such as the Constables of Burton Constable and the Fairfaxes of Gilling brought their servants, cooks, maids and chaplains to Scarborough so that during the season the 'Catholic congregation must often have swelled to over a hundred'. Yet even as late as 1780 there were still only 24 resident Catholics in the town. Until 1755 mass was said in lodging houses; afterwards a mass-house was founded by a bequest of the Crathorne family. In 1788 a Catholic priest lived in Low Conduit Street and in 1800 one had a house in Westgate. The first Catholic chapel was built in Auborough Street in 1783, but it was not until 1809 that ' a more commodious place of worship was erected' on the same site for as many as 400 people. Scarborough's Catholic community was growing even more rapidly than the town's.

However, the religious movement with the greatest popular appeal in Scarborough, as everywhere else in the country during these years, was Methodism, not Catholicism. John Wesley first rode to Scarborough over what he called 'the huge mountains' from Robin Hood's Bay in July 1759. Thirty-two years later, when Wesley died at the age of 88, and after he had made as many as 13 visits to the town, there were 621 Methodists in Scarborough. No doubt Wesley's powerful presence and his inspiring sermons were mainly responsible for the growth of Scarborough's Methodist congregation, but the town had its own converts before his first visit.

As early as 1756 Thomas Brown (1731-1811) hired a room on Whitehead Hill for prayers and preachers and a few years later he built a preaching house in Bennett's Entry in Foster's Yard near the old

Shambles. By 1770 Scarborough had become the head of a Methodist circuit which included Malton and Pickering and employed two resident preachers, Thomas Lee and Thomas Carlile. Two years later, Wesley preached 'in the shell of the new House', then being built in Church Stairs Street. When this Methodist chapel was finished it was said to accommodate nearly 300 people. What Wesley described as 'one of the neatest and most elegant preaching-houses in England' soon proved to be too small and inaccessible. In 1813 it was pulled down and replaced by a less 'elegant' but much larger building in Bird Yard, Cross Street. Here Scarborough's Methodists worshipped until they acquired the Queen Street site in 1839. Appropriately, these abstemious people built their new chapel and hall on the ground which had been occupied previously by the Blacksmith's Arms.

By comparison, Scarborough's Baptists had much earlier origins, yet for long lacked numbers, leadership and organisation. Admiral Sir John Lawson was described as an Anabaptist in the 1650s, yet there is no evidence that Scarborough then had a Baptist congregation or gathering. Furthermore, like many other religious radicals of that time, he died and was buried as an Anglican.

The founder of Scarborough's Baptist congregation was the Reverend William Hague (1736-1831). Though originally a Wesleyan, Hague had a Baptist chapel built at the western end of Longwestgate in 1776-7 for 38 communicants. According to Hinderwell, by 1811 this number had grown to 63 'beside many occasional attendants'. Like the Quakers, but unlike the Methodists, who still used St Mary's graveyards, the Baptists had their own burial ground next to their chapel on Longwestgate. Hague, 'the venerable Pastor', as Hinderwell called him, was a minister for 48 years, preached at the age of 85, and died in his 95th year. By the time he retired in 1816, his Ebenezer Chapel had been enlarged to seat 500 people.

The spectacular success of Nonconformity in the town excited the jealousy of Scarborough's Anglicans, no more so than when a non-denominational Lancasterian school was opened in 1810. Joseph Lancaster was one of the pioneers of the monitorial method of teaching and a voluntary school – so-called because it was paid for by voluntary public subscription – was founded in Scarborough using this method of instructing poor children in basic literacy and numeracy. The first Lancasterian school was built in a field on the north side of the Rope Walk (now Rutland Terrace), not far from the Anglicans' Amicable

Society School and clearly in competition with it. An attempt to appease the borough's Anglican bailiffs by offering them positions on the governing body of the new school was abruptly rebuffed. 'The magistrates do not choose to accept office without the approbation of the body corporate', was the curt reply from the Town Hall to the invitation. It was followed immediately by a council vote to grant five guineas to the school of the Amicable Society! Nevertheless, whereas the Anglican school could as yet count only 60 or 70 pupils, its Lancasterian rival soon had nearly 400.

Not all the members of Scarborough's oligarchy were so narrow-minded and bigoted. Thomas Hinderwell was a veteran trustee and generous benefactor of the Amicable Society, yet in his will he also left £20 to the Lancasterian school and the same sum to the School of Industry. The last was originally called the Spinning School and established in Longwestgate in 1788 by Scarborough ladies to educate and clothe twenty poor girls. However, after spinning ceased to be a common domestic activity, the school was united with the School of Industry, opened in 1808 in Cook's Row. Here about 100 girls were taught sewing and the rudiments of education, or, in Hinderwell's contemporary words, 'the principles of virtue' as well as the skills of 'useful domestic labours'.

However, in spite of the well-meaning efforts of voluntary subscribers and humane benefactors, most of Scarborough's children received no formal education at all and remained illiterate and innumerate. Even when state assistance to the voluntary schools was finally and reluctantly voted in 1833 it was so miserly that it made little difference. Parliament granted more money annually for the upkeep of the royal stables than for the nation's schools.

Charity

When it came to the relief of extreme poverty there was at least some compulsory provision. Ever since Elizabethan times every parish was required to levy rates on property owners and maintain genuine paupers out of the proceeds. Scarborough's poor rate assessments show a steady increase throughout the eighteenth century. In 1708 just over £100 was collected; by 1733, more than triple that amount; and by the 1790s, the figure was running at more than £1,000 a year, reaching a peak of £2,737 in 1801. After a fall in subsequent years, the assessment rose again to nearly £3,000 in the 1820s.

Depending much on the economic circumstances of the time, the numbers of elderly paupers and infants too young to be apprenticed in St Thomas's poorhouse varied from year to year. In 1810 there were 70; by 1830 there were 91, 63 adults and 28 children under the age of 14, of whom eight were classed as idiots or lunatics. In addition, the parish doled out sums of money, and sometimes food, coal and blankets, to those judged to be deserving 'outdoor relief'. In 1810, 240 people were receiving weekly allowances ranging from ninepence to one shilling and threepence each. When the children and other dependants of these outdoor recipients are included, the total number of Scarborians then benefiting from parish relief might have been almost a thousand, out of a borough population of less than seven thousand.

In accordance with an Act of Parliament passed in 1747 'for the relief and support of maimed and disabled seamen and the widows of such as shall be killed or drowned in the merchant service', Scarborough's shipowners and masters elected a president and 15 trustees to collect, hold and dispense a charity fund set up for the purpose. By law the owner of every ship registered at Scarborough was from now on required to pay sixpence a month into the fund for every crew member during the time his ship was at sea or in service. During the next five years this fund accumulated £1,019 15s. 2½d. – a striking illustration of the large number of vessels then registered at Scarborough and actively in service at sea in time of war. Consequently, in 1752, the trustees resolved to build a second refuge to that of Trinity House, to be called Scarborough Merchant Seamen's Hospital.

Half an acre of pasture 'without Auborough' on the north side at the junction of Greengate (North Marine Road) and 'King Street' (Castle Road) was bought for £90 and a fine stone building of 25 apartments raised on it. There was no shortage of approved applicants: all 25 apartments were always occupied by up to 100 men, women and children.

However, though the new system of compulsory relief worked well, Scarborough's old Trinity House hospital in St Sepulchre Street, dependent largely on voluntary subscription collected by the local Society of Owners and Masters, became increasingly inadequate and dilapidated. Some re-building and extending took place in 1785, but money for repairs and renovation was hard to find.

In 1825 Thomas Hinderwell's will had included a legacy of £100 to be used eventually for the re-building of Trinity House. Three years later, Richard Williamson, a shipowner who lived in Quay Street, donated another £400 for the same purpose. Nothing more happened until January 1832 when Robert Tindall, then president of the Society, drew the attention of the trustees to the deplorable condition of their building which then had 68 adults and children living in 27 decayed rooms. Tindall recommended that the hospital should be demolished and re-built, either on the present site or one closer to the Merchant Seamen's Hospital.

Events now moved forward rapidly. 'Mr Sharp, Architect of York', was employed to draw up a plan for a new Trinity House, provided the plan did not cost more than £10. By June 1832 Sharp's classical design had been accepted and subscriptions to the value of £1,393 had been promised. In little more than a year a new hospital was finished and occupied. For reasons of economy the same site in St Sepulchre Street was used and much of the old stonework incorporated as footings and rubble into the new building. The one extravagance was a sculpted external frieze above the entrance, for which the Society paid an extra £20.

Christ Church

The inconvenience and inaccessibility of St Mary's had long been a source of common complaint, particularly of visitors to Scarborough. Rather than climb the steep hill and stairs to the parish church, 'stars and ribbons' were known to have attended even some of the dissenter chapels more considerately located in the town. Despite the ambitions and efforts of Dr Falconer, St Mary's remained Scarborough's only place of Anglican worship.

Finally, in October 1826, a foundation stone was laid to what nearly two years later was consecrated as Christ Church. After prayers and a sermon at St Mary's, given by the vicar, John Kirk, he and 'a vast concourse of visitants and inhabitants' proceeded to the site of the intended new church in Bean's gardens. Mr Bean had been persuaded by the corporation to relinquish a sizeable area on the west side of Huntriss Row in exchange for the corporation's St Catherine's Close, then valued at £300.

That the corporation was closely involved in this sectarian enterprise is evident from the list of subscribers, given in the third posthumous edition of Hinderwell's *History*, published in 1832. Predictably the biggest donations, each of £155, were made by Henry, earl of Mulgrave, and the duke of Rutland, and by their protégés, the borough's two Members of Parliament, Edmund Phipps and Charles Manners Sutton, who each gave £70. The two bailiffs at the time, Edward Hebden, banker, and George Nesfield, brewer, had their names inscribed on the brass plate placed underneath the foundation stone. Even the two churchwardens, appointees of the corporation, Henry Fowler and William Thornton, had their names written on the plate above those of the two architects, P. Atkinson and R. Sharp.

When Christ Church was completed and consecrated by the archbishop of York in August 1828 it had cost about £7,000, less than £2,000 donated by private subscription and £5,000 granted by Parliament's commissioners for building churches. The commissioners were pleased to describe the finished work as 'elegantly chaste and amply commodious'. Not the least of Christ Church's benefactors was Sir John Johnstone, then one of Yorkshire's Members of Parliament; the 'worthy baronet' had provided the sandstone from his quarry at Hackness.

Christ Church more than doubled Anglican accommodation in Scarborough. Half of its 1,300 places were in rented pews, and the other half on free benches. An upper west gallery was built for charity children of the Amicable Society's school. Nothing could have been better calculated to fuel the wrath of the town's Nonconformists. In a borough with only 8,000 inhabitants there were now seats in two Anglican churches for more than a quarter of them, far many more than there were practising Anglicans to occupy them; whereas the Methodists, Independents and Baptists, denied any public assistance national or local, were obliged to worship in overcrowded and inappropriate buildings. Twice they had successfully prevented attempts to put the costs of Christ Church on the church rates, but they could do nothing to block the parliamentary subsidy.

Cliff Bridge

Barely a month after he had witnessed the laying of Christ Church's first stone, senior bailiff Hebden attended another foundation ceremony, this time for Cliff Bridge.

If St Mary's church was inaccessible, the spa wells under South Cliff were even more so. Spawers and bathers alike frequently deplored the difficult, even perilous, journey they had to undertake to reach the sands from St Nicholas Cliff and the steepness of their return ascent. Falconer's New Road, owned by the corporation since 1819, ran down into Ramsdale valley, but at times of heavy rainfall it was deep in mud or even under flood water. Alternatively, the footpaths zigzagging down from the Cliff tested all but the young and fit; the elderly and invalids, who could not afford the cost of hiring sedan chairs, must have been prevented from taking the sea or spa waters.

As so often happened before, the initiative for a solution came from outside, not inside the corporation. In October 1826 the bailiffs received a letter from Robert Cattle, sheriff of York and later lord mayor of that city, who proposed that a company should be floated to build a bridge across Ramsdale linking the Cliff with the spa. From now on events moved with amazing speed. The Scarborough Cliff Bridge Company was established on the first day of November 1826 by a meeting held at the George Hotel in Coney Street, York. To the Company the corporation granted a 99-year lease at five shillings a year for the land to be used by the bridge and a new footpath leading from its southern end down to the wells. The whole enterprise – bridge and terraced path – was estimated to cost £4,500.

The following month Scarborough corporation closed another agreement whereby the Company leased the spa wells, the staith, the spa buildings and undercliff behind them for 99 years at an annual rent of £20. In truth, the corporation was relieved to be rid of what had long been a financial burden as receipts from subscriptions fell and the costs of maintenance rose alarmingly.

The Bridge Company conceded that Scarborians could continue to take the spa waters without paying for them, but like everyone else they would have to buy tickets to cross the bridge. Charges for the use of the bridge by pedestrians were later fixed at five shillings for an annual ticket and three shillings for a fortnight's pass. Reduced rates were made available for families and servants. For each crossing bath and sedan chairs were charged an extra sixpence. Consequently, as one local commentator wrote later, crossing the Cliff Bridge was 'a walk from which improper classes are excluded'.

By the time the bridge was finished in the summer of 1827, 450 ten-pound shares had been issued, a third of them bought by

The newly-built Cliff Bridge, by J Stubbs, 1827

people living in Scarborough, but the whole project had cost almost twice as much as the original estimate: the bridge itself, more than £7,000 and the buttressed, terraced way to the spa, more than £2,000. It was therefore found necessary for the Company to offer another 150 ten-pound shares and raise the remainder by debentures at five per cent.

The investment proved unprofitable for the Company's shareholders, but the result was a magnificent engineering work of great value to Scarborough. The bridge, now 173 years old and largely in its original condition, is 414 feet long, with four iron arches set on three huge tapering stone pillars more than 70 feet high. The iron was cast in Bradford in the West Riding; the stone was quarried locally at Cloughton. From the south end of the bridge a new promenade, measuring 350 yards long averaging 10 yards in width, sloped gently down to the spa wells. Whether on foot or by chair, spawers and bathers could now reach the sands without fear of falling or drowning.

The completed bridge was first opened to the public on a fine, sunny day in July 1827. Between the firing of the cannon at six in the morning and the start of the procession from the Town Hall in Long Room Street to the Cliff which was at ten o' clock, the *Yorkshire Gazette* estimated that upwards of 10,000 spectators had gathered on both sides of Ramsdale to witness the ceremony. The procession, preceded by labourers, stone-masons and carpenters carrying their tools, included the bailiffs, Hebden and Nesfield, the town clerk, John Woodall, who was also treasurer of the Company, members of the committee and shareholders, and a brass band. On the Cliff they were joined by the archbishop of York, 'the venerable prelate', who was to give his name to Vernon Place, the site of Christ Church, and was also responsible for the names later given to Harcourt Place and York Place. After the band had played 'God Save the King' and 'Rule Britannia', the former several times, bailiff Hebden expressed his thanks and the corporation's to Robert Cattle, projector of the bridge. More speeches followed, including an eloquent one from Sir John Johnstone.

In the afternoon, the Royal Mail coach passed over the bridge, and on its return at full gallop a sailor stood on its roof 'to the imminent danger of his own life and to the very great terror of the multitude of spectators'. Finally, at five in the evening, 80 gentlemen sat down to a sumptuous dinner, price 12 shillings, at Donner's Long Room. Simultaneously, dinners were being eaten and toasts drunk in nut brown ale in public houses around the town. It was indeed a day of special significance in Scarborough's history.

Rotunda Museum

Unfortunately, Christ Church was not the only new building in Scarborough to be made of soft Hackness sandstone. In April 1828, only months before archbishop Vernon consecrated the church, the newly-founded Scarborough Philosophical Society began to erect its museum on the terrace below St Nicholas Cliff close to the new bridge.

The principal projectors of this enlightened enterprise were Sir John Johnstone, first president of the Society, Thomas Duesbery, Robert Tindall, junior, chairman of the building committee, William Smith, 'father of British geology', and naturalists, William Bean and John Williamson. Johnstone provided the stone; Duesbery, nephew of the late Thomas Hinderwell, gave his uncle's collection of fossils and manuscripts; Smith, Johnstone's land steward, designed the circular plan of the building and the exhibition of its contents; and Bean and Williamson added their knowledge of local fauna and flora. Williamson gave up his occupation as a gardener to become first keeper of the museum, a post he filled for the next 27 years.

The Rotunda Museum 1829. The two wings were added in 1861.

The Rotunda Museum, finished and opened to the public in 1829, was built in the Roman Doric style. It was both elegant and functional. Smith suggested to Sharp, the architect, that a circular plan would provide the best way of showing the geological stratification of the coast from the Tees to the Humber. The basement contained the Society's library, the keeper's room and a laboratory; the principal room, lit from a dome above, housed an unmatched collection of fossils displayed on sloping shelves in their chronological order; and the gallery's round walls, reached by a moveable staircase, were painted with a colour picture of local geological formations.

Lack of funds, all supplied by local voluntary donation, meant that the Society's plan to add wings to the Rotunda had to wait another generation. Also, admission charges – one shilling for an adult and

213

sixpence for a child under 14 – were in effect prohibitive for all but the well-to-do. Sharp's building, for which he was paid £20, cost nearly £1,300, and its furnishings and fittings a further £250, but every penny was well spent. If for no other reason, inside the museum there was now proof, for those willing to believe it, that the earth had not been created in 3000 BC or thereabouts. The contribution of 'Stratum Smith' to modern science, and in particular biological evolution, was now on public display there.

As Theakston's *Guide to Scarborough* of 1840 noted, until recently the town had few structures that were 'elegant or attractive', but in the space of only three years, from 1827 to 1829, in Christ Church, the Cliff Bridge and the Rotunda Museum it had acquired three edifices of both beauty and usefulness. Despite the subsequent criticism of the commissioners of inquiry into municipal corporations, members of Scarborough's unreformed ruling body had not been entirely unworthy or inactive. These three additions to the borough's architecture, all within close proximity to each other, had added greatly to Scarborough's reputation as a place of fashionable resort.

The Headland. Aerial view taken from out at sea.

A reconstruction of the Roman watchtower.

The burning of Scarborough by Hardrada in 1066.

Scarborough castle. Henry II's castle keep, showing the damage done during the Civil War.

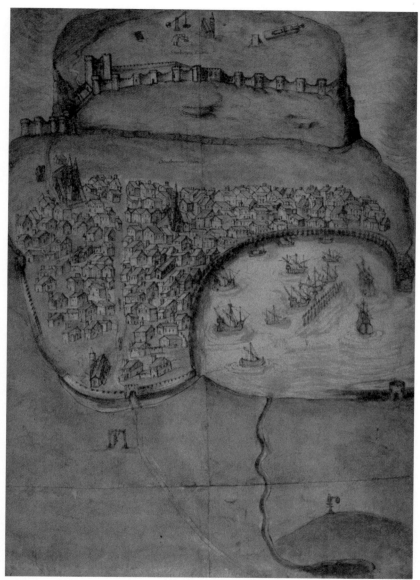

Engineer's plat. The first image of Scarborough circa 1538.

Holiday-makers on Scarborough Beach 1770. Painted by T. Ramsey.

The Grand Hotel.

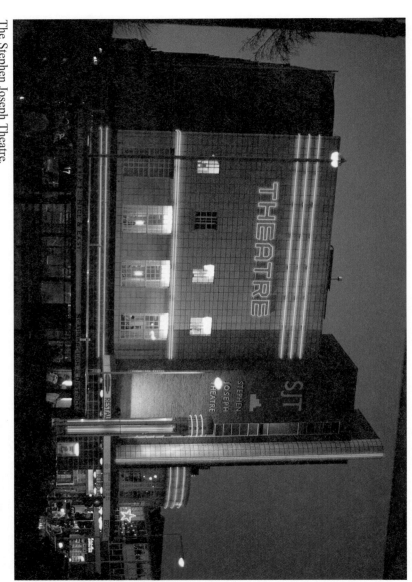

The Stephen Joseph Theatre.

12

POLITICS

Pocket Borough

Between 1715 and 1831 there were 36 parliamentary elections and bye-elections held in the borough of Scarborough, yet only seven of them were contested. During this long century, through the financial and ministerial power of the Treasury and the local influence of its officers in customs and ordnance, central government exercised control over at least one and often both of the constituency seats. Party politics rarely entered into differences of support; personal and family rivalries were more relevant when elections were genuinely contested; and a truly independent candidate was most exceptional.

The record of the Osbaldestons is not untypical. William Osbaldeston (1688-1766), a Whig country gentleman of Hunmanby, sat for Scarborough for 30 years, except when he was ousted between 1747 and 1754. He died as one of the borough's Members in September 1766. He owed his seat entirely to government favour and the local support of his relative John Hill, commissioner of customs from 1723 to 1747 and governor of Scarborough castle from 1744 until 1753. In the words of the official history of the House of Commons: 'He is not known to have spoken in the House', but voted steadily for Walpole and his successor in government. William's own successors continued the undistinguished family tradition. Fountayne Wentworth Osbaldeston (1696-1770) at the age of 70 inherited his brother's seat and held it until his own death four years later. Again, the official historian's comment reads: 'There is no evidence of his having spoken in the House'. Finally, George Osbaldeston (?1753 -1793), who succeeded to part of his great uncle's estate in 1770 and adopted his surname, was returned for one of Scarborough's seats in 1784. During the next six years in the Commons he voted with Prime Minister Pitt and never opened his mouth to speak.

Government electoral influence was usually wielded through the medium of one or two of the greater aristocratic landowning families in the district – in particular, Lord Fitzwilliam of Malton, Lord Carlisle of Castle Howard, the dukes of Rutland and the lords Mulgrave. In Lord Egremont's electoral survey of c.1749-50 Scarborough is there described as 'in Lord Carlisle's [pocket] for one and, if properly managed, both'. Savage Mostyn was Carlisle's unsuccessful candidate in the bye-election of 1744. However, three years later, Roger Handasyd, Carlisle's choice, received the same number of votes as Edwin Lascelles to oust William Osbaldeston, on one of the few occasions when there were more than two candidates for the two seats.

The 1761 parliamentary election was unprecedented in that there were originally four candidates nominated for Scarborough's two places: William Osbaldeston, the sitting Member, John Major, Jenison Shafto and George Cockburne. Several competing interests were represented by these men. John Major (1698-1781) was born in Bridlington, became a ship owner and iron merchant, and made a great fortune out of carrying troops and military supplies to the continent in the wars of 1740-48 and 1756-63. He was the government's agent with the backing of Lord Newcastle. In the sharpest contrast, Jenison Shafto, who stood in the Lascelles' interest, was a notorious gambler and racehorse owner. Ten years later, he shot himself after 'a change of fortune on the turf'. Cockburne, controller of the Royal Navy, was another government nominee. In the end, rather than upset Osbaldeston, the government withdrew Cockburne's candidature and found another safe seat for Shafto, leaving John Major with a walk-over. So no poll was taken at Scarborough after all.

By 1768, when the next general election took place, the arrival of Lord Granby on the Scarborough scene had changed radically the situation there. Granby was commander-in-chief of the army and master-general of the ordnance, positions which guaranteed him government support and strong electoral influence in the borough. Later, his principal rival, Lord Fitzwilliam, claimed unkindly that Granby had 'gained a footing' there 'by getting drunk with the mayor [sic] and corporation'. But the marquess did not need to use such methods of persuasion in Scarborough. For the next sixty years Granby's family, Manners by name, the dukes of Rutland by senior title, invariably held one of the town's two parliamentary seats.

In 1768 Granby put up his illegitimate son, George Manners.

Even by Scarborough's deplorable standards, there was exceptionally heavy bribery. Manners got 29 votes, Osbaldeston polled 24, and Major was third and out with only 22. Two years later, on the death of Fountayne Wentworth Osbaldeston, Granby's man, Ralph Bell, fought Sir James Pennyman for the vacant seat. Bell lost narrowly and Granby died suddenly at Scarborough. When George Manners died in 1772 his place in the House of Commons was taken by Granby's son-in-law, George Carpenter, the Earl of Tyrconnel, but he had to spend £2,500 at Scarborough to get in. Tyrconnel held the seat for the next 22 years, though he was still expected to pay the 44 members of the corporation to keep it. The fifth duke of Rutland, grandson of the marquess of Granby, had died in 1787, leaving the duchess and her brother, the duke of Beaufort, as his trustees. Consequently, in 1796, Beaufort's son, Lord Charles Henry Somerset, secured one of Scarborough's seats for the Rutland interest. Again there was no poll but a good deal of treating.

At the next election in 1802, however, there was both a contest and a poll. A local banker and Town Hall leader, John Woodall, was nominated by George Osbaldeston's widow, who doubtless had the future prospects of her son in mind. Woodall received only seven votes, not nearly enough to win a seat, but enough to put the duke of Rutland's brother, Lord Robert William Manners, into second place. Nevertheless, the duke was delighted by the result and later came to Scarborough even though only 26 votes had been cast for his brother.

Finally, in 1806, the Rutland seat was taken by Charles Manners Sutton (1780-1845), eldest son of the archbishop of Canterbury. Sutton held the seat until 1832. He was one of the most distinguished of the many distinguished men who have represented Scarborough in parliament. In 1817 he was chosen Speaker of the House of Commons, a chair which he held until 1834, believing that his place at Scarborough would always be safe. At the time of his appointment he wrote confidently: 'I have no grounds for suspecting, what has never yet occurred, at Scarborough, either opposition or petition.'

From 1790, until the Great Reform Act of 1832, Scarborough's other seat was in the permanent custody of the Phipps family of Mulgrave castle near Whitby. As early as 1779, the Honourable Charles Phipps, second son of Constantine Phipps, first Baron Mulgrave, and captain in the Royal Navy, won a Scarborough seat in the Admiralty interest. Five years later, however, he lost the place and a substitute had to be found for him at Minehead. Meanwhile, his eldest brother, Constantine, who had succeeded as the second Baron Mulgrave in 1775, represented a number of other constituencies – Lincoln, Huntingdon and Newark.

In 1790 the Mulgrave seat was taken by yet another brother, Henry Phipps (1755-1831), one of the most gifted of that gifted family. Henry's military career took him from an ensign in the First Foot Guards in 1775 to the rank of major general 20 years later. However, after the death of his elder brother, he succeeded to the title as third Baron Mulgrave and surrendered his seat to the youngest of the Phipps brothers, Edmund (1760-1837), in 1794 when he was called to the House of Lords. Later, Henry Phipps became governor of Scarborough castle, a post he held until his death, Secretary of State for Foreign Affairs in 1805-6, First Lord of the Admiralty 1807-10, and finally Master General of the Ordnance from 1810 until succeeded by the Duke of Wellington in 1818. By that time, now the Earl of Mulgrave, he had been struck down by what was described as 'universal paralysis'. Though still only in his sixties he was said to have the 'look and power of a man aged 90', and was too feeble even to write a letter.

Meanwhile, Edmund Phipps was combining a successful military career with what must have been a largely unoccupied seat in the House of Commons. Starting in 1780 as an ensign in the 85th Foot he was regimental colonel by 1809 and a full general ten years later. He served throughout the French Revolutionary and Napoleonic wars, often abroad in places such as Gibraltar, Flanders and Madeira. Like his elder brother Henry he was a personal friend and political ally of William Pitt the younger, and like his brother he also opposed the abolition of the slave trade and restrictions on flogging in the army. Both believed that 100 lashes was not an excessive military punishment. Edmund was MP for Scarborough from 1794 until 1818 and then again from 1820 until 1832. Like his brother Henry he too suffered from paralysis, but in his case it was caused by 'bad sherry' contaminated by white lead and affected only his right arm which 'hung down like the fin of a turtle'. For this reason he was nicknamed 'the Governor of Finland'.

During the interval from 1818 to 1820 when Edmund Phipps was not one of Scarborough's Members, the seat was kept warm by his nephew, Constantine Henry Phipps (1797-1863), first son of Henry. Unlike his father and uncles, Constantine was considered too clever for the army; he chose a political and diplomatic career. Also, in the sharpest contrast to the rest of his family, his politics were Radical and Whig, not Tory and reactionary. At Cambridge, where he was president of the Union, he dispensed with studies and 'made free use of his liberty as a nobleman by passing much of his time at the theatre in London, allured by the charms of a very respectable actress, whose portrait hung over his chimney-piece'. Clearly destined for the greatest responsibilities, Constantine was Governor of Jamaica from 1832 to 1834, Secretary of State for War and the Colonies in 1839, Home Secretary from 1839 until 1841, ambassador to France from 1846 until 1852, and finally ambassador to Tuscany from 1854 until his retirement in 1858. In 1838 this second Earl of Mulgrave had become the first Marquess of Normanby, the title still held by his descendants at Mulgrave.

Though the Manners and Phipps families duopolised Scarborough's parliamentary representation for more than half a century they left only a shallow and largely temporary impression on the town. It is therefore not surprising that today all that remains to recall these two families are street names – Mulgrave Terrace, Rutland Terrace and Belvoir (the Leicestershire home of the dukes of Rutland) Terrace in the Crescent.

Great Reform Act 1832

On 4 June 1832, after the Great Reform Act had passed all its parliamentary stages and received the royal assent, a bonfire was lit in Newborough. That evening a bigger bonfire was built on the foreshore sands and kept going until well into the following morning with tar barrels and old ships' timbers. Later that day, 44 dolls, dressed as members of the corporation, were paraded through the main streets and down to the seashore where they were gleefully buried in a deep hole in the sands. It was the end of an old and the start of a new era in the nation's and Scarborough's long parliamentary history. Scarborough was no longer a borough in the pockets of two aristocratic families; it kept its right to two Members and its former constituency boundaries, but from now on the franchise ceased to be the exclusive property of the 44 members of the Common Hall. Only 33 electors had voted in the last election contested 30 years earlier; henceforth all adult male residents owning houses of annual rental value of at least £10 would qualify for the franchise.

219

Significantly, neither of the two sitting MPs, Speaker Manners Sutton and General Phipps, cared to risk themselves before the new electorate. Edmund Phipps refused to stand again because in his words, 'any person patronized and favoured by them [the corporation] would be looked upon with jealous eye by the new electors'. The old order was represented only by Sir Frederick William Trench (1775-1859). Veteran of the French wars, who had served in Flanders, Sicily and Spain, Colonel Trench was related to the duke of Rutland by marriage and had held Cambridge, a Rutland borough, since 1819. As a Tory he had opposed the Reform Bill in all its stages and on 6 June he had told Scarborough's shipowners that the Act was 'uncalled for, rash and revolutionary'.

Trench had friends in the maritime interest at Scarborough because he was known to have promoted it in the House of Commons. In recent years, when the borough's own Members, the Speaker and General Phipps, had been unable to speak on Scarborough's behalf, the colonel had done so. As a result, several of the shipowners and master mariners, including two of the Tindalls, Robert and James, voted for Trench.

On the other hand, the colonel was vilified in a series of public handbills produced by J. Bye, Scarborough's radical printer, as an out and out reactionary who supported slavery, flogged his soldiers and ill-treated his Irish tenants. Not only was Trench the 'obsequent nominee of a certain Duke [Rutland] whom the town has little to thank for', but he was also an Irish landlord without any local connections – the corrupt lackey of a corrupt corporation.

The two Whig candidates who opposed Trench were depicted as altogether superior. Both Sir John Vanden Bempde-Johnstone (1799-1869) and Sir George Cayley (1773-1857) were Reform candidates, unsullied by association with the discredited occupants of the Town Hall. Both were country gentlemen: the Johnstones had owned the nearby Hackness estate for nearly 150 years, whereas the Cayleys had been at Brompton since the early seventeenth century. Johnstone, the second baronet since 1807, was well regarded locally as a serious-minded, educated, benevolent landowner. In 1827 he had been one of the principal founders of Scarborough's Philosophical Society and a year later chief projector of the Rotunda Museum, built to house its geological exhibits. Sir George's political and personal credentials were even stronger. The sixth baronet had been born in Paradise House near

220

Sir George Cayley at the age of seventy

St Mary's church and was already widely admired as an affable, considerate landowner, prolific inventor and brilliant scientist. Cayley was not a party hack and he had no gift for oratory, but he was respected as a sincere reformer and truly independent spirit.

Though 508 men were eligible to vote under the new franchise, in the event only 384 did so in December 1832; it seems that 32 of them abstained and another 92, for a variety of reasons, failed to register themselves. Each elector was allowed two votes, but only 685 votes were cast and openly recorded by the town clerk in the poll book. Johnstone came head of the poll with 285, Cayley second, with 255, and Trench, bottom, with only 145. The Whigs and reformers were triumphant; the Tories, who made up the great majority of the corporation, were decisively defeated.

What part bribery and coercion played is impossible to assess, but there was certainly plenty of treating. In August the corporation held a dinner in honour of Manners Sutton and 16 public houses offered free ale, known as 'blue drink', in support of Trench. However, according to the *Leeds Mercury*, only 'idle boys and children' took part in 'blue processions' and only they were seen in the beer shops 'taking their first lesson in drunkenness'. There is no doubt that Edward Donner, one of the bailiffs, who was also a member of Trench's election committee, made political use of his well-stocked wine cellar, just as J. Houson, proprietor of the Bull Hotel, freely offered his premises for Whig dinners and meetings.

The fickleness of Scarborough's new electorate was illustrated little more than two years later, in January 1835, when the same three candidates again presented themselves at the polls. By now the enthusiasm for reform had waned; slavery had been abolished; yet otherwise little seemed to have changed. Even one of the Whig MPs was disillusioned and disappointed by events since the heady days of 1832. Sir George was now a most reluctant candidate who stood for re-election only because he could not find a replacement. Now only half the electorate bothered to vote and Trench, who had been at the foot of the poll, was now placed top with only 176 votes, Johnstone came a close second with 161, and Cayley was ousted with 122. There had been no seismic shift of political allegiance: the main difference between December 1832 and January 1835 was that though Trench had kept all his supporters and added a few more, Johnstone, and especially Cayley, had lost theirs to abstainers.

When Sir George Cayley addressed his diminished band of followers in Houson's Bull Hotel on the night he acknowledged defeat, he told them that without radical reform of the corporation the Reform Act of 1832 was itself only 'an incomplete guardian' of their liberties. His good news – though by then it was widely anticipated – was that the Municipal Corporations Bill would soon become law.

On Wednesday and Thursday, 27 and 28 November 1833, two of His Majesty's commissioners, Fortunatus Dwarris and S.A. Rumball, appointed to inquire into the state of municipal corporations, held their first investigation in Scarborough's Town Hall. Facing them to answer their formidable list of sixteen searching questions was a committee consisting of the town clerk, John Woodall, senior; the two bailiffs, John Woodall, junior, his son, and William Thornton; the two coroners. Edward Hebden and Henry Fowler; the two senior members of the corporation, Anthony Beswick and William Travis; and Edward Donner, son of the former bailiff and wine merchant of the same name, and the corporation's solicitor. Cross-examining the corporation's spokesmen were Samuel Byron, shipowner and number 36 in the Third Twelve, and local solicitors, John Hesp, G Davies and William Page.

In effect, Dwarris and Rumball sat as judges and jury, the Town Hall committee was counsel for the defence, and the cross-examiners, led by Byron, were counsel for the prosecution. In the dock on trial was Scarborough borough council and corporation.

A fortnight after the inquiry the corporation committee reported that the town clerk had successfully answered all the commissioners' questions; and it rebutted 'the frivolous and unfounded charges and misrepresentations attempted to be advanced by its avowed opponents', principally Mr Byron and his lawyer associates. Travis was presented with a silver plate for 40 years service to the town and his unrivalled knowledge of the borough's constitution and customs. The Old Guard was unrepentant and defiant: it published its own partial version of the events in the Town Hall of 27, 28 November 1833 and in August 1835 petitioned the House of Lords, thanking it for resisting the Municipal Corporations Bill and asking the lords to exempt Scarborough from its reforming provisions!

So one-sided was the corporation's report that in January 1834 the commissioners were obliged to publish their own 'candid and essentially correct statement of what passed' during those two decisive days in Scarborough's history. The commissioners' report proved to be the most comprehensive and damning review of the town's form and practice of government and also revealed how strongly they were resented by some leading burgesses. Not that much had changed, it seemed, since Scarborough had had its own version of the Peasants' Revolt in 1381.

For the past 500 years annual elections to the Common Hall held on or after St Jerome's day had continued with only minor adjustments. Only on the death or resignation of a member of the corporation could a new man be brought into it from outside. The notorious 44 were still a self-perpetuating, closed body. Once elected, in effect a place was guaranteed for life.

After election neither residence in the borough nor attendance at Common Hall meetings was required. Henry Byron, father of Samuel, placed at six in the First Twelve, had resided in London for the last four or five years; Thomas Dewsbury lived in Beverley; Dr Nathaniel Travis, son of William, had his home in Malton; George Taylor lived in Filey; and Stephen Armitage had gone to Van Dieman's Land! Yet all of these men had reserved seats among the 44. When this matter was raised before the commissioners, Byron also cited the example of Christopher Coulson, collector of customs at Whitby, who had been an absentee member of the corporate body for 30 years. But the worst case quoted was that of Thomas Dewsbury, ranked 22nd in the Second Twelve, who had 'been away 45 years and attended once at a Hall out of curiosity'. The only defence offered by Travis was that all of these absentees had been householders in Scarborough at the time of their election. As for attendance, Byron might have raised the example of John Maling, who had been a member for 20 years and not entered the Town Hall once during the 90 meetings held in that time; or that of Valentine Fowler, who was still in the Second Twelve, but had managed only three meetings out of a possible 70.

The charge of nepotism – or what the commissioners politely described as the 'great prevalence of family influence in the corporation' – was also easy to substantiate. In 1833 there were five Woodalls, father and four sons, three of whom had been bailiffs; five Fowlers; three Travises, father, son and nephew; three Coulsons and three Whartons. If the commissioners had cared to look further back to 1811, they would have discovered that of 84 men who had sat in the Town Hall there were 11 Fowlers, six Woodalls, four Coulsons, four Tindalls, four Travises, three Whartons, and two each by the name of Wilson, Turner, Reed, Porrett, Nesfield, Donner, Byron and Beswick – 50 places in all filled by 15 families.

When Byron insisted that as many as a quarter of the council was 'unfit and improper', elected by a 'peculiar junta' of a small group of families, Travis counter-attacked by accusing Byron of trying to get his brother admitted. At this point commissioner Dwarris intervened to cool down the adversaries; this was an enquiry into a system, he said, not an investigation of personal character or qualification. Nevertheless, the commissioner's conclusion, that 'the manner of election may cause suspicion', implied his dissatisfaction with present and past procedures.

According to Byron's blunt accusations there was political favouritism in the choice of minor as well as major offices of the corporation. For example, the newly-appointed pinder, he alleged, had got his post by voting for colonel Trench; or as Byron colourfully expressed it: 'his ratting to the Corporation party the night before the last election was the cause of his appointment'.

Such party political prejudice even extended to the administration of justice by the bailiffs in the town's courts. Mr Page contended that bailiff Woodall had recently fined a policeman only five shillings for a most brutal assault on a tradesman's wife in her own house because the constable was 'blue', that is Tory.

One of the most heated altercations came when Byron asked the committee to account for the expenditure of £37 during the election of 1832. When Travis explained that the money had been distributed amongst 'the poor', Byron almost exploded with anger: 'Well', he said, 'that is the greatest burlesque on the word charity that I have ever heard. I wonder what the clergy would say to it; it is a gross perversion of the word. I ask Mr Travis if it was distributed to 18 publicans, who nearly all had 2 guineas each, in order to favour colonel Trench's election.' All that Travis could say in reply was that 'by poor' he had 'meant the populace'. Even the corporation's own version of this event was that 12 of the bribed innkeepers were electors who 'to their credit voted for Col. Trench'!

According to Byron, even the granting of publicans' licences was rigged. He cited the case of a new licence recently given to Bleach

House in Ramsdale because the premises was owned by a member of the corporation. Indignantly, coroner Fowler declared that there was no personal favour in granting the licence: 'it was granted for the public good', he explained, 'being in the road to the Mere'. 'Much the same as Driffield is in the road to York from hence', was Byron's sarcastic rejoinder.

Though the commissioners were able to report a healthy balance in the borough's current finances – annual income £1,015, annual expenditure £850 – more detailed investigation revealed some alarming facts about both sides of the audit. Money received from Newcastle and Sunderland levied on coal shipments from there amounted to more than £500 a year and exceeded expenditure on the harbour, but this was hardly to the Town Hall's credit. Byron asked drily whether the surplus had been spent on 'eating and drinking and other such useful purposes', but Travis's reply that the old harbour was kept in good repair was so softly spoken that it was entirely lost to the audience. The truth was that Vincent's and the island piers, for which the corporation was directly responsible, were in a 'disgraceful' condition, and 'the former little better than a nuisance'.

Much the same was said about other properties in the care of the corporation. Even the committee had to confess the poor state of the town gaol and the house of correction. Travis admitted that neither had exercise yard or garden. Donner agreed that the house of correction in effect was a place of solitary confinement. Page said that the stench there was 'abominable'. The commissioners subsequently wrote that both prison and house of correction were very much out of repair and extremely unhealthy. They made no comment on what they called 'another place of confinement called the black-hole'.

Recent sales of corporation properties also provoked a number of sharp exchanges. Lands to the value of £1,834 had been sold, but only by private agreement and without public advertisement or competition. Four of the purchasers were councillors, members of Woodall's bank, including bailiff John Woodall. Mr Davies said that if the corporation continued to sell property which it had held for 576 years, since 1257, it would soon be unable to meet its liabilities, such as debt repayment. 'Oh no', replied Travis, 'there is ample property for all purposes.'

However, it was also pointed out that the corporation was often ill-served by the poor returns it received in rent from some of these same properties. For instance, the whole of St Nicholas Cliff, one of the town's most valuable sites, had been let out for 50 years at five shillings a year. In this particular case the lucky tenant was not named, though the suspicion aroused was that he must have good friends in the Town Hall. Furthermore, some council rents were both trivial and antiquated. When Mr Page asked why he had to pay rent to St Thomas's church which had not existed for nearly two centuries, he was told that all the houses on the west side of Tanner Street, with back doors opening on to what had been St Thomas's churchyard, had to pay for the privilege; and the annual return to the Town Hall for these rents amounted to £3 18s. 1d.

When the matter of the corporation's annual accounts was first raised there was another warm encounter between Byron and Travis. In a voice too low to be heard in the chamber, Travis admitted that the accounts were audited privately and not circulated even amongst the members. Byron responded by saying that many members of the Common Hall never saw them; a dozen large folios were laid on the table during the meeting when other business was proceeding; and if he had tried to examine them he would be sent to Coventry. At that point, a 'distinguished personage' on the corporation benches grumbled, 'You're there already.'

Samuel Byron was the only member of the corporation who wanted it radically reformed, but he had many allies outside the Town Hall. Stung by their defeat in the January 1835 general election, Scarborough's liberals were determined not to allow their political enemies any further successes. Cayley's loss had been a serious blow; Johnstone's failure to give full support to the Municipal Corporations Bill was as unexpected as it was disappointing. Consequently, in the spring of 1835, the town's reformers established what they called the Scarborough Society for the Protection and Extension of Civil and Religious Liberty. They advertised their views in a monthly publication called *The Burgess*.

According to the first issue of *The Burgess*, dated 2 March 1835, the Society had been formed to return 'two liberal candidates of known good moral character, not drunkards, or those who would squander their property'; to protect tradesmen against political intimidation; to ensure the full registration of eligible voters; to address petitions which 'embodied the real sentiments of the town' to counter corporation petitions which did not; and, by reducing election expenses, conduct a 'war of principle against gold'. From now on, until its nineteenth and last issue in September 1836, *The Burgess* conducted a most effective editorial and correspondence campaign against the old corporation and its members and supporters.

Once again the issue of 'blue leases' – excessively generous tenancies of corporation land and properties granted to political allies – was raised in the pages of *The Burgess*. The lease of part of St Nicholas Cliff for 50 years at a ridiculous rent of five shillings a year was already common knowledge, thanks to the probing investigation of the royal commissioners, but now other examples were revealed for the first time.

The Burgess discovered that Messrs Morrison and Chapman had been given a seven-year lease at ten shillings per annum on the foreshore sands which, in the absence of competition there, meant that they could charge what they wanted for the hire of their bathing machines. This, commented the editors, was 'really paying too dear for blue [Tory] votes'. Moreover, whereas previously corporation leases were usually of one year duration, now they were being doled out to friends and potential adherents for a minimum of seven years. Addressing a House of Commons committee on this subject in July 1835, E.S. Cayley, one of the county's Whig Members, complained 'that if this Bill [Municipal Corporations] does not quickly become law, they [Scarborough council] will have leased away the whole of the corporate property'.

By the middle of 1835 it was evident that the reformers were winning the propaganda war with the reactionaries. The corporation's own petition against the Municipal Corporations Bill was endorsed by only 115 signatures, whereas the address to the House of Lords, expressing the contrary view of Scarborians, had more than ten times that number – 1152. Scarborough's Tories were now so alarmed that they set up their 'Loyal and Constitutional Association' in the town; but as more and more evidence of the corruption, mismanagement and self-indulgence of the old corporation was publicly exposed the more certain became its demise and the expulsion of its members. Before the Bill was finally passed into law everyone in Scarborough knew that the 'blues' were doomed and the triumph of the 'orangemen' was both inevitable and imminent.

In accordance with the terms of the Municipal Corporations Act, 549 rate-paying , adult, male residents of Scarborough were eligible to select the borough's new council on 28 December 1835. The old borough's boundaries were retained but now it was divided into wards, North and South, each with nine council seats. Predictably, *The Burgess* was uncomplimentary about the Tory candidates who stood for these new places in the Town Hall: 'seven of them are old corporators; three will be the mere tools of these seven gentlemen; one is a renegade Whig; four are a sort of nondescript, partly Whig and partly Tory; and two may be regarded as something more than Whig'. Facing these seventeen conservatives were nineteen so-called liberal reformers, none of whom, except Samuel Byron, had previously sat on the council.

Four days later, on 1 January 1836, *The Burgess* declared triumphantly that the Tories had met 'with the most signal defeat' in all but one of Yorkshire's corporate boroughs. Apart from Ripon, the reformers had won overwhelming majorities. In Scarborough they had taken 17 of the 18 seats. Only one of 'the old corporators', John Woodall of Belvoir Terrace, had survived the slaughter. In the North ward, Byron had come top of the poll with 193 votes, John Hesp fourth with 173. Dr Peter Murray, chairman of the Society for the Protection and Extension of Civil and Religious Liberty, came third in the South ward, well above such defeated old corporators as Henry Fowler, William Travis, and John Wharton. James Henderson, who held the old corporation's lease on St Nicholas Cliff, received a derisory 47 votes. The elevation of six elected councillors to be aldermen left six more places vacant and these were soon filled by six more reformers, including John Rowntree, the Quaker grocer of Bland's Cliff. Significantly, Samuel Byron, the man who had done most to discredit the old regime, was chosen by the new councillors to be the first mayor. As one commentator said, the last mayor had been tossed in a blanket; this one was carried into office on the shoulders of its burgesses.

Within only a few weeks of taking office, the new council was functioning in ways quite foreign to its predecessor. The new town clerk, John Uppleby, unlike John Woodall, his predecessor, was chosen by the council and was not a member of it. The new office of treasurer was also outside the body of the council but answerable to it. The council now met regularly at least once a month, its members attended conscientiously and its business and decisions were reported publicly. Obsolete posts, such as netherd and warrener, were abolished. Other offices within the choice of the council, such as chief police constable, harbour master and coroner, were soon to be filled by competent, professional men.

In contrast to the lethargy of the old corporation, the new council immediately set to work on town improvements. As early as March 1836 a proposal was agreed to 'macadamize Queen Street and Tanner Street'; by July plans had been drawn for a new prison on a site by the workhouse to cost upwards of £2,500. Henceforth, surpluses of harbour revenues would be spent on improvements and repairs to the piers and lighthouse, not on corporation feasts.

Between 1827 and 1835 the tavern expenses of the late corporation for audit, election, Shrove Tuesday, Perambulation and St Jerome's day dinners had come to the astonishing total of £1,480, more than the average annual income of the borough. The old corporators had found every occasion – such as oiling the locks of the Common iron chest, letting out market stalls or the sale of corporation lands – to consume quantities of wine and punch. The dinner held in honour of Manners Sutton had cost £130 18s. When the new council proposed to pay mayor Byron £20 a year to cover his onerous expenses, there were several complaints from townsmen: serving the borough was itself sufficient reward, there should be no further financial benefits or perquisites. As the editors of *The Burgess* so rightly remarked on the return of the new regime to the old Town Hall, this was the beginning of 'an important era in the history of the town – an era which the future historian will dwell upon with peculiar interest.'

13

SCARBOROUGH ABOUT 1840

Victorian and Edwardian Britain

In 1801 the first official census recorded the population of the British Isles as nearly 16 million, half of them living in England and almost a third in Ireland. By the census of 1911 this overall figure had nearly trebled to over 45 million, though as a result of famine and emigration, the Irish share had fallen to one ninth. More remarkable was the urbanisation of these people: in 1801 only one in five lived in towns whereas a century later it was four out of five. The contrast between rural and industrialised Yorkshire was particularly stark: by 1911 the East and North Ridings each had fewer than half a million inhabitants and the West Riding had 2.7 million.

If the eighteenth century had been an age of almost continuous foreign wars, the century that followed the battle of Waterloo (1815) was the most peaceful in British experience. Apart from the Crimean War with Russia (1854-6), all Britain's armed conflicts were with indigenous peoples in Africa and Asia to consolidate and extend the global empire. By 1914 the former colonies of white settlement had become the Dominions of Canada, Australia and New Zealand and the Union of South Africa; British India had a population in excess of 400 million; Burma, Malaya, Singapore and Hong Kong had become British possessions; and many of the richest parts of Africa from Cairo to the Cape, inhabited by 40 million people, had also been brought under British rule. Yet this world-wide, free-trade empire rested not so much on the firepower of the Royal Navy or Britain's tiny volunteer army as the financial, commercial and industrial dominance of the mother country. Empire was an expression rather than a source of Britain's power and wealth.

The nineteenth was Britain's century: no other state, before or since, has dominated the world's economy as Britain's did then. Britain was the workshop, the banker and the exchange market of the globe. Sterling was the money of international finance. Half the tonnage of merchant shipping on the seas was British built and owned. Even as late as 1880 more than 40 per cent of all manufactured trading goods were made in the United Kingdom. London was the largest and richest city on earth.

Peace abroad was matched by peace at home; there were occasional riots but no revolution. Political change came slowly and without violence. By stages – in 1832, 1867, 1884 and 1885 – the House of Commons reformed itself to become more representative of the nation. The secret ballot (1872) and legal curbs on candidates' expenses (1883) almost eliminated electoral corruption. Britain became a constitutional model. First borough then county local governments were opened up to rate-paying electorates. The dire consequences of trade recession, bank collapses, industrial injury and the premature death of the breadwinner were mitigated by the Cooperative movement, friendly societies and trade unions. Factory Acts cut excessive working hours and ended child labour. During the last quarter of the century Education Acts compelled school attendance up to the age of 12. Even work-houses – originally intended to reduce the costs of public charity by deterring the feckless – were by this time acting as hospitals and caring for orphans and the elderly.

Though such improvements were not evident until the second half of the century, the lives of millions were longer, more secure, more comfortable and happier than they had ever been. Smoke pollution, contaminated drinking water and appalling overcrowding in the 'new' towns reduced life expectancy there in the 1830s to below 30. Yet by 1911 urban life expectancy had risen to 51, only five years fewer than in the countryside, thanks to the huge Victorian investment in sewers, water supply, street cleaning, housing and hospitals.

Yet even before 1914, when the hundred-year peace was shattered, Victorian optimism and dynamism had begun to ebb away. The British birth-rate had been declining since the 1870s; army recruitment for the Boer War (1899-1902) revealed an alarming number of stunted, unhealthy young men; and surveys at that time in London and

York showed that up to 30 per cent of their inhabitants lived lives of poverty and squalor. The import of cheap American grain brought down bread prices, but undermined the profitability of British cereal farming. Between 1881 and 1901 the number of farm workers fell by 300,000. Against increasing foreign competition and tariff-protected markets, after 1905 British exports stagnated; and the rapid growth of trade union membership and militancy threatened the country's industrial stability. Abroad, the Boer War also exposed British world-wide vulnerability to the rising power and ambitions of the United States and Germany. In response, Britain was obliged to abandon 'splendid isolation' by making an alliance with Japan and colonial and defence agreements with France and Russia, her old enemies.

The Liberal governments of 1905-14 tried to come to terms with these domestic concerns with welfare schemes for old age pensions, labour exchanges and national insurance against sickness and unemployment, whereas the Conservative opposition favoured the abandonment of free trade for tariff protection. However, by the summer of 1914, the most menacing threat seemed to come from neither organised labour nor the Kaiser's battleships: the grant of Home Rule to Ireland had brought the United Kingdom to the brink of civil war.

In these circumstances, Scarborough's success as a middle-class health and retirement resort and working-class Bank Holiday destination derived from the nation's accumulation of industrial and commercial wealth and rising living standards. All but the very poorest people could now save for at least one day a year at the seaside. Shipbuilding and its allied trades had given place on the foreshore of South Bay to bathing machines, donkeys, sand castles and performing pierrots. A declining minority of 'old-towners' lived by fishing. The railways brought an ever-increasing number of long and short-term visitors, though most of them came still mainly from the industrial West Riding. Except for exclusive South Cliff, all parts of the expanding town were now connected by electric tram. After the mid-Victorian development of South Cliff came the lower middle-class movement into the North Side. By 1914 residential and recreational Scarborough – now widely admired for its 'gardens by the sea' – had almost reached the furthest limits of its medieval boundaries.

Walking the Boundaries

Even as late as 1840 Scarborough was not much bigger in built-up area than it had been 500 years earlier at the time of the Black Death. To the south of the town there were now the Cliff footbridge (1827), which spanned Ramsdale and led to the Spa promenade, and the newly-opened Gothic Saloon (1839); but the South Cliff above and behind the Spa was still bare of buildings, apart from a windmill on Ramshill where St Martin's church now stands. In effect, Ramsdale ravine still marked the southern boundary of the town and the Rotunda Museum (1828) was a conspicuous, isolated outpost on its northern slope. In the valley itself only the middle of Scarborough's three medieval water-mills, known then as Plantation mill, survived.

To the west of the town development outside Newborough Bar had been slow and piecemeal. Apart from Christ Church (1828) and the Oddfellows' Hall (1840), the new buildings in this area, once occupied by Bean's Gardens, were more residential than public. Two new terraces of private houses, Brunswick Place and York Place, running south from Falsgrave Walk (not yet called Westborough) were under construction. The first six three-storey houses in York Place, all faced with fine dark-brown ashlar, were already finished. With their bow windows rising from ground to roof level they must have appeared a most handsome row of superior-class homes for the well-to-do.

Even more dignified was newly-completed Belvoir Terrace, so-called, according to a distinguished visitor in 1839, 'in honour of the Duke of Rutland, who, although he had ceased to be absolute patron of the borough, is still as much revered as ever by its inhabitants'. (The visitor spelled the name 'Beavor', the correct pronunciation though not the correct spelling of the duke's home in Leicestershire.) What was once called White Bread Close or Great St Nicholas Close and had been intended in 1790 by Dr Falconer to be the site of his projected chapel, had become the Crescent Gardens. Here, on its northern side, separated from Belvoir Terrace by a new road leading out of York Place, there was now another terrace of half a dozen houses, 'distinguished by size and greater pretensions'. Whereas the New Buildings on St Nicholas Cliff of the 1760s and those put up by Huntriss a little later were intended as lodging houses for visitors, Vernon, York and Brunswick Places, Belvoir Terrace and the Crescent, all built in the 1820s and 1830s, were conceived as permanent residences for Scarborough's richest families.

234

Gothic Newborough Bar 1847 - 1890

Even grander were the four private houses already built on the south side of the Crescent Gardens – Wood End, Warwick House (later Londesborough Lodge), East Villa and Grove Villa – all superior, detached, stone mansions set in their own extensive grounds overlooking Ramsdale valley. A fifth, between Wood End and Warwick House, called Broxholme, was built in 1844-5. A century later it was to become Scarborough's Art Gallery.

On the north side of 'Without the Bar', Bull Lane and its continuation, recently renamed Aberdeen Walk, defined the limit of the town's development in this direction. Though the borough no longer kept a bull on it, what is now the lower end of Victoria Road was then straddled by the town Common. Open arable fields and pastures still separated Scarborough town from Falsgrave village. The oldest of Scarborough's windmills stood alone on the highest point between them.

Since at least the early years of the fifteenth century a windmill had occupied this same hill site. For centuries it had belonged to the borough, but since 1784 when Thomas Robinson successfully petitioned the Town Hall to erect a new 'fantail' mill, it had been owned privately. In 1840 it was run by Samuel Newton. Writing in 1787, James Schofield

235

had described it as 'a noble wind-mill', and now more than two hundred years later, though much altered, it survives as the Old Mill Hotel in Mill Street, still a prominent and attractive feature on Scarborough's sky-line.

Northwards, in 1840 Scarborough town still ended abruptly just outside its medieval boundary of the New Dyke and Richard III's unfinished stone wall. Beyond them there was only a scattering of buildings in open fields and closes. Richard Wilson's 'asylum' consisted of a row of fourteen single-storey, brick houses of two rooms each, built in 1836 'for the use of decayed mariners'. Apart from an addition of 1922 in the same Gothic style, Wilson's almshouses have survived largely unchanged, whereas the National Schools for Girls (1836) on Limekiln Hill and for Boys (1837) at New Dyke, built for Anglican children, have long since disappeared without trace. The same fate has also swept away the Merchant Seamen's Hospital (1752) which once stood at the junction of what became North Marine and Castle Roads.

Opposite the Merchant Seamen's Hospital one important improvement to the borough's facilities had recently appeared. In less than rapid response to the severe rebukes of the municipal commissioners, in 1842 the reformed Town Hall regime had built a new prison and house of correction. They stood at Local Place, the northern end of what was still called Tanner Street but would soon recover its medieval name of St Thomas Street. The corporation raised the money by sale of Ramsdale closes, better known today as the Esplanade. The new borough gaol boasted separate cell accommodation for men, women and boys and an exercise yard at the back. A year later the old Newborough Bar with its notorious prison cells was completely demolished and eventually replaced by a higher and wider gateway.

Beyond Local Place, Greengate (North Marine Road) and Peasholm Lane (Queen's Terrace and Queen's Parade) ran northwards still through fields and pastures. Two more windmills, Albion and Greengate, stood in open country. Wrea Lane (Dean Road) led only to Scarborough's principal brickfields and works on land soon destined to be used for the town's new workhouse. The borough still employed a pinder to gather up stray animals and his compound or pinfold was then behind the Merchant Seamen's Hospital on the site of what later became the Fire Station.

Scarborough town and Falsgrave village even together then covered only a small fraction of the 2,160 acres of the extensive liberty of Scarborough borough. The Municipal Corporations Act of 1835 had abolished Scarborough's medieval form of government but it had not diminished its borough boundaries. In 1837, when these boundaries were ridden and surveyed, it took four days to circumnavigate them.

Along the shore of the German Ocean (not yet renamed the North Sea) Scarborough stretched from Peasholm Gap in the north to White Nab in the south. Inland its limits were defined on the north side by Peasholm beck, which divided it from the royal manor of Northstead, Irton and Falsgrave moors to the west, and Cayton parish on its southern perimeter. Much of this area, such as the recently enclosed Weaponness – by 1840 more commonly called Olive or Oliver Mount – was pasture and rough grazing. Closest to the edges of development some of the land was cultivated as gardens and allotments for fruit and vegetables.

The main drainage of the borough, later submerged below modern roads, was still to be seen on the surface. Raincliffe spring, which rose in Sandybed, not Raincliffe, and was a stream of some volume, ran its meandering course along what became Whin Bank, Wykeham Street, Gladstone Road and Columbus Ravine. Eventually it joined Peasholm beck before together they entered North Bay through Peasholm Gap.

In contrast, Millbeck, the outflow of Scarborough Mere, which ran into South Bay, was already partly buried beneath man-made crossing points in upper and lower Ramsdale; and the Damgeth, which once cut through the middle of the old town, was now entirely underground, except when heavy rainfall brought it to the surface.

Falsgrave springs on Gilduscliff (Spring Hill) were still Scarborough's main source of water supply. The underground iron pipes from there fed three open public troughs in the lower town. Since 1828 they also fed and filled the largest covered receptacle for water in England, a brick reservoir in Workhouse (later Chapman's) Yard. Forty feet in diameter, 20 feet deep with a domed roof another 20 feet high and covered in clay, the reservoir had a capacity of more than 200,000 gallons. William Smith's brainchild ensured minimum wastage and continuous supply even in midsummer to the oldest parts of the town. Nevertheless, by the early 1840s, there were repeated complaints of water shortages: Smith had not anticipated such an enormous increase in demand. According to one report, 'the town was so ill-supplied with water that on some occasions it was almost impossible to get enough to drink'.

237

Getting There and Back

Besides a scarcity of good, clean water, Scarborough suffered from another serious disadvantage, which in 1840 might have seemed permanent – its geographical remoteness. Two centuries after Mrs Farrer's momentous discovery of mineral springs it was still almost as much an expensive ordeal to reach Scarborough from any distance as it had been in her time.

These were still the days of horses and coaches and carts. Travel overland was costly, tedious, time-consuming and uncomfortable, even for those few who could afford the best means. The royal coach link from London leaving York every morning at seven and arriving in Scarborough before noon was the safest road passage, but it carried only seven passengers, four inside and three on the roof. Weary and relieved, travellers tumbled out at the Blue Bell or Talbot inns. The mail was then taken down to the post office at 14 Merchants Row.

During the season from May until October there were eleven coaches altogether running to and from Scarborough. Houson, proprietor of the Bull hotel, and Lee, proprietor of the Golden Lion at Leeds, ran a daily service, except on Sundays, between Scarborough and Leeds in the Original Old True Blue or Four Inside. The journey on the turnpike went through York, New Malton, Yedingham, Snainton and Ayton and took between six and seven hours. From Leeds inside passengers paid eleven shillings (55p.), outside seven (35p.). From York the fares were eight (40p.) and five (25p.) shillings respectively.

Rival coaches, the Old True Blue, the Blucher and the Transit, made the same journeys at the same prices but operated to and from the Blue Bell and the Talbot inns. To and from Hull, via Filey, Bridlington, Driffield and Beverley, the royal mail, the Wellington and Magna Charta ran daily services during the season. Their link was with steam packets from London and coaches from the south which came through Lincoln and used the Wintringham ferry across the Humber. Finally, the Royal Union coach made return daily trips between Scarborough and Whitby.

One ominous portent of things to come was first seen reported in the *Scarborough Herald* of 8 August 1839. The Old Original True Blue was then advertised as leaving the Bell and the Blacksmith's Arms daily for York where passengers going on to Leeds would board the train for the final stage. In reply, Houson and Lee declared in the same issue that their Original Old True Blue would continue to travel between Scarborough and Leeds entirely by road 'at greatly reduced fares'! This was the first local shot in a war still being fought between road and rail.

Longer distance travellers who had the means might prefer one of the steam packets. During the summer northerners would find either the *Neptune* or the *Eclipse* waiting for them at Newcastle, and southerners one of the same at Hull, to complete their journeys by sea. In good weather the packets were certainly smoother than coaches and in all weathers faster than sailing ships. When George IV passed Scarborough in August 1822 on his way north in the royal yacht towed by a steam packet, 'they were going so swift through the water it was with great difficulty that Dr Travis presented a loyal address to the monarch'.

Finally, there was always the slowest and least comfortable of all road travel, that by carrier's cart, a means available to those of modest or negligible resources. There were twice weekly carts to and from as far away as Leeds, Hull and Pickering, carrying produce as well as people. Like the stage coaches they operated from Scarborough's inns and public houses: from the Bay Horse at 8 Queen Street, the Fountain in Leading Post Street, the Star and the King's Arms in King Street, the White Bear at 8 St Helen's Square, the Old Globe at 16 Globe Street and the London and New Inns in Newborough.

Granville's Scarborough

Among the visitors recorded in the weekly *Scarborough Herald* of 1 August 1839 was Dr Augustus Bozzi Granville. Elsewhere in that issue he was described as 'the celebrated and talented traveller' and, to repay the compliment, two years later he published a glowing report of what he had seen and thought in his *Spas of Northern England.*

Dr Granville had no complaint about Scarborough's water. On the contrary, after explaining that women carried water from the three conduits to private houses and inns at a penny a pint, he praised 'Falsgrave water' as 'rather hard but well-favoured and limpid'. Indeed, the doctor had nothing but praise for this 'Queen of English sea-bathing places', as he called Scarborough. He was 'enchanted' with what he described as 'a bay of Naples on the north-east coast'. Though a century earlier earls, marquesses and dukes had been as 'thick at that spa as berries on a hedge' and Scarborough was then what Brighton had become, it was still 'the most pleasing' of all the English spas he had visited.

Granville was even more pleased with the food at the Bell where he lodged than he was with the water. He sat down to a 'well-decked table' of 'good-looking bread, excellent tea, tea-cakes, muffins, new-laid eggs ... cold beef, raised pies, shrimps and potted and marinaded fish'; and that was just for breakfast! Not surprisingly, fish of the finest quality – turbot, haddock, cod and sole – were served at prices much lower than in Harrogate or London.

Throughout Scarborough the cost of meals, drink and accommodation was much cheaper than anywhere else Granville had stayed. All the lodging houses provided four meals a day and a bedroom for between four shillings and sixpence (22½p.) and six shillings and sixpence (32½p.) a day. Even Mrs Reed charged only a half guinea (52½p.) extra for weekly accommodation in her Royal Hotel on Long Room Street.

For the most affluent 'spawers' who brought their families, servants and private coaches, separate houses and stables could be rented at ten guineas (£10. 50p.) a week. The best house overlooking Cliff Bridge cost 13 guineas (£13. 65p.) a week during the season from 1 July until 12 October, but afterwards could be had for half that price.

However, Granville had come to Scarborough not to indulge himself with its food and drink but to inspect its spa and bathing facilities, and again he was not disappointed. First of all, he was most favourably impressed with Scarborough's natural position and scenic splendour, midway along a coast of 33 miles from Robin Hood's Bay to Flamborough Head of spectacular cliffs and 'the finest sands in England'. Scarborough's own South Bay sands were 'the purest' he had ever seen and made 'the best riding-ground in the world'.

On these flat, firm, clean sands Granville counted between 30 and 40 bathing machines, 20 of them, 'the largest and best', belonging to Joseph Chapman. Sea-bathing, Granville concluded, 'imparts vigour to an infirm constitution' and 'restores a morbid frame', though there is no evidence that he wrote from personal experience. However, the doctor did inspect some of the indoor sea-water baths. On the Cliff, the baths owned by Dr William Travis had marble interiors and were supplied with the purest salt water, warm and cold, administered by shower, pump, drenching or vapour. Newer baths, belonging to Dr William Harland and Mr John Champley, were also luxurious, particularly the former. Dr Harland charged only half a crown (12½p.) for use of his 'boudoir-like' and 'coquettish' establishment. It seems that Granville did not venture on to the foreshore to sample Vickerman's baths or down to the harbour to look at Weddell's: he would have found both inferior to those on the Cliff.

Half a crown a month was now the toll charge for pedestrians using the Cliff Bridge, which spanned Ramsdale ravine, 'a chasm 400 feet wide with a depth of nearly 80 feet'. Here Granville was gratified to encounter so many distinguished visitors making their 'afternoon promenade'. Their presence showed that with 'a very large number of the superior classes' Scarborough still retained its 'natural attraction'. The Cliff Bridge was more than a convenient route to the Spa and a promenade for visitors: from it there were 'grandstand' views of the horse-races held over the sands below every August. If Granville had stayed on for these races, which then marked the zenith of Scarborough's season, on two consecutive days in late August he would have seen thoroughbreds compete in six sweepstakes over 1½ or 2 miles across the broad width of South Bay.

Granville was enthralled by the Rotunda Museum. To him it was 'a most delightful source of amusement and intellectual gratification'. He failed to point out that admission charges of two shillings and sixpence a month for individuals and five shillings for a family ticket effectively excluded all but the well-to-do. Even more exciting was Mr McBean's private collection. At 7 Vernon Place during twenty years of exploration of the local cliffs and shores he had amassed between sixty and seventy thousand fossils and shells. The doctor was privileged to see them.

Of Scarborough's other visitor attractions Granville was less enamoured. Mrs Reed's hotel, formerly Donner's Long Room, had a spacious ballroom, but the dancing there was 'mediocre' because the company was unsociable to the point of incivility. 'This should be reformed, and the sooner the better', he concluded pompously. Significantly, Long Room Street was soon to be renamed St Nicholas Street, its earlier description. One resident who approved of the change was John Woodall. His new house at No 22 opposite the Royal Hotel would not have been built near a place thronged with noisy, inebriated, pleasure-seeking visitors to the town. Even Scarborough's theatre in Tanner Street was poorly attended, according to Granville. He counted only nineteen in an audience listening to 'a bewitching widow of a late

241

**South Steel battery and Weddell's
bath-house from East Pier, by J Stubbs, 1827**

gallant life-guard officer', who was much appreciated in London but apparently not, with the exception of the doctor, in Scarborough.

Of what should have been his principal concern, the Spa, Granville wrote little and even less that was enthusiastic. The new saloon, Wyatt's turreted 'castle' in the Gothic style, opened as recently as July 1839, did not much appeal to him perhaps because its interior decoration was still unfinished. Granville had no eye for architecture. He also complained, in his typically practical way, that gravel walks on the landscaped slopes behind the new building were 'sloppy in wet weather'.

As for the two Spa wells he did not doubt the therapeutic claims made for them but pointed out that confidence in their medical virtues was undermined when there were so many conflicting analyses of their chemical properties. He recommended that the authorities invite a professional and authoritative opinion.

Though Granville's purpose, in his own words, might have been 'to describe things as they are', what he had to say about Scarborough as a privileged, short-term visitor was necessarily

242

superficial and partial. Probably he never ventured below the Bell and he showed no evident interest in the harbour or the town's many industries and occupations. In a passing reference he wrote of the 'primeval huts and cottages of the fisherman and the mariner' and 'the red-brick dwellings of the humbler classes ... thickly huddled together' and 'canopied over by hovering clouds of blue smoke'.

The Other Scarborough

For information about the Scarborough that Granville ignored we have to look at other contemporary sources, particularly White's *Directory*, published in 1840. In that year, as in many past centuries, the sea, not tourism, provided the town with most of its employment and income. Visitors might regard Scarborough as a 'general resort for persons of distinction and families in the middle ranks of life', but for the majority of townspeople the sea was their livelihood, during as well as out of 'the season'.

According to White, there were 186 vessels of all kinds belonging to the port of Scarborough. Their crews numbered 1,535 men and boys. These figures match closely with the numbers of ships and seamen paying muster roll levies in 1845. In that year approximately 180 ships and 1,300 seamen paid the levy. Not all the seamen were natives of Scarborough and now only a few of the ships registered were built there, but the registers show that the town was still an important 'ship-mart' if no longer a major ship-building port. According to Theakston's *Guide* of 1841, in 1825 six ships with a total tonnage of 1,561 were built at Scarborough; in 1831, only three; in 1839, only two; and in 1840, only one of 325 tons.

The Tindall shipyards were producing fewer but bigger ships mainly for the Far East and Mediterranean carrying trades. The *Persia* (1838), the *Fortitude*, (1842) and the *Medway* (1845) were all over 500 tons yet still launched from their confined slipways on Sandside. Owned and operated by the three brothers, William, James and Robert Tindall, each had a crew of about 20 merchant seamen. The only other major shipowner of Scarborough ships was Thomas Burlinson Walker. He specialised in running and hiring out brigs and barques of about 250 tons. In 1845 Walker owned no fewer than 21 of these vessels, each of them carrying between five and eight crewmen.

Apart from the Tindalls, only three other boatbuilders at Scarborough were recorded in White's *Directory*: Thomas Armstrong, Robert Skelton and James and Thomas (sic) Smith. In fact, as registration figures show, Armstrong built two, the Skeltons four and the Smiths, James and William, four boats, all fishing yawls of about 50 tons, in 1840.

Sailmakers were now even scarcer: only two of them, George Fowler and Mosey Shaw, were named by White. Even more ominous is the absence from his *Directory* of the many traditional crafts associated with wooden shipbuilding, such as joinery, carpentry and rope-making. By 1842 the old rope-walks that once ran in the Castle Dykes and along the length of what later became North Street had disappeared. Tyson's map of that year noted only one surviving Rope-Walk as an alternative name for High Tollergate or the middle section of Castle Road.

However, if shipbuilding and its many allied trades were in rapid decline, Scarborough still had 52 men listed as shipowners in 1840, only four fewer than in 1832. Many of these owned only part shares or at most a single vessel, but a few, as well as the Tindalls and Walker, had substantial mercantile investments. For example, George Willis, who lived in one of the new York Place houses and would be elected mayor in 1854, owned five ships averaging 400 tons each and altogether employing nearly 70 seamen. Matthew Smith had seven vessels. Thomas Hick, senior, who lived in Howe House, Falsgrave, had six ships and shares in at least two more. Thomas Purnell, who served as mayor in 1839-40 and was elected for a second term in 1845, is listed as a shipowner and so are Samuel Beswick, the veteran councillor; Henry Fowler, collector of customs and leading Wesleyan Methodist; and John Champley, proprietor of the Cliff baths.

The old harbour was still quite a busy port. According to Theakston's *Guides* of the 1840s, exports from Scarborough were mainly of corn, butter, hams, bacon and saltfish. Imports consisted of coals from Newcastle and Sunderland; timber, flax and iron from the Baltic; brandy and apples from France; geneva (gin) from Holland; wine from Portugal; and groceries from London. Duties levied on this trade were worth nearly £2,000 in 1840, but the extension to Scarborough of the privileges of the bonding system more than doubled these receipts from 1841 onwards.

In 1840 Scarborough had 37 resident master mariners, a decline from the 59 listed in 1823. Only two of them, John Dye and

Old Sandside in the late nineteenth century

John Harrison, lived outside the old town, at 2 and 4 Brunswick Terrace. Seven had addresses in Princess Street, five in Longwestgate, five in Castlegate, three in Cook's Row, two on Sandside, and the rest on Merchants Row, St Sepulchre Street, Tuthill, the Dumple, Quay Street and the two Sandgates. Here again the physical separation of down-town Scarborough, the working harbour, and up-town Scarborough, the middle-class resort, is evident. Not surprisingly, all seven of the fishmongers in White's *Directory* lived near the waterfront on Sandside, on Quay Street or in the Bolts, amongst the fishing community.

Even the distribution of inns, taverns and beerhouses underlined this social spectrum from the poorest in the lowest parts of the old town to the most affluent in upper Newborough and Without the Bar with a middle band between them. The most exclusive were the Bull, the Royal, the Talbot and the Bell. According to Scarborough's first newspaper, the *Herald*, in the summer of 1839, Houson's Bull had a duke, a marquess and a countess; the Royal had two earls and their wives; the Talbot entertained Sir Henry and Lady Boynton; and the Bell had Dr Granville.

245

The resorts of fishermen, shipyard craftsmen and town labourers were the 19 beerhouses and the 30 or so public houses nearest the harbour; and separating these two extremes were the taverns such as the Bay Horse in Queen Street, the Star and the King's Arms in King Street, the Old Globe in Globe Street, and the London, George and New Inns in Newborough catering for 'the middling sort'.

Nearly all the better-class lodging houses named in White's *Directory* and the *Scarborough Herald* were on the south side of the upper town overlooking the Bay: on Merchants Row, Bland's Cliff, Leading Post Street, King Street and St Nicholas Cliff. It was already customary to advertise a 'sea-view' and to charge extra for it. Significantly, there were no public houses or taverns on St Nicholas Cliff, the most sought-after location for visitor accommodation.

In the sharpest contrast, common lodging houses, as they were called, were invariably situated in the depths of the town, and, in the words of a government inspector, were often 'in a wretched state'. Migrant Irish labourers and their families, travelling tradesmen, stranded seamen and the poorest lived and slept side by side in stinking squalor without washing facilities, ventilation, clean bedding or even daylight. Of the 26 common lodging houses inspected in 1852 under new parliamentary regulations, seven with 85 beds were immediately condemned as unfit for human habitation and refused registration. Their addresses were Bird Yard, off Cross Street, St Sepulchre Street, West Sandgate and Custom House Steps.

If upper Scarborough was still largely the preserve of 'the better sort' and 'spawers', the Poor Law Amendment Act of 1834 had effectively made the borough the involuntary home of all the district's paupers. Previously, Scarborough took care of only its own orphan children and elderly destitute; from now on its workhouse was grossly overcrowded with the paupers of 33 neighbouring townships from as far as Staintondale to the north, Snainton to the west, Sherburn to the south-west and southwards to Filey.

That in some respects Scarborough in 1840 was still little more than an overgrown village by the sea is illustrated by White's list of 12 'cowkeepers' resident in the town. Only two of them had homes in Falsgrave; the others had addresses in the heart of the town. Thomas Jackson actually lived in Town Hall Yard, behind Long Room Street. Every morning, except on Sundays, cattle and sheep were driven down Falsgrave Walk and Newborough Street to be slaughtered in the Old

Shambles. Of the 17 butchers named by White, seven had their shops in the Shambles and five others had addresses in neighbouring St Helen's Square. Live cattle were also brought down into the town for sale at the Thursday weekly market in Newborough Street and two annual fairs held there on Holy Thursday and old Martinmas Day. The only restriction on livestock movements through the streets of the town was that they took place before eight in the morning.

Crime and Punishment

Though the municipal commissioners of 1833 found that there were 'few places so quiet and orderly' as Scarborough, the private accounts of the town's two serjeants-at-mace and their constables paint a less favourable and more accurate picture.

Despite harsh punishment inflicted on convicted offenders, there was much petty theft in Scarborough. Transportation for seven years was the standard sentence for stealing 'jet from a warehouse', or 'wood', or 'cloth from the Talbot Inn', or a sovereign from a country man, or ninety pounds from a visitor. The value of the goods stolen seemed not to matter much. Handling rope pilfered from Tindall's shipyard cost a local man three months in the House of Correction, whereas stealing napkins from the Bull Inn put Francis MacDonald in Northallerton's House of Correction for two years. Perhaps Francis was a persistent offender; but the same draconian sentence was meted out to George Ward found guilty of carrying off a coat from a man playing in a field on Oliver's Mount. Scavenging from ships wrecked on the shore was a common practice; if you were caught it would reward you with six months hard labour.

There are fewer reported cases of poaching than in former years, but poachers still suffered severe retribution. Charles Garbut was summoned before Scarborough magistrates for taking 'a hare out of a snickle (trap) which he set himself' on Oliver's Mount. He was fined the huge sum of £5 and ordered to pay ten shillings (50p.) costs.

Smuggling, particularly of spirits, remained commonplace and profitable. Most of the liquor served so cheaply in Scarborough's inns and lodging houses was 'duty-free'. That so few cases came into the borough court suggests that it was regularly overlooked because too many residents and officials were engaged in it. In February 1840 three men were fined £5 each for conveying brandy into the town, but they were French!

There were many cases of coin forgery brought before the Quarter Sessions. Such offences were described variously as 'uttering base coin in the form of shillings' or 'paying [in] bad silver'. In most instances 12 months in Scarborough's own House of Correction was the sentence imposed. The usual penalty for vagrancy, a common offence, was a week or a fortnight of hard labour in the local House of Correction.

Girls who tried and failed to conceal the births of their bastard children were no longer flogged through the streets by the bellman; instead they were sent to Northallerton prison for six months. Fathers of such illegitimate offspring who refused to pay maintenance as ordered by the court were sentenced to a fortnight in Scarborough's new gaol.

Scarborough's constables used to burn bad meat at the market cross in St Helen's Square; now 'a basket of unsound Beef' was confiscated by them and the butcher who tried to sell it fined one pound.

On behalf of the coroner and magistrates the constables attended cases of violent and suspicious deaths. In Scarborough at this time there seems to have been an unusual number of suicides, by hanging from bed-posts, in the privy, in a stable, in the gateway to the Workhouse, in the Plantation, 'from the back gates of the New Inn', and 'in his home at 19 Princess Street'. Mary Readman's self-inflicted death was exceptional: she 'cut her throat with a raysor'. In all these cases, however, the unfortunate deceased was pronounced 'insane' or 'lunatic'.

Unexplained deaths were invariably explained 'by the visitation of God'; the first appearance of the phrase 'death from natural causes' occurs in a coroner's verdict of March 1844. Children were particularly vulnerable to death by burning, scalding and drowning in house wells. Abandoned babies were discovered in St Mary's churchyard and 'in a ditch near the Common New Barn'.

However, in other respects, the municipal commissioners were right: murder, manslaughter and public riot were all rare in Scarborough. The death of a youth of 14 run over by Hannah Wilkinson on the sands in 1845 was probably accidental. The young woman killed in her bed in Tanner Street at one o'clock in the morning was the victim of 'the effects of lightning', not a jealous lover. At midsummer 1845 there was only one prisoner for trial but he escaped from custody a day before the sessions!

As in any town at almost any time in the past and present there were drunken brawls on Saturday nights; but the only regular and serious disturbances of the peace were caused by the distribution of free beer at elections. Colonel Sir John Trench, who fought the parliamentary elections of 1832, 1835, 1837 and 1841, the last three successfully, was especially lavish with his bribes. In 1832, for instance, he gave '49 caps and as many comfortables' to the fishermen and sailors who had carried his flags on election day and on other occasions he paid for dinners and theatre tickets; but most of his treats were liquid. Parliamentary elections were the only events recorded when extra constables were hired to quell public riots in Scarborough's streets.

Schools and Churches

Some entries in White's *Directory* of 1840 illustrate Scarborough's character as a middle-class resort. The town boasted two resident artists: Matthew Baynes, junior (1793-1866), at 14 Palace Hill is less famous than the other, Henry Barlow Carter (1804-68), who was then living at 16 Queen Street. Carter was born in London and settled in Scarborough after his marriage there in 1830. Ten years later, when S.W. Theakston, bookseller, librarian, stationer and printer at 45-46 Long Room Street, decided to publish a new visitors' guide to the town he employed Carter to draw 22 pencilled sketches to illustrate it. During the next 20 years Carter gave Scarborough an unrivalled collection of superb watercolour paintings, many of them to be seen today in the borough's own art gallery, and his third home in the town, at 16 York Place, became an academy for many aspiring artists.

For its size Scarborough had an extraordinary number of schools, day and boarding, most of them small, private, fee-paying 'academies'. Theakston's *Guide* of 1841 listed no fewer than seven 'schools for young gentlemen', five of them offering boarding, and four 'for young ladies', one of them boarding. Queen Street was then an educational centre. Apart from Carter's drawing school at number 16, there were academies at 21, 32 and 36. William Potter ran his academy at 1 Albion Place and Ambrose Glenton Tyson, who published a map of the town in 1842 and invented a system of shorthand, also ran a private school at 33 Longwestgate.

William Merry was the first layman after a long line of Anglican clergymen to be headmaster of Scarborough's grammar school. In 1838 he succeeded the Reverend Joseph Skelton and held the post until 1852. During his first ten years he took the school in St Mary's church and boarded some of the boys at his home at 5 King Street. His advertisement in the *Scarborough Herald* of July 1839 provides the best description of what he had to offer:

> Mr Merry continues to receive into his house Young Gentlemen who are carefully instructed in English, Latin and French languages; the Mathematics, and all the detail of a Classical and commercial Education. The health, private comfort and correct deportment of the pupils receive diligent superintendence, and no pains are spared to ground them thoroughly in whatever is undertaken to be taught.

Boarders aged 12 paid 25 guineas (£26. 25p.) a year and those under 12 three guineas (£3. 15p.) less. Day boarders, who presumably were provided with meals but not beds, were charged 10 guineas (£10.50p.) and day boys only four guineas (£4. 20p.) a year. Washing and French lessons were each two guineas (£2. 10p.) extra. Young gentlemen were provided with towels and a pair of sheets which had to be returned.

However, if resort Scarborough had so many fee-paying academies for young gentlemen and young ladies, the lower town had a concentration of places for the poor. Sarah Brown taught 50 working-class girls at her School of Industry in Cook's Row. Here they learned reading, writing, arithmetic, knitting, sewing and other skills of domestic husbandry. Dr Murray had founded an Infant School in 1827 in St Sepulchre Street and by 1840 there were as many as 140 children under the age of six in his 'fostering care'. They were the lucky ones: most children of the labouring poor had little education and often less care.

At all levels, education was still the preserve of religious bodies. In Scarborough, as elsewhere in the country, the Anglicans were well established and provided free schooling for as many children as they could afford. Their National Society schools for 75 boys and 65 girls now received conditional grant aid from the state, whereas their Amicable Society, financed entirely by voluntary subscription, clothed, educated and sometimes fed as many as 80 children aged between nine and fourteen. At their Lancasterian school on Castle Road the

Nonconformists took in 300 day pupils regardless of religious denomination.

According to Theakston's first *Guide* of 1840, 'probably no town in the empire, of the same size, possesses a greater number of places for worship of God than Scarborough'. When current construction was completed the town's churches and chapels would have seats for everyone of its 9,500 inhabitants. Theakston's figures were probably accurate, but how many of these places would ever be occupied he neglected to say.

Scarborough's oldest, and between 1649 and 1828 only, church, St Mary's was said in 1840 to have seats for at least 1,100 and perhaps as many as 1,500 parishioners. To meet the increasing needs of a rising population and to raise more money the town's Anglicans had merely added galleries to the interior. Apart from the few assigned 'for the use of the poor' in the north St Nicholas aisle, nearly all St Mary's ground-floor box pews and upper gallery seats were rented by their occupants. Nevertheless, despite income from pewholders and many rich benefactors, the parish church remained shabby and neglected, as well as overcrowded with pews if not people. A picture of the western front published in 1812 seems to show a tree growing out of the south-west corner of the building; and the interior of St Mary's had become so inconvenient and 'barbarous' that the archdeacon of the East Riding refused to hold his annual visitation there. Not least of the objections to the misuse of Scarborough's only parish church was that after nearly two centuries of 'temporary' occupation the master and boys of the grammar school still monopolised the whole of the south transept, which had been divided into upper and lower floors. It was in these ugly surroundings that the Reverend Michael Hodsell Miller, vicar since 1828, served his congregation with two Sunday sermons, morning prayers three times a week and monthly communion.

Shortly after Miller was presented to the vicarage by Lord Hotham, Christ Church was consecrated by the Archbishop of York. With accommodation at least equal to that of St Mary's, yet free of galleries, lofts and box pews, the new church soon proved a serious rival. Situated in Vernon Place it was far more accessible for 'the politer parts of town' than the old parish church on its lofty hill-top site.

If Christ Church was originally intended to suit the needs of the well-to-do visitors and residents of Scarborough's western suburb, St Thomas's chapel, in the lower part of town, was built 'chiefly for the accommodation of the poor'. Unlike Scarborough's medieval church of St Thomas, this new chapel in East Sandgate was dedicated to St Thomas the apostle and martyr. Appropriately, its foundation stone was laid on his feast day, 21 December 1839. To £1,400 raised by private donation the Incorporated Society for the Building of [Anglican] Churches added a grant of £300 on condition that at least 330 places would be free to allcomers.

Thanks to parliamentary subsidy and generous gifts from wealthy benefactors, in only 12 years the Anglicans had almost tripled their accommodation in Scarborough, but it seems highly unlikely that they ever had the attendance to fill all of it. In contrast, the Nonconformists in general, and the Methodists in particular, were growing in numbers far greater than their seating capacities. The growth of the Wesleyan movement was spectacular and much of it was at the expense of the established church.

Though probably overcome by prejudiced enthusiasm, one local commentator declared that 'Wesleyan Methodism may be said to grip the town at all points'. The third Wesleyan chapel in Scarborough, built in Queen Street and opened in 1840, reflected the remarkable success of this denomination. Costing £7,000 and noted for its 'admirable acoustic properties', the new chapel had seating capacity for about 1,600, three times that of its predecessor, but it was frequently packed with nearly 2,000 worshippers. Underneath the ground floor little Wesleyans were given Sunday schooling and adults practised at their Saturday night band meetings. The whole building was heated by two formidable stoves called Gog and Magog.

The Wesleyans were counted the most 'respectable' Dissenters; primitive Methodism appealed more to the poorest, particularly the seafaring community of the lower town. When William Clowes first came to Scarborough he found the 'preaching room' at 4 Globe Street too small and instead addressed 'a prodigious mass of hearers, more than could hear me' on the sands. Other open-air meetings were held at the Castle Dykes. The first Primitive Methodist chapel in St Sepulchre Street on the site of the Franciscan friary was a 'home-made' structure, put up by the local fishermen in 1821. By 1840 it had to be enlarged and improved to seat up to 600. The chapel was well used: there were three Sunday sermons, another on Friday evenings, prayer meetings on Mondays and Wednesdays, and fellowship groups on Thursdays.

Another place favoured by God-fearing fishermen, visiting as well as native, was the Bethel on Sandside. For two centuries 'this ignoble and paltry-looking building' had been Scarborough's Common Hall and magistrates' court. Then, in 1800, when the councillors moved up to Long Room Street, the Quaker Tindalls bought it from the corporation to be a 'place of religious worship for sailors and fishermen'. Unlike every other chapel in the town its services on Tuesday and Saturday evenings were non-denominational. Baptists, both kinds of Methodists, Presbyterians and Independents, numbering up to 300, all attended on equal terms.

Meanwhile, the Baptists on Longwestgate, under their preacher, the Reverend Benjamin Evans, with about 150 communicants; the Independents in St Sepulchre Street, led by the Reverend G.B. Kidd, with up to 500 members; the Roman Catholics, in Auborough Street, with about 80 members; and the Plymouth Brethren, who met twice a week in their King Street chapel, altogether spanned the full range of Christian worship and belief in Scarborough.

Summary

As a commercial port, shipbuilding harbour and fishing market, by 1840 Scarborough no longer enjoyed its former prominence. Now overshadowed by Hull and Whitby, its harbour was valued mostly as a place of refuge for sailing vessels, especially colliers. Yet even in this respect its best days were in the past: the new steam ships were not so vulnerable to tide and tempest; its old harbour was too confined to accommodate larger vessels; and new coalfields and canals were undermining the monopoly of Newcastle and Sunderland.

Scarborough's future as a health and recreation resort was also less than promising by 1840. Few of the aristocracy favoured it any more. Taking the Spa waters internally was no longer fashionable. The numbers bathing in salt water, indoor or in the sea, had never compensated for the loss of those who had formerly taken the mineral springs, on site or in bottles. Scarborough, it seemed, could not prosper merely as a seaside resort. The season which opened in late June, reached a peak at the end of August, and petered out during October was too brief to sustain further expansion. Visitors had once spent two months at the Spa; now they came for only a fortnight or even only for the horse-races in the last week of August. The shortness of the season was already an insoluble problem. Sea-coal had rescued Scarborough from stagnation at the beginning of the seventeenth century; mineral springs and salt water had provided it with a new role and profitable vitality a century later; and now, two hundred years after Mrs Farrer's discovery, the town was in need of another impetus.

14

STEAMPOWER

The Railway

One kind of violent death was reported to Scarborough's coroner on 23 September 1844 as 'killed on the works of the railroad near Seamer'. So, even before the first locomotive arrived at Scarborough, the 'iron horse' had already taken its human toll; but during the next century the railway was to bring far more benefits than costs to the town.

At 1.45 p.m. on 7 July 1845 the steam engines, *Hudson* and *Lion*, pulled 35 carriages into Scarborough's new railway station. They had left York at 10.30 that morning and, after 'receiving ovations at every station on the way', were greeted warmly by the mayor, Thomas Weddell, and members of the Town Council. Crowds of curious spectators had lined the last mile of the route from Falsgrave; all Scarborough's shops were closed that day; and the distinguished passengers from York, who included George Husdon, 'the Railway King', were treated to a celebration luncheon by the corporation at the Town Hall.

The first railway train into Scarborough from York was seen at the time to be an important event in the history of the town, yet no one present could have foreseen its momentous, long-term consequences. Most local people thought the steam engines would provide faster and cheaper freight to the towns of the West Riding for Scarborough's fish; they would have been amazed, and perhaps horrified, to learn that eventually the railway would transform their elitist resort into an excursionist mecca for millions of holiday-makers.

Without navigable river or man-made canal and more than 40 miles from any centre of dense population, Scarborough had had to wait for the railway to connect it to the rapidly-growing wealth and population of the industrial West Riding, the Midlands, London and Scotland. It was George Hudson – who had persuaded his fellow shareholders in the North Midland Railway to invest £260,000 in the new line – who described Scarborough hopefully as 'the Brighton of the North'. Two years later, the opening of a branch line to Bridlington linked Scarborough with Hull.

In his notorious pamphlet of 1840 George Knowles of Wood End had warned Scarborians that they would rue the day that their town was linked by rail with the outside world. He predicted that the railway would bring only penniless vagrants and they would drive away the rich and respectable who had made Scarborough into a fashionable watering place. In years to come, he wrote, 'the novelty of not having a Railroad' would be Scarborough's best recommendation!

Knowles was much mistaken. For a long time yet, apart from concessionary excursions on public holidays and occasional Sundays, the new trains were beyond the reach of even the working classes. Migratory labourers and destitute travellers were still obliged to journey on foot or by cart.

Writing in May 1848, a correspondent of the *Scarborough Gazette* explained the circumstances of rail travel to the town in precise terms. He complained that the cost of a single first-class ticket from York had been raised from nine shillings (45p.) to ten shillings (50p.). He could have opted for a second-class seat, for which the fare was seven shillings (35p.), but instead chose 'the Tub', an open, third-class carriage, for which he paid five shillings (25p.). However, there was a fourth alternative, which he intended to use for his return journey – 'the Government Train'. The fare for this, at a penny a mile for the 42 miles, would be the cheapest at three shillings and sixpence (18p.).

The 'Government' or 'Parliamentary' train was the product of Gladstone's Railway Act of 1844. This Act required all railway companies to run one cheaper train every weekday in each direction, stopping at every station, running at a speed of not less than 12 miles per hour, with covered carriages, and charging no more than a penny a mile.

In practice, however, even a penny a mile was more than the average, long-distance traveller could afford; one 'Parliamentary' train a day, however lengthy, could hardly make much difference to the numbers who might want to come to the seaside from Leeds, Hull or Sheffield; and excursion Sunday trains did not have to conform to

Gladstone's regulations. Moreover, the daily service between York and Scarborough, even during the summer season, amounted to only four trains each way. Out of season, for eight months of the year, there were only three trains a day, and none on Sundays, except the mail train. Such was the dissatisfaction with these early trains that in November 1848 a horse-drawn omnibus was revived between Scarborough and York on Monday, Wednesday and Friday.

In the event, the railway brought an increasing number of prosperous seasonal visitors to Scarborough from greater distances, thousands of adult and child excursionists on day trips, but as yet no great influx of holiday-makers with time and money to spend enjoying themselves. There were no bank holidays until even later; and Sunday travel and pleasure-seeking were frowned upon by the sabbatarians. One day a year at the seaside, 'the trip', was the most that millions of hard-working, poor families could look forward to. The *Gazette* was always careful to distinguish between 'visitors', who stayed overnight in hotels and lodging houses, and those it chose to call 'holiday-people' or 'pleasure-seekers', who came to Scarborough for only a few hours and added little to the income and employment of the town.

Waterworks

In the twenty years between the census of 1821 and that of 1841 Scarborough's resident population grew from 8,188 to 9,503, an increase of only 16%. During the next twenty years, by 1861, it had grown to 17,284, an increase of nearly 82%. Nothing like this expansion had ever occurred before. It was so remarkable that those who summarised the census returns of 1861 felt obliged to offer an explanation. In the words of their report: 'The increase of population in Scarborough is attributed to the extension of railway communication and improvements in the town, which is resorted to as a watering-place during the season.'

The received and usually unchallenged assumption is that the arrival of the railway from York in the summer of 1845 transformed Scarborough from an old-fashioned, middle-class spa town into a thriving, popular seaside resort. However, the romance of the railways has obscured the prosaic truth that the prosperity of mid-Victorian Scarborough owed at least as much to the steam water pump as to the steam locomotive. In fact, the Scarborough Water Act of 1845, the most

257

important improvement in the town, was as vital to its future as the contemporary York-Scarborough Railway Act.

The Scarborough Waterworks Company was founded in 1844 by John Woodall and ten other local business and property owners. Town Hall suspicions that public interest would be sacrificed to the private profits of share-holders were allayed by undertakings from Woodall and his associates that were written into the Act of Parliament passed in June 1845. In return for a monopoly of water supply to Scarborough and Falsgrave, the Company agreed to limits on charges to private homes and guaranteed that the three public conduits would remain open for free domestic use every day from 6 am to 9 pm. As a result, the Act gave the Company control of the supply pipes, the Workhouse Yard reservoir and all the existing sources of water in Falsgrave, Stoney Haggs, Staxton, Flixton and Cayton.

Yet none of these changes would have added one drop of water to Scarborough's inadequate supply: the crucial innovation was the introduction of Trevithick steam pumps at Cayton Bay. Here, every day, 400,000 gallons were lifted about 60 metres to a reservoir holding a million gallons and from there conveyed by water main along the line of Filey Road down to Scarborough.

From now on nearly every householder was certain of a reliable flow of clean water for baths, closets, kitchens and laundries, and every location, not merely those close to the fixed water points of the old town, could become residential. In particular, the southern and western perimeters of Scarborough could expand outwards. From 1845 onwards several old and new hotels and lodging houses were advertising that they had 'plenty of good water'. Such was the increasing demand for water that in 1853 a new steam pump, nearly twice as powerful as its predecessor, was installed at the Cayton cliff works; and two years later, the old reservoir at Seacliff was abandoned in favour of one at Osgodby Top with four times its capacity.

Scarborough's sewage system was also radically improved at this time. In 1848 a new main sewer pipe, three feet in diameter, connecting with those in St Sepulchre Street, Merchants Row and West Sandgate, was taken through and beyond the West Pier. Discharging much of the town's waste on to the south sands of the foreshore was at last ended. In the same year, when cholera raged in other towns, coastal and inland, Scarborough escaped without a single reported case. As always, gravity and the cleansing motion of the tidal North Sea were

Scarborough's great natural advantages, but on this occasion the town authorities acted with alacrity to suppress what were euphemistically described as 'nuisances'.

The 1830s and 1840s were years of extraordinary increases in urban population so that for the first time in history more English people lived in towns than in rural communities. Nowhere was this urbanisation more rapid than in the West Riding of Yorkshire where by 1851 there were no fewer than ten towns with populations exceeding 10,000, from Leeds with over 100,000 to Doncaster with 12,000. The growth of Scarborough's residential population from 8,760 in 1831 to just under 13,000 twenty years later might be seen therefore as a natural part of this phenomenon, except that unlike its industrial neighbours the town had no great influx of migratory workers.

What made Scarborough a special case was its avoidance of a high death rate from contaminated food and water diseases, particularly typhoid fever and cholera. As Edwin Chadwick's sanitary report of 1842 emphasized, the high incidence of infection and mortality in industrial towns was due much more to squalor than poverty: a continuous, adequate supply of clean water and an efficient system of sewerage were the only remedies. In 1840 the streets of Leeds were said to be unpaved with overflowing sewers and offensive drains. Four years later, when Woodall formed his Company, Engels wrote that Bradford, Halifax, Barnsley and Huddersfield were no healthier than Leeds.

'Vital Statistics', the title of a chapter in Theakston's third edition of his *Guide* published in 1847, provided proof of Scarborough's superiority as a healthy town. Whereas deaths from diseases of the respiratory organs amounted to one in three in the United Kingdom, in Scarborough they were little more than one in five. The air was cleaner in Scarborough, not just because it stood open to sea breezes, but because it had none of the industries which caused so much atmospheric pollution. Fourteen per cent of the nation's population was over 70, but in Leeds this figure dropped to below eight. In Scarborough nearly one in five of the residents was more than 70. Dr John Dunn, Scarborough's resident surgeon, concluded that his fellow townsmen and women had a three times better chance of reaching 70 years than the inhabitants of Manchester. At 181 in every thousand live births, infant mortality in Scarborough was exceptionally low; nationally the figure was 214, and in Leeds it was 277. In the 1840s these were some of the town's 'vital statistics' which Dr Dunn attributed to Scarborough's equable climate, low rainfall and predominantly mild westerly winds. He made no reference to Scarborough's water supply or disposal of sewage and nuisances.

Hotels and Lodging Houses

The *Scarborough Herald*, arguably the town's earliest newspaper, was never more than a seasonal broadsheet, advertising accommodation and listing the names of summer visitors. It was born in 1834, and lived precariously and fitfully until it expired in 1846. Its successor, S.W. Theakston's *Gazette*, also began life in the summer of 1845 as a seasonal advertiser, but eventually evolved into Scarborough's first weekly newspaper. Together, these early issues of *Herald* and *Gazette* reveal the impact on the town made by the railway from York and the water main from Cayton.

By 1848 new terraces had been built, most of them to accommodate visitors. On South Cliff, above and behind the Spa, lodgings were advertised at almost every number between one and 31 on the Esplanade, a new address, and at Belmont Terrace overlooking Ramsdale. Opposite the new railway station there were also more new addresses – Westfield Terrace, Hanover Place and West Parade – where substantial houses had gone up for the benefit of well-to-do lodgers. For instance, Mr Barry, the builder, offered for sale no. 2 Westfield Terrace, comprising drawing, dining and breakfast rooms, four lodging rooms, three attics and servants' quarters.

On the north side too there was similar rapid development. Mulgrave and Rutland Terraces now stood on North Cliff and the east side of Greengate was now fronted by Albert and North Marine Terraces. What was soon to be called the Queen's Hotel, the first of its kind on the north side of the town, was finished and put up for sale in July 1848.

There was also much new investment and improvement in the established lodgings on St Nicholas Cliff. William Wood described his houses and cottages there as 'desirably situated in the most healthy part of the town', with uninterrupted views of the sea and sands, and within a few minutes walk of the Cliff Bridge, the Spa Saloon and Pleasure Gardens. There was no reference to the railway station, only a claim that every house had 'a plentiful supply of good water'. No 2 Cliff, which now belonged to Mrs Jefferson, had been recently 'fitted up with every article entirely new and of the best material' without sparing expense. The Countess of Athlone stayed there in August and September 1848 and Anne Bronte died there the following May.

Scarborough's leading hoteliers were well aware of the difference the railway might make to their business prospects. Mrs Reed had recently 're-entered' the Royal Hotel, refurnished and extended it by adding the late Edward Donner's house, and taken a lease on the refreshment rooms at the railway station. Mrs Reed also owned the Bull Hotel, which she now advertised inaccurately as 'nearer to the railway station than any other house'; while the new proprietor of the Crown, 9-11 Esplanade, informed potential guests that his 'omnibus' and cabs would be waiting for the arrival of their trains.

John Fairgray Sharpin (1821-95) might have been new to the hotel business but with extraordinary foresight he soon grasped the opportunities the railway now offered Scarborough and in particular the Crown. In 1845 at the age of 24 he took a 12-year lease on the premises. By the summer of 1847 he had enlarged the Crown by adding spacious dining and ballrooms and, thanks to Trevithick's pumps and the Scarborough Waterworks Company, had installed 'hot, cold and shower baths'. Advertising on the front page of the *Gazette*, he declared that his hotel was 'now ready for the reception of Families'.

To some extent Sharpin revived the attractions of the former Assembly Rooms of the previous century and succeeded in bringing back to Scarborough their clientele. In September 1847 the Crown held the first of what were to be many grand balls. Dancing began at 9 p.m., single tickets were five shillings (25p.) and family tickets for five cost one pound. In the words of the *Gazette*, 'with his usual liberality', Mr Sharpin provided refreshments at no extra charge. Upwards of a hundred residents and guests attended. So great was its success that henceforth Sharpin made the ball a weekly event during the season and employed the Cliff Bridge band from the Spa to supply the music. In July 1848 the Crown opened a spacious billiard room.

Sharpin's handsome, leather-bound visitors' book contains the names of some of the most distinguished and affluent in the country. In 1848 the archbishop of York and the bishop of London graced the Crown with their presence. In subsequent years Sharpin's guest list included such names as H.O.Wills, the Bristol tobacco manufacturer, and millionaire millowners from Lancashire and the West Riding.

261

George Knowles had warned fellow Scarborians that the railway would bring only 'a greater influx of vagrants, and those who have no money to spend'. Mrs Reed, John Sharpin and the town's other high-class hoteliers were soon proving him entirely wrong. No doubt they, and Knowles, were pleased to note that the carriages conveyed by the first excursion from York to Scarborough were all 'first-class'. The strict class consciousness of the railway companies meant that their upper-class customers need not fear having to travel with the 'riff-raff'.

Sharpin's meteoric success was a product of the railway and astute commercial advertisement. Only six years after he took out the Crown lease he was elected to Scarborough Town Council, and in 1853, at the age of 31, he was chosen mayor of the borough, the youngest ever to hold that office. Three years later, he bought two houses in Huntriss Row, demolished them, and in their place built new Assembly Rooms.

Ever since the last of the Long Rooms had been absorbed by the Royal Hotel in 1840, Scarborough had lacked the traditional amenities of the eighteenth-century assembly rooms. Sharpin's new Assembly Rooms in Huntriss Row, opened in June 1857, were meant to fill the void and cater for an ever wider market. At ground level there was a well-equipped billiard room, a spacious concert and lecture hall above it, and a photographic gallery on the top floor which on the first night displayed a panorama of the Crimean War. The following year Charles Dickens gave two readings there from his famous works. Later, when Sharpin introduced a wine and spirit merchant's business on the premises, Edward, Prince of Wales, became his most valued and valuable customer. The royal coat of arms that once decorated the walls of the Assembly Rooms is now displayed in the Rotunda Museum.

By 1860 Scarborough had a dozen first-class hotels charging up to ten shillings (50p.) a day. In addition to the long-established places such as the Royal, Talbot, Bell, George, Castle and Bull, all situated in or near Newborough, there were now new ones on what twenty years earlier had been green-field sites – the Crown on the Esplanade, the Victoria on Falsgrave Walk, the Queen's on North Marine Road, the Albion on Castle Road, and the Princess Royal on Filey Road. To these had also been added boarding houses and hotels – such as the Albert on North Marine Road, Swift's Boarding House on Blenheim Terrace, and the Railway Hotel, Without the Bar – costing four or five shillings (20 or 25p.) a day for bed, breakfast, dinner and tea, and catering for the increasing number of commercial travellers and holiday-makers of comfortable means. Whereas the best hotels always advertised their high-class wines and spirits, there were also now Thornham's and the York Temperance Hotels, both Without the Bar, and Thomas Whittaker's Temperance Hotel in Newborough. For some Victorian visitors cheap liquor was not an extra inducement but more of a deterrent.

Paxton's Music Hall

The revival of Scarborough as a resort for well-to-do summer visitors encouraged the Cliff Bridge Company to invest in an enlargement of Wyatt's Gothic Saloon, the promenade that served it and the gardens on the cliff behind. In 1856 the Committee was instructed by the shareholders to engage Sir Joseph Paxton for the purpose.

Paxton was already well known in Scarborough as a visitor there, but better known more widely as designer of the pavilion of the Great Exhibition of 1851 which had lately become the Crystal Palace. As head gardener for the Duke of Devonshire at Chatsworth he was also well regarded as an architect of parks and gardens as well as the buildings associated with them.

Paxton's ambitious proposals were carried out promptly. The promenade was extended southwards and on it there arose a permanent, circular, covered bandstand and beyond that a three-storeyed observation tower. Between Wyatt's Saloon, which lost its towers but was kept as a refreshment room, and the bandstand appeared Paxton's new music hall, built of stone carried by sea from Staintondale. Finally, running northwards at the foot of the cliff, a carriage drive was constructed which allowed access to all the Spa buildings regardless of weather or tide. Altogether, these substantial improvements cost the Company about £30,000.

The money was well spent and proved a profitable investment. From July 1858 when Paxton's Hall opened until 1876 when it was destroyed by fire, the Company paid dividends averaging 7%, despite the considerable costs of repairing storm damage, particularly that of 1861. By 1871 annual revenue exceeded £10,000, the proceeds of more than 100,000 tickets. At the height of the season there were sometimes as many as 4,000 people at the Spa.

When the Committee, in response to constant complaint, was compelled to increase the number of water closets and lavatories and charge fourpence for gentlemen and twopence for ladies, the income more than covered the wages of attendants. However, since the ten water closets all discharged directly through the sea wall on to the sands used by bathers, the Committee was persuaded to convert them to earth closets.

Whether there was any confusion between supply to the Spa wells and outflow from the closets is not known, but the two wells were now sunk in the promenade below ground. That 'the bear-pit', as it was called, remained unaltered suggests that by this time there were very few drinkers. Visitors now came to the Spa for almost every kind of entertainment other than its mineral waters. Nevertheless, considering the relative decline in the social status of the Spa's customers, there were surprisingly few reported cases of misbehaviour there. In 1848 there were reports of 'disorderly assemblages on the bridge and walk after dusk, more especially on Sunday evenings'; in 1862 the two Misses Chambers were said to have conducted themselves in an 'unseemly' way; and in 1871 the police were called in to rid the area of prostitutes.

Terms of admission to the Spa betrayed a strong sense of class differentiation. Even the cheapest, a day ticket for a servant, cost sixpence (2½p.). Distinction was made between a weekly ticket for one person costing 2s. 6d, (12½p.) and the same for a servant which was a shilling cheaper (7½p.). Nurses attending children were counted as one of a family for which the charge was 10s. (50p.) for a week and £1 11s. 6d. (£1. 57½p.) for the season.

Market Hall and Eastborough

In April 2000 Scarborough Borough Council approved a proposal to permit a street market to trade on Thursdays in St Helen's Square. Whether councillors were aware that this decision was a total reversal of their predecessors' policy is doubtful: in 1852-3 Scarborough's Market Hall had been built for the deliberate purpose of taking market stalls off the town's streets for ever.

For many years past there had been repeated complaints from visitors and residents about the noise, odours and obstruction caused by the markets in Newborough. The cattle market that had once blocked lower Queen Street every week had been removed to Local Place on the edge of town, but on Thursdays Newborough's wide thoroughfare was lined on both sides with rows of stalls. Hotels fronting Newborough which accommodated 'respectable' family guests, such as the Bell, the George, London and New Inns, were now suffering from what was a medieval practice.

In a vain attempt to reduce congestion and answer criticism, in 1845 the Town Hall had introduced new regulations regarding street markets. Only poultry, butter and eggs were to be offered at the northern end of St Nicholas Street; St Thomas Street marketers were restricted to pottery and hardware, where previously they were allowed to sell pigs; the upper end of Newborough would have sales of baskets, ropes and books only; and the lower end, at the junction with Queen Street, would specialise in clothing, shoes and hats. Rate-paying stall holders trading in Newborough on days other than Thursday were required to pay sixpence (2½p.) a day and non-rate-payers a shilling (5p.)

Secondly, there was growing opposition, particularly from the public health authorities, to the site of the Old Shambles – to the slaughter-houses there, the herding of cattle, sheep and pigs down Newborough, and the manure they deposited en route. Consequently, in 1852, the Town Council endorsed the proposal of the newly-formed Public Market Hall Company to end both nuisances by building an indoor market on the same ground as the Old Shambles. Royal assent was given to a parliamentary bill to this effect in May 1852.

The borough surveyor, John Irvin, was employed to prepare the Company's plans for Scarborough's first indoor market. To make room for a building 50 metres long and 35 metres wide an extensive area occupied by butchers' shops, slaughterhouses and tallow and bone yards had to be entirely cleared. Not least of the casualties were several old public houses – the Elephant and Castle, the Wheatsheaf and Letters in Cross Street, the White Bear and Fountain in St Helen's Square, and the Stag and Hounds, once entered by a flight of steps over the entrance to the Old Shambles. The mayor, John Hesp, officially opened the finished Market Hall in August 1853. Altogether it had cost the Company £16,000, which included £9,000 for the site.

The Old Shambles had gone, but in an age without refrigeration Scarborough still needed fresh meat close to its shops and houses. Local butchers were now forbidden to kill animals on their premises so a new public abattoir had to be built for the town. Consequently, a new site was found on Wrea Lane, then on the perimeter of the built-up north side, though still far too close to the new residential terraces of William

Street. From now on cattle for slaughter were herded down the Common Lane, which was soon to be re-named Victoria Road.

The Scarborough Public Market Act of May 1854, replacing but confirming its predecessor of 1852, did not end all market trading in Newborough. On special occasions, Holy Thursday, the Thursdays before and after St Swithin's Day, and old Martinmas, the last coinciding with the annual hirings of farm servants, market stalls were still set up in Scarborough's main street. Not until 1896, when the Home Secretary was persuaded to issue an abolition order, were these annual fairs ended. Scarborough corporation then had to pay the Market Company £300 as compensation for its loss of tolls on market stalls.

However, the construction of a permanent indoor market and the closure of Newborough's weekly street markets gave the corporation an opportunity to create a new direct, wide thoroughfare linking the harbour with the upper town. The Act of 1854 allowed the Borough Council 'to divert or alter the course of the streets called Leading Post Street, St Sepulchre Street, Dumple Street, St Helen's Square and Cross Street'; to block up 'the thoroughfare called the Shambles and Bennett's Yard'; and 'to make a new thoroughfare between the Dumple and Cross Streets'. As a result, during the next two years, the upper end of Eastborough, a new name, was opened by widening Carr Street and extending it down the slope to join the lower end of Merchants Row. The narrow dog's leg of Leading Post Street was by-passed. Finally, the Act of 1854 also permitted the removal of three obstructions to street traffic: the middle water conduit at the junction of St Sepulchre Street, the Dumple and Leading Post Street and the public fountain and weighing house in St Helen's Square.

The loss of these medieval survivors and other old buildings, such as the Mariners' Tavern, were tolerable prices to pay for the only major change in Scarborough's ancient street layout that has ever occurred. Anyone aware of the narrow crookedness of Leading Post Street and upper Merchants Row must feel gratitude for the clearances and realignment of 1856.

Cemetery and Workhouse

In 1856, 12 acres of land on the northern outskirts of the borough called Chapman's Pasture were bought by the corporation from John Bell, owner of the Queen's Hotel, for £3,000. They were to be the site of Scarborough's first public cemetery.

During the past few years the town had been rapidly running out of burial space. The Anglicans had taken and used up all the available land surrounding St Mary's church; the Baptists had only a small plot at the western end of Longwestgate; the Wesleyans, an even smaller one in Queen Street; the Quakers were confined to the ground in front of their Meeting House in St Sepulchre Street; and the Catholics had no place of their own near the new chapel between Auborough Street and Tollergate. With a population of about 15,000 the borough's average number of annual deaths now exceeded 320, and as yet all corpses were interred and none cremated.

However, as with so many other controversial issues of the time, religious differences obstructed practical solutions. As elsewhere, Scarborough had no non-denominational cemetery because historically burials were a religious responsibility, not a civic duty, and some Anglicans resented and resisted the loss of their long-standing monopoly. Nevertheless, despite pulpit claims and wishful beliefs, the English were not even predominantly Christian, and now only a minority of them were practising Anglicans. The census taken on Sunday 31 March 1851 revealed that of a total population of nearly 18 million only seven million had attended any place of worship on that day. Moreover, though the parish of Scarborough was particularly well provided with Anglican places at St Mary's, Christ Church and St Thomas's, those occupying them were outnumbered by the town's Catholics and Dissenters.

Nevertheless, the Reverend John William Whiteside, vicar of St Mary's since 1848, was determined that his Anglican dead should be awarded separate and privileged ground in Scarborough's new public cemetery. He insisted on his own mortuary chapel, exclusively for members of the Church of England, and a wall or iron railings to distinguish them from the Dissenter dead. In the end a compromise was reached: the Anglicans would have the eastern half and the rest the other western half, but there would be no railings of demarcation. Despite the objections of Dr Whiteside, the Anglican and non-Anglican mortuary chapels built in the centre of the burial ground on each side of the main entrance avenue were connected by an archway supporting a bell tower and spire. The same bell rang for both chapels. Ten of the 12 acres were enclosed by one continuous brick wall surmounted by coping stones and railings. However, whereas the Anglican dead on the east side were given a three-metre perimeter wall, the others on the west had to be content with one less than half that height. Francis Place, publican of the Ship Inn at Falsgrave, was the first to be interred in the new cemetery in May 1857. If he had any religious beliefs they are not recorded.

Readers who know Dean Road cemetery as it is today might be interested to read Theakston's comment on it in his *Guide* of 1858: 'it may be visited with pleasure; its neatly-kept walks and well-trimmed beds, the beauty of its situation, and the extent of view around, rendering it an additional adornment to the town and neighbourhood'. Any reader who doubts that the past is a foreign country should visit Dean Road cemetery now.

The Ordnance Survey map of Scarborough in 1852 offers some indication of the location and extent of the Union Workhouse at that time. Hemmed in between North Street, Waterhouse Lane and St Thomas Street, and deprived of some of its limited garden space by the construction of William Smith's covered reservoir, Scarborough's workhouse was clearly inadequate and unsatisfactory. Though built more than a century previously it was still serving a far greater area and a far greater number of inmates than originally intended or expected. The only separation made was between men and women, otherwise the aged, infants, sane, insane, innocent, criminal, unemployed and idle were all housed together.

Consequently, Scarborough's elected Board of Guardians advertised for architects to come forward with plans for a modern building and in July 1858 they accepted the designs of George and Henry Styan of York. The site chosen for the new workhouse was north of the town on the west side of Wrea Lane in what was then open country. Later that year the Board agreed to a builder's tender of just over £5,000.

By December 1859 the buildings were finished. The aged paupers were provided with the convenience of a horse-drawn omnibus 'furnished by Mr Reed of the Bull Hotel' to convey then to their new home. The rest of the inmates, orphan children, physically handicapped and mentally deranged, had to walk there.

By mid-Victorian standards Scarborough's new workhouse was a model: it had gas lighting, plentiful water, effective drainage and good ventilation. The infirm, able-bodied, sick and young were all separately accommodated. On rising ground parallel to Wrea Lane - or Dean Street as it was now usually called - there were three blocks of buildings. The first block had offices and the Board room; the second contained living quarters for the able-bodied; and the third, on the highest ground, housed the infirmary and sanatorium for infectious cases. The children had a school room. Vagrants were segregated from the others in their own ward.

Workhouse numbers varied and depended on economic circumstances, but the trend was inexorably upwards. The 92 inmates, 44 male and 48 female, of 1861 had become 140 by 1874 and up to 250 by the end of the century. Even so the numbers receiving 'outdoor relief', usually in the form of free coal, clothing, blankets and cash, also continued to rise. During hard times of high unemployment and bad weather, such as the late 1870s, those deserving outdoor relief exceeded a thousand, costing rate-payers up to £100 a year.

Borough Gaol

What had once been Wrea Lane, then Dean Street, was lengthened and changed to Cemetery Road, and finally became Dean Road, already had a workhouse at one end and a burial ground at the other when in 1866 it acquired a prison between them. Is there any other street that once accommodated the destitute, the criminal and dead all at the same time?

Significantly, the borough's police force had been almost doubled in strength in 1866. Where previously a chief constable, two sergeants and 17 constables had kept law and order, the force was then raised to 27 constables, three sergeants and a superintendent. The chief constable's annual pay of £60 became the superintendent's salary of £120 per annum. The average constable's wages were a pound a week. Since about 2,000 arrests were made by the borough police in 1865, no one could claim that they were overpaid or underemployed.

Though little more than 20 years old, the borough gaol on Castle Road was clearly inadequate to house Scarborough's growing number of thieves, vagrants, prostitutes and habitual inebriates. Just as the Board of Guardians had determined that the borough should have the best workhouse, so now the Borough Council decided to have a model prison. Designed by versatile architect William Baldwin Stewart and the borough surveyor, Alexander Taylor, the Dean Road gaol cost £8,755 and was opened for inmates in October 1866.

Because it became a Council depot as early as 1899 and has remained so ever since, Scarborough's former prison has survived into the twenty-first century remarkably unchanged: a hybrid of Victorian folly and medieval anachronism. The entrance still consists of two round-fronted crenellated towers on either side of a machicolated gateway. Here there are loopholes for non-existent archers and chains for an imaginary drawbridge. The governor's lodgings were in the north-side gateway tower. The whole site was enclosed by a battlemented brick wall nearly five metres high with interval towers.

The central prison block had 36 cells for male prisoners, all four metres long and two metres wide, and other accommodation for 12 women and four debtors or juveniles. On the ground floor were offices for the governor, chief warden and porter and waiting rooms; on the first floor there was a chapel, infirmary and surgery; and in the basement there were coal cellar, kitchen, clothing store, fumigating closet, 'itch cell' and windowless punishment cells. Outside this main building there were exercise yard, wash-house, stone breakers' shed, blacksmith's shop and stables.

However, as a prison Dean Road gaol had an unpromising start and short life. Its first inmate was a horsebreaker called William or Walter Scott, who was on remand waiting to stand trial on a charge of robbery. He soon discovered that the ventilation grille in his cell was insecurely attached to the wall and after passing through the hole he let himself down the outside wall of the block on a rope made of blankets. Once outside the prison block he found an old bedstead and clothes prop and used them to climb over the perimeter wall. Before its mortar had dried out Scarborough's new gaol had failed to fulfil its principal purpose.

Scott's escape was not the reason why Scarborough's municipal prison lasted only 12 years. In 1878 Disraeli's Conservative government passed an act which effectively nationalised the prison service. Local authority gaols like Scarborough's, however new and well managed, were all closed down. Other prisons were brought under the direct control of the Home Office in London, which imposed a uniform system throughout the whole country. Henceforth, Scarborough had only police cells for temporary accommodation; sentenced prisoners were dispatched to Northallerton or York.

15

MID-VICTORIAN HEYDAY

Valley Bridge

According to one contemporary local source, not usually given to exaggeration, on 1 July 1865 Scarborough witnessed 'the greatest processional demonstration' in its history: it was the day when Ramsdale bridge was first opened.

Though the private Valley Bridge Company, not the corporation, was responsible for this new public crossing of the town's old natural frontier, it was generally recognised as an event of the utmost importance in the history of the borough. The mayor, Ambrose Gibson, had authorised the procession and other celebrations of the inauguration, and all the town's bodies – the schools, friendly societies, churches and chapels, Volunteer soldiers, coast-guard, Royal Naval Reserve – as well as members of the corporation turned out in full force and panoply to parade from the town hall to the Westwood end of the bridge.

As early as 1849, Robert Williamson, manager of the York City and County Bank and Scarborough borough treasurer, had won permission from the borough council to build a carriage bridge across Ramsdale ravine that would connect the upper town and railway station with South Cliff. However, by 1854, when the five-year permit expired, the bridge was still no more than a paper plan. None the less, Williamson refused to drop the project and in 1861 seized a new opportunity. In September of that year an accident occurred at York that appeared to solve Williamson's problem. The North-Eastern Railway Company was then constructing a new road bridge over the river Ouse to link the railway station with the city centre. When one of the 300-ton iron girders slipped from its supports it knocked three more of the same into the river. Two workers were crushed to death, three others drowned. Williamson had the four girders rescued from the river bed and transported to Scarborough.

Even so there were still many obstacles and objections to a Ramsdale road bridge. The corporation would have preferred to build and own the bridge but eventually the costs were considered prohibitive: it had already borrowed heavily to pay for the new gaol. Also, the position of the proposed bridge raised some resistance and much heated argument since Williamson wanted it to cross the valley through and over the Plantation which would cause the loss of many trees and shrubs. Finally, there were those townsmen, like Sharpin, who opposed the bridge on principle because they feared it would carry hordes of excursionists from the railway station to the elitist environs of South Cliff.

In the end compromises were reached in the Scarborough Valley Bridge Company Act which received the royal assent in June 1864. There was a provision in the Act that, with the consent of at least sixty per cent of the shareholders, the Company could sell the bridge to the corporation, which would then be permitted to levy rates and borrow for its purchase and charge tolls for its maintenance. The Act also required the Company to align the approaches to the bridge from Westborough to Ramsdale Road so that no damage was done to 'the trees and public promenade called The Plantation'. Thirdly, the Act specified a tariff of tolls: sixpence (2½p.) for a horse-drawn omnibus carrying more than eight passengers; threepence (1p.) for any horse-drawn vehicle; fivepence (2p.) for every score of pigs, sheep or lambs; half a penny (0.2p.) for every head of cattle; and half a penny for every pedestrian. If there had been any danger of *hoi polloi* invading exclusive South Cliff, the half-penny toll would be sufficient to encourage them to head straight towards the foreshore sands and amusements. Even Sharpin was now reconciled to the bridge.

The Valley Bridge Company and Valley bridge proved to be a profitable success. Robert Williamson, first chairman of the Company, died before the bridge was opened, but other local subscribers such as Robert Tindall, Henry Fowler, William Rowntree, Edward S. Donner and J.J.P. Moody, the town clerk, pressed the work to completion. Altogether the bridge cost £28,163 but in 1891 the corporation bought both the Company's assets and the bridge for £36,000. Also in accordance with the terms of the Act of 1864, once the corporation had cleared all its debts and dues on the bridge, in 1919 it was made toll-free.

Grand Hotel

Two years after the Lord Mayor of London was invited to open Valley bridge his successor returned to the town, again with his state coaches, horses and servants, this time to preside over the opening of Scarborough's Grand Hotel.

Like Valley bridge, the Grand Hotel was the product of private, not civic, enterprise, and an illustration of the dynamism, optimism and engineering skill of its designers and builders. In 1862 the Scarborough Cliff Hotel Company bought the most valuable and desirable cliff-top site in the town: it paid £30,000 for just over three acres on the east side of St Nicholas Cliff. Cuthbert Brodrick (1822-1905), the architect, was already well-known and admired for his Town Hall and Corn Exchange buildings at Leeds, but at Scarborough he was faced with a formidable task. Once he had demolished Mrs Cockcroft's terrace of boarding houses he was left with an extremely awkward site – an elongated triangle on the precarious edge of a crumbling cliff. Brodrick's solution was so ambitious and expensive that by 1865, with the hotel only half finished, the Cliff Company ran out of money and credit and was liquidated. Though £100,000 had already been invested, Archibald Neil, a Leeds business man, and his Grand Hotel Company bought all the assets for a mere £43,000 and completed Brodrick's design.

Whether the ornate and heavy Grand Hotel *[plate 7]* is the most handsome building of its kind remains a matter of taste, but that it was the largest and most advanced in Europe in 1867 is indisputable. Using six and a quarter million bricks made at Malton's works, where Malvern Crescent now stands, Brodrick had constructed a V-shaped calendar colossus. The Grand Hotel had four domed towers representing the seasons, 12 floors on the seaward side for the months of the year, 52 chimneys for the weeks and 365 bedrooms for the days. Because it was built on the edge of and into the cliff slope the seaward side rose to 160 feet whereas that facing St Nicholas gardens was only 112 feet high.

Interior furnishings and fittings were as lavish and luxurious as the exterior sculptured stone and brickwork. There were 30 lounges and public rooms and 11 miles of carpeting on corridors and staircases. Each private room had four kinds of water supplied – hot and cold, fresh and salt. A miniature railway ran through a tunnel underneath the building to carry laundry to a boiler house on the sea front below. What was then described as 'the hydraulic ascending room' was probably the first hotel lift in the north. As a guarantee of the highest quality of service and cuisine, the Grand's first manager was Augustus Fricour, formerly of the Hotel Mirabeau in Paris.

The Grand Hotel represented Scarborough's heroic but ultimately vain attempt to remain an exclusive resort for the well-favoured visitor. Full board, which included admission to the hotel's quadrille dances, cost £3 10s. (£3. 50p.) a week. Evening diners were charged a minimum of six shillings (30p.) a head, and according to house rules 'ladies will not wear bonnets [and] gentlemen will wear dress or frock coats'. Even Winn's Crown Hotel charged only eleven shillings (55p.) a day for full board in private rooms with servant attendance; and the town's cheaper but best hotels – the Queen, Royal, George, Bull, Talbot, Bell, Blanchard's, York and Railway – were then offering dinners at a third of the Grand's prices and daily terms for less than five shillings (25p.).

North Bay Rock Gardens and Pier

Apart from the tall houses along Blenheim Terrace overlooking North Cliff and the new lodging houses running on either side of what had now become North Marine Road, by 1860 little had been done to extend Scarborough into North Bay. Theakston's *Guides* of the 1850s offered the visitor nothing more than a scenic walk through Barrowcliff Plantation. Like most of the north side of the borough this wooded ravine, also known as Wilson's Wood and now as The Glen, belonged to John Woodall, but he was pleased to permit the public access to the footpaths to and through it. Starting from the Whitby Road, either at Peasholm House or opposite the Queen Hotel, the visitor was invited to tread the path which ultimately became Peasholm Drive and then Manor Road until he returned to Scarborough by way of Falsgrave. On the land between Scalby Road to the west, Peasholm beck to the north, North Marine Road to the east and southwards to Trafalgar Street in 1860 there was not a single dwelling house; and most of that ground, more than a thousand acres, belonged to John Woodall.

The public grounds known as the Rock Gardens were the earliest attempt to exploit the tourist potential of the North Cliff. They extended down the steep cliff side from Blenheim Terrace Road above to the sea shore of North Bay below, ten acres in all with a sea frontage of about a quarter of a mile. Further north, what was later to become Queen's Parade, was then no more than a dirt track called Peasholm Lane.

After entering the gardens opposite Rutland Terrace by way of a domed Moorish temple, the visitor descended a covered stairway winding down the cliff to a wooden assembly hall. Said to be capable of holding 3,000 people, the hall was described as a 'covered musical promenade' where concerts, plays, balls and even circuses were held and performed throughout the whole year.

In fact the Rock Gardens were a commercial fiasco: they closed down in less than two years. Whatever their other defects, they were in the wrong place on a precipitous and unstable cliff too distant from most of the town's hotels and lodging houses. Josiah Forster Fairbank, the local engineer, who had promoted the Rock Gardens, persuaded the Town Hall that the only solution was a bay-to-bay tunnel excavated under and through Castle Hill. Permission to dig out such an underground tunnel approximately 600 metres long was first given by the council in 1865 and renewed in 1870, the second time with the addition of tramlines. However, though Fairbank continued to press his project and received the council's support as late as 1894, nothing came of it; and long before then what was left of the Rock Gardens had crumbled away and slipped into the North Sea.

Despite this early setback, the North Bay was the location of Scarborough's first and only experiment with a pleasure pier. Originally, maritime piers served entirely practical purposes: they afforded protection to vessels in search of sheltered anchorage, and they provided safe loading and unloading places regardless of weather and tide. By Victorian times Scarborough had three harbour piers all serving these functions, but none of them were of much interest to visitors. The harbour was for fishermen, shipbuilders and merchant seamen, not for holiday-makers. However, during the 1860s, a new kind of sea pier came into existence. Blackpool's North Pier opened in 1863 and Brighton's West Pier three years later. Both were no more than platforms or promenades for the recreation and amusement of pleasure-seeking visitors. Carrying dance halls, concert rooms and eventually machine arcades, the seaside pier gave the illusion of being at sea without actually leaving *terra firma*.

North Bay 1897   [Frith Collection]

Scarborough's North Bay pier, built between 1866 and 1869, was a modest, minimal construction: initially it cost its shareholders only £6,000, half the cost of Blackpool's and a fifth of Brighton's. Nevertheless, since at least half the capital investment for it came from local hoteliers, landowners and professional men, the North Bay pier illustrates how far Scarborough was changing from a spa town into a popular seaside resort. Unfortunately, the pier suffered from the same handicaps as the Rock Gardens – isolation and inaccessibility. Its original owners soon went bankrupt and it was eventually sold at auction for the knock-down price of £1,240.

Prospects for the pier were greatly revived in 1886 when the borough council bought the whole of the undercliff between the Castle Holms and Peasholm beck, previously known as Tintinholms. The area was drained, stabilised, landscaped and laid out in gardens with footpaths, shelters and a bandstand. At the same time a carriage road was built between the undercliff and the sea linking Peasholm Gap with the entrance to the pier. In 1890, the eldest son of the Prince of Wales, Albert, Duke of Clarence, formally opened the Royal Albert Drive and the Clarence Gardens; and at the same time the Scarborough Promenade Pier Company began an expensive improvement of their new acquisition. Promenading was no longer sufficient to attract paying customers and all existing seaside piers had to be enriched with pavilions, concert rooms and other places of entertainment.

276

Accordingly, the Company spent £10,000 redecking the walkway, installing electric lights, providing 'automatic machines' and building a row of shops at the landward entrance and a pavilion at the seaward end.

The North Bay pier enjoyed something of a revival during the 1890s and might have survived much longer had not a violent storm swept it away in January 1905, little more than three years before the Marine Drive finally connected the two bays. Both the Rock Gardens and the pier were premature: they preceded the development of the North side of Scarborough when they should have been part of it. In another way also they were defeated by an excess of Victorian optimism: neither were well enough designed and constructed to withstand the powerful forces of nature – the erosion of boulder-clay cliffs and the raging violence of the North Sea.

Bathing and Baths

Throughout most of the eighteenth and well into the nineteenth century sea-bathing at Scarborough was conducted in much the same manner. Men, women and children mixed together at the southern end of South Bay on the sands and in the sea near the Spa. Most of them undressed and dressed in bathing machines and many men bathed in the nude. If there were any complaints before the 1840s about men exposing their nakedness in public they are not recorded.

However, Victorian sensitivity was soon scandalised by what could be seen in South Bay Scarborough between June and October. In September 1847 an anonymous correspondent of the *Gazette* criticised the arrangements made for bathing which he wrote were 'in defiance of decency and ill-calculated to keep up the character of a place so long celebrated for refinement'. He suggested that male and female bathers should be separated by Millbeck, men to the north, women to the south. In response to this and other complaints, the following summer the town council ordered that gentlemen should be prohibited from bathing south of Millbeck and that Walshaw's machines on this stretch of the beach would be reserved for women and children only.

This compromise suited no one. John Walshaw protested that he would lose all his male customers; Morrison and Richardson, his principal rivals, continued to offer their green and red top machines to both male and female, 'opposite the old Terrace Cliff, the safe part of

277

the beach'; and those who objected to mixed naked bathing anywhere had been ignored.

During the 1850s the complaints increased in number and strength. The self-described 'father of a large family of girls, from 10 to 18' deplored this 'crying evil', whereby 'every physical attribute' of gentlemen was 'unblushingly exhibited' and 'perfectly distinguishable from the windows of houses, the promenade, and the beach', as not only 'indelicate but indecent'. Gentlemen who insisted on bathing without any clothing should be exiled to a length of the shore which was clearly marked and 'beyond the Saloon to the south'. Scarborough was the only place, he continued, where naked bathing was permitted during daylight hours; at Brighton, only after sunset did 'swarms of evil-stained mechanics' make their way to the sea when 'their dusty frames' were 'not distinguishable from the promenades'.

With some reluctance the Town Hall passed its first Indecent Bathing bye-law in 1861. All bathers were now required to change in machines and no one above the age of 12 was permitted to bathe on any beach in the nude. Nevertheless, the bye-law was still frequently broken by gentlemen who followed the traditional mode practised and recommended by Dr Wittie and plebeian excursionists who did not possess or bring swimming drawers. A second, stronger bye-law was passed by the council in 1867. Bathing machine proprietors were now made responsible for ensuring that all bathers were decently covered during the daytime and ordered to hire out drawers to all men who did not have their own.

Naturally, Walshaw, Morrison, Richardson, Crosby and the other machine owners were indignant that the council had ducked its responsibilities and made them into beach policemen. As Walshaw asked mayor Robert Champley in the council chamber: 'How do we force men – particularly upper-class ones – into bathing drawers against their wills?' To such a question there could be no satisfactory answer.

As a result, the town hall found it necessary to impose more stringent bye-laws in 1882 and 1892. The last threatened naked bathers over the age of 12 with a fine of two pounds; decreed that no bathing should take place between 8pm and 8am; ordered men's and women's bathing machines to be segregated and male and female bathers to keep at least 25 yards apart! For the first time the council also laid down maximum charges for the use of bathing machines – sixpence (2½p.) for adults for half an hour and fourpence (2p.) for children. However, such were the impracticalities of enforcement and the persistence of long-standing tradition – not to mention natural instinct – that photographic evidence provides proof that at least until 1914 some defiant men continued to undress on the open beach and swim in the nude.

Indoor bathing had for long been the exclusive privilege of the upper class visitor to Scarborough; but the decline of the expensive, even luxurious establishments and the appearance of new public baths on the foreshore indicated the social changes that were taking place in the town's clientele. By the 1860s Dr Harland's baths in Vernon Place had become the Sanatorium. Its proprietor, Dr Craig, was clearly more concerned with the medical value than the sybaritic pleasures of bathing. Champley's baths had gone and so had Weddell's overlooking the harbour. Even McBean's baths on the Marine Promenade were now advertised as making 'very reasonable charges'.

For the season of 1859 new public baths opened on the foreshore at the foot of Bland's Cliff: they were altogether different from their predecessors. Instead of a classical and restrained exterior, these new baths were built 'in the Saracenic style of architecture' with 'a lofty Mooresque water tower and dome' and 'a minaretted chimney shaft'. In other words, these indoor public baths were the first of the vulgar and colourful buildings that eventually would decorate the whole length of the south foreshore. Inside, 'a tidal swimming bath' drew its tepid water directly piped from the sea. There were 'dressing boxes' for at least 50 bathers, a ladies' plunge bath, and hot and cold showers.

Two years later, the Royal Northern Sea-Bathing Infirmary opened its doors only yards away from the public baths. In both appearance and purpose the contrast between them could hardly have been greater. The public baths were run by a private company for profit; the Infirmary was a charity hospital financed by voluntary subscription for the relief of the afflicted poor who were expected to benefit from sea-bathing and sea air. With their red and white brick arches and 'Moorish' roof the public baths were deliberately garish and extravagant, whereas the Infirmary was designed by the eminent architect W.B. Stewart in a most dignified and handsome style.

The Sea-Bathing Infirmary, which was later renamed St Thomas's Hospital, accommodated up to 52 male and female patients and possessed what was then every modern amenity. The upper part of the south-facing windows were fitted with perforated zinc so that incoming sea air was 'diffused uniformly', not experienced as a draught.

Aquarium and Foreshore Road

If Scarborough's Grand Hotel was bigger and better than any yet built in Britain's seaside resorts, ten years later when it opened in 1877, Scarborough's 'magnificent marine temple' was the greatest in size and scope of any existing aquarium in the world.

Like so many of the town's major improvements at this time the aquarium was the creation of private enterprise and profit-seeking. The Marine Aquarium Company, with initial capital of £37,500, was registered in June 1874 and thirteen months later the Scarborough Marine Aquarium Act received the royal assent. McMillan, architect of the Brighton aquarium which opened in 1872, was employed at Scarborough to design a superior model. On a two and a half acre site underneath the Cliff footbridge, where formerly there had been horse and carriage stables and sheds, the Company invested the colossal sum of £110,000 in a gigantic underground labyrinth. From start to official opening on Whit Monday 1877 the work took three years.

The ambitious intentions and nervous concerns of the Marine Aquarium Company were already evident in the introductory terms of the authorisation Act of 1872:

> Whereas during the summer season large numbers of excursionists visit Scarborough from the manufacturing districts and other places, and the Aquarium may at times be greatly crowded, and from the nature of the property, and its liability to damage by mischievous or ill-disposed persons, it is expedient that special provision should be made and bye-laws provided for the protection of the Aquarium ...

In short, the riff-raff would be excluded by high entrance charges and the ill-behaved deterred by punitive fines. No dogs were allowed; smoking was strictly forbidden; drunkenness would not be tolerated; acts of vandalism would be heavily penalised; and anyone who failed to report or hand in lost property might incur a fine of up to five pounds. When residents were allowed a preview in the week before Whit Monday the entrance charge was a shilling.

There was a vogue for aquaria in the 1870s, but nothing like Scarborough's subterranean promenade could be found anywhere else.

In 1876 Queen Victoria had been delighted to accept from her favourite prime minister, Disraeli, the title of Empress of India, and McMillan had followed the contemporary fashion by decorating the interior in a series of Indian architectural styles imitating mosques, Hindu temples and rajahs' palaces. After passing down a wide staircase and through a sumptuous court, the visitor came to a vast dining room richly decorated with colourful, patterned tiles and supported by iron pillars. Beyond this was a reading room provided with books, newspapers and magazines and further still two corridors, one to the right with a row of freshwater tanks, the other to the left with sea-water tanks. Further still there was a seal pond and water cascade and finally the largest tank in the world holding 75,000 gallons of water. In the words of an advertisement: ' ... caves and grottoes abound ... A hospital is provided with tanks for the reception of fish and for their treatment when sick.' The Company claimed that their aquarium could accommodate up to 5,000 visitors at any one time.

Scarborough's Aquarium was a financial failure. After the disastrous summer of 1879 when the wet, cold weather ruined seaside holidays as well as farmers' crops, the Company never recovered; by 1881 it was effectively bankrupt. Though the borough council excused it from rates for a whole year, sales of entrance tickets were inadequate to cover even the Company's interest debts. The Spa company would not pay even £17,000 for it. Eventually in 1886 it was bought by William Morgan, manager of Blackpool's Winter Gardens, and his associates for a mere £4,500.

By that time radical changes had been made to save the Aquarium by bringing it down market. Captain Webb, the Channel swimmer, spent 60 (or 74, depending on the source) hours in the big tank and then amazed onlookers when he climbed out without assistance. Other smaller water tanks had been converted into shops and stalls. There was soon a Japanese theatre, alligator pond, aviary, tea and monkey houses. To these alterations to the interior were added new popular attractions such as performing acrobats, cyclists, and free phrenology lessons and head examinations. Mme Leva, 'the Electric Lady', would oblige you with a shock if you dared to touch her; and the 'Clock-Eyed Lady' had eyes that registered the time of day. The People's Palace and Aquarium, as it was now appropriately renamed, opened daily from 9am to 11pm during the season for an admission charge of sixpence (2½p.). In 1893 the Aquarium acquired a summer swimming pool; in 1907, another theatre; in 1909, a skating rink; and finally, in 1913, a menagerie with tigers and lions. It had become Scarborough's subterranean equivalent of Blackpool's Tower.

The history of Scarborough's Aquarium from 1877 until the outbreak of war in 1914 is a miniature mirror of the history of nearly all seaside holiday places during these years. Mid-Victorian, middle-class preoccupation with serious self-improvement offered little commercial return; like Blackpool's Winter Gardens, Scarborough's Aquarium had to diversify and descend the social ladder in order to survive. What began as an educational institution to promote the study of marine biology, zoology and geology was soon replaced by a fun palace, a place of cheap entertainment. Secondly, the location of the Aquarium made certain its initial failure. By 1880 most of the summer visitors to the south foreshore were working-class day trippers who had neither the money for nor the interest in a subterranean promenade built in an exotic style which did not have even a liquor licence.

By building the Foreshore Road in 1877 to coincide with the inauguration of the Aquarium the borough council had acknowledged that this area, once lined with raft yards, sail lofts and shipping storehouses, was now to be given over entirely to recreation and amusement. However, though the road made the Aquarium more accessible from the lower town, this only made its fate more certain. The affluent and educated visitors for whom the original Aquarium was designed preferred to confine themselves to the Spa, South Cliff and the quieter sands of North Bay. As a long-established corporation with uncontested ownership of the foreshore, Scarborough's municipal rulers could regulate and censor activities there which otherwise would have been swamped by hawkers, entertainers, stalls and bathing machines, not to mention pierrots, 'nigger minstrels' and donkeys; but they could not persuade the ever-increasing number of plebeian trippers to educate themselves on bank holidays.

Verity's Grand Hall

During its long and eventful history the Spa had survived a series of natural disasters ranging from a landslide that buried it to violent sea storms which threatened to sweep it away. Then, within three hours, in the late evening of 8 September 1876, the Spa suffered yet another, this time man-made catastrophe: Paxton's Music Hall, still less than 20 years old, was reduced by fire to a gutted wreck.

In many ways the fire marked another dividing line in the story of the Spa. Even though these were times of national depression, during the three years before it, the Spa's annual receipts had averaged £11,500 and dividends were as high as four shillings (20p.) on a £3 share; but in subsequent years, even after rebuilding, enlargement and improvement, the Spa company was never able to reach this level of profit.

In 1874 the Spa's receipts and accessibility had been improved by the opening of the South Cliff tramway; within two years it was carrying 3,500 passengers a day at the height of the summer season. This cliff lift – probably the first of its kind in the world and the earliest of three to be built at Scarborough – was operated by pumping water into tanks beneath the two cars as they moved in opposite directions.

The rapid development of the South Cliff, particularly after the completion of the Valley bridge in 1865, was another important reason for the Spa's profitable success during these mid-Victorian years. In 1871 the Spa Company had extended its ground control and 'secured its southern flank' by buying the undercliff 'below the Prince of Wales Crescent' between what was soon to be the South Cliff 'incline carriage-way' and later still the Rose and Italian gardens. However, the Company did little with its additional property: its chief aim had been to close down a beerhouse on the site whose presence so close to the Spa grounds offended the temperance susceptibilities of its shareholders.

Another asset enjoyed by the Spa in particular and Scarborough as a resort in general was the patronage of Edward, Prince of Wales. He visited the town in 1869, 1870 and 1871. Though he came to Londesborough Lodge as the personal guest of the Earl and Countess in the late autumn and his principal purpose was to massacre game birds on the Earl's extensive inland estate, the Prince did attend two evening entertainments at the Spa in 1869 and 1871 and on the second occasion brought his wife, Princess Alexandra. Such was the prestige of the royal couple and the sycophancy of the age that the artist, Thomas Jones Barker, and Oliver Sarony, the local photographer, conspired to produce what the historian of the Spa called 'this gigantic fraud' – a portrait of Edward surrounded by his admiring Scarborough subjects on the Spa promenade. Sarony sold 'places' and 'faces' on the picture for as much as 100 guineas.

After the Prince of Wales caught typhoid from Londesborough Lodge's notorious water supply and very nearly died of it, he never returned to Scarborough. Nevertheless, the royal connection was re-established and remained a long-term benefit to the town's reputation. That Edward had contracted the fever there was strongly denied by Scarborians, particularly since his father, Prince Albert, had died of the same disease just ten years earlier and his death had been attributed to the foul drains of Windsor Castle. On the other hand, Lord Chesterfield, a fellow guest at Londesborough Lodge at the end of October 1871, was also infected and died of typhoid fever a month later, so there seems little doubt about the source of the Prince's near fatal illness. As a result, though Queen Victoria and her family were highly regarded and frequently commemorated by Scarborians, she was careful never to set foot in the town that had so nearly 'killed' her eldest son.

How to rebuild the Spa after the disastrous fire of September 1876 was a bitterly contested issue that broke the unity of the committee of the Company. The two most senior members resigned. Edward Hopper Hebden, senior bailiff in 1826-7 when the Cliff Bridge was opened and first chairman of the new Company, had served on the committee for almost 50 years. John Woodall, his banking partner, and Scarborough's richest, property-owning resident, had been another original member of the committee and the Company's first treasurer. Together they owned nearly a tenth of the Company's 20,000 shares. Their joint resignation marked the end of the first phase in the history of the Company.

In simple terms, the argument was between those who wanted a cheaper option of restoring Paxton's hall and those who argued that an entirely new and larger building was required. Finally, after several months of ill-tempered in-fighting, the radical party won: the eastern facade of Paxton's hall was to remain but a much grander building set further back into the cliff would replace it. From 26 plans submitted, the Company awarded the commission to the London architects, Verity and Hunt.

The extreme winter of 1878-9 and the problems caused by cutting deeply into the undercliff delayed the building work. None the less, Thomas Verity's Grand Hall was finished by August 1879 and the formal opening took place the following summer. No member of the royal family could be persuaded to attend and the Spa committee had to make do with the Lord Mayor of London and the mayors of Yorkshire's boroughs.   For the opening ceremonies no expense was stinted: London's Lord Mayor was the guest of the Woodall's at St Nicholas House, but the Company paid out £750, most of it to the Royal Hotel which accommodated its invited visitors for four days at the rate of a guinea a day and eight shillings (40p.) for their servants.   Since the Company had already spent more than £70,000 on the building work of the past two years such expenditure was considered only modest and fitting.

Until 1880 anyone using the Spa footbridge as a way to the Esplanade and South Cliff was obliged to buy a Spa ticket.   However, two years earlier it was decided to widen the bridge and fence off a footway for pedestrians who were subsequently charged half a penny for the crossing.   The small cost of widening and fencing soon proved the wisest of investments.   During the first full year, the toll collector, who was paid a pound a week in wages, received £572 17s.1d. from over a quarter of a million users.

Yet if more visitors wanted to walk to and from South Cliff, fewer now came to the Spa.   The Company was never able to recover the profits of the pre-fire years.   During the 1880s dividends gradually fell.   Nearly half the cost of Verity's Grand Hall had been borrowed and gate receipts were insufficient to pay off the Company's swollen debts. In 1886 the £1 season ticket was reduced to 16 shillings (80p.) and the cost of day tickets halved from six to threepence, but to no avail. Receipts continued to fall.   At the popular end of the market the Spa could not compete with the Aquarium and the south foreshore.   The days when the Spa was Scarborough and Scarborough was the Spa had gone forever.

More Churches and Chapels

Between 1850 and 1870, and particularly during the 1860s, Scarborough acquired many of its largest and finest church buildings, though several of these were to be demolished a century later.

After radical evacuation, renovation and enlargement, St Mary's parish church was reopened for services by the archbishop of York in July 1850.   No attempt was made to restore the lost western towers or any parts of the lost chancel and north transept, but the architect, Ewan Christian, increased the ground floor area by re-building the St Nicholas aisle on the north side of the nave.   The most dramatic

285

change was made to the interior: all the galleries that H.B. Carter had shown so well in his paintings of 1848 were cleared out; and the boys of the grammar school were at last expelled and Farrer's Aisle restored to its original use. Whereas previously St Mary's had sittings for about 1,100, few of them free and mostly in box pews, after the clearances there were places for nearly 1,500, 246 of them free.

The total cost of the restoration came to about £7,000, most of it raised by personal subscription. At the head of the list was John Woodall, who gave £500, and his name was followed by those of the local county aristocracy and squirearchy – Hotham, Denison, Feversham, Langley and Johnstone – who each donated three figure sums. In his inauguration sermon, the archbishop warned the congregation of the manifest signs of relapse from the doctrines and practices of the Church of England, particularly those 'tending towards the abominations of papal Rome'.

No doubt the archbishop would not have been pleased if he had lived to witness the laying of the foundation stone of St Peter's Roman Catholic church in October 1856 only a short distance down the hill from St Mary's. Two years later, 'the abominations of papal Rome' were being openly declared there in the presence of Scarborough's growing Catholic community, most of it of Irish origin.

Even before Valley Bridge was built, the summer community on South Cliff had provided themselves with an Anglican church to suit their affluence and fashionable taste. St Martin's (1861-2) was one of the earliest yet finest works of the distinguished architect, George Frederick Bodley (1827-1907): dark, heavy and grand on the outside, cavernous but richly decorated and furnished internally. Bodley was responsible for St Martin's exquisite stained glass windows. St Martin's was far bigger than then, or perhaps ever, required: in 1862 it had free seating capacity for 1,500, yet even twenty years later the total resident population of the whole of south-side Scarborough was only 1,606.

No doubt during the summer season St Martin's was crowded with visitors, but the pleasures of public promenading for some outweighed the duty of Sunday religious worship. As the *Scarborough Gazette* of 19 September 1872 observed, leather-bound prayer books were conspicuous at the so-called church parade along the Esplanade long before church services had actually finished.

South Cliff United Reformed Church (often called Balgarnie's after Rev. Robert Balgarnie, its first Congregational minister) 1864-8

Meanwhile, Nonconformist places of worship were fast multiplying in Scarborough. The Congregationalists, who had finished their heavy Gothic Bar Church at the corner of Aberdeen Walk and Without the Bar only a month after St Mary's was reopened, followed it with their magnificent South Cliff church and steeple in 1868 and their unpretentious Eastborough chapel the next year. Not to be outdone, the Wesleyan Methodists raised their Claremont chapel on Castle Road in 1860; the Primitives their yellow and red brick Jubilee chapel in Aberdeen Walk in 1861; the Wesleyans their impressive Corinthian-columned Westborough chapel in 1862; and the Primitives a fourth in 1865 in St Sepulchre Street. In later more pagan times of these only the Westborough and South Cliff churches have survived as places of worship: Bar, Jubilee and St Sepulchre were destroyed in the 1960s; and Claremont and Eastborough have been put to more secular uses.

Finally, in 1867, the Baptists – who had outgrown their chapel in Longwestgate – built another church in the Gothic style with an oddlypositioned steeple and apse in Albemarle Crescent.

This extravagant outburst of church building was an expression of exceptional religious conviction, but it was also a product of Britain's leading role as workshop of the world. After the increasing size of iron steamships had forced the closure of Tindall's yard in 1863, Scarborough had no industry of size to call its own, yet it profited indirectly and greatly from the nation's extraordinary prosperity: its expensive new churches as well as its sumptuous new hotels were paid for out of manufacturing money. For instance, the foundation stone of South Cliff's 'triumphant' and 'spectacular' Congregational church was laid by Lady Salt, the wife of its chief benefactor, Sir Titus Salt, the West Riding textile millionaire and philanthropist. Sir Titus had granted the spacious site which was worth £1,500 and donated another £1,000 to the building fund.

Summary

Theakston's street plan of Scarborough in 1875 outlines the expansion of the town that had taken place in the years since the Ordnance Survey of 1852.

Albion Road, South Cliff

On South Cliff such old features as herring house, drying ground and windmill no longer existed. The roads leading from the Esplanade in 1852 – Albion, Alfred and Prince of Wales Crescent – had then been little more than promises, whereas by 1875 they were addresses for terraces of handsome, tall houses. Prince of Wales Terrace was complete. Across to the west side of Filey Road the Royal Crescent faced the building plots now laid out in Princess Royal Park. Behind the Crown Hotel there were now Crown Terrace and Crown Crescent. Two churches on either side of Ramsdale Hill (soon to be renamed Ramshill), the new Congregational, better known as Balgarnie's, and St Martin's, dominated the approach to Scarborough from the south. That this was an exclusive, residential and high-class visitor area was emphasized by the presence of detached mansion houses on both sides of Belmont Road and the absence of shops. There were no public houses at all. In 1875 South Cliff had four hotels, the Crown, the Prince of Wales, the Ramshill Inn, and the Cambridge. Finished in 1865, the Cambridge hotel was 'a study in elegance and refinement' with an excellent cuisine.

North Side development had been altogether different. There were now long rows of working-class homes in Oxford, James, William, Hope and Durham Streets, in contrast to what had been built on the seaward side of North Marine Road. Here, overlooking North Cliff, a long terrace of very tall, lodging houses stretched as far as the North Riding Hotel. On the west side of North Marine Road, beyond Trafalgar Square, which was now almost complete, there were still open fields as far as Peasholm. In splendid isolation stood the Alexandra Hotel (later renamed the Clifton) at the northern end of Queen's Parade.

Westwards there was a glaring contrast between the streets of small terraced houses running off Victoria Road – Victoria, Hoxton, Nelson, Cambridge, Albion and Belle Vue – for 'the artisan classes', and the series of huge detached villas set in Westwood Park overlooking the railway line. Falsgrave's extension eastwards and Scarborough's Westborough suburb had now filled the green-field gap between them, though some surviving names such as Stoney Causeway (Londesborough Road), Folly Lane (Westover Road) and Love Lane (Belgrave Road) were reminders of a rural and more romantic past.

By the 1850s and 1860s large groups of working-class railway excursionists were spending days or even weekends at Scarborough. In 1865 the town was said to have had 15,000 to 20,000 visitors at a time during the summer season when its resident population, according to the census of 1861, was still only 17,204. However, unlike other northern seaside resorts, such as Blackpool, Bridlington or New Brighton, which had no historical connections with upper-class clientele, Scarborough was slow and reluctant to adapt to a more democratic market offering the cheapest accommodation and entertainment. The textile workers of Bradford and Halifax preferred Blackpool; and the metal workers of Sheffield went to Bridlington or Cleethorpes rather than Scarborough. Bridlington was known as 'Sheffield by the sea'. Like Bournemouth and Eastbourne, Scarborough tried to protect its exclusive reputation or at least preserve it in certain parts of the town. The affluent 'marine suburbs', Hove outside Brighton and Cliftonville alongside Margate, were matched by South Cliff, the 'New Scarborough'. Not even the Valley Bridge could span the social chasm that separated the Esplanade from the south foreshore. The guests of the Grand, Crown, Royal, Pavilion, Cambridge and Queen hotels on the one hand and day trippers crowding the South Bay sands on bank holidays were worlds apart.

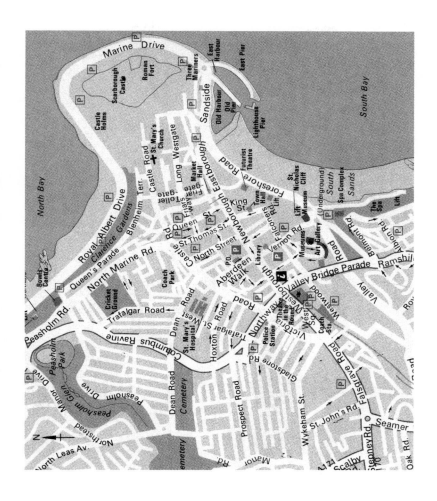

Street Plan of Central Scarborough

Scarborough remained one of the very few provincial resorts that was still fashionable enough to attract wealthy visitors from long distances and not just from its hinterland. Valley Bridge, the Grand Hotel and other palatial new ones such as the Cambridge and the Pavilion, the North Bay pier, the Aquarium and finally Verity's Grand Hall were all indications of contemporary confidence in Scarborough's future as a high-class seaside holiday town. In 1851, with nearly 13,000 permanent residents, Scarborough ranked eighth in population behind the other resorts, Brighton, Great Yarmouth, Dover, Hastings, Gravesend, Ramsgate and Torquay. With 65,000 residents Brighton dwarfed all the others. Blackpool then had only 2,564 inhabitants, Morecambe still only 1,301. Thirty years later, by 1881, with a population that had increased by 136%, Scarborough's 30,504 had brought it up to sixth position behind Brighton, Hastings, Great Yarmouth, Southsea and Southport. Scarborough, in the words of the census report, was still 'fair mistress' of England's north-east coast.

16

'DEVELOP SCARBOROUGH MAJESTICALLY'

According to the official census returns of 1881 and 1911, the population of Scarborough and Falsgrave had increased during these years from 30,504 to 37,224. However, this increase had taken place entirely in the last two decades of the nineteenth century since the comparable census of 1901 had then recorded the borough's population as 38,161. Probably for the first time since the Civil Wars of the 1640s the number of the town's inhabitants had actually fallen during the early years of the twentieth century.

An explanation for this surprising decline in residential numbers is difficult to find. There were 350 more households in 1911 than in 1901 mainly as a result of the new house-building that had occurred during these years on the northern perimeter of the town; but average family size had fallen from 4.3 to 4 and the average number of occupants per house had also declined from 4.4 to 4.2. Both were low figures by national standards. Moreover, whereas, in 1901, 780 houses were found to be uninhabited, ten years later their number had risen to 1,076.

Though as yet there were no official unemployment figures (Scarborough's first Labour Exchange opened in Huntriss Row in February 1911), we know that the first decade of the twentieth century was plagued by many widespread industrial disputes brought on by periodic trade depressions. In some of these years emigration, mostly to Canada and the United States, reached a quarter of a million. Despite a significant fall in death, especially infant mortality, rates, the population of the United Kingdom as a whole rose only slowly during these increasingly troubled years. In this context, the fall in the number of Scarborough's inhabitants makes some if not complete sense. Clearly, there were other local factors at work: during this period Bridlington's population rose from 12 to 14 thousand whereas Whitby's dropped from 11,700 to 11,000.

Compared with other English seaside resorts Scarborough's growth between 1881 and 1911 in population terms was modest. In 1881 Scarborough had ranked sixth behind Brighton (107,546), Hastings (42,258), Great Yarmouth (37,151), Southsea (34,226) and Southport (33,763). By 1911, having been overtaken by Bournemouth (78,674), Southend (62,713), Blackpool (58,371), Eastbourne (52,542), Dover (43,645), Hove (42,173) and Torquay (38,771), it had slipped to thirteenth.

Part of the reason for Scarborough's comparative lack of success as a popular holiday resort was its physical distance from the principal places of demand – the northern industrial towns and cities. Whereas the south-east coastal resorts benefited from their proximity to the enormous number of Londoners and Blackpool and Southport were within 50 miles of five million potential visitors, Hull was more than 50, Leeds 66 and Sheffield nearly 100 miles by rail from Scarborough.

A comparison with Blackpool during these years is illuminating. In 1865 Scarborough was said to have had a maximum of 15,000 visitors at any one time and still only 20,000 on bank holidays in the 1890s compared with Blackpool's claim to have entertained as many as 150,000 day trippers during the same bank holidays. Scarborough received 450,000 holiday-makers (a quarter of a million of them staying at least one night) during the summer of 1890, but Blackpool had two million in 1893 and nearly four million by 1913. Scarborough's share of a rapidly growing market was falling.

The census of 1911 also revealed how Scarborough had become predominantly a seasonal retreat for holiday visitors and a retirement home for the rich and elderly. Since 1851 the age profile of under-15s had fallen from 33.7% to 25.5% and the percentage of over-60s had risen from 11% to 12.1%. These figures should be set against the national averages in 1911 of 30.6% and 7.4% respectively.

In Scarborough, as in other seaside places, a low birth rate was matched by a low death rate. As a result of the many beneficial reforms permitted by the town's Improvement Act of 1889 it was still able to claim that it had a high standard of public health and hygiene. By 1905 Scarborough was said to be 'well equipped with public conveniences'; the borough's busy sanitary officers were compelling publicans to provide urinals and houseowners to install water closets and ventilate soil pipes; and there was now in place a system of compulsory notification of infectious diseases. A smallpox hospital was built above

Scalby beck in 1903 and a new sanatorium for consumptives opened the following year. Between 1880 and 1904 the borough's annual death rate fell from 20.06 to 14.68 per thousand of its population, well below the national average, and deaths from infectious diseases and tuberculosis were particularly low for an urban community.

There was a relative scarcity of young men aged between 15 and 39 (only 15% in 1911 compared with the national average of over 20%) and a relative surplus of females of the same age group (24.6% against the national average of 21.7%). In Scarborough females outnumbered males by seven to five. Of the 6,871 employed women nearly a third were indoor domestic servants and another third worked in lodging houses, hotels, shops, laundries and cafes. The villas of South Cliff accounted for a large number of chars, cooks, housemaids and dressmakers.

Seaside resorts were characterised by winter poverty and summer over-crowding and Scarborough was no exception. Unemployment was especially severe during the times of trade depression and when winter weather stopped building. Peasholm Park was begun in December 1910 to provide work for 100 local men who were paid a pittance by the council and given a midday meal of sausage and mash. A year later 60 otherwise unemployed manual labourers dug out the park lake. In contrast, during the summer, Scarborough's headteachers often complained that children were taking casual jobs instead of attending school and, to make room for guests, some of them were sleeping in garden sheds and damp basements.

The decision made by the town's rulers in 1882 to make no further extensions or major improvements to the harbour marks a significant signpost in the history of Scarborough: from now on its destiny was perceived to be seaside not seafaring.

The spread of housing during the last two decades of the nineteenth century was mainly in three directions. There was an extensive development of terraced streets west of Gladstone Road and what was to become the upper end of Columbus Ravine. A block of streets named after heroic explorers and navigators – Livingstone, Franklin, Nares, Murchison, Raleigh, Nansen and Gordon – and another series running west to Manor Road – Hibernia, Caledonia and Britannia – filled the green field areas on both sides of Prospect Road. Subsequently, during the next decade, the last open spaces east of Manor Road were built over with Ramsey and Lyell Streets.

Southwards, Scarborough (which had absorbed Falsgrave in 1889) stretched its tentacles down the west side of Seamer Road. Here the names of poorer, working-class streets, built for the local railway and gas workers, reflected Scarborough's mixed political allegiances. Salisbury and Beaconsfield, current and former Conservative prime ministers, were followed by Ewart, Gladstone's middle name. The 'Grand Old Man' had died in 1898 and the town recognised his eminence by naming a main road, a street and lane after him. His two Liberal successors, Lord Rosebery and Herbert Asquith, were also honoured with street names in this part of the town.

Ribbon development along Seamer Road was in marked contrast to the superior villas that had arisen on both sides of Ramshill Road. Aristocratic labels, such as Granville and Lonsdale, revealed the pretensions of their builders and residents.

Yet even as late as 1899 virtually no houses had been built beyond Trafalgar Street East. What was to become the lower continuation of Columbus Ravine was then still the bed of Raincliffe spring which ran into North Bay through Peasholm Gap. Cemetery Road led only to the cemetery. The explanation for this is simple: most of the land on the north side of the town still belonged to the Woodalls.

John Woodall of St Nicholas House was known as 'Shade Woodall' because he wore a patch over the eye he had lost as a result of smallpox. However, the nickname might well have had another meaning: John Woodall loved trees. He planted them everywhere – in the Valley, at the Mere, on Oliver's Mount, down St Nicholas and King's Cliff below his home, and on Barrow Cliff, overlooking Peasholm beck, the town's northern boundary. He was not interested in building houses, but he was concerned to preserve open spaces for the recreation and exercise of fellow Scarborians; and he had no financial need to sell land.

When John died in 1879 he left his estate to his widow Mary Eleanor, who died four years later, and their three sons, John Woodall, Charles William and Edward Henry. Then, in 1899, an extensive area, now known as Victoria Park, bounded by Cemetery Road, Peasholm beck, Columbus Ravine and North Marine Road, was sold by the Woodalls to the Walmsley brothers, two Leeds builders, for future housing development. By 1902 Langdale Road was almost complete and Tennyson Avenue and Moorland Road soon followed. 'Avenue' was by now preferred to 'street' or 'road' and Ashville, Beechville, Elmville and Mayville Avenues were all finished by 1912. Protests from these new householders persuaded the Council to change Cemetery into Dean Road.

If Scarborough was failing to capitalise fully on the growth of popular taste for seaside excursion and entertainment this was also the result of deliberate policy, not just accidental remoteness from Leeds and Sheffield. The decision-makers at the Town Hall were usually more concerned with quality than quantity. The resort was coming 'down-market', but reluctantly, slowly and within limits; its fate was still largely in the hands of the villa residents of South Cliff and Weaponness Park, not the amusement moguls of the Foreshore. A glance at the lists of repeatedly-elected councillors with names such as Whittaker, Rowntree, Tonks, Boyes, Sinfield and Morgan reveals a strong commercial interest, but these men were not merely wealthy business successes: they had sincere civic pride and moral conviction. Most of them were driven by religious faith. Their purpose, in the words of Meredith Whittaker, was to 'develop Scarborough majestically' and not to build another Blackpool on the North Sea coast. And in Harry Smith they had the most talented and dynamic borough engineer in the whole country.

Parks and Gardens

Two centuries ago Scarborough's earliest recorded public gardens were owned by William Bean. They then occupied an area between what became Westborough to the north, Vernon Road to the east, Belvoir Terrace to the south and York Place on the west. In his *Guide* of 1787 James Schofield referred to Mr Bean's 'universal gardens' which then supplied the town with 'every fruit' and 'elegant vegetables'.

Despite Scarborough's northerly, maritime location and its notorious summer sea frets, Mr Bean had 'perfected a pinery' which also produced grapes, melons, peaches, nectarines, apricots, plums and pears 'every day of the season, of the very best kind'. For a subscription of five shillings a head or ten shillings and sixpence for a family the garden walks were open to the paying public during the season. Sometimes Mr Bean hired a band to play music to his summer evening visitors. A view of the site drawn about 1830, after Christ Church had been built on part of it, shows rows of long greenhouses where the Oddfellows were later to erect their hall.

After the disappearance of Mr Bean's, the gardens known as Mr Walshaw's, on the town's northern perimeter, and Short's, overlooking Burr Bank, are features of the maps of the 1840s and 1850s; but they seem to have been entirely horticultural and not intended to entertain visitors. However, during the 1830s, the private fenced gardens belonging to the lodging houses on St Nicholas Cliff were amalgamated to form a single, enclosed area. The Cliff gardens were laid out with paths, lawns and shrubbery and surrounded by a low, stone wall with railings and half a dozen arched iron entrances. They were open only to residents and lodgers of the Cliff, however, not to the general public. The same restriction applied to Scarborough's even more exclusive Crescent gardens.

Not until 1853 did the Cliff Bridge Company advertise for a head gardener at 16 shillings (80p.) a week to take charge of the walks and plantations in the undercliff behind Wyatt's Saloon. Six years later, as a result of the extensions and improvements designed by Sir Joseph Paxton, the head gardener's wages were raised to 21 shillings (£1.05p.) a week. Floral beds were planted on the steep slopes between the balustraded stone staircases and in 1862 a summer house was built above them. Further landscaping of the undercliff south of Paxton's Hall took place after 1861 when eight acres of land were bought by the Company and planted with trees.

By that time the corporation's work of transforming Millbeck Dale or Ramsdale into a free, public park was well advanced. The last of the water corn mills was demolished and the mill dam, fed by the Mere, converted into a duck pond. What had been a dirt Mill Lane in 1860 was metalled and widened to become Valley Road. The Plantation became the People's Park. Four years later Plantation House was swept away to make space for one of the piers of the new Valley Bridge. Scarborough's People's Park was the first to be opened throughout the year and without charge to both visitors and residents. In 1912 it was re-christened Valley Gardens.

After erosion had wiped out the ill-fated Rock Gardens, the North Cliff remained undeveloped until the corporation purchased the whole length of the undercliff below Queen's Parade from the Castle Holms as far north as Peasholm Gap. Between 1886 and completion four years later the cliffside was drained, landscaped, laid out in gardens and saved from further movement (it was hoped) by a sea wall and carriage drive. The total cost to the ratepayer was said to be £50,000!

Ramsdale mill dam and plantation, by J Stubbs, 1827.

The main features of these Clarence Gardens were the pretty bandstand set in an excavated hollow and a wooden, rustic bridge that gave access to 'Flagstaff Hill', a nearby natural mound. For those who came to listen to the music but did not pay for the seats around the bandstandthe hill was used as a free grandstand. Between 1888 and 1906 the music was provided by a committee of North Side boarding-house proprietors; they hired bands, vocalists and sometimes pierrots. From 1907 until the outbreak of war in 1914 ended further open-air entertainment here Catlin's pierrots performed every season, paying the corporation an annual rent of £250. The Clarence Gardens survived the First World War but were afterwards the casualties of the winter landslide of 1921-2 and the major stabilisation of the undercliff that was necessary in 1923. The bandstand was removed to Falsgrave Park.

Meanwhile, in 1889, the corporation had purchased the four-acre field, previously called Great Northstead, which separated Peasholm Lane from Peasholm Gap. In honour of the Princess of Wales it was re-named Alexandra Field, and used as a children's playground with part let off for allotments and donkey pasture. Not until the winter of 1907-8 did work begin to convert Alexandra Field into two public crown bowling greens and at the southern end an arena with open stage

299

for performances. To afford shelter from cold northerly and easterly winds these two sides of the area were protected with high earth embankments. After the particularly wet summer of 1909, however, the council decided to put up a glass roof over the 'theatre', though for the season of 1910 only the front seats and apron stage were actually covered. What was to become the Floral Hall theatre was not finally finished until 1912, by which date it had cost Scarborough's ratepayers £2,950. Cardow's Cadets were the principal performers until they were succeeded in 1912 by George Royle's Fol-de-Rols.

By 1914 the corporation had also extended its control of the southern undercliff beyond the Spa. Between 1885 and 1895 the ten acres of the Holbeck cliffside were drained, terraced and converted into lawns and flower beds. In 1911 Holbeck Gardens were much enhanced by the presentation to the town of a handsome clock tower to commemorate the coronation of George V. The donor was Alfred Shuttleworth, resident of Red Court on the opposite side of the Esplanade. A year later the corporation bought George Lord Beeforth's 13-acre estate for £5,500 – his Rose Garden for £3,000 and the woodland beyond it for £2,500. During the next two years the two were converted into the Italian Gardens which consisted of rockeries, a lily pond, new rose beds and a pergola shelter.

Scarborough's widespread fame for beautiful gardens and well-kept public parks owed much to the initiative and enterprise of Harry W. Smith, who was borough engineer from 1897 until his retirement in 1933. During these golden years, despite the standstill imposed by the war of 1914-18 and its aftermath, Scarborough's 55 acres of 'public pleasure grounds', as he called them, grew to 350 acres.

The St Nicholas Gardens, originally opened to the public in 1900, were Smith's first contribution to this wonderful achievement. Two years earlier the Woodalls had sold their home, St Nicholas House, to the corporation for £33,575. Besides the house itself, which became the nucleus of the new Town Hall, the sale included a shop and house at 22 St Nicholas Street, the Exhibition Hall on the Foreshore and between them about two acres of steep undercliff. So what had been the Woodalls' private back garden was transformed into another of Scarborough's public parks, a protected greenery overlooking the splendid panorama of the foreshore sands and South Bay.

Harry Smith's greatest achievement, however, was Peasholm Park. In 1911, as its first venture beyond Scarborough's ancient borough boundaries, the corporation bought about a dozen acres of the royal manor of Northstead from the estate of the Duchy of Lancaster. Since the land consisted mainly of a barren mound set in a muddy depression known as Tucker's Field, the Crown was no doubt pleased to be rid of these allotments and piggeries. Besides there was no question of the surrender of obsolete manorial status: the office of steward of Northstead – 'an office of profit under the Crown' – continued to be used, as it had been since 1844, to allow a member of the House of Commons to vacate his seat.

Starting briefly in the bleak winter of 1910-11 and resumed the following winter, employing mainly the cheap manual labour of the otherwise unemployed, Harry Smith's design of a lakeland park and pleasure garden gradually took form and shape. Peasholm Hill became an island, surrounded by a lake of four and a half acres, which was fed naturally by the waters of Peasholm beck and Raincliff spring. Northstead manor house was exposed, excavated and then drowned beneath the level of the new lake. The stylistic theme adopted by Smith was Japanese: the hump-back wooden bridge to the island, the boathouse on the lakeside, and the pergola-like entrances were the original structures to which in later years were added other oriental features such as the island pagoda. Altogether, at its official opening in June 1912, Peasholm Park was said to have cost just over £2,000, and this figure included investment in rowing boats and canoes as well as boathouse, bridge, shelters and seats! Never had Scarborough's ratepayers enjoyed a better bargain for their money.

When Harry Smith addressed the Institution of Municipal and County Engineers at Scarborough in May 1915 he was able to report two more of his ambitious enterprises that were close to fulfilment. As early as 1900 the council had obtained parliamentary authorisation to construct a new bathing pool on Scarborough's seashore, but it was not until 1912 with the purchase of the South Cliff gardens that an ideal site for Smith's plan became available. Work began in 1913 and, despite the outbreak of war and the German bombardment, the pool was built in time for the 1915 season.

The South Bay oval swimming pool was 350 feet long and 180 feet broad and varied in depth from seven to two feet. At every high tide it was replenished with incoming fresh sea water. The outer concrete sea wall was wide enough to serve as a promenade for bathers and a viewing grand-stand for spectators. On the landward side there was another concrete public walkway 25 feet wide over a subway whichled from the dressing rooms to the open pool. There were 76 'boxes for gentlemen' and 61 for 'ladies', and additional dressing areas for schoolchildren, hot and cold showers, lavatories, first-aid and attendants' rooms. Above and behind the pool and changing rooms a series of terraces were cut into the cliff side for a café and rows of beach bungalows. Smith was able to tell his fellow engineers that so far total expenditure on the pool and terraces came to £31,695. Not least of the benefits of the South Bay pool to Scarborough's future was that it provided effective and permanent stability to what had been a very unstable cliff.

Blackpool had to wait until 1923 for its South Shore pool, Margate until 1927, and Folkestone and Ramsgate even longer, while Scarborough's pioneer of open-air sea-water bathing was a spectacular success. For instance, in 1926 the local press announced that 3,500 spectators had paid sixpence (2½p.) each to watch the weekly 'aquatic display'.

Secondly, by 1915 Smith's scheme for the development of Scarborough Mere was also well advanced. What had once been a 40-acre lake and swamp but had been diminished to a quarter of that size by silting and railway embankment was now being dredged, extended and landscaped. In the summer of 1913 the council had fitted out a small fleet of rowing boats and canoes for public hire and built a landing stage and café on the northern edge of the lake. The waters were stocked with coarse fish and anglers charged sixpence (2½p.) a day to catch them. It was another decade before the Mere and its man-made islands fulfilled Smith's plan and another waste land was transformed into a beautiful public amenity which was also, in his own words, 'a sound venture financially'.

Roads and Rails

The rapid physical expansion of the town and the changing forms of transport in the decades before 1914 brought about revolutionary innovations. Scarborough had pioneered the cliff tramways – the South Cliff serving the Spa was opened as early as 1875 and the Central near the Grand Hotel followed in 1881 – but because of its narrow streets and steep gradients the town was slow to adopt a modern system of internal transport. Though horse-drawn buses first appeared on Scarborough's streets in 1879, significantly their routes avoided the old town and the seashore.

One obstacle to free movement, the Bar that narrowed the main road between Newborough and Westborough, was bought by the corporation in 1876 and at last demolished in 1890, but little could be done about Eastborough's mountainous gradient.

Nevertheless, after royal assent had been granted in 1902 to a Bill which empowered the Edmundson Electricity Company to begin construction, five miles of tram lines were laid down by May 1904 at a cost of £96,000. By agreement Scarborough corporation was entitled to half the profits when they exceeded five per cent of running costs and an option to buy the system from 1915 onwards.

Scarborough's electric trams were an instant success: in their first two and half days 15 open-top cars carried 22,000 passengers on five basic routes for one or twopenny fares. Later, a special sixpenny Grand Tour covered the whole network and included a walk in Alexandra Gardens with the driver as guide. When the Company tried to suspend operations at the end of the 1910 season, the Town Hall successfully compelled it to run a reduced winter service for residents.

However, rising summertime takings failed to counterbalance rising wintertime losses. When the Marine Drive was opened in 1908 the tramway was not built along it, presumably because of the danger from heavy seas and the risks from wet, salty air. And plans to extend the lines to South Cliff were also dropped. Finally, in the face of increasing and damaging competition from motor vehicles, the Company sold out to the corporation for £20,000 and the corporation closed down the service in favour of the United Bus Company. The last tram left the West Pier at 11 pm on 30 September 1931 and reached the depot off Scalby Road between Hampton Road and Wykeham Street fifteen minutes later; its journey marked the end of another era in Scarborough's transport history.

As early as 1881 the Council had set up a committee to consider the practicalities and problems of a shoreline road linking the two bays. A year later Sir John Coode, the distinguished engineer, was able to recommend the construction of a promenade that would stretch all the way from Peasholm Gap to the Foreshore running around the foot of the Castle headland. The Royal Albert Drive in North Bay was finished in 1890, but the remaining Marine Drive that would link it with Sandside proved a far more lengthy, expensive and formidable undertaking. Though the foundation stone was laid in June 1897, the road was not opened for public use until April 1908. What was estimated to cost about £25,000 and take three years to build eventually cost about £125,000 and was eleven years in the making. Time and time again huge seas and gales swept away gantries, steam cranes and rail trucks. Civil engineering technology was pushed to its limits. Even as late as January 1908, when the Drive was completed, another storm moved the retaining wall up to 16 inches and left a deep, wide crack in the road surface. The official opening ceremony finally took place in August 1908 when it was performed by Prince Arthur, Duke of Connaught, one of Queen Victoria's sons, accompanied by his wife and their daughter, Princess Patricia.

No doubt the North Side would have developed as Scarborough spread outwards, but without the Marine Drive as well as the electric tram service along North Marine Road it is unlikely that Smith's ambitious plans for Alexandra Gardens and Peasholm Park would have materialised so early. Another motive behind the Marine Drive was coastal protection. The Castle headland was now secured against major losses from coastal erosion. Since 1890 there have been no massive rock falls from the sea cliff. *[plate 1]*.

The construction of the Marine Drive had yet another significant consequence: it led the council to buy up all the property on the harbour front of Sandside, demolish it and build a widened thoroughfare. The old sail lofts, boat yards and warehouses were cleared away. Spread Eagle Lane disappeared for ever. Fortunately, the irregular building line of Sandside was preserved and remains essentially intact today, whereas the harbour frontage was altered when the Herring Industry Board built the North Wharf there in 1925-7.

As far as external transport was concerned, the railway was still king until well beyond 1914. Whether day excursionists or residential holiday-makers, the overwhelming number of visitors to Scarborough arrived and left by train. Such was the volume of passenger traffic during the season that Scarborough had to have a new railway station at Londesborough Road, opened in 1908, an extended platform, and four extra miles of railway track to accommodate more carriages. The new line to Whitby, dating from 1885, required a tunnel under Falsgrave Road and a succession of road bridges to span its northward progress. After 1918 more and more private cars and public chars-a-bancs were to be seen on the roads to Scarborough, yet as late as 1934 Alderman F.C.

Whittaker (1882-1963) could describe, without exaggeration, the road between Malton and Spital Corner as little better than 'a donkey trot'.

Schools

During the 1850s and 1860s almost as many new school buildings were springing up in Scarborough as churches and chapels; and the purposes of some of their builders were as much religious as educational.

A new Wesleyan Day School was founded in 1856: the foundation stone for its home on the north side of Friars' Entry was laid at the beginning of 1858. Within a short time it had gained about 200 regular pupils, most of them infants, and a reputation for good order and efficiency, if not academic distinction. A newly-appointed teacher there was warned by her employers not to succumb to the 'temptation' of 'urging the children forward to meet the mistaken demand for intellectual results'. Working-class children had to be trained for work not educated to think.

From the established church authorities in Scarborough there was soon a competitive response. A new National school, St Thomas's, next to the church of that name, opened on Tuthill in August 1858. Its purpose was to provide basic numeracy, literacy and religious grounding for the children of the seafaring community on Sandside.

By this time the local Anglicans were increasingly embarrassed by the consistently uncomplimentary comments on their two old National schools on North Cliff. In the words of an inspector's official report of 1855: '130 ignorant boys [and girls] ... attend very irregularly'. He could find 'nothing of educational influence' in either the boys' or girls' school, and both over-crowded, one-roomed buildings were in poor condition. Consequently, in 1859, the old schools were demolished and replaced by one combined building on the south side of Castle Road for 140 boys and 140 girls. It was to be called St Mary's National School.

Not to be outdone, in 1861 the non-sectarian subscribers to the Lancasterian school sold their old building on North Cliff and erected new premises on land then called 'Back o'Danyell's' or Low Tollergate, subsequently St Mary's Walk. The girls entered the school from Garibaldi Street, the boys from Lancaster Street, at the opposite end. 'Gaffa' Watson, the headmaster, lived above the school rooms. Pupils paid fourpence a week in advance, or only twopence if their parents successfully pleaded poverty. By 1870 the Lancasterian school was admitting an average of 300 boys and girls a day, a number exceeded only by St Mary's.

Meanwhile, the oldest of Scarborough's children's charities, the Anglican Amicable Society, was also looking for improved accommodation for its school. At a cost of £2,000 a new combined school on the same site as its predecessor, between North Terrace and Castle Road, was opened in 1864 for 36 girls and 50 boys. With nearly 400 voluntary subscribers, rent from its received property at Cockhill Close on South Cliff, £5,500 invested in government stock, and an annual income of £542 from church collections and bequests, the Amicable Society was the town's richest charity. Most of its spending money went on clothing rather than schooling. The boys were given a new suit, cap, jacket, trousers, waistcoat, two shirts, stockings and boots; the girls got a new dress, hat, apron, boots and stockings. At Christmas there was a further issue of warmer clothes, and every January a dinner treat of roast beef and plum pudding. Twice a year, in memory of their benefactors, the boys and girls were each given sixpence.

By contemporary standards, Amicable children were Scarborough's fortunate few. In 1870 a total of 18 schools of very variable quality claimed to admit 2,370 children between the ages of five and 12, which meant that a further 1,400 had no schooling at all.

It was to fill such yawning gaps in elementary instruction throughout the country that Gladstone's Liberal government passed Forster's Education Act in 1870. The voluntary, religious schools were to survive and continue to receive state grants for attendance and efficiency, but from now on they had to face rivalry from the new Board schools which were undenominational, rate-supported and run by rate-payer-elected School Boards.

The implementation of the new Education Act once again aroused sectarian jealousies in Scarborough as elsewhere. Local Anglicans, Catholics and Wesleyans had no intention of surrendering their children to the 'godless' Board Schools and made every effort to maximise their numbers. Extensions were built to the St Thomas's schools. A new National school, St Martin's, opened on South Cliff. The Catholics made haste to draw more infants into St Peter's.

The nine places on Scarborough's first School Board were keenly contested and the return of one each of Catholic, Congregational and Methodist, four of the so-called 'unsectarian' party and two

Anglicans in effect gave the last a disproportionate advantage. In these circumstances, not surprisingly, the Anglican Amicable and National schools prospered independently whereas most of the non-Anglican schools were soon absorbed by the Board.

As early as 1874, the Lancasterian school, with 340 regular pupils, came under the authority of Scarborough's Board 'unconditionally and free of debt'. Four years later, the School of Industry on Cook's Row, which then had 90 girls under its wing, was taken over by the town's Board. The Wesleyan Day School survived until its building was knocked down in 1892 to make way for Scarborough's new hospital.

At the outset the Scarborough School Board decided to build three new schools in the borough with accommodation for 1422 children – an infants' school at Falsgrave, a so-called Central School for 800 boys and girls off Trafalgar Street West in fields behind the borough gaol, and a third mixed school on Longwestgate. With remarkable energy and speed this ambitious target was almost immediately achieved: by 1875 the three newly built schools had a total of 1239 children on their registers and an average attendance record of nearly 75%. Since attendance was not made compulsory until 1881 and parents were required to pay twopence a week for each child, this was a great achievement.

Gradually attendance figures at all Scarborough's elementary schools, voluntary and Board, improved. Fees for Board schoolchildren were remitted from 1875; average attendance rose from 80% in 1891 to 87% by 1901, after all Board school pence were abolished and two more Board schools, Gladstone Road and Friarage, were opened. In the words of one of Her Majesty's inspectors of schools: 'The School Board of the Borough of Scarborough continues to meet all demands in a liberal spirit.'

Under the chairmanship of a succession of enlightened and far-sighted men, notably William Rowntree and Meredith Whittaker, Scarborough School Board became one of the most progressive in the country. Long before Mundella's Act made attendance compulsory the Board employed a school attendance officer or 'kidcatcher'; and from the earliest years the Board schools had classes in science, navigation and practical cookery, not just the three Rs, reading, writing and arithmetic, for which central government paid grants. Not content with providing pupil-teacher classes and several at Standard VII, in 1897 the

Board resolved to build a separate school 'for upper standards' or 'higher grades'. Such post-elementary schools then in existence were run only by county boroughs such as Manchester and Birmingham and the London County Council, whereas according to the 1891 census Scarborough and Falsgrave had a population of only 33,776; and in 1897 the school-leaving age was still only 11!

Nevertheless, Scarborough's own Central Higher Grade School opened in November 1900 in a most handsome, brick building on the northern Plantation slope at Westwood. Of the original architect's plan only the basement swimming pool and the caretaker's house did not materialise. On three levels there were basement gymnasium, laundry, two dining rooms and a joiner's shop with 40 benches; on the main floor, a hall, 12 classrooms and library; and on the upper floors, physics and chemistry laboratories, art room and two staff rooms.

Scarborough's superb Higher Grade School was so advanced that it was illegal. According to the Cockerton judgement of 1900, the 336 boys and girls at Westwood were not elementary pupils and therefore, under the Act of 1870, could not be lawfully maintained out of the borough education rate. Fortunately, to save the school from closure, the town council took it into its tender care as an 'organised science school' financed out of central funds under the Technical Instruction Act of 1889. Since these funds were raised by an extra duty of sixpence a gallon on spirits they were then known as 'whisky money'. So, in this roundabout way, in 1901 Scarborough's newest school became the Municipal School or more familiarly to locals, 'The Muni'.

Moreover, when the Balfour Education Act of 1902 made the North Riding of Yorkshire County Council the authority for secondary schools, Northallerton wisely delegated responsibility for Scarborough to the borough's own education committee. Consequently, instead of becoming a county grammar school, Westwood remained 'The Muni'.

Under its two talented headmasters, A.S. Tetley (1902-16) and D.W. Bevan (1916-22), the life of the Muni was short but outstanding. In 1910 the inspectors praised the school for its academic successes and its flourishing extra-curricular activities which included Literary, Debating, Natural History and Dramatic Societies, French and Rambling Clubs, and School Choir and Band.

Two features distinguished the Muni from other grammar schools of the time: the presence of girls and the importance given to science subjects. Classes were separate but the boys and girls mixed in assemblies and on equal terms in all the out-of-school activities. Of the 22 county major scholarships won by the Muni students in the first 20 years, 13 went to sixth-form girls. On average the girls stayed on longer and in the highest classes they outnumbered the boys. Science was strong at Westwood because it had begun in 1901 as a school of science and four of its original staff of six were science graduates. Some of the country's best grammar and public schools would have envied the Muni's laboratories and lecture theatre. As a scientist Bevan broke the long-standing monopoly of classical heads of grammar schools; for many years he was president of Scarborough Field Naturalists.

If the Muni was a pioneer of progressive secondary education, Scarborough still had many examples of more traditional places of schooling. In 1867 there were no fewer than 30 different 'academies' housed mainly in the town's Victorian villas. Even as late as 1890 there were still 29 small, private schools, ranging from the exclusive Wachter Mesdemoiselles French Ladies school at 4 West Street to Fairbank's in Waterhouse Lane; and several other educational institutions of greater size and repute.

After St Mary's had expelled the town's grammar school from Farrer's Aisle in 1848, its survival depended on a succession of laymen who took boys into their own houses in Scarborough. William Merry (1838-52) kept the school at 5 King Street; James Sykes (1852-61) taught in York Place; and Thomas Swalwell (1861-72) rented a room in St Thomas Street near his home. In Sykes the town councillors made a bad choice: he nearly killed the grammar school. Joshua Rowntree, grandson of the founder of the Scarborough grocery store, who was born in Princess Street in 1844, went to Sykes at the age of eight. Of this schoolmaster he later wrote: 'He believed much in dunce-caps and in caning. I have seen five boys whacked and perched up at once.' Within a year Joshua was withdrawn and eventually sent to Bootham's Friends School in York as a boarder.

When Swalwell took over there were only four 'scholars' left, yet within three years he had 70 day boys in the school and another five boarders living at his home. He offered mathematics and classics; there was no science teaching, no library, no gymnasium and a neighbouring field was rented for games. Swalwell's revived school in St Thomas Street might have been the nucleus of a permanent grammar school but in 1872, when the town's leaders were preoccupied with the consequences of Forster's Act, it closed.

Coincidentally, in the same year, Scarborough got its first purpose-built grammar school on South Cliff. While the vicar of St Mary's, the Reverend Richard Frederick Lefevre Blunt sat on Scarborough's first School Board, the first vicar of St Martin's, the Reverend Robert Henning Parr, was thinking of higher matters, educationally speaking. 'On my coming to take charge of this parish nine years ago', he wrote, 'I formed an opinion that a great need in Scarborough was a middle-class school. I mean a school which should rank above the National schools and elementary schools [and] shall be vastly superior to ordinary private schools…'

The result of Parr's vision and endeavours was St Martin's grammar school on Ramshill Road, designed by the same architect, George Frederick Bodley, as St Martin's church but in a Tudor not a Gothic style. However, inside the red brick exterior there was only one large barrack-like school room to seat up to 100 boys with a sliding partition to divide it into two when necessary. Nevertheless, despite its lack of modern facilities, the school soon justified Parr's optimism.

St Martin's success is not hard to explain. It had the blessing and the powerful backing of the Anglican establishment which included gentry families such as the Worsleys of Hovingham and the Legards of Ganton. Not until Scarborough College opened in 1900 as a mainly boarding school did it have to face any local competition. The nearest grammar school was Lady Lumley's at Thornton Dale, 15 miles inland, and situated at the heart of middle-class South Cliff it was perfectly positioned to receive the boys for whom it was intended.

After the demise of Swalwell's school only James Wheater's Academy in Albemarle Crescent might have taken its place. That it had a good reputation is rather surprising, however, in view of the experience there of Thomas Laughton, younger brother of the famous actor Charles. In his autobiography Thomas recalled: 'It was a wretched school…Mr Wheater was a dapper little man who taught with a cane in his hand. One day he seized Charles by the collar and flogged him in front of us all…I refused to go back. When father discovered the reason, we were withdrawn from Wheater's.' Subsequently the two Laughton brothers were sent to the Jesuit college at Stonyhurst.

In 1915 Wheater closed his 40-year-old academy. Most of the boys and much of his furniture went up to St Martin's school. In the same year St Martin's opened a preparatory extension for boys under 12. By this time, under its fourth headmaster, Charles Frederick Turnbull

(1905-22), the school had more than doubled its numbers from 60 to 130 and the staff had increased to seven - the head, four full-time assistants, and two part-time, a music master and an art mistress.

An amazing range and variety of public examinations were now taken at St Martin's – for the Royal Society of Drawing, the College of Preceptors, Cambridge Local, and Leeds and London matriculation. Admission to the senior school was at 12 but few boys stayed beyond 15 when they then went into the civil service, the post office, customs and excise, or the merchant navy. Soon after Turnbull arrived part of the old school was equipped with laboratory sinks, benches and shelves so that the natural sciences could be taught in the new practical and experimental way as they were at the Muni. In Yorkshire, only Archbishop Holgate's at York, with its short-hand and land surveying, and Lady Lumley's with its Hebrew ('two shillings extra') had something more to offer than St Martin's curriculum.

Not that St Martin's grammar, at least in its earlier years, was much more humane than Mr Wheater's academy. The former's second headmaster, Whitley (1879-82), a Cambridge classics scholar, had a brief career at Scarborough because it was said that his right arm was not really strong enough for the job; whereas his successor, Thomas Raven (1883-1905), who stood well over six feet tall, gave the school its nickname 'Smartins'. On one occasion 'Tommy' caned every boy in the school and then sent them all home. Raven had no degree and taught all subjects in the senior school from Greek and Chemistry to book-keeping.

Sport

As late as 1882, in his chapter on 'Places of Amusement and Recreation', Scarborough's historian, Joseph Brogden Baker, recorded that only one of his so-called 'manly sports', cricket, was played in the town at that time. However, during the next three decades, though they never attained the national reputation of cricket at Scarborough, hockey, tennis, golf, football and lawn bowls all found permanent and prestigious places in the town's sporting calendar.

First formed in 1849, Scarborough Cricket Club was originally known as the Queen's Club because it met in the Queen Hotel on North Marine Road and played on the field opposite which was rented from John Woodall. Until 'a handsome pavilion' was built there in 1864 and between 1872 and 1874 the area was fenced and levelled, the ground was little better than a bumpy cattle pasture. Consequently, during these early years, important cricket matches were played on the Castle headland. It was here in 1868 that an Australian Aborigine XI, identified by their different dress colours such as Tiger pink, Dick yellow and Mosquito magenta, trounced Scarborough by 10 wickets. The *Scarborough Post* reported that 4,000 spectators had been treated to 'three days' amusement' by 'the Blacks' who were 'dressed in their native costume'.

Yet the Castle headland was hardly suitable as a cricket ground. Even in August 1868 the winds up there had been so strong that steel bails had to be used, 'this being an innovation not relished by the players'. Moreover, the land belonged to the War Department which decreed that no admission charge could be made, so that Lord Londesborough, the chief patron of invitation games, found himself having to defray the considerable costs of bringing visiting teams to Scarborough and accommodating them during their stay. After his sponsorship of a challenge match on Castle hill in 1871 the baron insisted that a better place had to be found in future, and this prompted the improvements on the North Marine ground soon afterwards.

Thanks again largely to the financial support of Londesborough and two other local, landed gentlemen, Sir Harcourt Johnstone of Hackness and Sir Charles Legard of Ganton, the three original trustees, Scarborough Cricket Club had the means to buy the freehold of their ground from the Woodalls in 1877. Of the £7,000 spent on the purchase and further improvements which included a new pavilion, £2,500 was raised by the sale of 26 building plots which were eventually occupied by boarding houses fronting North Marine Road.

By this time Scarborough Cricket Festival had already become an annual feature of the national cricketing calendar. The first nine-day festival in early September at the end of the summer season had already occurred in 1876, and from then on its fame and that of Scarborough as a cricketing venue went from strength to strength. W.G. Grace made his first appearance at the festival in 1885 and struck 174 runs for the amateur Gentlemen against the professional Players. Yorkshire played its first county fixture there in 1894.

Gradually the facilities of the North Marine ground were modernised and extended. The present red-brick pavilion replaced its primitive predecessor in 1896. New concrete 'stands' were added at the north side in 1926 and on the west boundary in 1956. The festival's close links with the MCC and the Yorkshire County Cricket Club ensured its permanency and success. As Scarborough grew as a holiday town so did the festival as a popular end-of-season attraction; the two were intimately inter-dependent – a first-class sporting and social event for a first-class resort.

The North Marine ground was much more than a cricket field: in its early days tennis, hockey, football and even outdoor bowls were also played there and on the neighbouring Recreation Ground. Scarborough Lawn Tennis Club shared the ground with the cricketers from the 1880s and the first Yorkshire Championships were held there in 1906; and Scarborough Football Club held its matches there from 1879 for nearly 20 winter seasons. It was at North Marine Road that Scarborough made its first appearance in the Football Association cup.

Hockey festival players eventually preferred the firm, flat sands of South Bay whereas the other sports found more suitable and exclusive homes elsewhere on the outskirts of the town. Opened in 1911, the Yorkshire Lawn Tennis Club's ground on Filey Road was described as 'the Wimbledon of the North'; it had seven hard and thirteen grass courts, a fine pavilion, open and covered stands surrounding the two centre courts, and a tarpaulin roof to protect them from the rain.

Association football finally found a local home of its own in 1898 at the Athletic Ground on Seamer Road. However, lacking the upper-class sponsorship of cricket, tennis or golf, even at amateur level the Scarborough club struggled to survive. As a winter sport football also had the disadvantage of having to depend entirely on residential supporters and until the 1920s match attendances were too low to finance a professional team.

In contrast, golf was then a game played only by the well-to-do. Founded in 1903, South Cliff golf club was one of the earliest in Yorkshire. Initially there were only nine holes in Deepdale under Oliver's Mount, but eventually the course was extended across the Bridlington Road to eighteen holes. The North Cliff course started with only six holes in Northstead straddling Burniston Road, and the Club, founded in 1911, did not acquire its present full-size links until 1928.

Lawn bowls is an outdoor game older than any other played at Scarborough, or arguably anywhere else in England. In 1688 Tory mayor, Thomas Aislabie, was ignominiously tossed in a blanket by the local soldiery on the 'Old Bowling Green'. John Cossins' first street plan of the town, drawn in 1725, shows this green to have been on the western side of upper Blackfriargate (Queen Street). Bowling Green House in this location appears on the Ordnance Survey map of 1852 and the green itself might still have existed until built over by the Catholic Convent in the 1880s.

The 'new' bowling green is harder to identify: probably, during the eighteenth century, it ran parallel to the west side of Long Room Street behind the Assembly Room and at the back of London Inn. On this site the 'new' green would have served mostly 'spawers' rather than residents.

Both these greens, 'old' and 'new', were the traditional flat ones. Crown green bowls was originally a Pennine game and brought first to the east coast resorts at the end of the nineteenth century by holiday-makers and immigrants from the West Riding. The earliest known crown green on land behind the Castle Hotel in Queen Street had a short life; bowlers complained that it was too small and confined. In response, the council offered a more spacious and suitable green on its Manor Road site which was opened by mayor William Morgan in August 1902. Three years later, the newly-formed Borough Bowling Club became its permanent tenant.

From now on new bowling greens were laid all over the town. Mayor J.W. Rowntree opened a flat green in Clarence Gardens for the beginning of the 1907 season; two greens, one flat and one crown, in Alexandra Gardens, date from 1908; and the flat greens on South Cliff were first played on in 1909. Robert Laughton, the hotelier, laid a private green next to his Pavilion Hotel. In these early years bowlers used flat and crown green indiscriminately; there were no leagues, only 'friendlies'; and Manor Road was the scene of the principal competitions where the Boyes and Hospital cups were played.

Politics

The Great Reform Act of 1832 had minimal repercussions on Scarborough's parliamentary politics. After the Whig triumph of that year the old, anti-reform order returned with the restoration of the Tory, Sir Frederick Trench, in the elections of 1835, 1837 and 1841, along with the leading, but conservative, Whig, Sir John Johnstone of Hackness.

The local landowning interest remained strong. Besides Sir John, who retained his seat almost without interruption from 1832 until his death in 1869, the Earl of Mulgrave represented Scarborough for the Whigs during the years from 1847 until 1857 when he was appointed governor of Nova Scotia. Sir Harcourt Johnstone, Sir John's heir, succeeded his father unopposed in 1869 and sat as a Liberal for Scarborough until raised to the peerage as Baron Derwent in 1881. Other wealthy landowners who represented Scarborough in the House of Commons were William Forester Denison (1834-1900), who sat briefly as a Whig in 1859 until he followed his father as Baron Londesborough the following year; and Sir Charles Legard of Ganton, who was Conservative MP for the borough during Disraeli's government of 1874-1880.

Scarborough's electorate remained small, property-owning and entirely male. Even after the Reform Act of 1867 doubled the franchise, there were still only 4,246 votes cast in the borough by 2,500 electors when the resident population exceeded 20,000. Consequently, in 1885, Scarborough was one of the ancient parliamentary boroughs that lost one of its two seats.

Contrary to the received view, Scarborough was never a predominantly Liberal town. The Conservative party won one of the two seats in 1874 and the only seat in 1885 and 1892; and when the Conservative candidate lost it was by only a small margin. Scarborough's Tory candidate from 1884 until 1900, Sir George Reresby Sitwell (1860-1943), was second in 1884 (twice), 1886 and 1895, but on each occasion his defeat was narrow. The borough was fairly equally divided. The Liberal victory by Walter Russell Rea (1873-1948) in 1906 reflected a national landslide, yet in December 1910 his winning margin was only 52 votes out of 5,474 cast. By that time Sitwell had deserted to the Liberals because the Conservatives had refused him a peerage and the president of the local Conservative Association was William Francis Henry Denison, second Earl of Londesborough (1864-1917).

Until the Secret Ballot Act of 1872 ended voting in public, wooden hustings were erected outside the Town Hall in St Nicholas Street up to 1865 and then outside the Court House in Castle Road in 1868 and 1869. Here parliamentary candidates were nominated and addressed the electors; here votes were openly declared and recorded in the poll books; and from here results were announced.

As the electorate grew larger and more literate, elections were conducted increasingly by the printed rather than the spoken word.

315

Polling took place on several consecutive days and the town was plastered with placards and party posters. In 1880, for example, Newborough Bar carried a huge notice identifying Johnstone and Caine, the Liberal candidates, with 'Peace, Progress and Prosperity'. Since under Disraeli's Conservative government the country had just experienced two costly and avoidable wars in South Africa and Afghanistan, a succession of ruined harvests and an industrial slump, not surprisingly both Johnstone and Caine came top of the poll.

The election of 1895 was very closely fought. J. Compton Rickett, the Liberal, just beat Sitwell by a mere 24 votes out of more than 4,800. Photographs of the time show two sets of sandwich-board carriers: one line of bowler-hatted men on Sandside advertise Sir George's personal attachment to the Union Jack flag, while another flat-capped platoon proclaim that his Liberal opponent stands for 'Equal Treatment for Rich and Poor'.

National issues usually determined the outcome of parliamentary, and sometimes even municipal, elections. One question that nearly always came to the surface was that of licensing laws. Should Britain's permissive tradition which allowed anyone to buy a two-guinea licence to sell beer at any time to anyone of any age continue or should drinking be restricted or even prohibited altogether? In the broadest terms, the Conservatives and the Anglicans favoured freedom or only minimal control whereas the Liberals and Nonconformists campaigned for much stricter curbs on the sale and consumption of alcohol. Publicans, brewers, distillers and most hoteliers supported anti-temperance candidates and huge quantities of free beer and spirits were dispensed during elections.

In Scarborough the temperance cause was championed by Thomas Whittaker (1813-99), who as a young man in Preston had taken the pledge of absolute abstinence and then had become a salaried lecturer and propagandist for the British Temperance Society at the age of 24. After settling in Scarborough in 1849 as proprietor of the Temperance Hotel in Newborough, Whittaker soon found himself at odds with what he disparagingly called 'the Londesborough clique'. When in 1861, he suggested in a passionate letter to the local press that 12 members of the Whitby lifeboat crew had drowned because they were befuddled with spirits, his effigy was paraded through the streets of Scarborough, flogged, smeared with red ochre, and finally burned on the sands triumphantly.

Sir George Reresby Sitwell, baronet, 1860-1943.

From now on the battle lines were drawn. Against intense opposition, two years later, Whittaker was elected by South Ward voters to the Town Hall, where he had a place for the next 20 years with a break between 1873 and 1876. The hiatus was caused by the temporary victory of the brewers and their allies who drowned the South Ward with drink and unseated both Whittaker and his running-mate, Alfred John Tugwell (1831-1921). In 1874 prime minister Gladstone complained bitterly that his Liberal government, which had introduced new licensing limits, had 'been borne down in a torrent of beer and gin'; and it was not until he returned to office in 1880 that the Liberals were able to pass a law severely restricting candidates' electoral expenses.

By that time Thomas Whittaker had served a year as Scarborough's mayor, become a Justice of the Peace, and set up his own newspaper, the *Scarborough Evening News*, as a counter-blast to the *Scarborough Post*, organ of the local Conservatives, whose principal shareholder was Sir George Sitwell. Whittaker never offered himself as a parliamentary candidate, but his friend W.S. Caine was Liberal MP for Scarborough between 1880 and 1885 and president of the British Temperance League.

However, Whittaker died in 1899 a disappointed man. Since 1872 no advance had been made to curb drinking; there were still 115 licensed beer and public houses in the town; and babies were still dying of cirrhosis of the liver. On his tombstone in Dean Road cemetery is inscribed this defiant and angry declaration:

> 'Tell me not what strong drink has been, nor what it is intended to be. I know what it is now. It is Britain's curse, it is the God of this Nation.'

Another controversy that divided Scarborough's political leaders and split the Liberal party there was Irish Home Rule. When Gladstone's bill to give the Irish a Dublin parliament was defeated in 1886 by an unholy alliance of Conservatives and Liberal defectors, he went to the country on this single issue. Joshua Rowntree (1844-1915), Quaker pacifist, temperance advocate, founder of the Adult schools in Springfield and Roscoe Street, and defender of trade union and women's rights, was then Scarborough's mayor. Nevertheless, he resigned from the office (thereby forfeiting £50), and stood as Home Rule parliamentary candidate.

318

Thomas Whittaker 1813-99

The election of 1886, a straight fight between Unionist and Home Ruler, was unprecedented. Five former Liberal MPs for the borough opposed Rowntree, but he unseated the sitting Member, Sitwell, by 102 votes. The result was a tribute to Rowntree's sincerity and courage, rather than a measure of support for Home Rule in the borough. With only one exception, Scarborough was the only constituency in England to record a Liberal gain.

Joshua Rowntree sat through the Parliament of 1886-92 which was controlled by the anti-Home Rule majority of Conservatives and Liberal Unionists. However, in 1892, at the next general election, when Gladstone was returned for a fourth term as prime minister, Sitwell won back Scarborough by a narrow margin. Sir George had a special talent, it seems, for winning Scarborough when his party lost the country and losing it when the Conservatives swept to a national victory.

Irish Home Rule divided old friends and even families, as well as Scarborough's Liberals. John Woodall Woodall, who served on the town council from 1863 to 1889 and was mayor four times, remained loyal to Gladstone, whereas his brother, C.W. Woodall, joined Chamberlain's Liberal Unionists. Tugwell, a stalwart veteran of the temperance movement, took a strong line in support of the Liberal Unionists and so did Benjamin Fowler (1828-1910), chairman of the town's licensing bench, who had refused many applications from brewers and publicans. On the other side, E.T.W. Dennis (1847-1923), who had sold the *Mercury* weekly to the Whittakers and founded Scarborough's most successful printing and publishing business, became a Quaker and stood steadfastly by Gladstone. There can be no doubt that the vexed question of Irish Home Rule dealt a grievous injury to Scarborough's Liberals from which they never fully recovered, whereas the temperance issue produced mostly ill-tempered invective. When Sitwell won the election of 1885 his enemies alleged that his only supporters were 'drunken, swearing blackguards', publicans, brothel-keepers and 'fallen women'.

Joshua Rowntree's fair-minded benevolence might have cost him his life. In March 1900, at the height of the Boer War, when humiliating British defeats in South Africa were still freshly remembered, he invited Cronwright Schreiner, a Boer, to a reception at Rowntree's café in Westborough. The following evening Schreiner was to address a public meeting at the old Town Hall. However, before Rowntree's 'At Home' even started, a large and angry crowd had gathered in the street outside the café and had begun to hurl tomatoes and then stones at its windows. On police advice the reception was abandoned. Joshua escaped by a back door but was assaulted in Huntriss Row and had to find refuge in a neighbouring house. His home on Ramshill and the Rowntree family shops in the town were also attacked by stone-throwers. The mob remained in Westborough until dispersed by troops from Burniston Barracks.

Yet Joshua was undaunted. Nine months later with his wife he sailed to South Africa to investigate stories of concentration camps and atrocities and cruelties suffered by Boer women and children. He found many of the stories true and with characteristic courage and frankness reported them in a public statement. When the accuracy of Rowntree's findings was challenged in the House of Commons, Lloyd George defended his former colleague ending with the words: 'His word is as good as his oath.'

The outbreak of war with Germany in 1914 was a devastating blow to Scarborough's Quakers and to none more than the ageing Joshua. Only two years previously, at his invitation, a party of German Friends from Frankfurt had stayed in the town. Rowntree's last public speech, deploring the 'anarchic barbarism of war', was delivered less than three months before the Kaiser's battleships shelled his home town and five months before his death at Wrea Head, Scalby.

Fishing

During the 70 years from the arrival of the railway from York in 1845 to the outbreak of the First World War in 1914 Scarborough's fishing industry was transformed by a series of revolutionary changes.

Even before 1845 there were signs of a revival of various forms of fishing that had been overshadowed by merchant shipbuilding during the previous century. Scarborough's dried cod, marketed by London merchants, was sold as far away as Ireland, Spain and the West Indies. None could match the traditional skills of the local dry fish curers and as late as 1842 the East Pier was rented by them as a major curing station.

Scarborough's fresh fish went by road inland to Malton, York and even Leeds, but transport costs priced it beyond the pockets of all but well-to-do customers. At this time, surprisingly, little interest was shown by Scarborough's line fishermen in the herring shoals that passed down the North Sea between July and September, though in 1844 a smokehouse was built at the foot of Oliver's Mount.

In 1833, a new type of fishing craft, the yawl, had made its first appearance in the registry of Scarborough's Custom House. Smaller than the five-man boat, with only two not three masts, and only partly decked, the yawl was the original product of Robert Skelton's yard. During the next two years Skelton built 15 yawls for the fishermen of Scarborough, Filey, Robin Hood's Bay and Staithes.

The first trawling smacks had arrived at Scarborough as early as 1831. When more of these West Country vessels carrying fishermen and their families came the following summer they were strongly resented and physically attacked. Nevertheless, despite the initial hostility of Scarborough's xenophobic, line-fishing fraternity, trawling was soon established there and adopted by the natives. Within easy reach of the rich grounds of the Dogger Bank, Scarborough was regarded as an ideal location, more so when the outer harbour was dredged in 1844 to provide extra accommodation for home and foreign trawlers.

The railway opened a greatly extended and enlarged domestic market for fresh and lightly-cured fish so that even the poorest could afford to buy it. Instead of throwing back much of their catch of sole, haddock and plaice to avoid glutting the coastal markets, the trawlermen could now operate throughout the year and sell their fresh fish to domestic merchants. Until the mid-1860s when it was finally overtaken by Hull, Scarborough was Yorkshire's leading fishing port. Owners and merchants there, such as Abraham Appleyard, James Sellers and Henry Wyrill, dominated the local trawling industry. Sellers and Wyrill departed from the old custom when they bought vessels on mortgage instead of raising the capital in partnership shares. Their new trawlers, now being built at Scarborough, were much larger than their predecessors and much better equipped. Steel warps replaced ropes and steam-powered capstans took the place of manpowered ones. While the fishermen of Filey, Bridlington, Whitby and Staithes stuck to their old-fashioned line-fishing Scarborough's 40 trawlers joined the fleets of Hull and Grimsby and fished the waters of Denmark and Holland.

The railways also gave new life to the herring trade. During the summer season more and more boats from places as distant as Penzance, St Ives and the Isle of Man brought their heavy catches into Scarborough. In 1864, for instance, the Harbour Commissioners there reported the presence of 400 vessels, 100 in the harbour and another 300

Part of the herring fleet off Scarborough

outside, sending in their herring in small craft. The summer months were now dominated by the herring as they had been centuries earlier when Scarborough Fair flourished. It was at this time that the word 'kipper' came into use, allegedly another Scarborough invention of the local Woodger family.

The 1860s were also the best years for inshore fishing when the creel or pot ousted the traditional 'trunks' or 'hoops' that had been employed for so long to trap shellfish. In the 1820s Scarborough was reduced to only six active cobles, but by 1870 there were nearly 40 of them specialising in catching crab and lobster. Scarborough crab was now sold fresh as far away as Birmingham. However, the increasing scarcity and cost of cockle, mussel and limpet (known locally as flithers) bait and the depredations of indiscriminate trawlers soon put heavy burdens on inshore fishing. By 1890, when inshore trawling was at last banned, the damage to stocks was already irreparable.

Another radical innovation was the introduction of steam trawlers which could operate in dead calm as well as strong seas. The first one appeared at Scarborough in 1878; and during the next few years the port acquired a considerable fleet of adapted paddle steamers and purpose-built steam trawlers. However, diminishing catches and a general trade depression soon caused a rash of bankruptcies amongst owners. Edward Rawlinson, Henry Wyrill and Henry Lamble Woodger all went under between 1885 and 1887, and the death of James Sellers in May 1887 marked the end of an era in Scarborough's fishing industry. By the close of that year Scarborough's fleet of steam trawlers had dwindled from 27 to 16, and it never recovered.

Where Scarborough had pioneered, Grimsby, Hull, Shields and Aberdeen profited. Scarborough was disadvantaged by its greater distance from coalfields, its inferior engineering and repair facilities, and its lack of sufficient harbour space. Though the West Pier had been widened and lengthened between 1879 and 1882, it still could not serve a large fleet of these bigger vessels.

A similar fate befell Scarborough's herring boats. Landings of herring continued to rise and reached a peak in 1895, but the trade was increasingly controlled by outsiders. Scarborough was merely a convenient landing stage, curing station and point of inland dispatch. The East Pier, which had once been the site of white fish drying, for up to six months of the year now became the country's principal curing location. Scottish merchants brought in their own gangs of Gaelic-speaking girls from the Highlands who cleaned, split and packed the herring in barrels between layers of salt.

Between 1880 and 1914 Scarborough's own fleet of fishing smacks declined in number and relative importance. When the local smack owners tried to raise their diminishing incomes by demanding 6¼ per cent instead of the traditional 5 per cent of gross profits, their action provoked an unprecedented fishermen's strike. After a preliminary meeting in the Sandside Coffee House, 300 men paraded through the streets of the town and held a service at St Thomas's on Easter Sunday 1887. In the end a compromise was reached and the men went back to the boats; but there was no permanent solution to the problems faced by the old sailing smacks. The future belonged to the steam trawlers of Grimsby and Hull. By 1900 Scarborough no longer had its own trawler fleet, though at least one Aberdeen boat was crewed entirely by Scarborough men.

The line-fishing yawls also went into terminal decline. In the 1850s and 1860s some of them had grossed up to £1000 a year; by 1890 few of them earned as much as a fifth of that. By 1914 all of them had been broken up except the *William Clowes*, which was the headquarters of the Scarborough Yachting Club until it too perished in 1921. In-shore shell fishing from cobles had also declined since the heydays of the 1860s. Not until the First World War brought food shortages and sky-high prices could Scarborough's lobster and crab fishers afford the costs of motorising their cobles.

Though rising rapidly in numbers and prosperity during the 1850s and 1860s and then falling on increasingly hard times in succeeding years, Scarborough's fishing community remained distinctively and conspicuously different from the town's other resident and visitor population. Fishermen and their families did not mix much with day trippers and holiday-makers or have much to do with the lives and livelihoods of upper town dwellers. They had their own chapels and their own public and beer houses. The 'bottom-enders' lived in a closely-knit, homogeneous community in the jumble of narrow streets, dark alley ways and back yards from Princess Street down to the shore-line of Sandside. The contrast between Sandside and the south Foreshore was between getting and spending, work and play, hardship and pleasure.

In all its forms fishing required the active and full cooperation of whole families. The womenfolk collected the bait for lines and pots: the 'flither-girls' often walked great distances up and down the coast with their heavy wicker baskets in search of limpets, cockles and mussels. Nets were made and repaired by entire families working together. Though no apprentice was indentured at Scarborough after 1881, young boys were expected to follow their elder brothers and fathers as deck-hands and cooks. Because of this family intra-dependence fishermen were discouraged from marrying outside the community and encouraged to father large numbers of children. Those whose homes were 'below the pump' in Low Conduit Street were therefore inter-bred and inward looking. One of the main reasons given by George Alward for settling at Grimsby rather than Scarborough was the hostility to 'foreigners' of the latter's fishing confraternity.

On the other hand, according to the testimony of William Edison, who in 1882 had been chief constable at Scarborough for the past 16 years, Scarborough's fisher folk were law-abiding, God-fearing and respectable. Unlike at other seaports, at Scarborough there were no 'crimps', that is prostitutes who preyed on seamen when they came ashore with money in their pockets, and to his knowledge there was no instance at Scarborough of a fisherman refusing to go to sea because he was suffering from a venereal disease. Young men who deserted were usually country lads, not natives, who had gone 'up street' and got drunk there; homebred boys would not dare to defy their masters and shame their families. Partly because fishing was always a hazardous occupation requiring physical bravery, endurance and cooperation, and partly because most crew members were paid in profit shares not weekly wages, Scarborough's fishermen and their families belonged to a special community with a unique record of proud solidarity.

17

THE BOMBARDMENT AND AFTER

1914-39

Once the war with Germany had begun in 1914, Irish, colonial and industrial crises were submerged in a tide of united patriotism. This unity was soon fractured, however, by Irish republicanism, the resurgence of nationalist demands for self-government, and post-war slump. The armed uprising in Dublin in 1916, followed by the IRA's guerrilla warfare of 1919-21, achieved only partial success: Ireland was partitioned between a Protestant-controlled North of six counties, which remained within the United Kingdom, and a Catholic-dominated Irish Free State of 26 counties which drifted outside it.

Out of the carnage of the Great War came small but lasting benefits for the nation's education, housing and health. Women were at last given parliamentary votes, though they did nothing to save the Liberal party, a major casualty of total war. The 1914-18 war ushered in a generation of Conservative party dominance, punctuated by only two brief periods of minority Labour government in 1924 and 1929-31. Economically, too, there could be no return to 1914. Then the national debt had stood at £706 million; by 1920 it had rocketed to £7,875 million. Post-war industrial depression and chronic, mass unemployment eventually produced the General Strike of 1926 – an unprecedented and never-to-be-repeated challenge to Baldwin's Conservative government. After only nine days the strike fizzled out, leaving the trade unions, and particularly the coalminers, utterly defeated. During ten of the twenty inter-war years the number of registered unemployed exceeded two million.

Britain's population continued to rise, though now more slowly, from 40.8 million in 1911 to 44.8 million in 1931. The birthrate decline continued. For many of the employed workers in the new industries of the Midlands and South-east the inter-wars years were times of growing affluence and contentment. By 1939 there were two million, mostly British-built, private motor cars on the roads. In the words of A J P Taylor: 'The baby Austin ousted the baby.'

But the staples of the North – cotton, wool, coal, shipbuilding, iron and steel – remained depressed and lost between a third and a quarter of their labour forces. Millions struggled to exist on the dole. After the Wall Street crash in 1929, Britain left the gold standard, devalued the pound sterling, and abandoned free trade to protect its shrinking markets. Unemployment reached a peak of nearly three million in 1932. After the short-term revival of the war years, farming also was sunk in depression, and the rural population declined even further.

There were stark discrepancies between classes and regions. Only one in ten working-class boys, and even fewer girls, received a secondary schooling beyond the age of eleven. Most of the new semi-detached homes built in the 1930s during the housing boom were bought on mortgages by the white-collar and skilled employees in the new electrical, radio and car industries. Only one in ten working-class homes had fixed baths, and 35 per cent of all houses in 1939 were without electricity. There was no national health service: fewer than half the population was insured against sickness. Infant mortality was more than twice as high amongst unskilled as professional families. More than a third of young male volunteers were rejected by the armed forces as medically unfit. One per cent of the nation owned two-thirds of its wealth.

Nevertheless, from 1935 onwards, rearmament slowly revitalised the economy. There was much more money for leisure and entertainment. By 1939 nine homes out of ten had wireless licences; 20 million cinema tickets were sold every week; and professional sport, particularly cricket and football, attracted huge crowds. Football betting pools flourished. On the other hand, churches, chapels, theatres, music halls and public houses all recorded smaller attendances. Though more than half the British people never spent a single night away from home during the last twelve months of peace, a day trip to the seaside by motor coach or excursion train was an experience now denied to only the smallest minority. Eleven million workers were now entitled to a week's paid holiday every year.

Unfortunately, these improving times of low inflation, minimal crime, cheap private housing and rising material expectations for those in work were abruptly terminated by events on the European continent. Having failed to save Czechoslovakia from Hitler's greed, Britain and the empire went to war with Germany in September 1939 in a vain attempt to save Poland from the same fate. In 1914, even East-coast seasiders were unaware of the menace of the Kaiser's battleships; in 1939, everyone in Britain knew that the enemy's bombers would always penetrate even the best aerial defences.

The Bombardment 1914

Direct hit received by Scarborough Lighthouse

In 1969 it was Osbert Sitwell's last wish that after his death a copy of his favourite work, *Before the Bombardment*, should be buried with his cremated remains. Osbert's earliest foray into full-length fiction was a brilliantly-witty and unsparing assault on pre-war, upper-class culture – public schools, organized games, blood sports and the snobberies and petty preoccupations of the idle rich – set in a thinly-disguised Scarborough he called Newborough. The Grand was his Superb Hotel, the Spa became the Winter Gardens, his mother's relations, the Londesboroughs, were Lord and Lady Ghoolingham, god and goddess of the cricket festival, and his market hall, harbour and cemetery were all Scarborough's.

Nowhere is there a better and bleaker literary description of Scarborough as it was *Before the Bombardment*, yet as a former Grenadier guardsman, writing in 1926, Sitwell's memory was altogether embittered by his experience of what had happened *after* Scarborough's 'baptism of fire' in 1914. For him, as for millions of others who survived the slaughter, the world was to be utterly and irrevocably changed by the first great war of the twentieth century.

Soon after 8 am on 16 December 1914 two German battle cruisers and a light cruiser, heading southwards, emerged from the cold dawn mist off Scarborough's North Bay. Less than half an hour later the same warships disappeared northwards having fired upwards of 500 high-explosive shells into the town, castle and harbour. The bombardment did more than inflict panic, destruction and death on a totally undefended and unprepared seaside community: it marked a woeful watershed in the history of the modern world.

Until that fateful morning, for the winter residents of Scarborough, the war with Germany had been a commercial setback, not yet a human tragedy. On the day war was declared, 4 August, the town was enjoying a happy summer season. The Fol-de-Rols were drawing full attendances at the Floral Hall; the Theatre Royal and the Grand Opera House were doing well; Catlin's 'favourite pierrots' were as usual entertaining crowds on the foreshore sands; and Plaxton's builders had just finished a new restaurant, a new theatre and the Picture Palladium House in record time. The sun had shone in June and July and most of the hotels and boarding-houses had no vacancies.

The earliest ominous signs were an announcement from the LNER Company that rail excursions to the north-east coast were cancelled until further notice and the arrival at Scarborough railway station of 50 Territorial soldiers. As the bank holidaymakers made their way back home, Scarborough's grocers, who included J.L. Hopwood and John Rowntree and Sons, issued a public notice to their customers. Despite the war, business was to be 'normal'; richer residents were asked not to purchase goods 'in excessive quantities' for in doing so they would cause shortages and push up prices.

Hits received at the back of St Nicholas Parade

By September, as the first casualties to the British Expeditionary Force in Belgium and in the Royal Navy were reported in the press the mood at home was beginning to change, but there was always Christmas and the New Year to look forward to. Then came the Bombardment.

The damage inflicted on Scarborough's population and buildings by the 12-inch and 11-inch guns of the *Derrflinger* and *Von der Tann* was costly and extensive. According to the most recent thorough research, 489 shells killed 18 and injured 84 people, hit 209 properties, seven churches and ten public buildings. No part of the town was spared; almost every street suffered. The Grand Hotel alone received 36 shells causing destruction which cost £13,000 to repair. Some of the physical scars never healed. One shell went right through the lighthouse which had to be demolished and was not replaced until 1931; and the brick barracks of Mosdale Hall, which had not housed troops since 1878, was entirely wrecked.

According to the War Office statement, at all three places, Hartlepool, Whitby and Scarborough, shelled by the Germans that morning, 'there was an entire absence of panic'; but, in fact, out of Scarborough all the roads leading inland to Seamer, Ayton, Forge Valley and Scalby, were crowded with fleeing men, women and children. Aberdeen Walk's Post Office was packed with anxious people desperate to withdraw their life-savings; and the 8.25 am train to Leeds was long delayed because porters had to remove third-class passengers from first-class carriages by force. Some refugees travelled as far as London. Mayor Graham's announcement in the *Scarborough Evening News* that residents should keep calm and help others to do the same was a little too late.

The general assumption was that the bombardment would soon be followed by a German landing: Scarborough was about to suffer the fate of Belgium. Sir George Sitwell, who had taken cover in the cellar of Wood End during the barrage, made preparations to hide himself on an island in the Valley during the enemy's occupation of the town. The arrival in Scarborough that afternoon of the 8th battalion of the West Yorkshire (Territorial) regiment might have been regarded as a hasty attempt to repel a seaborne invasion, but in truth its main purpose was to restore public order and protect property from looting.

Ever since the bombardment many efforts have been made to sift the facts from the deliberate deceits of both German and British

332

government propaganda. German intentions were many and confused. A successful attack on English coastal towns would raise the morale of the Kaiser's navy particularly after the destruction of its Far Eastern fleet off the Falklands on 8 December. It would also deal a devastating blow to British security. The Germans had long resented the arrogant assumption that Britannia would always rule the waves. Also it was hoped that such a raid, posing a threat of military invasion, would persuade Asquith's government to keep more troops at home instead of sending them into the trenches of the Western Front.

In tactical terms, the raid was intended to provide cover for a mine-laying operation. As *Derrflinger* and *Von der Tann* pounded Scarborough, *Kolberg* laid at least 100 mines between Filey and Flamborough Head which were to take a heavy toll of local shipping. Finally, the best possibility for the Germans was that the attack would lead to the elimination of some of the Royal Navy's battle cruisers in the newly-seeded minefields and in an engagement with a superior fleet. Hipper's battle cruisers, retreating homewards, might pull Beatty's battle cruisers into the jaws of the whole High Seas fleet.

There is no evidence in German records that Scarborough was seen as anything more than a soft civilian target. Like Hartlepool and Whitby, it was chosen because it could be reached quickly under the cover of the long winter night; it was safely distant from the Royal Navy bases at Harwich and Cromarty; and it was conveniently opposite a gap in British minefields. Scarborough was neither military nor naval base. The 14th King's Hussars at Burniston Barracks were mustered, issued with 20 rounds of live ammunition each and manned their cliff-top trenches, but the German gunners ignored them and their quarters. Far many more shells hit hotels than either the castle or the harbour. German marksmanship was indiscriminate not incompetent. If the bombardment had any preferred target it should have been Scarborough's naval wireless and monitoring station in Sandybed. However, that many shells fell near but none on the station suggests only that the Germans were aware of its existence: it is most doubtful that they appreciated its key importance.

Two days before the raid, Admiral Jellicoe, in command of the British Grand Fleet, was alerted by Room 40 at the Admiralty in London that Hipper was about to attack the English North Sea coast. This vital intelligence had been gathered from the Admiralty's listening stations at Hunstanton and Scarborough, and thanks to the recent capture of three secret encoding books the 'boffins' in Room 40 could now read all the intercepted radio signals passing to and from the German High Seas fleet.

Afraid that this crucial advantage might be discovered by the enemy, Winston Churchill, First Lord of the Admiralty, made no attempt to warn the East coast ports of imminent onslaught. Instead, it was agreed secretly that Hipper's battle cruisers should be allowed to reach the English coast unopposed and then intercepted and annihilated on their homeward voyage. In the event, neither German nor British naval plans were fulfilled: poor visibility, confused and misunderstood signals prevented any major clash of battle fleets in the North Sea on 16 December 1914.

Nevertheless, the potentially decisive value (and limitations) of naval intelligence derived from wireless stations such as Scarborough's had been demonstrated. The 'Scarborough Raid', as the Admiralty chose to call it, was a critical event in the history of British intelligence. A month later, a German naval squadron was surprised, engaged and badly mauled in the battle of Dogger Bank; and 18 months later Jellicoe was given advanced notice of the exit of the High Seas fleet which led to the battle of Jutland. In both cases, this new kind of 'Scarborough warning' of impending German fleet movements was invaluable to the Royal Navy.

There were other far-reaching consequences of the bombardment: above all, its propaganda value for the British war effort was huge. Loss of life was far greater at Hartlepool than at Scarborough, but Scarborough's wider fame as a beautiful, seaside holiday playground made it a much better publicity target. 'Remember Scarborough' became second only to Kitchener's pointed finger and 'Your King and Country Need You' as the nation's most effective recruiting poster.

After the initial surge of August and September, when it was widely believed that the war would be over by Christmas, there had been a lull in voluntary recruitment. However, by December, when stalemate had been reached with trench warfare on the Western Front, it was clear that the British Expeditionary Force, virtually obliterated after the battle of Ypres in November, would need far many more soldiers for the following spring offensive. The Scarborough Raid therefore came with perfect timing. A poster produced by the recruiting office at St Nicholas Hall urged the 'Women of Scarborough' to 'Help to Avenge the

Slaughter of the Innocent Women and Children of Scarborough by Encouraging Men to Enlist at Once'. The popular national press such as the *Daily Sketch, Mirror* and *Mail* now had fresh ammunition to hurl at 'the Huns' and their 'barbaric Kultur'. The *Daily Sketch* called for a thousand volunteers for every shell fired on defenceless Scarborough.

The Bombardment's principal affect was to convince the British people that this was to be a hard-fought, costly and prolonged struggle. They had gone to war for gallant, little Belgium: now they were fighting for their own survival. British homes, British churches and schools, and British women and children were being targeted by a powerful and unscrupulous enemy. All the unprecedented restrictions now being reluctantly proposed and imposed by the Liberal government – press censorship, heavier taxation, import duties, a ban on emigration and licensing controls – became much easier to justify and carry through.

In retrospect the Bombardment had even wider significance. The deliberate German attempt to demoralise and terrify women and children blurred the distinction between armed combatants and civilians, which had been observed for generations past. In practice, the Geneva and Hague Conventions, which were meant to protect the innocent from the cruelties of warfare and had been endorsed by the German Empire, were hollow. 'Remember Scarborough' was the first signpost that pointed all the way to Coventry, Dresden and Hiroshima.

Aftermath

The Bombardment soon receded into a fading public memory. A comparison of W.H. Smith's *Scarborough Directory* of 1915 with its predecessor conveys nothing of the shattering experience of 16 December 1914. During the Civil Wars of the 1640s Scarborough was depopulated and took decades to recover whereas in 1915 only the Central of the town's six Wards showed a slight fall in burgess numbers compared with the previous 12 months. There had been no evacuation of women and children: in the North, North-West, East, West and South Wards increases in inhabitants were recorded. It seems that nothing much had changed. Alderman Christopher Colborne Graham (1857-1943), mayor since November 1913, stayed on for another year, and eventually for another four more until November 1919. The council of mayor, deputy-mayor, six aldermen and 18 councillors, three from each Ward, continued to be evenly balanced between Conservatives and

Liberals. Though the Foreshore Road and its seafront railings had received several direct shell hits, the public was still warned that 'any person sitting or standing on the iron railings is liable to a penalty of £5'. Standards of correct behaviour had to be upheld.

The appalling British casualties suffered at Gallipoli in 1915 and on the Somme in 1916 threw the German East-coast raid of 1914 into a new perspective. 'Hun' barbarism was now taken for granted and Scarborough's losses were insignificant compared with the whole nation's bereavement. As a result, when a German U-boat surfaced in South Bay on the evening of 4 September 1917, fired 30 shells at the town in 15 minutes, and killed three people, the event went almost unnoticed outside Scarborough. Damage and deaths were confined to the central district of the town – Hoxton Road, James Street, Eastborough, Longwestgate, Bland's Cliff and the Foreshore – and half the explosives had fallen harmlessly into the sea. According to Kelly's *Directory* of 1923 'no deaths resulted'. In fact, Scarborough's coroner, G.E. Royle, examining the circumstances of the fatalities, described the German perpetrators as 'devil's spawn', but conceded that 'in philosophy, music and the arts Germany has stood in the forefront'.

During the First World War Scarborough's fishing families suffered the most. Many fishermen lost their lives and more their boats and livelihoods to sea mines and U-boats. Uniquely, when in 1917 the U57 sank 13 Scarborough fishing boats, it rescued their crews and put them safely aboard a neutral Norwegian merchant ship. By the beginning of that same year, however, Scarborough had been effectively closed as a fishing port: its neighbouring waters had become too hazardous to operate. For the last two years of the war most of Scarborough's fishing fleet, altogether as many as 156 boats with a combined tonnage of 1,989, had joined the Scottish fleet and from Aberdeen went in convoy under the watchful eye of Royal Navy warships. Nevertheless, by the time of the Armistice of November 1918, 29 Scarborough fishermen had lost their lives at sea as a result of enemy action.

After the war there was a lengthy and not always good-tempered debate about the form and location of the town's memorial. In the end a committee chaired by Alderman Graham rejected Alderman Whittaker's proposal to adopt a design by Sir Edwin Cooper of a 'Temple of Remembrance' and build it in Valley gardens. Instead, the committee accepted a submission by the borough engineer, Harry Smith, of a stone obelisk, 75 feet high, which on Oliver's Mount could be seen from every part of the town. On 12 bronze plaques it recorded the deaths of 747 men, women and children when it was unveiled on the 26 September 1923.

Health and Homes

In his annual report of 1933, Dr Stanley Fox Linton, Scarborough's Medical Officer of Health for the past 20 years, warned the council of the imminent danger of visitations to the town of diphtheria and scarlet fever. There had been no epidemic during the past year and in the previous five years the borough had averaged only 67 cases of diphtheria with four or five deaths annually. However, he continued, 'if our turn comes a considerable number of unprotected children in Scarborough will die' and therefore parents must be persuaded to have their offspring immunised.

Fortunately, there was no repeat in the 1930s of the serious diphtheria epidemic of 1918-20, partly because Linton's ominous warning was heeded. During the 18 months from December 1933 to June 1935, 1,230 Scarborough children were immunised. There was only one death from the disease in 1935, one in 1936, and one in 1937. By that time an outbreak of measles was causing the local medical authority more concern: during 1936 the schools had reported 732 cases and in the following year 249. Altogether eight Scarborough children died of measles during this minor epidemic.

As Dr Linton frequently pointed out, Scarborough's residents and holiday visitors were lucky not to suffer the worst consequences of its poor milk supply. Year after year he complained of sub-standard, watered down and adulterated milk. Even as late as 1936, after polluted milk had killed 51 people in Hampshire, he reported that the percentage of milk samples declared unsatisfactory by the public analyst at Scarborough was worse than twice the national average; and this was 'not creditable to a health resort'. Perhaps the Hampshire lesson had been learned in Scarborough: in 1937 Linton was able to record a major improvement in the town's milk quality when only one sample out of 156 examined was found to contain tubercle bacilli.

Simultaneously, the good doctor was trying to persuade children to drink school milk. At the beginning of 1932, the education committee agreed to a milk club at Friarage School, and by 1934 four other local primary schools, St Mary's, St Martin's, St Thomas's and St

Peter's, had their own milk clubs. Tuberculin-tested, Jersey milk was supplied to these schools and sold to the children at a penny per third of a pint. After the price was halved and the education committee consented to provide free milk to undernourished schoolchildren with the poorest parents, by 1935 more than 3,600 bottles, three for every four under-12 children in the borough, were being consumed each school day.

None the less, malnutrition continued to be a problem in Scarborough: a school inspection in 1936 revealed that nearly one in five children were undernourished, rising to one in four of eight-year-olds. Three years later, though some improvement was evident, 99 children out of a sample tested of 899 were found to be sub-normal in terms of weight, height and health. By this time 600 schoolchildren were receiving free milk, half of them poor evacuees from West Hartlepool, Hull and Middlesbrough. Yet despite the obvious need for them, no free meals were provided by any of Scarborough's schools.

By 1937 Dr Linton was pleased to report that pulmonary tuberculosis was 'a waning disease' in Scarborough. Forty years earlier, he continued, 'it was not a rare thing to see the younger members of a family on reaching their early twenties die one after another of consumption of the lungs'. However, in Scarborough, over the three five-year periods since the war, 1921-5, 1926-30 and 1931-5, the average number of annual deaths from pulmonary tuberculosis had fallen from 34 to 30 to 24, and in 1936 the figure was 11.

If the general improvement in the health of Scarborough's poorer resident population was due only partly to better nutrition, another vital factor was housing. Throughout the inter-war years, and particularly during the 1930s, Scarborough council undertook several schemes of slum clearance and new house building.

In 1935 Frank Drake, headmaster of Friarage Senior Boys' School, edited the 'souvenir' of the National Union of Teachers' Conference held that year in Scarborough, and wrote one of the chapters on the town's history. In it he was unable to resist a personal attack on what he called 'a Philistine Streets and Buildings Committee' of the Town Hall which had been responsible for re-naming the former Dumple Street, recently swept away in 'a slum clearance scheme'. Friargate was the new name it had chosen for the new street of council houses. Drake's disgust was all too evident: 'It is not Friargate, it never was Friargate, and it never will be or can be Friargate', he declared. Historically, Drake was right, but since then Scarborough's 'philistine' housing committees have continued to confer redundant or even fictional medieval descriptions on council housing estates. However nonsensical the name 'Friargate', it has lasted much longer than the irate headmaster of Friarage School, and the occupants of slums who became council-house tenants were probably less concerned with their new addresses than with the welcome novelties of indoor flush toilets, hot water on tap and fixed baths.

One of the promises made by prime minister Lloyd George when seeking re-election in 1918 was that a peacetime government under his leadership would tackle the nation's acute housing shortage with 'new homes fit for heroes'. At the end of the war it was estimated that the country needed 800,000 new houses. Unlike many other towns, however, Scarborough's population had not outgrown its housing stock, but especially in the old town many hundreds lived in sub-standard homes without adequate heat, light, water or sanitation; and the cheap terraces thrown up in the 1850s and 1860s had become slums.

Financed by an extra penny rate and central government subsidies, Scarborough council became a slum-clearance and house-building authority during the 1920s. As early as 1923 many of the oldest and most unfit domestic properties, usually surrounding open, back yards, with names such as Hong Kong, Vasey's, Nesfield's, Oxley's and Poad's, had gone and nearly 100 new council houses had been built, most of them on the new Edgehill estate off Seamer Road. Under the Labour government's Wheatley Act of 1924, nearly 300 new homes were built with state assistance the following year, 183 by the council, and 28 demolished. Year by year more of the oldest addresses disappeared. By 1930, Adelaide Place, Althorpe's Yard, Boyes' Yard, Clarkson's Buildings, Dixon's Yard, Gambles Yard, Hall's Yard, Lownboro's Yard, Mast Yard, and many more had become rubble.

However, it was not until the 1930s, again with the necessary help of parliamentary subsidies for such purposes, that the council cleared whole streets and replaced them on the same site with new houses. A compulsory purchase order of 1933 relating to 94 dwellings in Cross Street and covering two acres of land was soon followed by another for its parallel neighbour Dumple Street and more for Globe Street, Ebenezer and Providence Place. By 1936, 13 areas of 5½ acres in all, affecting 412 dwellings occupied by 1,625 people were subject to compulsory purchase and clearance orders. At the same time, from 1934 to 1937 inclusive, of the 980 new houses built in Scarborough, 597 were the council's own. As Dr Linton reported with justified pride: 'Many people in Scarborough, never having seen these areas, cannot realise what has been done and is being done. But no one who knew the old Cross Street and Dumple Street district with its courts and alleys and hovels, and now views the transformation which has taken place, can fail to appreciate …what this means to the health and well-being of the people, especially the children, who lived there.' In addition, one of the most beneficial improvements during this time was the substitution of water flush toilets for pail closets. By 1936, the 1,700 pail closets which had existed in the town 15 years earlier had nearly all gone.

Another major advance in the town's welfare also took place about this time: on Friday, 23 October 1936, the Duke of Kent officially opened Scarborough's new hospital.

Scarborough's first 'hospital' had begun as a medical dispensary 'free of charge to the indigent sick' and financed by the 'benevolence of the public'. Its first purpose-built home in Elders Street opened in 1859 and took its first in-patients six years later. When the Elders Street building proved too small, a new hospital was built in Friars' Entry on the same site as the old Wesleyan Day School. When it opened in 1893 it had 50 beds. Most of these were occupied by sick and wounded servicemen during the 1914-18 war. However, by the 1930s, though Friars' Entry then had 70 beds and an out-patient department and was recognised as a training school for nurses, it too had been outgrown by Scarborough's medical needs.

Accordingly, a new eight-acre green-field site on the Woodlands estate was purchased and plans approved for a hospital of 140 beds with space for 140 more. The whole scheme, which cost £135,000, and subsequent running costs were paid for entirely out of voluntary donations, collections, subscriptions and various contributory insurance plans. Only 12 beds were set aside for private, fee-paying patients and 12 more for maternity cases which the corporation financed. Nevertheless, no expense on fabric, fittings, furniture and equipment was spared. As the official brochure claimed without exaggeration, Scarborough hospital was all that modern skill and design could make it, with its fire-proof buildings, insulated walls and ceilings, central heating, electric lifts, X-ray department, two operating theatres and a separate nurses' home with 60 bedrooms. Though long since retired as borough engineer, Harry Smith designed the lay-out of the spacious hospital grounds with lawns, garden, orchard, greenhouse, nursery and two tennis courts, all surrounded by a perimeter of planted shrubs. In 1937 the old hospital was let to the National Joint Committee for Spanish Relief to house child refugees from the Bilbao district of northern Spain.

During the 20 inter-war years territorial Scarborough changed more than at any time previously since king John had given Falsgrave manor to the borough. Scarborough spread out and thinned out. Peasholm Park and the sea front bungalows and promenade in North Bay beyond Peasholm Gap represented the town's first incursion into the royal manor of Northstead, but it was not until after the First World War that the corporation bought the freehold to the whole of the estate from the Crown for £49,345. At that time the resident population of these 468 acres was only 41. Then, in 1934, more than another thousand acres were taken into the municipality, 376 from Scalby Urban District on the north side, and 896 from Scarborough Rural District to the west and south. Again, these lands were mostly pasture and wood with a population of only 667. As a result of these significant additions, since 1913 the borough's total area had grown from 2,362 to 4,185 acres.

Yet simultaneously, as a consequence of slum clearance, national economic recession and the inexorable decline of Scarborough as a fishing and trading port, the population of the borough rose only slowly and slightly. The national census of 1921 had produced a figure of 46,192, but since it was taken in late June it overestimated the number of permanently resident inhabitants by nearly 19 per cent: the true total would have been close to the 37,201 recorded by the 1911 census. In 1931 the next census returned a total of 42,384 residents. However, unofficial estimates made by the Town Hall in subsequent years – 41,818 in 1934, and 40,910 in 1937 – suggest that the gains of the 1920s were being gradually eroded during the following decade, despite the borough's territorial growth. The combined effect of these two developments – area expansion and stable or even declining population – was that the density of residence per acre fell from 16.9 in 1921, to 15.3 in 1931, and 11.2 in 1951, when the borough's population was still only 43,985.

In his annual report for 1923 Dr Linton had stated that 'the unsavoury areas in the town are the main factor in keeping our death rate above the level found in other towns of the same size' and therefore slum demolition and re-housing would make Scarborough a much healthier place for its residents. In 1923 Scarborough's death rate was

12.2 per thousand compared with that of 10.6 in similar-sized towns and a national average of 11.6. In other words, though not Dr Linton's, Scarborough had long since lost its enviable reputation as one of the most salubrious towns in the country.

Despite the persistent exertions of Linton and his supporters on the council, there was no improvement during subsequent years in the town's death rate. On the contrary, in 1937, at 12.7 per thousand it was still above the average for England and Wales of 12.4. Though infant mortality rates in the borough had fallen from 71 per thousand in 1923 to 56 in 1937, this was in line with the national trend and no better than the national record. During the same period, Scarborough's birth rate, which for long had been well below the national average, continued to fall: in 1923 it had been 15.5 and by 1937 it was down to 13.2 per thousand. Throughout the 1930s there was an excess of deaths over births so that any increase in the town population would have been the result of immigration.

Two final sets of statistics might help to explain why Dr Linton's optimism was ill-founded. Whereas once St Mary's churchwardens had paid pennies for fox heads, the corporation depot in Dean Road now paid threepence a head for dead rats. Throughout the 1930s the average number of dead rats received each year was 4,000. Secondly, during the same decade, the average number registered as unemployed every January was about 2,500 men and nearly 1,000 women. Whatever the opportunities and rewards of summertime work, the winters in Scarborough were as bad if not worse than ever. In truth, it seems that the borough's medical problems were at root economic rather than sanitary.

North Side

No part of Scarborough changed more radically during the inter-war years than the North side. By 1939, nearly all the area east of the Scarborough-Whitby railway line had been put to residential or recreational use. The only extensive grass lands left were North Cliff's 18-hole golf course and the playing fields of Burniston barracks and the new primary school at Northstead.

Harry Smith's ambitious plans for development of Northstead had been interrupted by the war. However, as soon as funds were available and urged on by Alderman Sir Meredith Thompson Whittaker (1841 - 1931), who was mayor during the first two post-war years,

Smith's schemes were rapidly implemented. The outright purchase of the whole of the Northstead estate in 1921 and central government grants to aid the use of direct labour at a time of high unemployment removed remaining planning and financial obstacles. The destruction of the north end of Clarence Gardens as a result of cliff landslips since 1917 had been a serious setback, but Smith's extensions of and additions to Peasholm Park more than compensated for their loss.

By 1924 Wilson's Wood had been transformed into the Glen. A deep ravine and impenetrable wilderness of undergrowth had become a beautiful, landscaped, woodland walk. Peasholm beck now filled a lily pond, ran over miniature waterfalls, under stone bridges, entered a children's paddling and boating pool before finally dropping into the Park lake.

Like John Woodall, Harry Smith loved trees. As he once told his deputy: 'If you do nothing else, wherever you can, plant a tree. It will be there when you have gone.' Though not so well cared for as they once were, and no longer labelled with their botanical names and countries of origin, Smith's rich variety of trees and exotic shrubs are still in the Glen nearly 60 years after his death.

In 1925 North Bay promenade was extended northwards as far as the bulge where Peasholm Dale reached the shore and the Corner Café at its southern end was opened. With its ballroom for dances and concerts the Corner Café represented one of the corporation's boldest ventures into municipal catering and entertainment. Altogether, the promenade extension and café complex cost the ratepayer £32,000.

Soon afterwards Peasholm Park was much improved by the addition of many new attractive features – a bandstand set in the lake, a miniature golf course on the north bank above it, a Japanese pagoda on top of the island, a waterfall cascading down a rock cliff below it, and several oriental statues and sculptures brought from Kirby Misperton Hall. At night the island was floodlit and around the edge of the lake the lights from hundreds of electric bulbs strung between poles were reflected in the water. Scarborough now had its own modest and tasteful illuminations. In 1930 the North side also got its own cliff tramway, Scarborough's third, linking Alexandra Gardens with North Bay promenade.

The North Cliff golf course had a wooden clubhouse and three holes on the landward side of Burniston Road and six more between the road and North Bay. The fifth hole was deep down in the natural valley, which in medieval times was called Mickledale, and the sixth was high above it on top of the plateau to the east. According to a popular legend, George Horrocks, then Scarborough's entertainments manager, was one day at the sixth green when he heard quite distinctly the conversation of players faraway and down below at the fifth. Mickledale was a natural amphitheatre and soon to become the site of Britain's most celebrated, permanent, open-air theatre.

In 1928 the North Cliff golf club moved its course northwards to its present 18-hole location straddling Burniston Road to make way for 'the North Bay Pleasure Gardens' in Mickledale. The following year an open-air roller-skating rink and ten hard tennis courts were opened by mayor Abraham Moore on the plateau above the gardens and work began below on the miniature railway and the open-air theatre.

Of all the many new developments on the North side none captured the public imagination and interest more than the miniature railway. For nearly a mile it ran from Peasholm to Scalby Mills station platforms through tunnels, under bridges, and along Peasholm Dale and then parallel to and above the sands of North Bay. The first locomotive, *Triton*, was an exact scale model of the LNER's Gresley engines, but instead of steam it ran on diesel, and pulled five open coaches capable of carrying 100 passengers. The mayor, Alderman 'Billy' Butler, was at the controls of *Triton* when it first pulled out of Peasholm station in May 1931. Scarborough's miniature train was such an instant success with adults as well as children that in 1932 *Triton* was joined by its younger twin, *Neptune*, and the two operated simultaneously in opposite directions. The single fare was threepence.

By that time the open-air theatre was ready. All the most optimistic forecasts were soon fulfilled. Everyone of the 7,000 seated audience had a clear view of the island stage set in the middle of the lake and illuminated with 40 million candle power, and all of them had perfect hearing of musical note and word of song. The theatre was leased by the corporation to Scarborough Operatic and Dramatic Society which selected and produced each new annual show, hired principal professional performers, and recruited as many as 200 'extras' from amongst its own members. In July 1932 Sir Edward German's light opera, 'Merrie England', was chosen for the opening summer season. In subsequent years, until the sequence was broken by the Bohemian Corporal, 'Tom Jones' (1933), 'Hiawatha' (1934), 'Carmen' (1935), 'Merrie England' again (1936), Gounoud's 'Faust' (1937), 'Tannhauser'

(1938) and 'Bohemian Girl' (1939) were performed before full and appreciative attendances.

The total bill for Northstead Manor Gardens, as Mickledale was renamed in 1935, was £53,588. Besides the open-air theatre, which had cost £11,308, the children's boating pool, water-chute, lakeside toilets and shelters and miniature railway had cost Scarborough's ratepayers nearly £40,000 and the tennis courts, skating rink and café on the plateau another £3,000.

The open-air theatre was opened by Sir Maurice Jenks, Lord Mayor of London, who was rewarded for his presence with the freedom of the borough. His wife, the Lady Mayoress, was given the honour of opening Glen Bridge, the culmination of the council's long-term plans to bring Scarborough into the motor age.

When Valley Bridge was taken over by the corporation in 1891 there were only horse-drawn carts and omnibuses making the crossing between South Cliff and Westborough, and though electric trams ran through the town between 1904 and 1931 none was allowed to trespass on the exclusive environs of 'New Scarborough'. However, the rapid increase in motor traffic during the 1920s and the new developments on the North side prompted some councillors, notably the forward-looking Meredith Whittaker, to support a series of road-widening schemes that would permit easier movement between south and north Scarborough. The first obstacle was Valley Bridge.

The corporation had abolished tolls over the bridge as early as 1919, but work to widen and strengthen it did not begin until 1925 and was not finished until the opening in July 1928. Since two-thirds of the £160,000 bill had been paid by central government, appropriately the ceremony was performed by Mrs Ashley, wife of Wilfred Ashley, then Minister of Transport. For such an important event at the height of the summer season there were surprisingly few spectators. Nevertheless, the long procession of motor cars which made the first crossing and the total absence of horse-drawn vehicles signified that Scarborough had now entered the new age of the internal combustion engine.

For men like Meredith Whittaker, Valley Bridge was only a beginning: Scarborough had to have a wide thoroughfare that would link the bridge and Westborough with Columbus Ravine and the North side. When faced with stubborn opposition, in October 1927 he refused to serve again as the borough's next mayor. 'I am not prepared any longer to sit evening after evening listening to the drivelling chatter of a municipal mountebank', he wrote in a letter to the then mayor, John Bielby. Without the opportunity to 'pursue a policy of further developing the attractions of the town', he continued, 'this life, in my case, is closed'. Now in his 87th year, the proprietor of the *Scarborough Evening News* and *Mercury* and father of the council chamber, Sir Meredith was clearly angry with what he regarded as blind obstruction and petty penny-pinching.

Though he did not live long enough to see the fulfilment of his dreams for Scarborough, when Whittaker died in 1931 preparations for what would be called Northway were then already well advanced. By October 1929 Westfield Terrace opposite the railway station had been reduced to rubble and Albion Street was about to suffer the same fate. A new swathe, dual-carriageway width, was being cut through from Westborough to the head of Columbus Ravine, Scarborough's new gateway to the North side.

Harry Smith finally retired in October 1933. After receiving a gift from the corporation of six Chippendale chairs and a cheque for £309, he declared proudly that during the past 36 years he had spent a million pounds of rate-payers' money. Perhaps Smith's departure explains why little more was done in North Bay during the next few years. On the north side of Peasholm Gap, where G.B. Rawling had once stored his bathing-machines, for a time there was only a shabby circus called Astley's, which the corporation took over and made into a children's boating pool. The 'Puny Pool', as it was promptly called, had an undistinguished but fortunately brief existence before it was converted into a modern, outdoor bathing pool in 1938. At a cost of nearly £30,000, the council built accommodation for bathers, seating for spectators, and a swimming pool 230 feet long and 60 feet wide filled with sea water that had been filtered and chlorinated and heated to a temperature of 68°F. The North Bay bathing pool proved to be the last major improvement on the North side before another war put a stop to further progress.

Entertainment

Meanwhile, after many years of decline, though still under the management of the Cliff Bridge Company, the fortunes of the Spa had taken an upward turn. Shareholders who had once received five per cent dividends in the 1880s could expect less than half of that by 1910. An

346

attempt to revive the sale of bottled spa water produced no profit and only provoked the old controversy over the right of Scarborians to have it free at the source.

Moreover, there were other, deeper causes of acrimony between town and Company. When the Company had first been given its 200-year-old lease in 1837 its land was outside residential Scarborough and almost valueless whereas, by the beginning of the twentieth century, South Cliff with its fashionable Esplanade, gardens and high-class hotels had become the most sought-after site in the borough. However, though the corporation's undercliff gardens were free to the public, the Company charged even ratepayers to walk on its promenade, footpaths and terraces. Consequently, when it was proposed that the Town Hall should pay £5,000 to the Company for the unused land south of the tramway and exchange more than 4,000 square yards of sands in front of the Spa wall for less than 2,000 square yards of Spa land at the top of the undercliff next to the Esplanade, there was resistance and resentment on both sides.

Nevertheless, the deal was finally struck and the plans of both were completed in time for the 1914 season. The corporation acquired more seafront ground for bungalows and bathing huts and the Company widened its promenade. Sir Edwin Cooper (1874-1942), who was born in Nelson Street, designed 'the boldly handsome sweep seawards, familiarly known as 'The Bulge', and on it a new bandstand, alfresco café, marble forecourt and graceful terrace steps behind them.

A new lease of life for the Spa's musical tradition also occurred at this time. After 22 seasons under the brilliant direction of Herr Meyer Lutz, which ended in 1892, the Spa band had passed through a dull period. In 1909 one of the shareholders named them the 'undertakers' because they wore black suits and black stove-pipe hats and their music was more suitable for funerals than festivals. Then, in 1912, the Spa committee appointed Alexander (Alick) Maclean at a personal salary of £450 as their new conductor. Initially contracted for only one season, Maclean stayed on until his death in 1936, and under his direction the Spa orchestra achieved new levels of prestige and popularity.

Though its main buildings escaped major damage in December 1914, the Spa languished and was neglected during and after the 1914-18 war. However, in its centenary souvenir of 1927, the Company was proud to declare that 'a period of placid obscurity is ended' and 'a new era has dawned'. Under the capable control since 1924 of manager Will

347

Emerson and thanks to the skilled workmen of F.W. Plaxton, who in 1925 had built a new ballroom, 'Scarborough Spa' had become 'the most lustrous pleasure-place in Britain'. From now on there would be dances throughout the year and during the season twice daily, 'evening dress optional but desirable at the evening dances'.

The range of middle-class attractions and entertainments offered at the Spa during the 1927 and subsequent seasons was almost as impressive as the claims made for them in advertisements. Maclean's orchestra played three times a day and its music was broadcast to every corner of the site. The Spa Bijou orchestra played afternoons and evenings in the alfresco café, or the children's corner café if the weather was inclement. There were three different programmes every week at the Spa theatre and five special galas, with fireworks, dancing and cabaret, during the summer. For indoor refreshment there were five cafés, a buffet and a soda fountain; for outdoor recreation there was a putting green. The Spa well in the north pump room was open daily from 8am to 5pm and customers who suffered from rheumatism, neuritis, dyspepsia or indigestion were invited to take the water au naturel, aerated or in tablet form.

Little was now heard and much less drunk of the Spa waters that had once made this place in Scarborough the focus of its visitor appeal. Even by 1914 the south well was closed and never re-opened. After the war the water was sold mainly bottled or in tablets by Clarke's Aerated Waters Company to convalescent homes. When the United Bus Company replaced the trams in 1931 and required a wider turning space, the north bandstand was demolished and the pump room buried underneath a concrete kiosk selling ice-cream and soft drinks. Finally, after several attempts to re-open the wells, in 1981 analysis revealed that both sources were seriously contaminated and unfit to drink. By that time Scarborough had long since ceased to be, in Dr Granville's famous phrase, 'the Queen of English Watering Places'. As Dicky Dickinson, 'Sovereign of the Spaw', might have lamented:

> Fair, fair and full of fame,
> But Scarborough town is not the same:
> Where is the Spaw, where I gave the law,
> And nought did lack but a kingly name?

While the Spa continued to cater for Scarborough's minority of 'up-market' visitors, the Foreshore remained the mecca of the multitudes. During the inter-war years there was a significant increase in the number and variety of places of popular indoor amusement, particularly in the provision of 'picture palaces'. As horses and trams gave way to motorcars and charabancs, so live theatres were superseded by cinemas.

Scarborough's original popular 'umbrella', the Aquarium, once accurately described as a 'subterranean palace' but now an increasingly dilapidated Gala Land, still offered 'a ceaseless round of entertainments' which included exhibitions, concerts, dancing, circus sideshows and billiards. However, to prevent its inevitable closure, the council reluctantly took it over in 1921 in the hope that it might still have a profitable future.

Northwards, along the Foreshore Road frontage, Will Catlin (1871-1953), beach pierrot and entertainments impresario, still held sway. His Olympia Picture Palace claimed to have 'luxurious seating' arranged on a gradually sloping floor which allowed everyone a full view of the silent screen. Nearby, his New Arcadia, first opened in 1909, offered performances of Catlin's troupe of 'Royal Pierrots'. Its unique moveable roof, which in a matter of minutes could convert an outdoor to an indoor theatre, covered 2000 seats. Newest and most palatial of all was his Palladium Picture House constructed in white glazed Carrara marble and designed in 'the Italian Renaissance style'. When it first opened in the summer of 1914 it claimed to be the most modern cinema in Britain.

Catlin's most prestigious creation came in June 1921 when his Futurist Super Cinema, erected on the site of the Arcadia, first opened its handsome doors. No expense was begrudged: the organ alone cost £5,000 and the total bill came to £80,000. Silent films were shown with organ or orchestral accompaniment every evening and two afternoons a week all year round. There were upholstered seats for up to 3,000 customers. On the ground floor an American Ice Cream and Soda Fountain Saloon was said to be the first of its kind in the country. Catlin never did anything by halves.

By this time the old Londesborough theatre in Westborough had been renovated and modernised to show motion pictures, and Aberdeen Walk had also acquired its Picture House for the new medium of public pleasure. In this context of intensifying competition, the ailing

Theatre Royal in St Thomas Street, Scarborough's oldest, finally expired in 1924.

Though originally constructed in 1767 and remodelled in 1859, when it was the town's only place of entertainment, the Theatre Royal had been given a new lease of life by Henry Mayhew after brief closure in 1882-3. Mayhew, was manager as well as proprietor from 1886 until his death in 1919. However, by 1913, to survive, the Royal was obliged to show silent films during the winter months.

Attempts to convert the Royal into a full-time cinema were frustrated by the poor condition of the neglected building. In 1928 the council bought it only to knock it down so that this section of St Thomas Street could be widened to accommodate motor traffic. Today there is only a blue wall plaque on the shops and night club which occupy its former site to indicate that a theatre had once stood there for 150 years. Reports received of the ghostly presence of Edmund Kean, Mrs Siddons, Ellen Terry and other famous actors and actresses who once appeared alive at the Theatre Royal cannot be entirely discounted.

The Capital cinema was opened in 1929 to take early advantage of the new talking pictures. Fortunately, its heavy ornate white ceramic façade in Albemarle Crescent was no longer fashionable in the next decade when Oscar Deutsch was building his movie-house empire. Scarborough's Odeon, one of 37 of that name opened in 1936, was on a clearance site opposite the railway station at the start of the new Northway thoroughfare. The corporation leased the ground for 99 years at an original rent of £780 a year. The Odeon's central, prominent location, spacious, modern interior and tasteful, art deco style soon made it the most popular and profitable place of public entertainment in Scarborough.

The Odeon was officially opened by Sir Kenelm Cayley of Brompton. Amongst the distinguished guests also present was Charles Laughton (1899-1962), Scarborough's own film star, who had been born nearby in his parents' Victoria Hotel, the eldest of the three sons of Robert Laughton. In 1908 the Laughtons moved from the best commercial hotel in the town across the road to the Pavilion, three times bigger and far grander. According to his younger brother, Tom, it was probably Will Catlin who had first infected Charles with the theatre bug. From his local success as Willy Mossop in an amateur production of 'Hobson's Choice' at the Arcade in 1923, Charles had gone on to the West End, Elstree studios and finally Hollywood, while Tom ran the

Pavilion and from 1935 onwards rescued the Royal Hotel. When the Odeon opened, Tom Laughton was Scarborough's most successful hotelier and long-standing councillor for Weaponness ward, and Charles had achieved immortality and an Oscar for his 1933 portrayal of Henry VIII.

Enlightenment

If the sacrifices and experiences of the 1914-18 war made British politicians sensible of the bad housing endured by many of the working class, they also alerted them to the backwardness of the nation's education. The defeat of the semi-literate French by the well-schooled Prussians had prompted Forster's Education Act of 1870 which established the elementary Board schools. The initial shocks of Boer War defeats led to Balfour's Act of 1902 which made secondary education the responsibility of counties and county boroughs; and the Great War brought forth Fisher's Act which raised the minimum school-leaving age from 12 to 14 and abolished elementary school fees.

Unfortunately, the ideals of Fisher's Act of 1918 were soon blunted by the cruel constraints of central government economies. To meet the need for many more school places the North Riding Education Committee had planned to build two new secondary schools in Scarborough, one for boys and one for girls, and to convert the Municipal School into an elementary high school for 11 to 14-year-olds. However, such progressive hopes were nullified by the so-called 'Geddes Axe' of 1921 – drastic cutbacks in Treasury spending brought about by economic recession and high unemployment. Fisher's Act was emasculated, though the chief victims were Scarborough's girls, not its boys.

In 1922 the 'Muni' ceased to be co-educational. All its 150 girls were unceremoniously expelled and forced to take up new quarters in what *The Mercury* called a 'totally unsuitable building'. Westlands, at the bottom of Westbourne Grove, had been built in 1877 to house Miss Woodhead's private girls' boarding school, but had been evacuated after the Bombardment. Though under Miss Woodhead and her successor, Miss Wood, the school had flourished, the empty building was bought by the North Riding County Council because it was cheap, not because it was best for a much larger girls' day school.

351

That the secondary education of girls, however gifted, was valued less highly than that of boys, however dull, was evident at the formal opening of the Girls' High School in December 1922. The ceremony had to be held in the nearby Victoria Hall of Holy Trinity because Westlands had no assembly room big enough for the occasion. The chairman of the North Riding Education Committee described to the girls, their parents and teachers what he regarded as 'the two objects of secondary education': 'first to enable the clever child to set his (sic) foot on the educational staircase ... and second, to raise all children to a level of sweet reasonableness'! He failed to explain what clever girls were expected to do with their educated cleverness. Dr Philpotts, Mistress of Girton College, Cambridge, the distinguished guest speaker, was even blunter. She did not recommend a University degree for girls unless they intended to teach and therefore remain unmarried.

It took the North Riding County Council another 17 years to provide the long-suffering girls with an appropriate home. Finally, in September 1939, when the rest of the world was preoccupied with other matters, 350 girls and their teachers were transferred from their 'rabbit warren' of Westlands to a new purpose-built school at Sandybed. Set in open, green field countryside with tennis courts and hockey pitches, the new Girls' High School had an assembly hall where all of them could gather every day. When headmistress Miss Elsa Glauert chose 'Per Ardua Ad Astra' ('Through Difficulties to the Stars') as her school's maxim perhaps she had in mind the inadequacies of Westlands and her aspirations for a future Sandybed, rather than the Royal Air Force, which adopted the same motto soon afterwards in 1923.

In the greatest contrast, the magnificent 'Muni' was to be exclusively for Scarborough's boys. In 1921 St Martin's grammar school had passed into the care of the North Riding; the Anglican church and its supporters could no longer maintain it sufficiently. The last administrative link between the established church and secondary education in Scarborough was finally broken. Two years later, the 130 boys of St Martin's came down Ramshill, crossed Valley Bridge, and joined the boys of the old 'Muni' which then became Scarborough High School for Boys. Coeducation at the secondary level, which had been such a radical feature of Scarborough's Westwood project, was suspended and did not overcome prevailing prejudice until comprehensive reorganisation in 1973.

The amalgamation of two different and hitherto rival schools worked remarkably well. Under Raymond King (1924-30) and then Henry Marsden (1930-61), the Boys' High became one of the leading grammar schools in the county. By 1939 it had doubled its number to 500. A preparatory department with entry at the age of eight was added in 1927 so that some boys were at Westwood for ten or eleven years. Gradually the curriculum was enriched: German became a main school subject in 1931; Biology in 1933; Geometrical and Machine Drawing in 1941. After 1926, 50% of the main school places were being awarded to County Minor scholars, and the school soon retained a small but outstanding sixth form of scientists, linguists and historians. Much to the delight of Henry Marsden, in 1939 the Boys' High became one of 20 grammar schools in the north of England eligible for Hastings scholarships at Queen's College, Oxford. Two years earlier, the school had taken up rugby instead of soccer and despite the lack of adjacent playing fields – the one amenity the Westwood planners had not included – soon earned a fixture list in cricket and hockey as well as rugby of some of the strongest schools in Yorkshire.

The First World War had also revealed an alarming shortage of British merchant seamen. So in 1917 Scarborough Education Committee with remarkable foresight and enterprise, established a new and unique school to prepare boys for service at sea.

The Graham Sea Training and Engineering School was so-called because its home and grounds, East Mount or Paradise House, were a gift to the town of Alderman Graham, who was mayor throughout the war years. Boys were admitted to the school at the age of 11 and were expected to stay for a minimum of four and a maximum of five years when the national statutory leaving age was only 14. For those whose parents or guardians were residents of the borough there were no school fees – another unusual concession at this time. The boys were given a general education in English subjects and Mathematics and special instruction in seamanship skills and marine engineering. School roll numbers gradually rose between the wars so that by 1939 there were 91 boys in the care of a headmaster, two certified teachers, a science teacher, and two special subject instructors – a master mariner and a teacher of metal-working and engineering.

The most noteworthy and best remembered possession of the Graham was its training schooner, the 100-ton *Maisie Graham*, which the school took over in 1925. Every summer for six or seven weeks the

Maisie Graham cruised between various ports on both sides of the North Sea, providing its youthful, voluntary crew with invaluable seafaring experience and often much enjoyment.

Scarborough council might have won a deservedly high reputation for its education policies, yet in the matter of public libraries its record was truly deplorable.

There had never been a shortage of libraries in Scarborough for those readers rich enough to pay for them. As early as 1733, for a seasonal subscription of five shillings (25p.), the town's visitors were able to borrow up to six books at a time from a shop in Long Room Street. By 1787, James Schofield, author of Scarborough's first guide, had 4,000 volumes for hire from his bookseller's store in Newborough. He was soon followed by other book salesmen and publishers, notably William Ainsworth and John Cole, whose subscription libraries catered for the middle-class customer; and they in turn by Soloman Wilkinson Theakston, whose library in St Nicholas Street was still functioning as late as 1904 when it was bought by W.H.Smith.

Apart from several circulating libraries, members of the Philosophical and Archaeological Society could borrow books from their Rotunda Museum, and from 1851 the Mechanics Institute had a membership library in the Oddfellows' Hall in Vernon Place. However, even when the Public Libraries Act of 1850 allowed boroughs to levy an extra rate to finance free municipal libraries, Scarborough corporation failed to respond. A poll of ratepayers taken in 1887 rejected a free public library in the town by 2,105 votes to 1,408, perhaps because there were now too many resident working-class literates. Andrew Carnegie (1835-1918), the Scots-born American multi-millionaire, offered Scarborough £5,000, £7,000 and finally £8,000 for a new building, yet even though the town could then have had a free public library for as little as a penny in the rateable pound, his generosity was spurned.

By the 1920s there were more than 600 Carnegie free public libraries in Britain but Scarborough was still without its own. At last, in 1924, when the Mechanics Institute offered their premises for a mere £1,850 on condition that the council took up the Public Libraries Act, here was an opportunity that even the miserly Town Hall could not miss. During the next five years the ground floor of the Oddfellows' Hall was converted into lending, reference and reading rooms and upstairs preparations were made to show the Harrison collection of stuffed birds and animals which had been donated to the town. William Smettem was appointed the first chief librarian, a post he was to hold with distinction until his retirement in 1955.

Scarborough's public library was finally opened by Sir Meredith Whittaker in June 1930. Almost immediately it was found to be too small for its 9,500 books and the 15,000 residents who applied for borrowers' tickets in the first full year, so that in 1936 an extension to the original Oddfellows' Hall was opened by Sir Meredith's son, Francis Croyden Whittaker (1882-1963), then serving his second successive year as mayor. Harrison's stuffed animals went back into storage and the first floor gained a concert hall, exhibition and lecture rooms. Downstairs a very fine private collection of local history sources donated by the Whittakers formed the nucleus of the reference library's Scarborough Room and space was found for a separate children's section.

Adshead Revisited

During the four decades from 1911 to 1951 that spanned the two world wars Scarborough's population rose by 7,609, an increase of 20.5%; but since the area of the borough had nearly doubled during these years by the addition of residential 'suburbs' such as Northstead, Barrowcliff, Edgehill and 'New Brighton' (Cornelian Drive), this represented an outward expansion not an increase in density.

Also, by the standard of other English seaside resorts, which now numbered well over a hundred, during this same period Scarborough's population growth was well below the average of 50%. At about 20% Scarborough's demographic increase was similar to that of Southport and Brighton, yet almost insignificant compared with that of Morecambe (205%), Skegness (192%), Blackpool (143%), and less than that of neighbouring rivals, Bridlington (72%) and Filey (47%).

Another point of difference was that whereas Scarborough's extra inhabitants occupied new semi-detached private and municipal houses and flats, the most 'successful' resorts, such as Skegness, Rhyl and Mablethorpe, owed their spectacular enlargement to bungalow, chalet, caravan and holiday camp construction. Nevertheless, in terms of resident numbers, Scarborough had held on to its position in the 'league table' of seaside resorts as 12th in 1911 and 13th in 1951.

Amongst major resorts Scarborough was most unusual in providing so many council houses for former slum dwellers while at the same time continuing to invest heavily in visitor amenities. By 1938 the council had built nearly 1,500 new homes at Edgehill, Prospect Mount, Barrowcliff and Northstead, and many more were planned for Barrowcliff. As the emeritus professor of town planning at London University, S.D. Adshead, commented on the town's housing and slum clearance record: 'Scarborough has done well.'

By 1938 Harry Smith had been succeeded as borough engineer by H.V. Overfield. It was Overfield who planned the North Bay swimming pool. In that same year, along with professor Adshead, he drew up a comprehensive and optimistic proposal for the town which was published as *The Future Development of Scarborough*. Together they made many carefully-considered recommendations designed to prepare Scarborough for the new era of motor transport; a new, direct road into the Valley from the A64 at Edge Dell which would afford better access to the finest approach to South Bay; a by-pass on the western perimeter of the town to link the four main routes, Filey Road, Seamer Road, Ayton Road and Scalby Road; the widening of several inner-town streets to accommodate two-way traffic; and the provision of many new coach and carparks for visitors' vehicles. Since travel in the future would be by air as well as road, they suggested that Scarborough should have its own 'aerodrome' on Irton Moor.

As for Scarborough's ageing Foreshore attractions, Gala Land, they wrote that it ought to be demolished and replaced by an underground ice-skating rink and surface carpark and gardens; and the 'New Olympia' should be pulled down to make way for shops, a swimming pool, dance hall, restaurant and rear carpark.

There was no question of standing still; Scarborough must continue to grow physically. The sea wall and promenade should be extended in one direction northwards to Scalby Mills and in the other southwards towards Wheatcroft Cliff. After Monkey Island had been flattened, Scalby Mills could become a pleasure park with swimming pool, open-air café and beer garden. For the more discerning clientele of St Nicholas Cliff there might be a new concert hall on Marine Parade and in the Crescent an indoor bathing pool and sunbathing terrace on the site of the White House. The town already had Londesborough Lodge for its medical baths; one day soon it should buy the two remaining big private villas, Wood End and Broxholme, and make them into municipal museum and art gallery.

Whether all of these bold recommendations of Adshead and Overfield would have been adopted by the council had not the war intervened is impossible to say and too hypothetical to discuss with profit. Some of them proved prophetical; others have never been seriously considered since. Scarborough is still without an airport; still has to rely on the old A64 approach for its principal connection with the outside world; and, more then 60 years after Adshead, is still waiting for a by-pass road.

Yet in 1938 Adshead and Overfield had good reasons to be optimistic about Scarborough's future. Holidays at the seaside were becoming ever more popular and accessible. When young Harry Hardcastle won £22 on a threepenny accumulator in Walter Greenwood's novel *Love on the Dole* (1933), both his father and sister had no doubts about how he should spend it. His father told him: 'Ah'd take that lass o'thine away on a holiday'; and Sally was more specific: 'That'll take you to Blackpool or the Isle of Man', she said. Grenwood's novel (and subsequent play) was set in Hanky Park, a grubby working-class district of Salford during the depths of the Great Depression. There and then a holiday of any kind was an unforgettable experience and 'holiday' invariably meant a trip to the nearest coastal resort. In 1933 and for some years to come the seaside was still a fairyland destination for millions of working-class families who had to live in the North's mining and manufacturing villages and towns.

During the 1930s, despite continuing high levels of unemployment in the industrial North, more and more lower-income families could afford a weekend or even a week rather than just a bank holiday away from their drab homes and smoke-ridden towns. By 1939 as many as eleven million people earning less than £5 a week were entitled to annual summer holidays with pay.

Moreover, as Adshead noted and other visitors to the town remarked, Scarborough was able to receive growing numbers of proletarian trippers without frightening away its traditional middle-class clientele. V.S. Pritchett made the point well in 1934: 'Scarborough is so cunningly devised by nature to perpetuate the amenities of the caste system ... The hills so divide Scarborough, in fact, that it has been able to tout for the masses without losing caste.' South Cliff and the Spa still catered for the well-to-do; the North side offered excellent sands and sea, comfortable family lodgings and outdoor recreation to suit the tastes and pockets of the skilled and professional; and the Foreshore was the playground for *hoi polloi*. The three took their different pleasures separately. When the author's working-class parents had a week's lodgings in Queen Street in August 1933 they never ventured as far as Peasholm Park and were only vaguely aware of its existence. Adshead concluded that Scarborough was 'better able to entertain all classes than any other seaside resort in England'.

Even fickle fashion was working in favour of the seaside. During the 1920s a suntan had ceased to be a stigma and become a social asset. The rich and leisured now envied and emulated the browned skin of the farm labourer and road mender and what better place to acquire the natural cosmetic than at the sunny seaside? All Adshead's projected bathing pools were embroidered with sun lounges and sun terraces. If anyone then knew what melanoma was the word was never spoken.

Yet there was another, unglamorous face to Scarborough. What astonished Harry Hardcastle more than the brilliance and beauty of the sea and the sands was that even in 'a holiday paradise' there could be poverty and unemployment. Scarborough was no exception; and it is this sharp contradiction between the perception and experience of the holiday visitor to the town and the sometimes harsh reality for many of its residents that has been one of the main threads of this chapter.

18

FROM BLITZ TO BINGO 1939-1974

There are two conflicting historical views of the affect of the Second World War on Britain. In the eyes of the political Left, total war promoted national solidarity and a welcome, common realisation that government had the means, if it had the will, to abolish unemployment and destitution. In the eyes of the political Right, the war fostered a dangerous, socialist delusion that the national economy was amenable to tight bureaucratic control. This clash of ideology was to pervade British party politics for the next half century.

That Britain stood alone and alone withstood Hitler and Mussolini in 1940-1 when nearly the whole of Europe as far east as Moscow had succumbed to them encouraged a British illusion that they were still the greatest power in the world. The unvarnished truth was that Hitler's army was destroyed by the Soviet Union; that Japan was brought to its knees by the United States; and that Britain's contribution to the victories of 1945 was far smaller but costlier, except in combatant casualties, than had been the case in 1918. The Second World War bankrupted Britain; and British imperial prestige never recovered from the humiliating surrender of Singapore in 1942. If the war did not cause the break-up of the British Empire, it certainly hastened it.

Yet, as with the First so with the Second, there were benefits for the British people who survived the war: long before it was over, the shape of a post-war welfare state was being fashioned. The Beveridge Report of 1942 outlined a scheme of comprehensive insurance that would protect every citizen 'from the cradle to the grave'. Here was a blueprint that assumed there could be no return to the privations and unemployment of the 1930s. Secondly, Butler's Education Act of 1944 guaranteed a free secondary schooling for every boy and girl up to the school-leaving age of 14, which would be raised, eventually, to 16.

Above all, the war led straight to the first majority Labour government (1945-50), which was pledged to nationalise 'the commanding heights of the economy' – coal, railways, electricity, gas, water, iron and steel, the Bank of England – and committed to full employment. But the most beneficial and lasting achievements of Attlee's ministry, at a time of extreme austerity, was the foundation of a national health service, which provided free medical care for the whole population; and the construction of well over a million, state-subsidized, council houses.

Though this Labour government was ousted by the electorate in 1951, the long Conservative rule that followed until 1964 made no fundamental changes in domestic policy. Even the process of de-colonization, which had begun with the grant of independence to India, Pakistan, Burma and Ceylon (Sri Lanka) in 1947-9, was not reversed or even halted by the Tory governments of Churchill (1951-5), Eden (1955-7), Macmillan (1957-63) or Hume (1963-4). By 1964, what Macmillan had called 'the wind of change', had blown through British Africa as well as Asia and liberated Ghana, Nigeria, Kenya, Zambia, Tanzania and Malawi. After the Suez debacle of 1956, which finally laid bare British weakness in the world, there was a general, reluctant recognition at home that the empire was all but over. Though Britain had its own nuclear weapons, their 'independence' from the USA was clearly fictional. In the face of communist Eastern Europe and Red China, the so-called 'special relationship' with Washington was one of growing dependence. The first British attempt to join the European Common Market was vetoed by President de Gaulle of France in 1963.

After the relative consumer affluence of the years 1954-64, the next decade under the governments of Harold Wilson (1964-70) and Edward Heath (1970-4) brought new, alarming social divisions and ominous evidence of economic backwardness. Welsh and Scottish Nationalists posed threats to the United Kingdom; Catholic revolt in Northern Ireland, aided and abetted by the IRA, led eventually to the imposition of direct rule from Whitehall in 1972. Student protest mainly against the American war in Vietnam erupted in widespread disorder in 1968. Meanwhile, devaluation of the pound in 1967 brought only temporary relief. Contrary to orthodox assumptions, by the early 1970s, both inflation and unemployment were rising at the same time. Finally, a four-fold increase in the price of Middle-eastern oil fuelled trade union demands for higher wages which culminated in the three-day working week and the coalminers' strike of 1974.

On the positive side, during the 1960s, there were major liberal reforms of the laws regarding censorship, homosexual conduct, divorce and abortion. Convicted murderers were no longer hanged to death. Eighteen-year-olds were given the vote. The Wilson years also witnessed a significant enlargement of educational opportunities: six new universities were opened; the Open University was founded; and a Ministry of Arts set up. Local education authorities were strongly encouraged to abolish the eleven-plus and establish comprehensive secondary schools.

Blitz

Whereas the outbreak of war with Germany during August bank holiday 1914 had taken Scarborough by surprise and the Kaiser's naval bombardment of the following December came like a thunderbolt out of the mist, Scarborians were already preparing for a second war long before it began in September 1939.

As early as 22 September 1938, on the day that prime minister Neville Chamberlain flew to Godesberg to meet Hitler and a week before he left again for the Munich conference, 60,000 gas masks arrived in Scarborough. They were stored in the Ebenezer chapel in Longwestgate and during the next few days they were issued to every man, woman and child in the town and nearby villages. Though gas attacks from the air never took place, fear of them was behind the apprehension that gripped the country at the time of the Czechoslovakian crisis and beyond. Why the North Riding of Yorkshire should have been the first county council to receive its quota of gas masks is not evident.

The Munich agreement at the end of September 1938 merely postponed the inevitable. Eleven months later, 1 September 1939, on the day the Germans invaded Poland, the first evacuees, nearly 5,000 children and their teachers mostly from schools in the Hessle Road district of Hull, reached Scarborough. The next day they were followed by another 1,879, also from Hull, in a party that included mothers and elderly people. Finally, on 9 September, 7,150 schoolchildren from Middlesbrough and Hartlepool swarmed into the town. Clearly, the industrial and dockland areas of Hull, Middlesbrough and Hartlepool were regarded as potentially prime targets for German bombers, but the main reason why so many evacuees were sent to Scarborough was because the town was known to have many empty beds and unoccupied rooms.

However, in September 1939, the Luftwaffe was preoccupied terrorising Polish people, and the panic soon passed. Within weeks nearly half of the earliest evacuees had returned home, and within a year there were fewer than 2,000 left. More than 4,000 visitors spent Christmas 1939 in the town assured that in the words of a local brochure they could look forward to 'a tonic holiday at Scarborough in 1940'. It was not to be: the so-called phoney-war of September 1939 to April 1940 was only a temporary respite, not a permanent immunity. Scarborough was declared a 'defence area' and received its first bombs from passing German aircraft in June 1940. In August, an eight-year-old boy was killed when a lone bomber dropped four explosives near the gas works in Seamer Road. In October, a parachute mine demolished and damaged an extensive area of Potter Lane, Short's Gardens, Anderson Terrace and Castlegate, killed four and seriously wounded 31 others.

Scarborough's own 'Blitz' occurred on the night of 18/19 March 1941 when up to a hundred German aircraft jettisoned high-explosives, incendiaries and land mines on the town and neighbourhood. The raid began soon after eight o'clock; when the all-clear sirens sounded at half past four the following morning, 23 town residents had been killed, hundreds injured and over a thousand buildings destroyed or damaged. One bomb killed seven in Commercial Street; another a whole family of six and a maid at 120 North Marine Road. Queen Margaret's school was flattened by a land mine. Fortunately, the girls had been evacuated to Castle Howard, but their building was never restored. E.T.W. Dennis & Sons, the printing works in Melrose Street, was gutted by fire and had to be completely re-built. The frontage of the Queen's Hotel in North Marine Road was so severely blasted that it was never repaired and was to be demolished in 1948. Fire engines from as far away as Middlesbrough and Northallerton were called in to put out Scarborough's blazes.

On 10 May there was another night-time raid. Many incendiary and high-explosive bombs fell on the town centre and South Cliff. Scarborough's Art School in Vernon Road was destroyed. Many other buildings, such as the Labour Exchange in Huntriss Row, were badly damaged. The Billiard Hall with 16 tables next to the General Post Office in Aberdeen Walk, having been weakened by the May air raid, suddenly collapsed the following July. It was never re-built. Leighton House flats at the end of Brunswick Terrace also never recovered from the blast damage and were eventually taken down in 1948.

If sending children to Scarborough to escape German bombs seemed not a little illogical after the events of March and May 1941, the last influx of evacuees, 1,439 in all, who arrived from London in July and August 1944, was well directed. Only London and the south-east of England were within range of Hitler's vengeance weapons, the V1 'doodlebug' or 'flying bomb' and V2 rocket missile, whereas Scarborough, it was assumed, had long since seen the last of its hit-and-run visitors.

However, by 1944, many Scarborough residents were heartily sick of evacuees. Most of the children had emerged from the poorest and most deprived homes in Hull and Middlesbrough; many of them were so dirty, infested and incontinent that they had to be cleaned at a reception centre before being allocated to billets; and a few were rebellious and even violent. They were not always welcome even when accompanied by a not ungenerous weekly allowance, excluding food, of five shillings (25p.) for an adult and three shillings (15p.) for a child. In some rare cases Scarborough's constables had to force evacuees on unwilling hosts. Fortunately, Hitler's V-weapon sites on the continent were soon over-run by Allied troops and Scarborough was then glad to be rid of most of its uninvited guests. On the other hand, some evacuees were so happy in Scarborough that they made it their permanent home.

For the duration of the war Scarborough ceased to be a seaside resort for happy holiday-makers and instead became a war zone and superior billet for many thousands of refugees and servicemen and women. Virtually every hotel in the town was taken over. One of the Royal Air Force's Initial Training Wings occupied the Grand; another found a home in Bramcote school. The Queen's hotel was already wrecked by British soldiers before it was blasted by a German bomb. The Pavilion, the Balmoral, the Crown, the Cambridge and the St Nicholas all had to accommodate a variety of service personnel. The Royal was lucky to give shelter to convent girls from Hull and their formidable Reverend Mother took virtual charge of the premises. Tom Laughton, its proprietor, decided that his hotel-keeping days were over for the duration of the war and joined the Army Catering Corps. Other public buildings were put to unusual uses: for example, the Methodist Jubilee chapel in Aberdeen Walk became an emergency rest shelter for bombed-out families and temporary home for the boys of Hull Trinity House Navigation School. At one time it seemed that there were more Kingstonians in Scarborough than in Hull.

Scarborough took on the appearance of a besieged citadel. Both beaches were declared prohibited areas; the undercliffs were sown with anti-personnel mines; some approach roads to the seafront were barricaded and guarded by armed soldiers. There was barbed wire everywhere along the foreshores. Scalby Mills hotel became the outpost of the local Home Guard who used the lower Scalby Beck as exercise ground and rifle range. Veteran Green Howards guarded the Wireless Station on Sandybed Lane. From April 1942 South Bay sands were reopened to the public during daylight hours, but swimming there was still banned because of the danger from sea mines. The North Bay pool was available to the public between June and September from 1943, though the indoor baths at Orleton School and the Aquarium were reserved for the Royal Air Force. Scarborough's streets took on a new, ugly appearance: after the March 'Blitz', over 1,500 air-raid shelters and 50 static water tanks were built in them.

Medical Officer of Health reports for the war years make revealing reading. Dr Fox Linton, who did not finally retire until 1946 after 33 years in office, was pleased to record that in 1943 there had not been a single road traffic accident death – a remarkable achievement considering the special perils of night-time bombing and black-out restrictions. Also in the same year, though the isolation hospital in Cross Lane had admitted 118 cases of scarlet fever, the incidence of infant mortality was the lowest in the town's recorded history. The following year there were only four deaths from diphtheria, the lowest number the borough had ever known.

Considering the extraordinary gathering of young, healthy service-men in the town and the number of girls whose fathers and husbands were away from home as long as six or seven years, it was not surprising that Dr Linton reported the first rise in Scarborough's birth rate for 20 years, and a much greater proportion of illegitimate births than previously. In 1943 the percentage of illegitimate births was 15%; the previous highest had been 13% in 1917, another mid-war year. After two decades of deficit there was now in Scarborough a natural surplus of births over deaths.

However, Scarborough's rat population was also increasing rapidly. In April 1940 the resident rodents at the Food Office in St

Thomas Street had consumed a large number of meat coupons sent in by the town's butchers. The Dean Road depot received 625 dead rats in 1943 and 615 in 1944 from the public, but the borough's 'rat catcher' toll of 1,588 in the first year was far exceeded by the borough's 'rodent operatives' catch of 3,951 in the second. Linguistic euphemism to disguise unpleasant facts was already practised at the Town Hall.

After the Second World War the acrimonious dispute that followed the First was not repeated: Scarborough already had an outstanding war memorial and there was neither enthusiasm nor money to pay for another one. The war memorial fund launched by mayor Johnny Jackson in 1946 had reached only £1,251 four years later, and this sum was scarcely sufficient to cover the cost of rearranging the old bronze plaques and putting up new ones on the east side of the obelisk on Oliver's Mount. Finally, on Remembrance Sunday 1950, over 5,000 Scarborians attended the emotional unveiling by mayor Rodney Chapman. The 12 new plaques were inscribed with the names of 353 soldiers and sailors, 216 RAF personnel, 22 merchant seamen, 70 civilians killed on active service, and 42 more who had died in air-raids – altogether 706 townspeople who had lost their lives.

Recovery

When the Spa reopened at Whitsuntide 1945 its buildings were then described by the *Evening News* as 'battle-scarred, needing repair and renovation'. They were not unique: the same words could have been used to describe most of Scarborough's war-torn fabric.

Some places took many years to recover from the war, and the Spa was one of them. The Spa Company under the chairmanship of Francis Whittaker (1945-51) struggled to keep alive, but as a life-long teetotaller he resigned when a liquor licence was granted to the ballroom. In some post-war years no dividends were paid to shareholders; even in the best they never exceeded five per cent. Like all seafront structures, the Spa promenade and sea wall took a terrible battering from the great storm of January 1953.

Six months later the Spa Company sold the footbridge to the corporation for £22,500. The penny toll was immediately abolished and the toll houses and gates removed from the north end the following year. Nevertheless, though the bridge was now free, the Spa Company continued to charge for their carriage drive, promenade and undercliff gardens, and there was no other level access than theirs to the corporation's South Bay pool, chalets and cafés. Finally, after protracted negotiation, for £110,000 and £2,000 more towards the Company's costs, Scarborough corporation bought the Spa in November 1957.

The immediate consequence of the corporation take-over was the end of entry charges to the promenade and Spa grounds; other major improvements took much longer to materialise. Some minor internal modernisation of the cloakrooms for the ballroom and seating in the Grand Hall was approved, but the borough engineer's plan to take the sea wall out another 100 feet and thereby provide more than 300 extra parking spaces was effectively blocked by the council's harbour committee. It was argued that such an artificial bulge would cause greater accumulation of sand on the foreshore, and access to the harbour was far more important than access to the Spa.

In November 1947, at a time of acute national austerity, Scarborough's Member of Parliament, Alexander Spearman, opened the first exhibition at the town's new art gallery in the Crescent. 'Through Three Centuries' consisted of 105 paintings and drawings of Scarborough by the earliest known artist, Francis Place (1647-1728) via the works of Francis Nicholson (1754-1844), J.M.W. Turner (1775-1859) and H.B. Carter (1803-67), to the most recent of John Piper and Frank Mason. Pictures were borrowed from the British Museum, the Victoria and Albert, the city art galleries of Leeds, Birmingham and Newcastle upon Tyne, and the private collections of Sir Osbert Sitwell, Alderman G.K.G. Pindar and Sir Meredith Whittaker. The exhibition was a superb illustration of the scenic splendours of Scarborough and its deserved fame as a subject for the most gifted of the nation's artists. Most of the pictures on loan were returned the following January, but Scarborough's art gallery had by then begun to establish itself as a place of considerable artistic importance. It was to be open free to the public every day of the week, winter and summer.

Scarborough corporation had bought Crescent House in September 1942 at the bargain price of £3,000. For the next five years it had been used as a children's nursery and welfare clinic. Then, when the clinic was moved to Roscoe Street rooms early in 1947, in its wisdom the council decided to convert this splendid building into an art gallery and also open its gardens and extensive grounds to the public. Since the Town Hall had already purchased its neighbours on either side, Londesborough Lodge and Wood End, from their private owners, this meant that all the gardens on the north side of the lower Valley Road would become a public park.

As early as 1925 the corporation had paid £6,000 for Londesborough Lodge to the West Riding millionaire wool merchant, Thomas Henry Fenton, who had bought it from the Denisons five years before. In 1929 the Lodge reopened as the municipal medical baths, the modern equivalent of the private establishments that over a century earlier had earned Scarborough the reputation of a high-class health resort. Yet the Londesborough medical baths were mainly for residents rather than visitors and offered them physiotherapy and chiropody as well as hydrotherapy and Turkish baths. Year by year, even after the advent of the free National Health Service in 1948 was expected to undermine fee-paying treatment, Scarborough's medical baths provided a welcome and popular amenity. In 1939 they had over 5,000 visits; by 1948 nearly 18,000 patient visits brought in over £3,150 to the council treasury; and even as late as 1972, a year before they closed, 3,656 customers received physiotherapy for their rheumatism and arthritis and another 1,978 enjoyed the Turkish baths.

The third house in this south-western corner of the Crescent, Wood End, had belonged to Scarborough corporation since its purchase from Osbert Sitwell in 1934. Sir George Sitwell had emigrated to his 'castle on the hill of the screech owls' (Montegufoni) near Florence in 1925, and none of his three children, Edith, who was born at Wood End, Osbert and Sacheverell, who was born at 5 Belvoir Terrace, cared to live in the family's marine villa. All the Sitwell furnishings were removed to Renishaw in Derbyshire and the house stood empty, neglected and almost derelict. Finally, in 1947, the council's libraries and museums committee decided on a new use for Wood End: the east wing would contain a natural history collection, the west would honour the Sitwell family, and the high, central conservatory would become a vivarium and snake-house.

In preparation, W.H.Smettem, director of Scarborough's libraries and museums, gathered together the literary works of the Sitwell family. In the restored oak room were now displayed the first editions of *Left Hand, Right Hand*, Osbert's much-praised autobiography, the original manuscript of *Miracle on Sinai*, his novel, and *Wrack at Tidesend*, his volume of verses, as well as the published and unpublished compositions of his father, sister and brother, kindly

367

donated by their authors. The west wing was repaired and converted into a home for the town's rich collection of natural history, which included Colonel James Harrison's specimens of extinct and rare animals and birds. Under the glass roof of the conservatory Indian python, puff adder, water moccasin, chameleons, iguanas, lizards and tree-frogs were kept in comfortable warmth.

When Scarborough's newest museum was opened in July 1951, Sir George was a conspicuous absentee: he had died in Swiss exile in 1943. However, Osbert and Edith did attend the opening ceremony despite the fact that during a preview a loose ceiling brick bounced on Osbert's head, ricocheted off the mayor and town clerk and finally felled the clerk of works. Osbert was convinced that his father's ghost had registered his disapproval of what had become of his beloved Wood End. Nevertheless, a visiting correspondent of *Yorkshire Illustrated* expressed only a common opinion when he wrote, 'Wood End is assuredly a pride to Scarborough and an asset to the county'. Entrance charges to the museum were to be sixpence (2½p.) for adults and threepence (1p.) for children. Even when confronted by the most daunting financial constraints, Scarborough's councillors and officers were still capable of forward-looking innovation and investment. Wood End was not expected to return a financial profit.

In 1937 Scarborough corporation had taken over the Rotunda, the town's oldest museum. W.H. Smettem had been directed by the council to report on the condition and contents of the Rotunda, and during the next three years he supervised the cleaning, sorting and cataloguing of its collection. However, after Wood End was opened in 1951 it was decided that the two museums should complement and not compete with each other. The Rotunda would transfer its fossils and specimens to the Crescent and become solely a museum of archaeology and history: its west wing would house Bronze-Age Gristhorpe man, Simpson's findings on Castle hill, and the recent Mesolithic discoveries of Moore and Clark at Star Carr; and the east wing would be devoted to the Roman and medieval periods. Scarborough was at last beginning to appreciate and display to the general public evidence of its eventful and significant past.

Meanwhile Scarborough had returned to the serious business of pleasing its holiday-making visitors. In 1951, after more than a quarter of a century in post, the council's second entertainments manager, George Horrocks, finally retired. Ever since 1925 he had been principally responsible for the corporation's summer galas, concerts, firework displays and all manner of visitor attractions. After the First World War the corporation had started to manage its own cafés and restaurants instead of letting them by tender to catering firms. Under Horrocks the council became the town's chief provider of refreshment and entertainment. In 1925 cafés were opened in Alexandra Gardens, Peasholm Park, at the Mere, on Oliver's Mount and at Peasholm Gap. Later, shops and kiosks were built in North Bay, on Royal Albert Drive and on the promenade extension at the end of Peasholm Dale. Between 1919 and 1932 the council's cafés and kiosks made an average annual profit of £8,000; during the austere post-war years of 1945-9 this figure had fallen to £6,000; but during the 1950s it rose again to over £13,000. The corporation made its own ice cream: in 1925 production was a modest 6,000 gallons (27,240 litres); by 1959 it had reached nearly 23,000 gallons (104,420 litres).

Yet George Horrocks is best known and most dearly remembered, not for his cafés and kiosks, but for the unique entertainment events he organised for Scarborough's visiting families. The first performance of miniature, mock naval combat on Peasholm Park lake took place in 1927. Three years later the council commissioned more miniature warships which re-enacted naval battles of the 1914-18 war. During the 1939-45 war these boats were ruined in storage by rot and woodworm, so Horrocks had a whole new fleet built to re-enact the battle of the River Plate fought in 1939. Half a century after the departure of Horrocks, Peasholm Park's twice-weekly naval warfare remains one of Scarborough's unique and most enduringly popular spectacles.

Another sea-faring theme, also attributed to Horrocks, was the 'Hispaniola'. Launched at Scarborough Mere in June 1949, this scaled-down pirate ship was a particular favourite with children for the next four decades. Every summer many thousands of excited children set sail in the 'Hispaniola' and then searched diligently for buried 'doubloons' on the Mere's 'Treasure Island'.

A third project, inspired but not implemented by Horrocks, was Peasholm Park's illuminated tree walk. First opened in the summer of 1953, at a cost of £7,000, the island feature consisted of pathways lit at night by overhead fairy lights and enlivened by plastic models of characters and scenes from well-known children's stories. Like naval warfare, 'Hispaniola', and the ever-popular North Bay miniature railway, Peasholm Park's tree walk was yet another highly successful example of council enterprise which appealed to children. Scarborough had become predominantly a family resort for people of all ages as well as classes.

Another popular revival on the North side was the open-air theatre in Northstead Manor gardens. Only the last of the eight pre-war shows had lost money, and for the 1945 season Scarborough's Operatic Society staged 'Merrie England' for the third time. From then on, summer after summer, Britain's biggest theatre went from one success to one even greater. Pre-war classical opera gave way to post-war musicals. Coach-loads poured in from all over the north of England twice a week during the season from May to September. After 'Robin Hood' in 1949, 'Vagabond King' in 1950, and 'Song of Norway' in 1951, came 'Desert Song' in 1952. On one evening during the last summer, 8,983 – many of them sitting on the grass verges and in deck-chairs – were squeezed in. By September, altogether 165, 561 had paid admission to watch and listen to 22 performances. Though the 1952 records were never exceeded, the shows continued to make a profit during the next few summers. On one night in 1955, 8,000 attended a performance of 'Oklahoma'.

The council's comparative neglect of the Spa was balanced by its concern to develop further the appeal of the North side. Along the shore southwards it seemed that Scarborough had reached a dead end, whereas northwards Adshead's glamorous vision of an amusement and pleasure park at Scalby Mills remained a tempting goal. The first and most expensive task was to extend the sea wall and promenade northwards from the bulge to Scalby beck and this major construction work was not finished until the early 1960s. The undercliff had to be cut back and 'Monkey Island', a popular playground for many generations, was eliminated entirely. However, the council's development of Scalby Mills was a disappointing imitation of the 'pleasure park' envisaged by Adshead and Overfield 30 years earlier: there was no illuminated archway entrance, no domed dance hall, no fountain, no children's boating pool, no bandstand, and no swimming pool. At the time many rate-paying residents thought that the new beach chalets, public house, carpark, shops and grassed area were too high a price to pay for the loss of Monkey Island and the natural charm of Scalby Mills.

In the circumstances of the 1960s perhaps a third outdoor public bathing pool was considered excessive and uneconomic. What Scarborough needed and should have had long before, for residents as much as for visitors, was an all-year-round, indoor swimming pool. If the Town Hall was slow to recognise this serious deficiency, the people of Scarborough were not. During the 1960s public demand grew and council resistance crumbled. Three sponsored walks of 40 miles to Whitby and back raised more than £11,000 between 1967 and 1970, and there were many other fund-raising events to prompt and embarrass councillors. When the Northstead swimming pool finally opened in January 1973 it had cost £220,000 altogether. Appropriately, the first users were many of the children from local primary schools who had done so much to make it possible.

Meanwhile, one promising post-war development was the growing diversification of Scarborough's economy which lightened the town's dangerous dependence on the seasonal holiday trade. Leading this healthy trend towards greater industrial activity was the coach-building firm of Plaxton's.

Frederick William Plaxton had started a joinery workshop in Bar Street in 1907. By 1914 he was employing plumbers, masons, plasterers and bricklayers as well as joiners and putting up handsome new buildings such as the Palladium cinema on the Foreshore, 'the most up-to-date picture theatre in the country', in record time. In the 1920s Plaxton's built the Futurist cinema and the new Valley Road bridge; but their new works on Castle Road began to specialise in bodywork for motor vehicles. In 1936 a much larger new factory on Seamer Road was opened and Plaxton's were now building motor coach bodies there for companies all over the country.

During the 1939-45 war Plaxton's made ammunition boxes; from 1946 they were putting bodies on Bedford, Commer and Austin chassis, building Green Goddess fire tenders and mobile canteens for the American air force. F.W. died in 1957 and was succeeded as chairman by his son 'Eric', who in 1961 bought a 45-acre green-field site for a new, expanded works at Eastfield. By 1972 Plaxton's employed 1,330 workers, most of them from Scarborough, a figure to compare with the 5,000 who were then employed servicing the town's holiday industry.

On a smaller scale, but of growing significance, were other light industrial concerns. Scarborough had a long history of printing and publishing and by the 1960s, to add to the long-established family firm of E.T.W. Dennis, whose printing house in Melrose Street had been entirely re-built after the fire of 1941, the town now had D.H. Greaves and G. A. Pindar. Son of the founder of Pindar's printers, George Kyte

371

Grice Pindar, had been mayor, alderman and leading councillor since the 1930s until his death in 1959. Eventually, this family firm would outgrow its adapted premises in the former Claremont chapel in Castle Road.

Other industrial companies had also moved into obsolete buildings in the town after the war. From 1946, Joseph May, a Leeds clothing manufacturer, employed over a hundred women on the top two floors of the old hospital in Friars' Way. A similar number of female employees worked for Sportcraft making outdoor sports wear in the former St Mary's school on Castle Road. J.B. Swift and Son was originally an ironmongery business in St Thomas Street. War-time munitions production pushed its workforce up to 250, and by 1964 Swift's Sheet Metal Works still employed about 200 men.

Since the end of the war an unexpected turn-around had taken place in the fortunes and function of Scarborough harbour. As long ago as 1934 the town clerk had informed the harbour commissioners that their debt to the council and therefore the ratepayers had now reached £60,000 and was increasing at the rate of £3,000 a year. Repairs and maintenance were costing more than the port's income and the council could not be expected to subsidise the commissioners indefinitely. As a result, in 1935, by Act of Parliament, all the material assets of the harbour commissioners were transferred to the corporation and the outstanding debt cancelled; but it was not until 1948 that the Town Hall at last resumed administrative control and responsibility for the whole of the harbour.

During the next few years ratepayer subsidy gradually declined until 1964-5 when the harbour's accounts finally showed a surplus, perhaps for the first time for two centuries. Under the capable direction of the new harbour master, Captain J.W.K. Hall, who held the post from 1950 until his death in 1972, the port enjoyed a new lease of prosperous life. When he took over the harbour had no trade except in fish, mainly because decades of neglect had allowed silting to reduce the depth of water so much that no sizeable cargo vessel could use it. However, in 1952, the corporation commissioned their own inshore dredger, the *Skarthi*, at a cost of £29,000, and within a short time vessels of up to a thousand tons were discharging at the North Wharf. During the next 20 years, under the captaincy of the redoubtable Sydney Smith, *Skarthi* earned many more times its original and running costs. When it was not working at home *Skarthi* dredged 22 other British ports.

In 1954 only four ships from abroad brought timber into Scarborough; by 1961 the number of foreign vessels unloading at the North Wharf had risen to 50; and by 1964 it had reached 129. The annual tonnage of foreign ships bringing cargo into Scarborough harbour went up from 616 in 1954 to 27,861 ten years later. Throughout the 1960s cargoes of timber, grain, fish, bricks, fertilizer and potatoes came in from Finland, Russia, Sweden, Germany, Denmark, Holland and Poland; but before the end of the decade the North Wharf had reached the limit of its capacity. When an attempt was made to increase berthing space and Scarborough's fishermen protested vigorously, their case was upheld by the government's Ministry of Agriculture, Fisheries and Food. Officially, Scarborough was still classed as a fishing port; its fleet, employing about 150 men bringing in an annual catch valued at about £200,000, had a higher priority than any number of merchant ships.

Health and Homes

During the two decades between the census of 1951 and that of 1971 Scarborough's resident population declined slightly from 43,670 to 43,070. Only between 1943 and 1948 had births exceeded deaths, and after this exceptional period the pre-war norm of low birth rate and high death rate returned. The sudden leap in residential numbers between the estimate of 1952 (41,740) and that of 1953 (43,470) is almost entirely explained by the enlargement of the borough southwards to include the new Eastfield council estate. Here, since 1950, more than 500 families, mostly from the old town, had been re-settled.

After the immediate post-war 'baby boom' there was a predictable national fall in the birth rate, but Scarborough's own rate of decline from 19.3% in 1947 down to as low as 12.04% in 1956 was the result of its abnormal age-profile. The 1951 census revealed that, in common with other coastal resorts to which elderly people were retiring in ever growing numbers, Scarborough had an exceptionally high proportion of 15.6% of residents who were over 65. This percentage was exceeded locally by only Whitby (15.9%) and Scalby (17%). Also, the borough's proportion of children under 15, which was just over 19% of the total, was the lowest of any area in the North or East Ridings. Furthermore, the high number of young people leaving the town to find employment elsewhere and the 122 who in 1956 alone migrated overseas also explain why Scarborough's marriage rate, 7.4% per thousand population, was less than half of the average for England and Wales. Bearing in mind all these facts, Dr William Goronwy Evans, Scarborough's Medical Officer of Health since 1953, predicted that the excess of deaths over births would increase in the future. He was right: by 1965, as these trends continued, more than one in five of the borough's inhabitants was over 65 and amongst them premature death from winter hypothermia had become a matter of medical concern.

On the other hand, infant mortality rates in Scarborough had fallen – down from an average of 26 in every thousand live births during the early 1950s to an average of 14 in the years 1968 to 1972. From 1944 onwards there had been no more infant deaths from diphtheria. There were still outbreaks of measles epidemics but the infection was mild, not fatal. Though pulmonary tuberculosis remained a medical problem, it now caused fewer deaths, thanks to mass radiography and earlier, more effective drug treatment. By 1972 scarlet fever and whooping cough had almost disappeared. Modern medicine now saved childhood and adolescence from most of their mortal perils. The principal cause of infant deaths in Scarborough was now accident at home.

The new adult health hazards were lung cancer and venereal disease. As early as his annual report for 1962, Dr Evans had warned the public of the dangerous effects of cigarette smoking. One third of all deaths in Scarborough that year had been the result of coronary thrombosis, chronic bronchitis and lung cancer – all three caused or exacerbated by inhaling tobacco smoke. His warning went unheeded: deaths from lung cancer, particularly amongst middle-aged men, continued to increase year by year.

Incidence of venereal infection also showed a disturbing upward trend in Scarborough: in 1963 there were only 46 new cases identified at St Mary's special hospital clinic; by 1972 this figure had gone up to 255. A graph showed that most attendances that year had taken place between May and October, reaching a peak in August. Gonorrhoea, it seemed, was mainly a summer holiday experience.

In keeping with the nation as a whole Scarborians were better housed by the 1970s than ever before. At the end of the war there had been an acute housing shortage: at least 800 people were without homes and well over a thousand lived in over-crowded, insanitary, unfit dwellings. Initially employing German prisoners of war, the council rapidly raised more than a hundred prefabricated 'temporary' homes on their newly-purchased Sandybed estate on the outskirts of the borough. Most re-housing, however, took place from 1950 on the Eastfield estate, which until 1 April 1953 was in Seamer and Cayton parishes beyond Scarborough's southern perimeter. Between 1950 and 1957 the corporation built 1,462 new homes, most of them at Eastfield. By the end of the 1950s Eastfield had its own shops, schools, churches, library and clinic, though not yet its own community centre. In 1972 it became one of Scarborough's six municipal electoral wards with its own three councillors sitting in the Town Hall.

The Butter Cross, West Sandgate

Having met the immediate housing emergency, Scarborough council then set about demolishing the poorest and oldest town dwellings. Throughout the 1950s and 1960s clearance of condemned houses went ahead in William Street, Wrea Lane, Regent Street, Atlas Place, George Street, North Terrace, Brook Square, St Mary's Street,

West Place, St Sepulchre Street, Mill Yard, St Thomas Walk, Whitehead Hill, Friars' Way, Longwestgate, Paradise Row and Auborough Street. Some old names disappeared forever. For instance, the south side of Low Conduit Street, including the seventeenth century cottages of Farrer's hospital, was swept away and replaced by new buildings re-addressed as Princess Square. The Butter Cross, once a conspicuous feature and subsequently a Grade One listed monument, was relegated to a hiding place behind the new building line. Low Conduit was the last reminder of Scarborough's medieval water supply; the name Princess Square had no historical validity.

One landmark in the social history of Scarborough was the closure in 1965 of the last of its registered common lodging houses at 4 Leading Post Street. Mrs Harvey, the proprietoress, had run the house for the past 15 years; her four surviving elderly male lodgers were charged two shillings and sixpence (12½ p.) a night for bed, light, heat and cooking facilities. Now she could no longer afford the improvements required by Scarborough's health department.

Another key moment in Scarborough's accommodation history came in 1968 with the end of the Friars' Way slipper baths. They had been opened by the corporation in 1949 in the out-patients' hall of the former hospital building to provide old-town residents with the washing amenities they lacked in their own homes. With some satisfaction the then Medical Officer of Health, Dr John Stokoe (1946-53), reported that 'the weekly bath has become almost a social event in the lives of a good many townspeople'. One young mother had come to Friars' Way every Friday night, put her five children in the bath together and proceeded 'to give them a good tubbing'. The charge for a bath was sixpence (2½ p.), a penny (½p.) extra for soap and twopence (1p.) more for a towel. Presumably the young mother had paid for only one bath not five.

According to Dr Stokoe's report for 1950, at that time about one in three of Scarborough's houses had no fitted bath and the corporation's newest facility had been used 16,000 times. However, as the town's early and mid-Victorian housing stock was demolished and more existing homes were modernised with bathrooms and wash basins, the number of slipper bath users gradually declined. During the last full year, 1967, when 13 houses in St Mary's Street came down, attendances at the slipper baths had fallen to 3,781.

By the end of the 1960s the borough council had practically stopped building new houses or flats, whereas private house building had once again become important. In 1968, a peak year, 242 new dwellings were built by private enterprise, a figure almost equal to the corporation's busiest years, 1952, 1953 and 1954. Most of these new private houses were on the North side of the town in Newby and Newlands. The council no longer demolished old properties to re-house their occupants; instead emphasis was now given to improvement of existing homes, regardless of their age or location. Year by year the town's older housing stock was inspected by officers of the health department. Homes which lacked the four basic amenities of bathroom, indoor water closet, water-heating system and food store were declared deficient and encouraged to seek improvement grants. By the 1970s overcrowding had ceased to be a residential problem; it was now welcomed by landladies when it meant that their boarding houses were full of guests and they and their own families slept in attics, cellars, corridors and garden sheds.

For many years there had been official disquiet about the condition and location of the Victorian slaughter-house at Wrea Lane. In his report for 1957 Dr Evans expressed his concern that the old buildings there could not be adapted to modern, hygienic methods, and their location so close to residential urban property was wholly inappropriate. It was therefore with some relief that he was able to record in 1964 that the new corporation-built abattoir at Seamer had opened in April and the old premises had been closed and would soon be knocked down.

Not that Scarborough's public health anxieties had been entirely allayed by the 1970s. Scarborians might now live in homes that were warmer, drier and more convenient and where they could keep their bodies and clothes freer of infection, but for reasons which baffled the local sanitary officials the town continued to be plagued with rodents. Until the 1950s the chief public health inspector had reported annually the tally of rat corpses found in the borough; by 1953 the number had fallen to about 2,000. By 1971, however, domestic infestation had reached such a critical level that John Pester, the chief inspector, felt compelled to draw attention to it in his annual survey. Furthermore, in the local press he appealed to builders, plumbers, electricians and other contractors, including the Gas and Electricity Boards, to make sure that they left floors and walls 'rodent proof'. During the past year nearly a thousand complaints had reached his department and during the next twelve months 300 premises were said to be overrun with common rats and another 800 with mice. Both rats and mice were becoming resistant to conventional control and to be overrun with common rats and another 800 with mice. Both rats customary poisons. The installation of central heating was thought to be one of the reasons why they were flourishing in Scarborough.

Still, 1971 was a far cry from 1871, when Dr J.W. Taylor had been appointed the borough's first medical officer of health. A century earlier both the birth and death rates in Scarborough had been about double what they had become by 1971: in a population of 25,000 there had been 835 deaths and 523 births, whereas in 1970, in a population of 42,080, there were 784 deaths and 514 births. In 1872 the high mortality of infants had to be accepted as inevitable; in that year alone 34 children had died of diarrhoea and dysentery and the last epidemic of smallpox in the town had killed 35 residents.

By the 1970s Dr Evans was not the only one to be increasingly perturbed by the increase in illegitimate births; despite the available services of the family planning clinic now open in Northway their numbers continued to grow. The war-time record of 15% of all births had become the norm by 1971 and 1972 when in each year unmarried Scarborough mothers gave birth to 85 babies. By comparison Dr Taylor had slightly fewer of such births to report but an appalling and sinister rate of mortality amongst them. In 1876, 19 out of 67 died before they were twelve months old; in 1877, 34 out of 73; in 1878, 36 out of 86; in 1879, 29 out of 77; and in 1880, 37 out of 73. His sad conclusion was that these babies were mostly the offspring of domestic servant girls who, to keep their employment, had to put them out to so-called 'nurses'. Deprived of their natural and proper sustenance, many of these babies starved to death.

Nevertheless, Dr Taylor had ended his first annual report on an optimistic note: now that sanitary matters had been brought so prominently before the public, he was sure that 'this beautiful town will ever retain the name which it so justly deserves, the Queen of British Watering Places'. Despite major improvements in public health and welfare, by the 1970s there were some who were beginning to question this proud title.

Ominous Signs

Though few of Scarborough's landladies and business men had much to complain about during the 1950s, towards the end of the next decade there were already threatening signs on the horizon for those willing and able to interpret them.

Fred Pontin, who had followed Billy Butlin and built holiday camps after 1945, began to open Pontinental centres on the Mediterranean coast from 1963. For £50, all inclusive, he offered British holiday-makers a fortnight in guaranteed sunshine. As late as 1967, a historian of the English seaside resort declared boldly: 'I cannot see the seaside ever losing its appeal'; but what he seemed to have overlooked was that warmer seas abroad lapped other foreign beaches. With the advantage of hindsight it is now clear that the 1950s and 1960s were the last golden years in the history of the English seaside playground.

In 1971, with 365 hotels, Scarborough was still ranked fourth behind Blackpool (2,055), Torbay (1090), and Bournemouth (1055), and ahead of Eastbourne (335) and Brighton (250), but its bigger hotels were already closing or coming down market. Three of the town's grandest hotels, the Cambridge, Pavilion and Balmoral, were all bulldozed in 1973. In 1964 Tom Laughton had sold the Royal which then entered a long period of decline and uncertainty. Two luxury hotels on South Cliff, the Wessex and Cecil, were converted into high-class flats. Without a regular supply of conference delegates to supplement the disappointing decline in the number of seasonal guests, there was insufficient profit to invest in modernisation. Hotel guests now expected central heating and en suite bedrooms.

The character and form of the seaside holiday was changing rapidly. By 1970 Scarborough already had 1,400 self-catering flats and flatlets, nearly all of them once part of former hotels and boarding houses. The domestic refrigerator, convenience foods, the prohibitive cost of employing servants, television and the private motor car – all contributed to the growing preference for self-catering and the decline of hotel profitability. More and more holiday-makers now chose caravans, chalets or even tents for their accommodation. Though personal disposable incomes were rising, a smaller proportion of them was being spent on the traditional week or fortnight at a seaside hotel or guest house.

During the 1960s the private motor vehicle was liberating a growing number from the captivity of the established seaside resort. By 1971, 67% of visitors to Scarborough came by car and only 13% by train. The increasing volume of motor traffic added to Scarborough's problems in other ways: access to the town from the West Riding, its main source of income and incomers, was severely delayed by bottlenecks at Tadcaster, York and Malton; many of its streets were too narrow to take two-way movement; and its carparking spaces were very inadequate. Above all, the family car brought freedom of choice: by the 1970s 'holiday' was no longer synonymous with 'seaside'.

Furthermore, seaside businesses of any kind could not expect assistance from a central government which had still to wake up to the evidence of their decline. Indeed, Edward Heath's government (1970-4) added greatly to the financial liabilities of hoteliers and the competition they were experiencing from smaller 'bed and breakfast' providers. The Fire Precautions Act of 1971 forced proprietors to introduce fire doors, fire escapes, smoke detectors and sprinklers. Two years later, the new Value Added Tax put an extra burden on hotel business while 'pirate' landladies evaded registration.

By 1971, though a fifth of Scarborough's working population was in manufacturing, nearly half was still dependent on the holiday trade which remained stubbornly seasonal. Fewer than a third of the town's hotels were open throughout the year and unemployment figures were high during the slack winter months. Every January, during the 1950s, well over a thousand men and women were registered as unemployed. During the following decade the total rose relentlessly, so that by February 1972 the out-of-work in Scarborough numbered nearly 2,500. The town's main economy was failing to provide sufficient livelihood for a growing number of its residents, and industrialisation was too slow to compensate for holiday trade losses.

Another ominous sign was the sudden, and at the time inexplicable, collapse of the open-air theatre. What had been a phenomenal success in the fifties turned sour in the sixties. 'Summer Holiday' in 1960 was more like washed-out winter; the 'Desert Song' of 1963 failed to live up to its predecessor in 1952; and in 1968 'West Side Story' was a financial disaster. Reluctantly, the council wrote off the Operatic Society's five-figure debt and leased the site to Don Robinson, a local business man, who put on 'It's A Knock-Out' there for the next 12 seasons. From 'Tannhauser' to 'It's A Knock-Out' in only 30 years showed how rapid and far the down-market descent had gone. Yet when another local business man, Frank Boyd, proposed to stage pop concerts at the open-air theatre, the council turned him down because the noise would 'distress the people of Northstead'. Here was another indication of the growing conflict between the two Scarboroughs – a popular holiday and leisure centre and a home for the retired and elderly.

By the 1970s, when even 'It's A Knock-Out' was beginning to lose its appeal, the future of the vast open-air theatre had become a perplexing problem and a growing embarrassment. The leader of the borough council, David Jenkinson, declared in 1972: 'We would never consider actually getting rid of it'; while others in the Town Hall were already saying quietly that it had become 'a white elephant'.

Critics attributed the failure of the open-air theatre to the unwillingness of visitors to sit outdoors in the damp and cold of English summer evenings, but Scarborough's indoor entertainments were also suffering losses in the 1960s. Television was killing the cinema.

The first casualty in Scarborough was the old Londesborough theatre in Westborough. Originally opened in 1871 and named after the town's aristocratic family (Lady Londesborough should have graced the opening with her presence but was indisposed with a coincidental cold), the theatre was lit by gas and could seat up to 1,200. However, just prior to the outbreak of war in 1914, in order to survive, the Londesborough had become a picture house with tip-up seats. As the oldest and least comfortable of Scarborough's five cinemas, once attendances began to fall off during the late1950s, its fate was inevitable. In September 1959, after a last full-house showing of 'Left, Right and Centre', starring local actor Ian Carmichael, the Londesborough closed its doors for good. The following year it was knocked down and replaced by faceless shops and offices.

By the 1960s it seemed that the only way to save a dying cinema building was to make it into a bingo hall. In January 1966 the Gaiety Cinema, formerly the Aberdeen Picture House which dated from 1920, re-opened as Corrigan's Gaiety Bingo Hall. Two years later, a similar fate overtook the Capitol cinema in Albemarle Crescent. Now the Odeon was Scarborough's only surviving full-time cinema.

Commercial bingo was first brought to Scarborough by the Corrigans, originally a travelling fairground family. Albert Corrigan, who was born in a caravan on Holbeck Moor near Leeds in 1904, settled in Scarborough in 1947. On the Foreshore Road he converted the Princess Hall, formerly a ballroom, into a permanent amusement arcade. Later, his brother James (Jimmy) bought the old Foreshore marine baths at the foot of Bland's Cliff, concreted the pool, and changed the mock

Moorish building into a 'pleasure palace' of slot machines and bingo stalls. He called it Coney Island.

Another major link with Scarborough's Victorian past was broken when Gala Land, previously the Aquarium, was closed down in 1966. Since 1926, the subterranean funfair had been leased out by the corporation to Bridge Bros Ltd, but forty years later it had become damp, malodorous and mostly empty, even in high season. In a belated, vain attempt to meet the growing challenge of the private motor vehicle, the corporation destroyed this cavernous labyrinth beneath the Spa bridge and converted it into a damp, malodorous and usually empty underground carpark. The whole cost was estimated to reach £358,870.

Though not fully appreciated at the time, the Beeching Axe, which fell on the Scarborough-Whitby railway line in 1965, was another damaging blow to the potential prosperity of both towns. The line inland, linking Scarborough with Pickering via Seamer, had ceased to operate in 1950; its closure excited little interest or regret. The Scarborough-Whitby line, however, which dated from 1885, was altogether different: its deep cuttings, tunnels and many bridges had been constructed at great expense and with admirable skill, and its coastal route via Robin Hood's Bay made it one of the most spectacular and beautiful in the country. Here was another opportunity missed; within a few years the line was built over and lost forever.

Finally, all was far from well with the fishing industry. Though it was yet too soon to tell how Britain's membership of the Common Market would affect Scarborough's fishermen, the rapid decline and virtual disappearance of the herring by 1970 was another blow to the town's economy.

Suspension of normal fishing during the war had allowed stocks to recover. Herring landings at Scarborough in 1953 amounted to 22,000 crans with a market value of £77,625. Ominously, however, 1954 was the last year when tunny fish, which followed and fed off the herring shoals, were caught off Scarborough. From then on fewer and fewer Scottish diesel drifters landed their catches between mid August and mid October and fewer girl gippers worked on the open piers gutting and boxing herring. By 1969 the local catch had fallen to 4,284 cran and for the first time in centuries, except during the war years, no boat from Bridlington, Great Yarmouth or Lowestoft put to sea in search of herring.

Railway Poster from the 1930s by Andrew Johnson
Broxholme – Scarborough's Art Gallery

The new purse-seine nets which could hold up to eight times the volume of the old drift nets and the Norwegian and Russian factory ships had done irreversible damage. It was the end of an era for Scarborough, which like other east-coast ports had relied so heavily and profitably on the great herring migration for nearly a thousand years.

FIN-DE-SIÈCLE 1974-2000

During the last quarter of the 20th century the British economy passed through two major recessions separated by an overheated boom. The scourge of mass unemployment returned, but now it was accompanied by inflation. By 1980 two million were registered as out of work and between 1983 and 1987 the number exceeded three million. About a quarter of Britain's manufacturing capacity, most of it in the old industrial areas, was wiped out. In 1983, for the first time in 150 years, Britain's imports of manufactured goods were more valuable than its exports. As a result, the government cut back severely on spending, especially that of local authorities, by capping rates and reducing the real value of rate-aid subsidies. Revenue was raised by the sale of council houses, but councils were not allowed to spend it. Similarly, central government receipts from privatisation and North Sea oil were used for current purposes and to keep down direct taxes, and not invested in capital projects or modernisation.

After the fall of Margaret Thatcher in 1990 there was another recession. The housing boom of the 1980s collapsed. Unemployment again began to rise towards three million, and this time the South was as badly hit as the North. In 1992 the Major government had to withdraw from the ERM (Exchange Rate Mechanism) (after five billion pounds had been wasted in its defence) because the pound was overvalued. By 1997, interest payments on the National Debt exceeded the government's total expenditure on education.

Margaret Thatcher, prime minister from 1979 to 1990, dominated the 1980s. She was the first party leader since Lord Liverpool (1812-27) to win three elections – in 1979, 1983 and 1987 – on the run. She took full advantage of the Labour party's disarray and fortuitous events. When Jim Callaghan's Labour government (1976-9) attempted to stifle inflation by placing a statutory limit on wage increases, it provoked public sector strikes in the so-called 'winter of discontent' in 1978-9, and his defeat in the subsequent general election. In 1982 Argentina invaded the Falkland Islands. Mrs Thatcher reacted promptly, vigorously and successfully to recover these distant and apparently valueless outposts of empire. The Falklands war was the last expression of British 'gunboat diplomacy', but it was popular enough to secure a second Conservative victory the following year.

The fortunate discovery and exploitation of North Sea oil and gas during the 1980s turned balance of payments deficits into surpluses from 1986; and it also relieved the British economy from its overwhelming dependence on coal. The defeat of the prolonged strike of the National Union of Mineworkers in 1984-5 effectively ended its power in British politics. Arthur Scargill was no more a match for Mrs Thatcher than General Galtieri had been. In 1987 the electorate gave her a third term. By that year trade union membership, which had reached 13 million in 1980, had fallen to nine million. The belief was born and fostered that Mrs Thatcher had at last blunted the blackmail of organised labour which had destroyed previous elected governments, both Conservative and Labour. However, after 1987, her government ran into a series of setbacks, which finally brought about her replacement by the emollient John Major. The hated 'poll-tax', rising inflation and interest rates, a huge deficit in the balance of payments, personality clashes with her chief cabinet colleagues and a Tory backbench revolt unseated the 'Iron Lady'.

After 18 years in office, by 1997 the Conservatives had discredited themselves in the eyes of the electorate presented with increasing evidence of corruption, or 'sleaze', as it was now called. The political and fiscal windfalls of privatisation had thinned out. British Rail had been broken up and sold off cheaply. The coal industry had been run down and then bought by a private company for next to nothing. The schools were subjected to ceaseless interference and reform, and a sustained attack had been made on civil liberties in the name of crime and immigration control.

In contrast, the political middle ground was now occupied by the leader of the New Labour party since 1994, Tony Blair. He had jettisoned the socialist objectives of common ownership. Just as Conservatives of the 1950s had once swallowed old Labour's nationalization of the 1940s, so now New Labour of the 1990s embraced Mrs Thatcher's privatisation of the 1980s. Blair also promised the people that he would not 'tax and spend', as his old Labour predecessors had done or threatened. His only radical change would be constitutional – devolution for Scotland and Wales, reform of the House of Lords, and a referendum on proportional representation. The result was a Labour landslide and the worst Conservative defeat in its entire history.

By 2000 all but the referendum on proportional representation was done, or about to be done. Blair was as bad as his promises. Unemployment came down; indirect taxes went up. Government spending restrictions on transport, health and education had been as severe under New Labour as they would have been under old Tory. No attempt had been made to reverse the fundamental changes made by 18 years of Conservative rule. New Labour was a government of business enterprise that had cut the umbilical cord with the trades unions.

Though Mrs Thatcher claimed to have 'rolled back the state', in fact the last quarter of the 20th century witnessed a significant extension of central government control. In annual review after annual review, local government were squeezed even tighter and local taxes had to be raised to make good the deficit. Town and county halls were replaced by Whitehall, which insisted on ever closer inspection of local services and spending. Local authorities became increasingly dependent on winning hand-outs from European, regional and national quangos. Lotteries loomed larger in the dreams of local directors of finance.

At the beginning of the 21st century, Britain was faced with one leading and unresolved question – whether to enter more fully into the European Union or to withdraw to its perimeter. Given the divisions within both New Labour and old Conservative on this vital issue, the question seemed likely to go unanswered for some time to come.

Reorganisation: Winner or Loser?

After 800 years of corporate self-government, as a result of the terms of the Local Government Act of 1972, in one important sense Scarborough ceased to exist on Sunday, 31 March 1974. On the following day the borough's old municipal identity was subsumed into a new administrative district. Some argued that the town had lost a superannuated daughter to gain a whole new family and that this was the last in a series of events which had begun in 1201 when King John had granted Scarborough's burgesses 60 acres of the royal manor of

Falsgrave. Other residents feared that the borough would be swamped by a largely rural hinterland.

Scarborough's own community was much the largest in the newly-created and enlarged borough. Of the district's population of 97,310, more than half belonged to Scarborough: 44,440 lived in the former municipal borough and another 11,536 in what had previously been Scarborough's rural district. By comparison, the other constituents – the former urban districts of Filey (5,336), Scalby (8,686) and Whitby (12,749), and the rural parishes of Folkton, Hunmanby, Muston and Reighton, previously in the East Riding, and of Whitby in the North Riding – were small in population though large in area. Scarborough had become the capital of a vast, mainly rural territory of over 200,000 acres, stretching from Scaling Dam in the far north, beyond Hunmanby southwards, and inland as far west as Snainton and Fylingdales. And the new borough council was responsible for 45 miles of Yorkshire's North Sea coastline which included three harbours at Whitby, Scarborough and Filey.

The newly-elected district council which first gathered in Scarborough Town Hall on 1 April 1974 was therefore very different from its municipal predecessor. In 1973 Scarborough's council had consisted of the mayor, Ida Slarke, her deputy, Jack Smith, seven aldermen, and three representatives from each of the six town wards – Northstead, Woodlands, Eastfield, Castle, Falsgrave and Weaponness – altogether 27 elected members. The new borough council had 50 elected members representing 20 wards. The new mayor, David Jenkinson, was a veteran Woodlands councillor, but his deputy came from Filey. All six of Scarborough's old wards had survived the reorganisation and each, apart from Eastfield, had gained a fourth representative, making 23 in all; so that even with the addition of the mayor the town had still less than half of the full council's number. Under the new Act the office of alderman had become merely honorary and Scarborough's aldermen had either retired or offered themselves for re-election.

From 1979, and in subsequent elections at four-yearly intervals, Scarborough gained an additional seventh ward, Central. However, all seven returned only three councillors each, making 21 out of the 49 members of the full council. In short, Scarborough's overwhelming demographic dominance was not reflected in its share of the Town Hall seats. On the other hand, as far as the permanent administration of the new Scarborough council was concerned, the town's predominance was undisguised. The chief executive, Russell Bradley, had been the old borough's deputy town clerk. All five principal officers, or directors as they were now called, were based in Scarborough and had their departments there. The new district was to be run from, if not by, Scarborough.

If Scarborough town dominated its own district, it in turn was dwarfed by England's largest county, North Yorkshire. Police, fire and social services, highways, libraries and schools were all county, not borough responsibilities, and they took away most of the town's revenue from taxation and the powers of its local councillors. By 2000, band D council-tax payers in Scarborough contributed £2 30p. a week to the Town Hall and £11 90p. a week to Northallerton's County Hall. Scarborough's concerns and interests as a coastal resort were shared by Whitby and Filey, its borough partners, but North Yorkshire was a vast farming and forested territory: 62 per cent of its area was National Park.

Nevertheless, even with the advantage of hindsight, it is far from clear whether the people of Scarborough derived more benefit than handicap from this re-arrangement of local government which is now more than a quarter of a century old. There are so many other historical factors and variables in the equation to confuse the answer.

In the first place, during the last 25 years, at both national and local level, there have been radical fluctuations in party political control. The Labour governments of Wilson and Callaghan (1974-9) were succeeded by the Conservative administrations of Thatcher and Major (1979-97), and they in turn by the New Labour government of Blair (1997-). These political upheavals at Westminster and in Whitehall were contradicted by the perverse electors of Scarborough. In 1983, when Mrs Thatcher was returned with a hugely increased majority, in Scarborough her party lost a long-held majority in the council chamber. In Falsgrave, all three Tories, who included two former mayors, were unseated by the three Labour candidates. Eight years later, in 1991, when the Conservatives were still running the country, local elections in Scarborough resulted in an unprecedented victory for a revitalised Labour group. Of the 21 municipal places, Labour won 16 and the Conservatives were left with only five; and for the first time Labour became the largest party in the whole district.

Finally, in May 1999, with a Labour government back in Downing Street after an absence of 18 years, Scarborough's Labour Party suffered a shattering defeat. Eastfield, which hitherto had always returned three Labour representatives, now turned its back on the party and ousted both the council leader, Mavis Don, and the current mayor, Fred Standing. The same punishment of its Labour councillors was inflicted by Northstead. Consequently, as the nation anticipated another Labour triumph in a general election, council leadership in Scarborough had returned to the Tories under Eileen Bosomworth.

What effect these seismic changes in party political control made to Scarborough is hard to find. Indeed, throughout these years, despite many changes in personnel and party labels, there was remarkable continuity and monotonous repetition. Some refrains never altered. There were persistent claims from the Town Hall that central government, whatever its political complexion or the state of the national economy, undervalued Scarborough's financial needs; and the result was an annual dirge of expenditure cuts and postponements and tax increases.

At the end of 1980, under the government's new block grant rate system announcement by Environment Secretary Michael Heseltine, Scarborough stood to lose £600,000, whereas Blackpool would gain the same amount and Bournemouth's allocation would rise from £2.5 million to £4.1 million. When Scarborough's councillors and the chief executive, Russell Bradley, met government ministers in Whitehall to protest about this unfair rate-support grant, they came away frustrated and disappointed. Russell Bradley said that Scarborough had been compared with Ryedale by civil servants who did not realise that it was responsible for 45 miles of coast and two major harbours! To those with historical perception it seemed that the bias against Scarborough which dated from the first Tudor monarch was still current in the capital.

Year after year the chief executive complained that Mrs Thatcher's government was blind to Scarborough's special needs and deaf to its petitions. In 1983 he told councillors: 'We are a major resort with minor resort resources'. From 1985 his successor, John Trebble, had no more success in persuading either Conservative or Labour ministers that Scarborough had exceptional financial burdens. By 1988 grant allocation from central government had fallen from 61 to 40 per cent of the borough's spending requirements. At the end of 1997, senior Labour councillor, Ian Stubbs, regretted that Scarborough had been 'treated most unfairly' by New Labour's latest restrictions on local borrowing and spending. The chief executive's simultaneous conclusion, that 'financial constraints on local government remain

390

severe and the need for the borough council to find savings within its revenue and capital budgets is a constant requirement', might have prefaced any one of the council's annual reports from 1975 through to 2000.

As a result, every year there were new economies proposed and practised. After a sequence of staff cuts, in 1982 Russell Bradley announced that the council had reached 'rock-bottom'. Yet the number of full-time employees in 1981, 1170, had fallen to 908 by 1988. Even so, by the year 2000, to achieve even further administrative savings, the Town Hall was planning to centralise all its departments in one location on the St Nicholas-King Street site.

To raise the capital revenue the council had to sell property. In 1980 Normanton Rise was auctioned off for £80,000 and the department of tourism transferred from there 'temporarily' to the council's Londesborough Lodge. Though this was described at the time by one councillor as 'a misuse of a very good building', more than two decades later Londesborough Lodge is still occupied by council officers. Financial necessity was the sole engine of policy.

Under the Thatcher government's 'right to buy' scheme, the council sold more than a thousand homes between 1982 and 2000, during which time its housing stock fell from 4,345 to 3,153. However, Whitehall allowed the council to spend only a quarter of the proceeds raised. By 2000 councillors were complaining that they no longer had the financial resources to maintain their houses and were proposing to offer all of them for sale.

Throughout the 1980s the council continued to put properties on the market. Town houses and shops on St Nicholas Cliff, Marine Parade and York Place, Seamer abattoir, Scalby Manor Hotel, Oliver's Mount farm were all auctioned for cash. By 1991, Michael Barrett, then director of finance, warned councillors that soon they would 'no longer have many assets to sell'. Five years later, the council had abandoned plans to restore the decaying South Bay pool, and decided to demolish unprofitable beach chalets, close the North Bay cliff lift, introduce charges for admission to Scarborough's museums, and increase them for the few surviving public lavatories. The following year Raincliffe and Row Brow farms and shops in North Marine Road were sold to finance capital investment. Yet during all these years of stringent economies and cuts in services and maintenance, Scarborough's householders were required to pay annual increases in rates and taxes usually well above the level of inflation.

The unpalatable truth was that the town's main source of income and employment, tourism, was failing to sustain the traditional forms of holiday and leisure amenity. In almost every sense Scarborough had entered a downward spiral. Fewer visitors spending less meant that Scarborough could no longer fund its loss leaders – such as parks, gardens and theatres – with diminishing income from what had once been highly profitable outlets – such as catering, chalets, deck chairs and outdoor entertainments.

The evidence was plain to see in the annual reports and abstracts of accounts published by the Town Hall from 1982 onwards. Nearly all the council's own facilities were soon losing money. Reaching a peak of over 150,000 in 1985-6, attendances at the Sports Centre on Filey Road had fallen to fewer than 100,000 by 1998-9; annual admissions to the indoor pool fell by 25,000 between 1994 and 1999; beach chalets that had once earned a surplus went into deficit in 1986-7 and never recovered; by the 1990s the council's own cliff lifts were taking less than they were costing to service and repair; and catering, that had once been so profitable, was running into the red by the end of the 1980s. Peasholm Park was only just holding its own financially and so was the miniature railway, but as early as 1982 the North Bay outdoor pool had become a serious liability. Putting up prices merely deterred customers. To cut losses the council had to lease out to tenants.

The renovation of the Spa and the opening of a London sales office in the early 1980s revived Scarborough's conference trade, but only temporarily. The 61,029 delegates who came to 371 conferences in 1987-8 represented about ten per cent of the town's visitors that year. A decade later, their numbers had slumped to 18,255, who attended only 46 conferences at the Spa. Even the number of nights visitors spent in caravans at Scalby Manor dropped by a third between 1996 and 1998. Only the council's car parks were raising significant revenue, though there were many complaints that their charges were too high. Significantly, whereas the council had doubled the printing run of official holiday guides during the 1980s to 200,000 a year, there was no further increase in the 1990s. And it was not only council attractions that failed to make ends meet: when the North Bay's Sea-Life Centre first opened its doors in May 1991, 20,000 visitors passed through them in two weeks, whereas during the whole of 2000 the Centre sold only 3,000 entrance tickets.

In January 2000 *The Times* recommended Scarborough in the winter to its readers, though only for a weekend break. The attractions of Britain's first seaside resort were listed as ice-cream, fish and chips, the Stephen Joseph Theatre *[plate 8]*, two museums and an art gallery which closed on Sundays. The following August the government in London announced its intention to launch an inquiry into the decline and decay of seaside holiday towns.

Between 1965 and 1999 the number of British subjects travelling abroad for their holidays soared from five to 27 million a year. When in September 2000 a further fall of 15 per cent in the number of people attending Scarborough's summer season indoor shows was revealed, the council's director of tourism blamed 'variable weather conditions', and the council's head of leisure services pinned responsibility on a rise in the cost of motor diesel fuel. Even for those who were best placed to take a strategic view the leaves were still obscuring the forest.

Town Centre: Supermarkets, Pedestrians and Parking

Another kind of revolution took place in Scarborough during the final quarter of the twentieth century – a revolution in the physical appearance and character of the town centre. As elsewhere in the country, the arrival of superstores and shopping malls, the unrelenting demands of the motor car and the irresistible economies of retail commerce changed utterly Scarborough's streets and shops.

Whether these radical changes were improvements or disasters remains a controversial subject. Scarborians like Louise Brindley, with strong nostalgic feelings, believed that 'the rot set in when they bulldozed the Pavilion, the Balmoral, the Londesborough theatre and Bar church'. 'They' were, of course, the councillors and officials in the Town Hall who from the 1970s onwards thought that these major structural alterations were unfortunate but entirely unavoidable if Scarborough was to prosper in the future. As Jonathan Allison, chief planning officer, said in 1982, the same year as Miss Brindley's outburst, when introducing another scheme of street pedestrianisation: 'If Scarborough is going to compete as a shopping centre, it must adapt to people's requirements and release them from harassment of traffic'.

In retail trade, as in the leisure industry, Scarborough was being brought down-market during these years. One by one the high quality stores, which had once catered for middle-class preferences and purses, had to give place to those that served the mass market. Anderson and Flintoff, Marshall and Snelgrove, Tonks and Rowntree, all disappeared. Tonks descended to Superdrug after Littlewoods had backed out; Rowntree became Debenham which was then bought by the Burton group; Marshall and Snelgrove in St Nicholas Street, one of the most prestigious department stores in the north of England, became Marshall House, which by the end of the century had turned into an abandoned, derelict shell with trees growing out of its upper blocked windows.

On the afternoon of Tuesday, 3 January 1984, the future of Scarborough's trading centre was to be determined. No fewer than five retail giants had made bids for four locations. ASDA wanted to invest £10 million in a superstore and car park for 500 vehicles on the Plaxton's works site on Seamer Road after the coach-building firm had moved out to Eastfield; both Fine Fare and Morrison's had made an offer for the council's Dean Road old prison and depot; Hillard's had asked for the United bus station at Westwood; and Proudfoot, a local family business, was asking for an extension to their existing premises at Eastfield. After a marathon session lasting nearly six hours, the town's fate was decided.

In the council chamber there was general agreement that Scarborough could carry only one more supermarket, so that in deference to local grocers and residents the Dean Road depot was saved from Fine Fare and Morrison's, and Hillard's got the Westwood site. However, the most crucial decision concerned ASDA. On the mayor's casting vote its application was rejected and when renewed five months later rejected again by 25 votes to 16. Since 1971 the number of vacant shops in the town centre had increased from 13 to 40 and there was a growing fear that a perimeter superstore would suck the commercial life-blood out of Scarborough. What the town needed urgently was a high-street, not a suburban, shopping mall.

What chief executive, John Trebble, hailed as 'the most valuable and significant redevelopment scheme in the history of Scarborough', the Brunswick Pavilion, took several years to materialise. Two years earlier, in 1987, two rival developers had confronted each other; but only one of them could win. In one corner, Clayform Properties advanced a far-reaching proposal to put £20 million into a new shopping complex they chose to call 'St Thomas Walk'. Against them, the Burton Property Trust offered a similar gigantic investment and new property fronting Westborough on the Rowntree site.

On the face of it, Clayform seemed to have the edge: already they had bought up all the freeholds in the earmarked area which included the Tesco store, the North Street multi-storey car park, Chapman's Yard and Waterhouse Lane. None of these properties had architectural merit and some of them were run down. In contrast, Brunswick Pavilion would require the destruction of the former Rowntree store, now owned by Debenham, listed Brunswick Terrace behind it, and the Quaker Meeting House in York Place. Furthermore, whereas the Newborough frontage to 'St Thomas Walk' was already pedestrianised and access roads on the North Street side newly made and widened, the Brunswick site was still surrounded by busy vehicle thoroughfares. Nevertheless, the Town Hall preferred Burton to Clayform, perhaps because the former offered up to 340 extra car park spaces whereas Clayform would have merely incorporated the existing North Street multi-storey.

In the event, though there was strong public opposition to the demolition of what remained of Brunswick Terrace and even more to the loss of the Rowntree building that had housed 'Harrods of the North', Brunswick Pavilion was completed with remarkable speed and efficiency. During the unpromising commercial circumstances of the late 1980s and early 1990s, the new shopping mall was regarded by councillors and officers as necessary to the revitalisation of the town centre. As David James, then director of tourism, noted in 1989, of the £135 million visitors brought annually into the borough, £40 million was spent in the town's shops.

Accordingly, when work started on the Brunswick project the council spent £2,000 on a firework display; and when the first phase was finished in July 1990 the mayor led a procession from the Royal Hotel accompanied by a jazz band, London's town crier (Scarborough's had a previous engagement), jugglers and clowns. Though a slump in high-street trading forced Burton to put its properties on to the market, the last phase was competed in October 1991.

The council's optimism about the Brunswick Pavilion has been largely vindicated. Nearly all of its 40 shops have been leased continuously, even in times of recession. In the past decade up to 165,000 customers a week have passed through its doors and up and down its escalators. On the other hand, the Balmoral site remains as 'undeveloped' at the end of the century as it was when Clayform first

Pedestrian Precinct

put forward their ambitious proposals for it.

One of the major reasons for the comparative stagnation of town-centre marketing during the 1990s was the radical reversal of Town Hall policy. Opposition to perimeter supermarkets now failed to prevent planning consent being given to two more – Morrison's, alongside the new A64 Seamer by-pass, and, most controversial of all, first Tesco, then Safeway, on the Gallows Close at Falsgrave. Moreover, most of the east side of Seamer Road, former railway and gasworks land, was gradually given up to retail outlets which competed with Scarborough town shops. In these changed conditions, it was not surprising that Scottish Widows, successor to Clayform, withdrew their plans, which in the words of one senior council officer would have breathed 'vitality and viability into the town centre'. Once undisputed queen of the Yorkshire coast, Scarborough at the beginning of the 21st century seemed more like a distressed damsel anxiously waiting for a rich rescuer.

Another sign of 'distress' was the continuing decline in the town's hotel business. Some of the bigger concerns, such as the Prince of Wales and Gibson's, survived transformed into luxury retreats for the elderly and well-heeled. Older, town-centre, formerly coaching inns experienced differing fates. The Castle in Queen Street was burnt down but phoenix-like eventually rose up again to become a handsome block of residential flats. Once the Old Bar, before that Miller's, and before that the Nag's Head, the Huntsman was preserved as a shoe shop. The Talbot, another eighteenth-century inn, survived only as an exterior. The Victoria became the Old Vic and the George was renovated as the New George. The Bell endured, but only just, and like the others had witnessed busier and better days. The Grand Hotel was bought by Butlin's.

Yet but for the council's policy of creeping pedestrianisation the town centre might well have suffered terminal decay. After the neglect of traffic management in the 1970s, between 1980 and 1992 a pedestrian zone stretching from the St Thomas – St Nicholas Street junction with Newborough to the York Place – Albemarle Crescent junction with Westborough was gradually laid down, and less successful attempts were made to create an inner ring road around it. North Street, Victoria Road and Somerset Terrace were all widened and a new link connection cut between North and St Thomas Streets. The Odeon and Falsgrave roundabouts were replaced by computer-controlled traffic lights.

However, there remained at least two insuperable obstacles: St Nicholas Street could not be widened to take two-way traffic movements, and of the five multi-storey car parks once envisaged for Scarborough centre only one existed by the end of the 1990s. Early plans to by-pass the St Nicholas Street bottleneck were abandoned. In the absence of effective park-and- ride facilities on the outskirts of the town, Scarborough's streets were unable to accommodate the growing numbers of motor cars. Parked cars on narrow, one-way streets were making the town's traffic thrombosis chronic, not just seasonal. As a consequence, in 2000 the council felt obliged to introduce a comprehensive and highly-contentious control of street parking, the results of which have yet to be assessed. As a declining seaside resort Scarborough could ill-afford to be regarded as anti-motorist.

South Side

After local government reorganisation in 1974, the town settled down to a drawn-out conflict between the new council's scheme to remodel the Spa buildings and a well-supported public determination to

South Bay and Oliver's Mount in 2000

preserve Verity and Hunt's Victorian creation. In the end, after a three-day hearing in January 1978, the Department of Environment's inspector remained unconvinced that the council's proposed drastic alterations were either necessary or desirable: he recommended the refusal of listed-building planning consent. As a result, the council was compelled to settle for restoration of the interior of the Grand Hall, repairs to exterior stone-work, and major improvements to the ballroom, Vita Dome and Regency Room. Altogether the cost was estimated to reach £5 million.

The official re-opening of the restored Grand Hall took place on 23 May 1981, just over a century after the original opening. This time the chief guest was Michael Montague, chairman of the English Tourist Board. All those present on this occasion could not but admire the great care, sensitivity and skill which had been invested in the work of restoration and modernisation. The Grand Hall's first decorative colours of pastel green and blue had been re-discovered under many layers of old paint and re-applied; air conditioning, central heating and modern lighting had been installed; and 2,000 new, tip-up, luxury seats could now be removed to storage whenever the hall was to be used for exhibitions. Max Jaffa was the leading performer at the first gala concert that evening; and the following day he began his 22nd consecutive season at the Spa.

The council's hopes that the refurbished Spa would enhance the town's reputation and success as one of the country's principal conference venues was not to be fulfilled in the long run. Delegate numbers seem to have reached a peak in 1987 when more than 60,000 attended 371 conferences, but there was no significant recovery from the recession in the early 1990s. By 1998 the figure had fallen to 24,885 at 51 conferences; and advanced bookings for 2001 were down to only 34 conferences attended by fewer than 20,000. By then Scarborough had long since lost the major political party and trade union assemblies to Blackpool, Brighton and Bournemouth, and many of its others to Harrogate.

One restoration that did not occur was that of the Spa waters. As early as 1967 Clarke's Aerated Waters and Bottling Company of Clifton Street lost its council licence to bottle and sell Spa water, and this marked the end of sales to customers. However, in 1986, councillors supported a plan to reopen the subterranean pump room beneath the Spa promenade which had been sealed over with concrete five years earlier. Unfortunately, these same councillors eventually decided that £65,000 was too high a price to pay, despite their previous acknowledgment of 'the unique significance of the Spa wells in the history of Scarborough and their potential interest as a tourist attraction'. Consequently, Scarborough's famous spa waters survived only as an undrinkable, brown trickle running down the outer wall of the promenade.

As long ago as 1938, Adshead and Overfield had recommended the demolition of the old Olympia building on the Foreshore Road and its replacement with a new combination of shops, dance hall, restaurant and indoor swimming pool. By 1975, the Olympia, originally built as a wooden fisheries exhibition hall 80 years earlier, had become an expensive embarrassment to the Town Hall; its once-popular dance floor was now an antiquated cinema.

The spectacular bonfire that completely destroyed the old Olympia's Funhouse amusements, cinema and lock-up shops in July

1975 was therefore regarded with some relief: it raised nearly half a million pounds from fire insurance which went towards paying for the renovation of the Spa; and at minimal cost to the council it cleared the site for redevelopment.

However, the new Olympia Leisure, put up by the Redcar Amusement Park Company in 1980 on the site leased from the borough council, was some way short in design, appearance and amenity of that envisaged by Adshead and Overfield. The ground-floor amusement arcade was like every other of its kind on every other seafront only uglier, and the so-called 'medieval village' shops on the upper level soon proved a commercial as well as a visual failure. In 1986 the shops became an ice-rink and later still the ice-rink turned into a ten-pin bowling alley.

Yet the fate of the Olympia was better than that of the Windmill, its Victorian neighbour on the other side of the cliff lift below the Grand Hotel. Pulled and deliberately burnt down in 1980, 20 years later the 'Windmill' remains as an empty, unsightly gap, waiting vainly for a developer to take it from the council's hands.

Sadder still was the fate of the South Bay swimming pool. Even as late as the 1960s the pool attracted thousands of holiday-makers and residents every summer, but at the end of the next decade daily receipts were sometimes as little as five pounds. Under-funded, out-of-date and out of fashion, this cold, sea-water pool was threatened with closure by 1980. 'Save the South Bay Pool' campaign, backed by the town's Civic Society and the South Cliff Traders' Association, forced the Town Hall to concede a reprieve. Various 'solutions' were put forward to save the pool, but none was favoured by the council, and the end came in 1989.

Deserted, derelict and surrounded by a grim security fence to keep out vandals, the South Bay pool still awaits an adventurous saviour. About its future only one thing is certain: after the instability of South Cliff was dramatically illustrated by the Holbeck slide of 1993, the physical structure of the pool must be retained to buttress the land behind it and withstand the force of the incoming sea.

One area of council planning policy which had mixed fortunes concerned the relentless spread of amusement places. Some councillors would have allowed crude market forces to prevail; fortunately, more of them held the view that slot-machine arcades should be confined to the popular Foreshore. With its 18 listed properties, Sandside ought to be preserved as a harbour frontage, and Eastborough should remain a shopping thoroughfare.

Though the council lost the first round on appeal in 1981, four years later it won a crucial victory by preventing no.4 Sandside, the Golden Grid restaurant, from becoming yet another place of electronic games, flashing lights and raucous music. Consequently, from then on, the Town Hall was able to launch a successful programme of repair and conservation which has greatly improved the appeal and appearance of Sandside.

Efforts by shopkeepers and café proprietors to undermine the Sandside Project, as it is called, were resisted and usually defeated, though the surprising concession of an extended lease to Luna Park was a serious setback for those who wanted the harbour to be reserved for sea-craft. Indeed, the loss of cargo trade and the continued decline of the local fishing industry during the 1990s had plunged the harbour's accounts into deficit, so that commercial calls intensified for more of it to be converted into a permanent 'pleasure park'.

Finally, the bold experiment to set up a commercial museum of Scarborough's history on Sandside lasted all too briefly. When Henry Marshall's 'Happy Hour Fun Factory' reopened in 1993 as 'Millennium Themes' it was universally and warmly welcomed, even though some of its 'history' was of doubtful accuracy. However, for whatever reasons, 'Millennium Themes' failed to attract enough paying customers for its owner and part of the building reverted to an amusement arcade at the end of the second millennium. Whether seafront Scarborough, in particular Sandside, would keep the oldest form of its historical character as working harbour and fishing port or become even more like South Shore Blackpool is still an open question.

Yet another indication of the decline of Scarborough as a visitor resort was the regrettable neglect and decay of Scarborough Mere. For 43 summers the 'Hispaniola' had given pleasure and excitement to countless numbers of children, but in 1993 it was removed from the lake and dry-docked in Peasholm Gap. Though the council then spent £350,000 dredging the Mere, no private developer could be found to regenerate the area. The Mere café was closed; the boats transferred to Peasholm Park. Plans to make the Mere part of an extensive country park on Scarborough's perimeter remained on paper. 'Hispaniola' was sold and re-launched as a South Bay pleasure boat. Whether the Mere can ever be revived as a visitor attraction remains a matter of discussion and speculation.

North Side

Donkey-rides on North Bay beach

Meanwhile attempts were being made by private business to revive the holiday attractions of North Bay. Don Robinson, managing director of Beach Management Limited, had secured a lease from the council on the six-acre site overlooking Northstead Manor Gardens. The redundant hard tennis courts and roller-skating rink were transformed into a miniature Disneyland for the 1969 season. Scarborough's new Zoo and Marineland had an aviary of 200 exotic birds, chimpanzees, sea lions, penguins, seals and otters. Two performing dolphins gave six shows daily in a small, heated pool.
Attached to it, the Adventure Park had dodgems, roundabouts and 'the largest slide in Europe'.

The Zoo and Marineland proved a major, if only temporary, commercial success: in its final year, 1984, it drew nearly half a million paying customers, and was the sixth most popular wildlife attraction in Britain, surpassing both Whipsnade and Edinburgh zoos. However, from 1985, when the site was converted into 'Mr Marvel's Showtime

USA Fun Park', it was all downhill. The installation of a complete American street in 1986 and the construction of a 90-metre-long chairlift in 1990 failed to restore its earlier profitability.

At the same time the council's own North Bay bathing pool was running further into debt. Even during good summers when more than 100,000 visitors paid admission, the deficit was still tens of thousands of pounds. As a result, in 1984, the pool was leased to Kunick Holdings, a partnership of Don Robinson and the former holiday camp owner, Sir Fred Pontin. At a cost of about half a million pounds they changed the 1938 swimming pool into a water-theme park, principally by adding two spiral water-shutes, each 165 metres long, then the longest in Europe, a 30-seat jacuzzi and a water cannon feature. By 1991, 'Watersplash World', as it was then called, was described by the BBC 'Holiday' programme as Scarborough's 'biggest tourist attraction'. *Daily Mirror* readers voted it fourth in a list of the country's top ten theme parks.

But it was not to last. Soon afterwards, Scarborough council was obliged to take back direct management of the pool, spend nearly a quarter of a million pounds on repairs, and again carry the financial consequences of falling attendances. During the summer of 1999, 'Atlantis Water Park', its latest name, admitted only 40,000, and the following year lost a staggering £200,000. By then the borough's director of tourism suggested that instead of opening from May until September it should only operate in the two peak months of July and August.

Yet on the North side not all was gloom and doom. Throughout the summers of the 1990s the laughter of many happy children could be heard in Kinderland. Designed by local architect John Stockill and paid for by Dudley Wallis out of the sale of his Cayton Bay caravan park, Kinderland transformed an overgrown allotment area and travelling circus site on Burniston Road into a delightful children's playground. Here there were no slot machines, no mechanical rides, no animals and no loud music, yet in its first two seasons, in 1985 and 1986, 275,000 visitors young and old passed through its welcoming turnstiles. Paying only one entry charge, they found picnic places, shops, cafeteria, and a rich variety of safe amusements which included a water chute and boating on Northstead Manor Gardens lake. Red uniformed 'girl Fridays' were employed to supervise the children as they climbed frames and ropes, descended slides, jumped on trampolines, or

403

simply played in sand pits. Nearby residents who had opposed Kinderland were soon some of its most enthusiastic supporters.

The biggest changes, however, took place at Scalby Mills, though here they were only indirectly the result of Scarborough's ongoing struggle to remain a first-class seaside resort.

In 1983 Scarborough council gave outline planning permission for Yorkshire Water Authority to invest £17 million in a new sewage disposal system. Hitherto nearly all the town's untreated waste had poured directly into the sea down two pipes, at Castle Head near the harbour, and Scalby Ness. Not surprisingly, tests showed that the bathing waters in both North and South Bays fell well short of the minimum standard of bacteriological quality required by a European Community directive of 1975. Consequently, Yorkshire Water proposed that all Scarborough's sewage should be pumped northwards under the Marine Drive and North Bay promenade to Scalby Mills. There it would be screened before passing out into the sea by a long outfall pipe.

Probably no proposal in Scarborough's history cost more money, aroused more heated argument and antagonism, and caused more mutual ill-feeling than Yorkshire Water's scheme. A local pressure group calling themselves 'Sons of Neptune' led the protest movement. Screening, they claimed, was insufficient treatment: Scarborough's bathing waters would still be contaminated by sewage sludge. The outfall pipe was far too short: tidal currents would bring the effluent on to North Bay sands twice a day. Scalby Mills was the wrong place for a sewage works and pumping station. Residents of Scalby Mills agreed, and so did many other outraged Scarborians.

Nevertheless, with only two brave exceptions, the borough's councillors accepted Yorkshire Water's assurances and rejected an alternative proposal that full-treatment works should be sited further north at Cowlam Hole. The 'Sons of Neptune' were derided by leading councillors as 'opportunist' disloyalists who were damaging Scarborough's sensitive reputation. In reply, officers and councillors were accused of endorsing a plan that was merely short-term and expedient because though it would put the miniature railway's Scalby Mills station out of commission for three years, it would also rid the council of a costly embarrassment – the New Scalby Mills Hotel, amusements and shops – with Yorkshire Water compensation.

In the event, Yorkshire Water and the Town Hall won the day, if not the argument. During the three years from 1988 to 1991 the railway tracks beyond the beach halt were taken up and Scalby Mills station demolished while sewage works were constructed underneath it.

North Bay in 2000.

The concrete and plate-glass buildings of 1966 and the long slide which had taken the place of Monkey Island were swept away and the site cleared for something entirely different.

On 31 May 1991 the Sea-Life Centre first opened its doors to the public. After the late-lamented Aquarium and the more recent Marineland, it was Scarborough's third attempt at such an undertaking and Britain's ninth, new-style, sea aquarium. There was some disquiet about the three dazzlingly-white, metal pyramids which now covered the aquaria. One Northstead councillor described them as 'appalling' and ruinous to North Bay's natural appearance, whereas their architect believed that they would be 'as fresh and exciting in 20 years' time' as they were when new. Yet there was no doubt about the centre's instant popular and commercial success: within three days its rays, flatfish, jelly fish and sharks had entertained 7,000 visitors and during the following year the British Tourist Authority awarded it one of its prestigious 'Oscars'. Next to the re-built Scalby Mills miniature railway terminus and the well-concealed sewage works, Scarborough's Sea-Life Centre seemed an improvement on what had preceded it there.

Finally, in 1993, just a decade after the 'Sons of Neptune' had identified it as the most suitable location, Cowlam Hole was chosen by Yorkshire Water for their new £30 million, full-treatment, sewage 'farm'. Scalby Mills no longer satisfied the latest European Union requirements. The new plant would become operational in April 2001 and thereby bring an end, at last, to Scarborough's sewage saga.

By the end of the twentieth century, Scarborough council's North Bay Leisure Parks information boards, though only a few years old, were out of date and misleading to visitors, if not residents. Peasholm Park no longer had an aviary or a pagoda in a Japanese garden on its island. The 70-year-old North Cliff lift, which once linked Alexandra gardens with Peasholm Gap and the promenade, had been judged too costly to repair and run and given away to Launceston in Cornwall. The beach chalets beyond Hodgson's Slack had disappeared, and so had the maze in Victoria Park; the first had been replaced by a waterlogged mini-golf course, the second by a mini-car park. The open air theatre in Northstead Manor Gardens was no longer recognisable as such: its terraces had been stripped of seating and its island stage now lacked scenery and changing rooms. As for Marvels and the so-called Scarborough Fair amusements, they now seemed forlorn and abandoned, and the gaunt, stark supports of the chairless, chair-lift looked like a relic of a bygone era. Only the white pyramids of the Sea-Life Centre appeared proud of their glaring presence – perhaps because they had recently given birth to several, smaller offspring.

Theatres

In 1989 another of Scarborough's favourite places of live entertainment, the Floral Hall, fell prey to the bulldozers. The building had stood unused since its last summer season in 1986, but four years earlier it was described as in a 'state of decrepitude' and its variety shows were unable to fill even half of its 1,500 seats.

During its 76-year history the Floral Hall had been more than enough to answer those critics of 1909 who had objected when the council borrowed £3,000 to finance its construction. George Royle's pierrots, the Fol-de-Rols, who returned every summer, apart from a break during the First World War, from 1911 to 1933, gave the Floral

Hall its foundation reputation. They were succeeded by Richard Jerome's 'Rolling Stones' until the outbreak of the next war in 1939. Then, during most of the post-war seasons until 1963, the Fol-de-Rols returned to the scene of their former fame.

However, it was in the later 1960s and 1970s that the Floral Hall staged its most popular shows – Dickie Henderson in 1964, Harry Worth in 1965, Mike and Bernie Winters in 1966, and Jimmy Clitheroe in 1967. By now television was dictating public, light entertainment, and in 1973 Charlie Williams, Yorkshire's black comedian, broke all previous box-office records after his appearance on ITV. More than a quarter of a million people queued, watched and laughed at his twice-nightly shows during a season lasting 14 weeks.

By the 1980s there were few leading comedians, singers or musicians who had not appeared at Scarborough's Floral Hall, but their appeal was wearing thin. As ticket sales dropped, the council tried different themes without much success. In August 1986 the *Evening News* theatre critic called the Hall 'an oversized tangerine fridge' and wondered how long Scarborough could get away with 'the sort of rubbish' he had had to sit through.

'Not much longer', in the case of the Floral Hall, was the answer to his question. At the beginning of 1987 councillors were told that half a million pounds would be needed to bring the old theatre up to modern standards of safety and comfort. Nearly all its external metal supports were severely corroded, its glass roof leaked every time it rained, and it lacked central heating. Given that the council had only just bought the Futurist and had been offered the ailing Opera House, the Floral Hall was clearly a theatre too many.

As a result the council's Floral Hall was replaced by the council's Alexandra Bowling Centre which opened in October 1989. The proposal to build a two or three-storey, multi-purpose leisure centre had been rejected on grounds of cost. Instead, the Town Hall opted for the cheapest alternative of a ground-floor, indoor bowls centre, despite the objections of Scarborough's home bowlers who preferred a south-side location on Filey Road. On the outside the contemporary 'aircraft hanger' seemed a heavy price to pay visually and inside bowlers were soon complaining of uneven playing surfaces, ill-positioned lighting and another porous, flat roof. Casual bowlers declined in numbers from 12,500 in 1994-5 to 8,200 in 1997-8. When the resident club refused to finance urgently-needed improvements without guarantees for the future of the centre, the council threatened to sell or lease it. By 2000 the future of the Alexandra Bowling Centre was in doubt.

Though the Floral Hall was the town's only fatal casualty, Scarborough's other theatres did not fare well. Originally what had been the Charles Adams Grand Circus dating from 1876, then the Prince of Wales theatre, later Zalva's Hippodrome, and from 1918 the Opera House in St Thomas Street, closed down in September 1971. Since 1946 the theatre had been run by the York Citizen Trust, which put on a play at Scarborough for a week and then another week at the York Theatre Royal. After 25 years, however, the Trust could no longer afford the mounting costs of maintaining a slowly decaying building in the face of declining audiences. At first, Scarborough's own volunteers, the Opera House Preservation Society, hoped to run and renovate the theatre, but after they were unable to raise the necessary funds it was bought outright by Don Robinson.

After gaining a new roof and expensive internal refurbishment, the Opera House was reopened and enjoyed something of a renaissance during the 1970s. There were successful summer shows, winter-time film runs, and occasional stage performances of highly popular groups such as UB40. But the Royal Opera House, as it had now become, soon felt the chill draught of the 1980s. In 1987, Mr Robinson's company, Kunick, sold the building to Jays's Entertainments, which was declared bankrupt five years later with unpaid debts of three million pounds. Finally, after live entertainment there had ceased altogether and the theatre had been leased out to different commercial operators who ran the cinema and the bars, the whole building was devastated by two major fires in 1996. Four years later, the Royal Opera House on St Thomas Street, twice incinerated, pronounced dead, but not yet buried, remains Scarborough's worst derelict eyesore.

Meanwhile, the Futurist on the Foreshore, Scarborough's largest theatre with more than 2,000 seats, was also struggling to survive. After Catlin's had converted it from cinema to theatre in 1958, it was bought by the impresario, Robert Luff, in 1967. Then, in 1985, at the end of protracted negotiations, Scarborough council paid what was claimed to be a bargain price of £320,000 to become the Futurist's new owner, though subsequent events suggested that it was too much and too late. A decade later, after the council had invested about £3 million in renovations, repairs and subsidy, the theatre was still running at an alarming loss. During the year 1998-9 the Futurist cost Scarborough's taxpayers £92,000. By this time there seemed little hope of attracting back the many famous groups and comedians who had once performed on its stage. The theatre and its adjacent buildings were put on the market by a despairing council now hoping that a capital-rich developer might put a high value on the potential of the site. As yet, there have been no takers, and prospects for the Futurist remain uncertain.

In the greatest contrast to this tale of theatrical woe has been the spectacular triumph of Scarborough's theatre-in-the-round. Stephen Joseph, son of Hermione Gingold, first came to the town to stage a season of plays in the concert room of the Central Library during the summer of 1955. The plays were performed 'in-the-round' in a room notorious for appalling acoustics. Box-office takings were so low that Stephen Joseph took part-time work as a coal-heaver and brewer's drayman to pay actors' wages. In the third season a young man called Alan Ayckbourn joined the company as assistant stage manager. After Stephen Joseph fell ill in 1965 (he died in 1967), his place was taken by Alan Ayckbourn as theatre director and resident playwright. From then on, every year, Ayckbourn's new plays were first acted in Scarborough before achieving national and international acclaim.

By 1975 Ayckbourn had won deserved, world-wide recognition, but in his adopted home town his brilliant, dark comedies were still being performed in the totally unsuitable concert room of the Vernon Road library. With lamentable lack of appreciation, Scarborough's council had failed to provide a new theatre or even an existing, redundant building for the now famous theatre-in-the-round.

Fortunately, councillors were saved from further ignominy when the former Westwood School became vacant as a result of secondary reorganisation, and in October 1976 Ayckbourn's company moved there from the library theatre. Westwood was a vast improvement on the library concert room, but it was an old-fashioned, purpose-built school not a modern theatre.

By the late 1980s, of the country's 80 surviving Odeons, Scarborough's was unique: it still had only one screen and it had kept most of its original 1936 features. However, it had been losing money for four successive years and its owner, the Rank Organisation, decided to close the town's only surviving, full-time cinema. It was therefore typical of the irony characteristic of such events that early in 1988, just months before it ceased to be a cinema, Scarborough's Odeon was awarded Grade Two listed status as a building of 'special architectural interest'. In practice, this meant that nearly all of the Odeon's external façade, including the shop frontages of 4 to 12 Northway, had to be preserved. On the other hand, to protect the structure from inevitable decay and perhaps destruction, some viable alternative use had to be found for it soon. Applications to turn the Odeon into yet another bingo bazaar were mercifully rejected by the council landowner.

After six years work and an investment of almost as many million pounds, the old Odeon was resurrected as the new Stephen Joseph Theatre. Scarborough council granted a 99-year lease to the ADMirable partnership of Ayckbourn, Lord Downe of Wykeham, and Charles McCarthy, deputy chairman of McCain Foods (GB) Limited – a nicely balanced triumvirate of literary genius, landed aristocracy and business acumen. The new interior was a highly skilful and tasteful combination of restoration and conversion. Instead of one gigantic cinema with a seating capacity of 1,700 with over 700 in the circle, there were now two theatres – a 400-seat auditorium in the round and a 200-seat studio theatre which could double as a cinema. To these were added an enlarged foyer, shop, restaurant and bar. Though annual grants from the Yorkshire and Humberside Arts Council, a lottery donation of £1.5 million from the Arts Council, and nearly half a million pounds from the European Union fund made completion possible by April 1996, credit should also go to all those hundreds of local benefactors who bought square feet of floor space at £25 a time.

Alan Ayckbourn had been made a freeman of the borough in 1986, awarded a CBE in 1987, and a knighthood in the New Year's Honours list of 1996, but the Stephen Joseph Theatre was the most rewarding recognition of his services to the world at large and Scarborough in particular. The town now has a theatre as well as a playwright it can be proud of. It also has an answer to those who complain constantly that Scarborough's former elegance had given way entirely to cheap seaside seediness.

Schools and Colleges

In 1973 another revolution took place in Scarborough – the town's schools went comprehensive.

The Butler Education Act of 1944 had made little difference to the form of secondary education in Scarborough. All places at the two high schools, the boys' at Westwood and the girls' at Sandybed, became free, but they remained very restricted and highly competitive. The North Riding Education Committee kept a tight rein on admission numbers. Girls who 'failed' the demanding Eleven Plus entrance examination for the county's high school might be offered places at the direct-grant Convent Catholic school in Queen Street, yet here also the intake was strictly limited. As a result, about four out of five of Scarborough's children left school at the minimum age of 14 (until it was raised to 15 in 1948), without any paper qualification. School Certificates were the preserve of the grammar schools.

The Butler Act decreed that there had to be a distinctive break at the age of 11; that all children beyond that age should receive a free secondary education; and that this should be one of three kinds – grammar, modern or technical – depending on the child's aptitude and academic ability. Though Scarborough's grammar schools were well established, its secondary moderns and technical schools did not exist. The majority of the town's youngsters still attended all-age elementary schools with infant, junior and senior departments.

It was partly to provide town-centre accommodation for Scarborough's secondary modern children then in over-crowded, all-age schools that the North Riding Education Authority decided to build a new 'flagship' high school on Woodlands Drive. The new Scarborough High School for Boys opened in 1959. Henry Marsden took his staff and boys to the outskirts of the town and the old 'Muni' building became Westwood County Modern School. Two years later, Marsden retired after 31 years as headmaster and was succeeded by Alec Gardiner.

During the 1960s the Act of 1944 was gradually implemented. A new secondary modern, mixed school named George Pindar after the late Alderman G.K.G. Pindar, freeman of the borough, four times mayor and long-serving borough and county councillor, was built by Plaxton's at Eastfield; a girls' only secondary modern, Raincliffe, opened on the Throxenby site; and the Catholic community established their own separate secondary school, St Augustine's, at Sandybed.

When Harold Wilson's Labour government strongly recommended comprehensive reorganisation to all local education authorities in 1965, there was little hope or fear that a county as conservative and Conservative as the North Riding of Yorkshire would take any notice. When Edward Heath's Conservative government took office in 1970 the abolition of the Eleven Plus seemed even more remote in the North Riding's largest town with two of the county's most successful grammar schools. Yet two years later the county's Education Committee put forward a comprehensive plan for Scarborough which the Conservative secretary of state, Margaret Thatcher, approved.

Still, Scarborough's secondary school reform was less radical than it might have been and many parents and teachers preferred. In 1973 the secondary moderns – Scalby, Raincliffe, Pindar and Filey – became 11 to 16 mixed comprehensives; the Boys' High School was abolished and its premises became a fifth 11 to 16 comprehensive, the Graham School; and the Girls' High School was replaced by a Sixth Form College. The Graham Sea-Training School was absorbed into the new Graham. The Catholics chose to have their own 11 to 16 comprehensive at St Augustine's. The new scheme was dictated by financial prudence more than educational conviction. Not a single new permanent building was constructed: accommodation for the extra year of pupils when the school-leaving age was raised to 16 in 1972 was already in place. Complaints that Scarborough had gone comprehensive on the cheap were ignored by the rate-payers. In 1975 the Labour government's abolition of direct-grant status forced the closure of the Convent school, Scarborough's last grammar.

More than a quarter of a century later, dissatisfaction with Scarborough's secondary schools is largely negative and nostalgic, rather than reasoned. Short of bussing teenagers long distances from their homes to schools, there are bound to be significant differences between the neighbourhood comprehensives at Scalby and Pindar; Graham and Raincliffe serve the town well; and St Augustine's has silenced its early critics who said it was too small. Under a succession of able principals and despite severe financial constraints, the Sixth Form College has flourished.

Scarborough never did get a secondary technical school, but it did acquire a technical college, which had two historical parents – the School of Art and the Technical Institute. Scarborough's School of Art originally dated from 1882, though it was not until two years later that it moved into a permanent home, formerly Harland's medical baths and sanatorium at the junction of Vernon Place and Falconer's Road. The school was self-financing until taken over by Scarborough corporation in 1919. From then on it was run as a secondary school. However, on the night of 10 May 1941 it was destroyed by German bombs and never re-built. Staff and pupils were transferred to the annexe of Westlands in

Westbourne Grove, previously the quarters of the Girls' High school and now occupied by the Scarborough Technical Institute.

The Institute had started in 1896 as an Adult Evening Class at the Central Board School on Trafalgar Street West. It secured a home of its own at Westlands when the girls moved out from there to Sandybed in 1939. Finally, in October 1961, after three years construction work on a green-field site next to Scarborough hospital, Scarborough at last got a purpose-built Technical College. Since then it has become the main provider of adult and further education in the Scarborough district, re-christening itself the Yorkshire Coast College in the 1990s.

After Westlands was emptied it fell into private hands and rapid decay. The council finally obtained a compulsory purchase order on the building, in 1985 demolished it, and later put up a good-looking block of flats on the site.

Meanwhile, Scarborough's long tradition of supporting private, fee-paying, boarding schools had continued throughout the twentieth century, and by the end of it two survivors were prospering.

Founded in 1893, with only three boys at first, Bramcote preparatory school on Filey Road, had nearly a hundred boys and girls a century later. In 1901 the school had acquired a lease on the five-acre North of England Lawn Tennis ground which it bought outright in the 1920s. This extensive area provided Bramcote with one of the finest recreational spaces of any school of its kind in the country. Throughout most of the twentieth century cold baths, fresh air, corporal punishment, vigorous exercise, compulsory Anglican worship and plenty of Classics were characteristics of Bramcote, but to endure and prosper, like any other prep school, it had to modernise its curriculum and humanise its regime. By the year 2000 Bramcote had an outstanding record of entrance to many of the major public boarding schools. With 62 boys and 32 girls between the ages of four and 13 and no fewer than 14 full-time staff teaching in well-equipped classrooms, the future looked bright for Bramcote.

Across Filey Road and up the hill, Scarborough College was also doing well. It too had started life as a small boys' boarding school at the beginning of the last century. By 1999 it had 350 boys and girls, many of them day pupils from the locality, between the ages of 11 and 18. Like Bramcote, Scarborough College had many enviable advantages: its main building was designed by Edwin Cooper and its playing fields were adjacent and spacious. However, also like Bramcote, from the 1980s it had been obliged to give the highest priority to academic achievement. Entrance into higher education had become all important. By 2000 its junior prep school, Lisvane, had moved from Sandybed to a new building on the same Filey Road site.

One South Cliff private school that did not survive was Orleton boys' prep. Founded in 1891 by Edward Augustus Cooper at 6 Belmont Terrace (now part of the Esplanade Hotel) for boarders only, it moved first to Sunninghill, a large house on the corner of Filey and Queen Margaret's Roads, and finally in 1910 to a purpose-built school at Wheatcroft, just south of Scarborough College. Orleton had its own indoor swimming pool, gymnasium and ten-acre playing field. After its founder's death in 1914, the school was run by his formidable, cane-wielding widow and her daughter. During the 1920s and 1930s they had a hundred boys on roll and a reputation for Spartan discipline and intense piety. Orleton boys walked to St Martin's on the west side and Bramcote boys on the east side of Filey Road to Sunday matins. However, in March 1940 the Royal Engineers moved into Orleton and two years later Mrs Cooper was declared bankrupt.

In 1948 what had been Orleton became the North Riding Teachers' Training College, specialising in preparing young ladies for the profession at the primary level. Extensions were made during the 1960s but during the following years the College was threatened with closure and only narrowly reprieved finally in 1985. By that time it had become the North Riding College of Education and was offering degree courses which were later validated by the University of Leeds.

With the benefit of further additions and improvements, by 2000 the college, now with 1,300 students, had become the Scarborough Campus of the University of Hull, offering three and four-year degrees in subjects as unusual as coastal marine biology, creative music technology, internet computing and leisure and tourism management, as well as the post-graduate certificate in primary education. Its reputation in fine art, dance and drama was second to none. At the end of the nineteenth century there had been serious hope that Scarborough might have its own university; 100 years later Scarborough Campus was as near fulfilment of this hope as anyone in the town could expect.

Parliamentary Politics

On 1 May 1997 something quite remarkable happened in Scarborough's parliamentary history: for the first time since 1918 the Conservatives lost their seat there, and for the first time ever a Labour candidate won it. What had been a Conservative heirloom became a Labour stronghold. Lawrie Quinn, the first successful Labour party candidate, won more than 45 per cent of the 54,321 votes cast, a swing of 14.7 per cent from the sitting Tory MP, John Sykes.

Since 1918 Scarborough had lost its exclusive right to send a representative to the House of Commons. From that year onwards the borough was obliged to share a Member with Whitby, which also forfeited its own separate representation. By the same Act of Parliament of 1918 the new constituency of Scarborough and Whitby was required to offer votes to all resident men over 21 years of age and women of 30 years and upwards. According to official figures, the new combined constituency had 34,578 electors. Scarborough 's own resident electors numbered 9,248 men and 7,821 women willing to admit to being over 30, whereas previously only 6,384 men had been eligible to vote.

In these unprecedented circumstances, with a high proportion of the male electorate absent from home and entitled only to a postal vote if they were registered, the 'Coupon' election at Scarborough was an extraordinary event. The Conservative Unionist candidate was the Hon. Sir William Gervase Beckett (1866-1937) of Kirkdale manor, Nawton, a well-connected banker and owner of the *Saturday Review*. Since 1906, against stiff opposition from local Liberals, he had clung on to the Whitby seat. Walter Rea, Scarborough's distinguished Liberal MP since 1906, had chosen not to contest the new division, and his place was taken by Captain Osbert Sitwell of Wood End, eldest son of Sir George. And for the first time at Scarborough, the Labour party fielded a candidate, John Watson Rowntree (1854-1933).

J W was born at 47 Newborough, had become senior partner in the family grocery business when his father, John, died in 1894, and had served the borough for 20 years as councillor, alderman and mayor in 1906-7. Nevertheless, whatever his local and personal credentials, in the over-heated atmosphere of this post-war election he was damned as a pacifist as well as a socialist. In the words of his most influential enemy, the pro-Liberal proprietor of the *Scarborough Evening News*, Meredith Whittaker, Rowntree was 'a Quaker Pacifist and Little Englander of the most pronounced type'. Rowntree's pledges to support wholesale nationalisation, council housing, the minimum wage, sex equality and the League of Nations made him even less favoured by Scarborough's voters.

The outcome was therefore inevitable. In a turn-out of only 60 per cent, Beckett won more than half the poll and recorded a majority of nearly 4,000 over Sitwell. Osbert's first and last foray into politics, like so much of his life, was both comical and tragic. Though Sir George financed his son's campaign, he was such an eccentric embarrassment to the Liberal cause that he had to be kept indoors until polling day. As a Grenadier Guards' officer and veteran of the Western Front, Osbert might have swept the jingoist vote, but his public denunciation of all wars as acts of wasteful wickedness was not calculated to win electoral support.

Finally, Rowntree came a very bad third with less than five per cent of the vote. Having failed to receive one eighth of the poll he forfeited his deposit of £150. Undaunted, J W declared that one day, before the end of the twentieth century, Scarborough would return a Labour Member of Parliament.

Beckett might have held Scarborough and Whitby until his death, but in 1922 he transferred his ambitions to North Leeds and allowed Captain Sidney Herbert (1890-1939), Royal Horse Guards, Eton and Balliol College, Oxford, to occupy his warm and comfortable Conservative seat. Against a succession of Liberal opponents, Herbert polled more than half the vote in 1922, 1923 and 1924 and nearly half in 1929. Another Rowntree hopeful, this time Howard, renewed the Labour challenge in 1929. He managed only 4,645 votes, about one in ten of those cast, even though his party for the first time in its history won the largest number of places in the Commons.

In May 1931 Sidney Herbert retired and his role was taken by another young army officer, Paul Latham (1905-55), Eton and Magdalen College, Oxford, who, despite his inexperience, succeeded in fending off the by-election challenge of the gifted Liberal candidate, J Ramsay Muir. This time the margin was only just over 2,000 votes. However, when the next general election came in October 1931 the Liberals could not find or agree upon a contestant and Sir Paul had virtually a walk-over against a little-known socialist opponent: his majority was 25,450. From then on Latham had effectively a life tenancy: only premature death voluntary retirement or scandal could unseat him; and the last seemed least likely

It therefore came as a complete surprise to most Scarborians in August 1941, as they were dreading the next unwelcome visit from the Luftwaffe, that Sir Paul suddenly resigned his seat. He was charged with 'disgraceful conduct and attempting to commit suicide', and the following month he was convicted by court martial, cashiered and sentenced to two years imprisonment. He was still only 36 years old. Searching round for a stop-gap, the Conservatives found Alexander Cadwallader Mainwaring Spearman (1901-82).

Alexander Spearman, Repton and Hertford College, Oxford, had failed to win a Commons seat elsewhere in 1935 and 1937. Far from temporary, however, Sir Alex, as he became in 1956, proved to be more enduring than any of his predecessors. During a quarter of a century he won no fewer than seven consecutive elections at Scarborough. Sometimes the Liberals got second place, as in 1945, 1959 and 1964, other times, in 1950, 1951 and 1955, it went to Labour, but Spearman was always comfortably top of the poll regardless of the national result. It hardly seemed to matter what happened electorally everywhere else: the Scarborough and Whitby constituency was one of the safest Tory seats in the country.

Spearman's electoral record was unprecedented, even for Scarborough, but his tenure of the seat was surpassed by his successor, Michael Norman Shaw. The first Conservative candidate since Beckett without an Oxford degree, or any degree at all, Michael Shaw had been rejected by the voters of Dewsbury in 1955 and by those of Brighouse and Spenborough in 1959. He had won the latter in 1960 only to lose it again in 1964. His adoption by Scarborough's Conservatives in 1966, after Spearman's retirement, was fiercely contested. There was strong support for Meredith Whittaker (1914-84), magistrate, proprietor and editor of the *Scarborough Evening News*, senior county councillor, founder chairman of Scarborough's Civic Society, and fourth generation in his family to play a prominent role in local affairs. Whittaker also had an Oxford degree and a fine second-world-war record as an officer in the Green Howards. None the less, for some Conservatives in Huntriss Row, notably the leader of the Young Conservatives, Harvey Proctor, Whittaker was much too independent and liberal-minded; they preferred someone more docile and old Tory. Shaw was adopted and won easily; Whittaker was rejected, stood for Doncaster, and lost. It was an outcome that many Scarborians regretted at the time and for many years to come.

Sir Michael Shaw's reign at Scarborough lasted 26 years. Like Sir Alex Spearman he also won seven elections on the run, usually with sizeable majorities, sometimes as high as 14,000 and never less than 5,000. By national standards the Liberal vote in Scarborough remained significant. Between 1959 and 1987, only once, in 1979, did Labour win a second place. The closest the Conservatives came to losing the seat was to the Liberal candidate, Michael Pitts, in February 1974.

In retrospect it seems that the wheel began to turn in 1992. After Sir Michael's retirement, the new Conservative nominee, John Sykes, failed to secure half the vote, the new Labour representative, David Billing, gained nearly 30 per cent of it, and the Liberals were relegated to third place for the first time since 1979. Five years later, and just in time, J W Rowntree's prediction came true. Sykes lost 10,000 of his previous votes, the Liberals slipped to below 15 per cent of the poll, and the chartered civil engineer once employed by Railtrack with a degree from Hatfield Polytechnic, Lawrie Quinn, broke the 80-year-old Tory stranglehold. By 1997 the Scarborough Division electorate had grown to 75,862 compared with the old borough's 6,384 eligible to vote in 1914.

It remained to be seen at the next general election in the next century whether the voters believed that New Labour was an improvement on old Conservatives. Given what had and had not happened under a Labour government since 1997, J W Rowntree, the socialist pacifist with a belief in state paternalism and council housing, would have been less than content with its record. Ironically, by the time that Labour at last won Scarborough, the party was no longer socialist.

Prospects

At the beginning of the 21st century Scarborough seems poised on the sharp edge between further, perhaps irreversible, decline and rejuvenation.

On the negative side of the equation are those powerful, prevailing forces which have been operating since the 1960s to undermine the viability of our traditional seaside resorts. For millions of British holiday-makers 'seaside' has come to mean some foreign, usually Mediterranean, shore; and Scarborough can no better compete with Benidorm's guaranteed sunshine than Blackpool or Bournemouth; and cannot wait for 'global warming' to work its miracle. Meanwhile, at home, the heaviest commercial investment in seaside locations by groups such as Butlin's has been in self-catering holiday villages in places such as Skegness, Bognor and Minehead, where virgin spaces and planning permission were readily available.

Domestic tourism, however, no longer means necessarily a visit to the coast: during the 1980s and 1990s the biggest expansion has been in forest centres, lakeside villages and theme parks – all inland locations. Whereas once there was only the seaside, now there are so many other attractions nearer home and easier to reach. Not least of these are the new retail malls such as Gateshead's Metroland, Sheffield's Meadowhall and Manchester's Trafford Centre, which have become the preferred choice for millions of car-borne day trippers. Shopping has become a major leisure activity.

Finally, the seaside town, Scarborough included, no longer offers the exciting and unique glamour and entertainment it once virtually monopolised. Its cinemas show the same films, its hotels the same television programmes; it has shops and bingo halls just like those everywhere else. It suffers from all too familiar problems of litter, graffiti and vandalism. To find somewhere totally different from home nowadays you have to travel far and abroad.

Scarborough lost its aristocratic clientele in the nineteenth century and its middle class appeal before the end of the twentieth, but de-industrialisation has robbed it of many of its potential working-class customers. The death of the coal, and the decline of the steel, engineering and textile industries have impoverished the urban communities of the North of England and Scotland which once provided Scarborough with much of its income and trade; and there can be no return to the 'good old days' when coach and train loads of factory workers and their families spent their 'feast' and 'wakes' weeks in the town's boarding houses.

Yet these irrefutable facts seem to have been ignored or only dimly perceived by Scarborians. In the 'Viewpoint' columns of the *Scarborough Evening News* the phrase most often repeated by complaining correspondents is still 'restore to its former glory'. As more familiar and much-loved buildings and places – the open-air theatre, the South Bay pool, the Royal Opera House, Scarborough Mere – languish abandoned and derelict, there are despairing cries for their restoration.

419

Nostalgia fattens on decay; wishful outweighs realistic thinking. There is no way back to the 1960s, let alone the 1930s, and what Scarborough needs urgently is revitalisation with the new rather than restoration of the old.

As Scarborough's decline took root, scapegoats and panaceas have multiplied. Chief of the scapegoats has been Scarborough borough council. Unaware of the remorseless fall in council income, and ignorant of the crippling restrictions imposed by successive central governments on local spending and borrowing, Scarborough's taxpayers have lost faith in the Town Hall. Startling illustration of this loss of faith has been the extraordinary volatility of the local electorate and the alarming decline of its participation. Councillors – particularly Conservative councillors – could once expect to retain a seat for life, or at least until retirement. Now there are no safe places in the council chamber. In 1983 only 27 of the former 49 were returned, and for the first time in living memory the Conservatives forfeited their overall municipal majority. By 1995 Weaponness was the only surviving Tory ward, yet four years later Labour was routed even in Eastfield where previously it had all three representatives.

During these same years there was a catastrophic collapse in voting turn-out, from an average of 70 per cent in 1979, to 40 per cent in 1987, and 34 per cent in 1999. In this last year fewer than one in four Eastfield electors bothered to go to the polls, whereas 20 years earlier the turn-out there had been 68 per cent. Apathy has become the political norm; and resentment the reaction of many.

When not blaming councillors for misspending their money, drowning Scarborians were clutching at passing straws. The most favoured panacea remains a dual-carriaged A64 which it is naively assumed would bring a ceaseless avalanche of big-spending motorists from West Yorkshire and then convey them back home speedily, eager to return to Scarborough at the earliest opportunity. This particular pipe-dream fails to address the question of what happens to this volume of vehicles when it reaches the outskirts of the town. In the absence of a long-overdue and effective park-and-ride scheme on the perimeter of Scarborough, an improved A64 would merely create a traffic tail-back stretching for miles and perpetual gridlock in the town centre. Though ease of access is an important consideration, visitors will come to Scarborough not because the journey is shorter but because the destination is different from and better than they can find elsewhere.

Another panacea that is more castle in the air than straw in the wind is the proposal pretentiously called 'Zenith'. This gigantic paper project to cover all 43 acres (17.4 hectares) of east Northstead manor with hotels, cinemas, holiday village homes, shops, cafés, restaurants, indoor pool and outdoor ski slope at an estimated cost of £250 million if implemented would totally transform the North side of the town and have a devastating impact on the rest of it. Yet Zenith has been enthusiastically embraced by the local press, by the borough's leading councillors and officers, and by its Member of Parliament as Scarborough's last, best hope for the future. Indeed, the editor of the *Scarborough Evening News* cannot believe that the town has a future without Zenith!

Mercifully, Zenith is out of proportion to the problem and the place: if successful, it would bankrupt Scarborough; if it was built and then failed, it would become an eyesore comparable in scale to the former Butlin's camp at Filey which has been a refuse tip for the past 15 years. Not surprisingly, however, no developer has been found in the world which would risk such a huge investment. Nearly six years after it was first unveiled, Zenith is still as distant from realisation as ever.

Fortunately, to arrest Scarborough's downward drift there is no need to transmute it into a miniature Disneyland or imitation Las Vegas: the town requires judiciously applied therapy, not a death warrant. Far from regarding a dualled A64 or Zenith as Scarborough's only salvation, there are in fact many positive signs of gradual rejuvenation for those who care to look.

By 2002 there has to be a radical reform of local administration. During the past 25 years what has been cumbersome, time-consuming, expensive and opaque, or even impenetrable, is to be altered to a new cabinet system of government. Only nine elected senior councillors will become responsible and accountable for their departments. Such a new departure promises to make the Town Hall far more efficient, professional and respected by taxpayers.

Secondly, there is now welcome evidence of regeneration. The future of council-owned neglected blackspots, such as the Mere, the South Bay pool, St Nicholas and Clarence gardens, Peasholm Park and the Glen, now looks better than for many past years. Also, private commercial investment is beginning to return to the town centre. Having saved the corner of Aberdeen Walk and Westborough from total demolition, Bristol -based Crest Nicholson has submitted outline planning permission for restoration and development of the North Street - St Thomas Street - Chapman's Yard area which includes derelict property. English Heritage is at last making Scarborough castle visitor-friendly, and English Rose is restoring the prestige of the Royal Hotel, Scarborough's oldest. North Yorkshire County Council has plans to concentrate all its Scarborough offices on another eyesore site – Marshall House and King Street. Most encouraging of all has been the splendid success of the Castle Pride Initiative, a multi-million-pound scheme to revive and repair many of the town's listed buildings, shop fronts and street furnishings. Launched in 1996 and financed jointly by Scarborough council and central government's regeneration challenge fund, through grant-aid the project has already rescued such important buildings as The Three Mariners on Quay Street and revitalised whole areas of the old town, particularly Eastborough.

Though tourism will probably remain Scarborough's principal source of income and employment, for some time it has been clear that the town's future well-being depends heavily on financial services and manufacturing. The Cayton Low Road has become a vital artery of commerce and industry. Scarborough Building Society, the second oldest of its kind in the world, continues to prosper and expand and will soon have its new headquarters out there. The growth of the Pindar Group, based mainly on its outstanding achievements in technical innovation, has been phenomenal. McCain Foods, which opened its first Eastfield factory in 1968 and its second in 1979, has become a major contributor to Scarborough's prosperity and welfare, not least through the exemplary efforts of its chairman Charles McCarthy, who was made a freeman of the borough in 1985. The Athletic Ground, home of Scarborough Football Club, has become the McCain Stadium. And Plaxton's, though no longer a family firm, remains an essential element in Scarborough's economy. When Eric Plaxton died in 1995 he left £10 million to the town.

During its long and eventful history Scarborough has played many different roles. In turn it has been royal fortress, international fish fair, harbour of refuge, shipbuilding mart, aristocratic assembly, middle-class retirement resort and, most recently, popular holiday destination. It could be said that Scarborough was Britain's earliest coastal resort and that it invented the seaside holiday. Throughout the centuries the town experienced contrasting periods of affluence and poverty, of prominence and insignificance, but thanks to the enterprise and tenacity of its people it has endured and expanded. Whatever the future might bring to Scarborough it will surely survive by building on the foundations of its distinguished past.

Conclusion

There are at least 17 Scarboroughs in the world, 14 of them populated. Of the three that are not inhabited, navigators steer clear of Scarborough reef, a coral outcrop off the Philippine island of Luzon, but look out for Scarborough hill a landmark on the approach to Portland in Oregan on the American Pacific coast; and Scarborough Bluffs overlook the north side of Lake Ontario in Canada.

The largest inhabited Scarborough, with a population exceeding 100,000, is a suburb of Toronto in Canada. There are three Scarboroughs in the Caribbean, the chief town of Tobago, and one each on the islands of Nevis and Jamaica. There are at least three Scarboroughs in the United States – one is in New York State, another is in Maine, and a third, which Americans cannot spell, is in West Virginia. Australia has three Scarboroughs, a suburb of Perth, a park near Sydney, and a beach at Brisbane. New Zealand's south island has two Scarboroughs on its east coast – one just south of Christchurch, which has a restaurant called 'Scarborough Fare', and another, further south still, at Timaru. Finally, there is a beach on Cape peninsula, near Cape Town, South Africa, named Scarborough.

Yet none of these, it goes without saying, can compare with England's Scarborough, in North Yorkshire, the first in the world of that name, the mother and father of all the others, and the only one rich in lengthy and significant history.

If Scarborough has given its name to communities and places in four other continents, it has also become part of the language of English folklore and proverb in several different forms. Most of these forms are now obsolete, but one was revived and popularised in modern lyric and another is still quoted in works of reference.

From as early as the twelfth until as late as the sixteenth century Scarborough was one of western Europe's principal fishing ports and markets, used by Flemings, Dutchmen and Danes and other North Sea fishermen, as well as Scots and English. Every summer the gigantic shoals of herring worked their coastal way southwards, passing the Shetlands in April and reaching Yarmouth by September. In July and

August they came close to Scarborough, attracting from near and far fishermen who brought in their catches to be salted, smoked, dried and sold. An entry in the order book of Aldeburgh (Suffolk) corporation for the year 1598 reads: '... every free inhabitant that should go after the f[east] of St John the Bapt[ist] fishing in Scarborowe seas should pay...'. The feast of St John the Baptist falls on 24 June. Sadly, the North Sea herring, once so plentiful, has been fished into near extinction, so that few are now to be found in 'Scarborowe seas'.

Herring was not the only fish associated with Scarborough and its annual fish fair. In 1491 Westminster abbey's kitchener bought his fish on the quayside of the Thames 'of a Skerborowe man in the schype', and in the abbey's accounts, 'haburdens', large salted cod, are referred to simply as 'Scarborough fish'.

So Scarborough fish were caught in Scarborough seas and sold at Scarborough fair. Though there are no references to fish in the words of the folksong 'Scarborough Fair', and the lovers who sing the verses might have been anywhere, in them there is one suggestive line: 'Betwixt the salt water all on the sea sand'. In medieval times the stalls of Scarborough fair were set up on the sands of the foreshore at low tide. On the other hand, since nearly two centuries separate the last time Scarborough fair was celebrated in 1788 and a song popularised by Simon and Garfunkel in the 1960s, the connection between them is probably more wishful than factual. In truth, terms derived from Scarborough's fame as a fishing port and market relate only to medieval times and practices and had become obsolete long before old Scarborough became new Scarborough.

However, 'Scarborough warning', meaning no warning at all, though medieval in source, has survived to the present day. Originally, Scarborough gained a gruesome notoriety for hanging thieves without benefit of trial or even delay – in other words, a locally approved lynch law. Later, Thomas Stafford's seizure of Scarborough castle in 1557 without prior warning and by subterfuge and deception gave 'Scarborough warning' a new currency. Used to mean a blow *followed* by a warning, the term subsequently became a commonplace of Elizabethan and Jacobean correspondence. When, totally unexpectedly, the Kaiser's battleships shelled the town one grey December morning in 1914, 'Scarborough warning' gained another sinister illustration.

Now, at the beginning of the third Christian millennium, a new but still ominous sense is given to 'Scarborough warning'. The term is

424

currently used as a comment on the sad deterioration of a place that once proudly and justifiably called itself 'Queen of the Yorkshire Coast'. The warning is given to other endangered coastal resorts not to follow Scarborough's recent example: not to allow sewage to flow directly into their bathing waters; not to damage a commercial heart by enslavement to suburban supermarkets; and not to destroy precious architectural heritage by pandering to the cheap, fashionable and ugly.

What hope is there for Scarborough's recovery in the twenty-first century? Will Scarborough survive supermarkets, traffic congestion and coastal erosion? Historical precedents are promising. Scarborough has suffered many catastrophes yet never been permanently defeated by any of them, man-made or acts of God. Consumed by fire in 1066, it literally rose from the ashes; in the later middle ages it was ravaged by plague, foreign wars and the corruption and greed of its own oligarchy; during the Civil Wars it was evacuated by its residents and repeatedly vandalised by soldiers; and during the next century it was gravely wounded by political schism and family vendetta. Natural disasters, such as the destruction of the great pier in 1613 and the collapse of South Cliff on to the spa in 1737 actually forced Scarborians to rescue themselves from their poverty and lethargy.

When old sources of wealth and importance became obsolete, the town found new ones to replace them. First there was the headland which attracted to it Roman signal station, Viking fort and Plantagenet castle. To rescue Scarborough from its decline as a fishing port and market, there came sea-coal to make it into a vital harbour of refuge. Mrs Farrer's momentous discovery eventually brought an entirely new source of income, employment and function to the town; and when drinking the spa waters began to lose its appeal sea-bathing took its fashionable place. Ship-building sustained Scarborough during the eighteenth century and long enough for it to survive until the coming of the railway made it ultimately into a popular holiday resort.

From its earliest pioneering days as a maritime retreat, Scarborough has gone 'down market'. Once the playground for the rich and idle aristocracy and landed gentry, it then became a residence for the professional and industrial middle classes, and latterly the day-out excursion destination for the populous. In their horse-drawn coaches the aristocracy once came to Scarborough for a season that lasted months; the middle class spent weeks there after arriving by train; and now in their motor cars the people come to Scarborough for the day.

Nevertheless, during the last two thousand years, Scarborough has been rescued time and time again – sometimes by outsiders for their own purposes and profit, but more often by its own inhabitants. Repeatedly, their energy, civic pride and determined persistence have reformed and revitalised a community that appeared doomed to stagnation and irreversible decline.

Bibliography

CHAPTER 1

Binns A.L. in Edwards M. (ed.), *Scarborough 966-1966* (Scarborough, 1966).

Brooks F.W., *The Battle of Stamford Bridge* (East Yorkshire Local History Society, 6, 1956).

Collingwood R.G., *The Roman Signal Station on Castle Hill, Scarborough* (Scarborough, 1925).

Faull M. & Stinson M. (eds), *Domesday Book: Yorkshire* (Chichester, 1986). Hey D., *Yorkshire from AD 1000* (1986).

Magnusson M. & Palsson H. (trans.), *King Harald's Saga* (1966).

Rimington F.C. (ed.), *The History of Ravenscar and Staintondale* (Scarborough, 1988).

Rowntree A. (ed.), *The History of Scarborough* (1931).

Salway P., *Roman Britain* (Oxford, 1981).

Smith A.L. *The Place-Names of the North Riding of Yorkshire* (Cambridge, 1928).

Wilson P.R. in Maxfield V.A. & Dobson M.J. (eds), *Roman Frontier Studies* (Exeter, 1991).

CHAPTER 2

Baildon W.P. (ed.), *Notes on the Religious and Secular Houses of Yorkshire* Yorkshire Archaeological Society Record Series XVII (1895). Baildon W.P. (ed.), *Monastic Notes,* YASRS LXXXI (1931).

Bond E.A. (ed.), *Chronicon Monasterii de Melsa,* Rolls Series 1 (1866).

Brown R.A. 'Royal Castle-Building in England 1154-1216, *English Historical Review* 70 (July, 1955).

Brown R.A. & Colvin H.M., 'The Royal Castles 1066-1485' in *The King's Works* II, (1963).

Brown W. (ed.), *Yorkshire Inquisitions,* YASRS XII (1892), XXXI (1902). *Calendars of Close Rolls. Calendars of Patent Rolls.* English B., *The Lords of Holderness 1086-1260* (Oxford, 1979). English B. (ed.), *Yorkshire Hundred and Quo Warranto Rolls,* YASRS, CLI (1996).

Farrer W. (ed.), *Early Yorkshire Charters* I (1914).

Goldthorpe L.M., 'The Franciscans and Dominicans in Yorkshire', *Yorkshire Archaeological Journal* XXXII (1936).

Hinderwell T., *The History and Antiquities of Scarborough* (3rd edn, 1832).

Holt J.C., *The Northerners* (Oxford, 1961).

Howlett R. (ed.), *Chronicles of the Reign of Stephen, Henry II and Richard I,* Rolls Series I (1884).

Lawrance N.A.H. (ed.), *Fasti Parochialis,* YASRS CXXIX (1967).

Pearson T., *An Archaeological Survey of Scarborough* (Birmingham, 1987).

Rowntree A. (ed.), *The History of Scarborough* (1931).

Rushton J.H. in Edwards M. (ed.), *Scarborough 966-1966* (1966).

Warren W.L., *Henry II* (1973).

CHAPTER 3

Binns J., 'Did Scarborough Burn?' *Transactions of the Scarborough Archaeological and Historical Society,* 35 (1999). *Calendars of Close Rolls. Calendars of Patent Rolls. Copy Translations of Scarborough Charters* (Scarborough, 1912).

Darby H.C. (ed.), *A New Historical Geography of England before 1600.* (Cambridge, 1973).

Dobson R.B. (ed.), *The Peasants' Revolt of 1381* (1970).

Dobson R.B. in Hilton R.H. & Ashton T.H. (eds), *The English Rising of 1381* (Cambridge, 1984).

Hamilton J.S., *Piers Gaveston, Earl of Cornwall 1307-1312* (Detroit, Michigan, 1988).

Hatcher J., *Plague, Population and the English Economy 1348-1530* (1984).

Heath P., 'North Sea Fishing in the Fifteenth Century: the Scarborough Fleet', *Northern History* III (1968).

Horrox R. & Hammond P.W. (eds), *British Library Harleian Manuscript 433,* 4 vols (Upminster and London, 1979-83).

Hoskins W.G., *Local History in England* (2nd edn, 1972).

Jeayes I.H. (ed.), *The White Vellum Book* (Scarborough, 1914).

Page W. (ed.), *The Victoria History of the County of York: North Riding* II (1923).

Public Record Office, Subsidy Rolls, E179/212/139, 152.

Richmond C.F., 'English Naval Power in the Fifteenth Century', *History* 52 (1967).

Roskell J.S. *et al.* (eds), *The House of Commons 1386-1421* (1992).

Somerville R., *History of the Duchy of Lancaster 1265-1603* (1953).

CHAPTER 4

Acts of the Privy Council. Ashcroft M.Y. (ed.), *Scarborough Records 1600-1660,* 2 vols (Northallerton, 1991).

Aveling H., *Northern Catholics: The Catholic Recusants of the North Riding of Yorkshire 1558-1790* (1966).

Baker J.B. *The History of Scarbrough* (1882).

Bindoff S.T. (ed.), *The House of Commons 1509-1558* (1982).

Binns J., 'Scarborough and the Pilgrimage of Grace', *TSAHS* 33 (1997); 'Scarborough versus Seamer: An Elizabethan Tale of Market Forces', *TSAHS* 34 (1999).

Calendars of State Papers Domestic.

Cartwright J.J., *Chapters in the History of Yorkshire* (Wakefield, 1872).

Chandler J. (ed.), *John Leland's Itinerary: Travels in Tudor England* (Stroud, 1993).

Chapman J. (ed.), *Scarborough Records,* 3 vols (Scarborough, 1909).

Clay J.W. (ed.), *Dugdale's Visitation of Yorkshire*, 3 vols (Exeter, 1899, 1917); *Paver's Marriage Licences,* YASRS XL (1909).

Dickens A.G. 'Some Popular Reactions to the Edwardian Reformation in Yorkshire', *Yorkshire Archaeological Journal* XXXIV (1939).

Hall B., 'The Trade of Newcastle and the North-East Coast 1600-1640' Ph.D. unpub. thesis, London Univ., 1933.

Hasler P.W., (ed.), *The House of Commons 1558-1603* (1981).

Hinderwell T., *The History and Antiquities of Scarborough* (3rd edn, 1832).

Hotham Papers, DDHO/55/1-33, East Riding County Record Office, Beverley. Nef J.U., *The Rise of the British Coal Industry,* 2 vols (1932).

Norcliffe C.B. (ed.), 'Paver's Marriages Licences' *YAJ* X (1889).

Rowntree A. (ed.), *The History of Scarborough* (1931).

Scarborough Corporation Records, DC/SCB, North Yorkshire County Record Office, Northallerton.

Sheils W.J. (ed.), *Archbishop Grindal's Visitation of the Diocese of York 1575* (York Univ. 1977).

St Mary's churchwardens' papers, PE 165/241, East Riding County Record Office, Beverley. St Mary's parish register 1602-82, MIC 5582, Scarborough Central Library.

Thompson E. (ed.), *Scarborough Wills,* 3 vols, Scarborough Central Library.

Willan T.S. *The English Coasting Trade 1600-1750* (Manchester, 1967).

CHAPTER 5

Ashcroft M.Y. (ed.), *Scarborough Records 1600-1660,* 2 vols (Northallerton, 1991).

Binns J., *A Place of Great Importance: Scarborough in the Civil Wars, 1640-1660* (Preston, 1996); (ed.), *The Memoirs and Memorials of Sir Hugh Cholmley of Whitby 1600-1657,* YASRS CLIII (2000); 'Captain Browne Bushell: North Sea Adventurer and Pirate', *Northern History* XXVII (1991), 'Sir John Lawson: Scarborough's Admiral of the Red', *Northern History* XXXII (1996).

Calendars of State Papers: Domestic; Venetian; Interregnum. Commons Journals. Historical Manuscripts Commission: *Lord Braye* (1877); *Portland* (1891); *Ormonde* (1903); *Pepys* (1911).

Lords Journals. Meldrum correspondence, HD36:2672, Suffolk County Record Office, Ipswich.

Newsbooks, I, *Oxford Royalist* i-iv (1971). Scarborough Corporation Records, DC/SCB, North Yorkshire County Record Office, Northallerton.

Schofield J., *An Historical and Descriptive Guide to Scarborough,* 1st edn, (York, 1787).

Thomason Tracts, British Library.

Wildridge T.T. (ed.), *The Hull Letters 1625-1646* (Hull, 1887).

CHAPTER 6

Baker J.B., *The History of Scarbrough (1882).*

Binns, J. 'Mr and Mrs Farrer', *Transactions of Scarborough Archaeological and Historical Society* 26 (1988).

Calendars of State Papers, Domestic. Copy Translations of Scarborough Charters (Scarborough, 1912).

Corbin A., *The Lure of the Sea* (1995).

Gent T., *History of Hull* (Hull, 1869).

Henning B.D. (ed.), *The House of Commons 1660-1690,* 3 vols (1983).

Hutton W., *The Scarborough Tour in 1803* (1804).

Jackson C. (ed.), *The Autobiography of Mrs Alice Thornton,* Surtees Society LXII (1875).

Pennant T., *A Tour in Scotland,* 3rd edn. (Warrington, 1774).

Penney N. (ed.), *The Journal of George Fox* (1924).

Rowntree A. (ed.), *The History of Scarborough* (1931). Scarborough Corporation Records, DC/SCB, North Yorkshire County Record Office, Northallerton.

Whittaker M., *The Book of Scarbrough Spaw* (Buckingham, 1984).

Wittie R., *Scarbrough Spaw* (York, 1660, 1667).

CHAPTER 7

Ashcroft M.Y. (ed.), Scarborough Records 1600-1660, 2 vols (Northallerton, 1991).

Barry J. (ed.), *The Tudor and Stuart Town* (1990).

Binns, J. 'Crime, Misdemeanour, Sin and Punishment in Seventeenth-Century Scarborough', *Transactions of the Scarborough Archaeological and Historical Society,* 31 (1995); 'Black Death at Scarborough', *Transactions of the Scarborough Archaeological and Historical Society,* 32 (1996).

Buckley J., *The Outport of Scarborough 1602-1853* (Scarborough, 1951).

Chapman J. (ed.), *Scarborough Records,* 3 vols (1909).

Harvey B., *Living and Dying in England 1100-1540* (Oxford, 1995).

Hearth Tax returns, Public Record Office, E179/216/462.

Henning B.D. (ed.), *The House of Commons 1660-1690,* 3 vols (1983).

Hutton W., *The Scarborough Tour in 1803,* (1st edn. 1804, 2nd edn. 1817).

McIntyre S.C. 'Towns as Health and Pleasure Resorts', D.Phil. unpub. thesis Oxford Univ., 1973;

'The Scarborough Corporation Quarrel, 1736-1760', *Northern History* XIV (1978).

Morris C. (ed.), *The Journeys of Celia Fiennes* (1949).

Thompson E. (ed.), *Scarborough Wills,* 3 vols (1931).
Tindall C., *The Tindalls of Scarborough* (1927).
Pearson T., *Paradise, Scarborough* (Scarborough, 1988).
Probate Wills in the York Registry, Borthwick Institute of Historical Research, York.
Scarborough Corporation Records, DC/SCB, North Yorkshire County Record Office, Northallerton.
St Mary's churchwardens' accounts, 1607-98, PE 165/241, East Riding County Record Office, Beverley.

CHAPTER 8

Borsay P., *The English Urban Renaissance: Culture and Society in the Provincial Town 1660-1779* (Oxford, 1989).
Hembry P., *The English Spa 1560-1815: A Social History* (1990).
Macky J., *A Journey through England in Familiar Letters,* 2 vols (1714, 1722).
McIntyre S.C., 'Towns as Health and Pleasure Resorts', D.Phil. unpub. thesis, Oxford Univ., 1973.
Morris C. (ed.), *The Journeys of Celia Fiennes* (1949).
Murray H., *Scarborough, York and Leeds. The Town Plans of John Cossins 1697-1743* (York, 1997).
Newspapers: *The Daily Gazetteer, The London Daily Post, St James Evening Post, York Courant.*
Porter R., *English Society in the Eighteenth Century* (1990).
Sedgwick R. (ed.), *The House of Commons 1715-54,* 2 vols (1970).
Thomson G.S. (ed.), *Letters of a Grandmother 1732-1735* (1943).
Ward C. & Chandler R., *A Journey From London to Scarborough* (1734).
Whittaker M., *The Book of Scarbrough Spaw* (Buckingham, 1984).
Withers letter, *Yorkshire Archaeological Journal* XII (1893).
Wittie R., *Scarbrough Spaw* (1660, 1667).

CHAPTER 9

Ainsworth W., *The Scarborough Guide* (York, 1806; Scarborough 1815).

Broadrick G., *A New Scarborough Guide* (Scarborough, 1806; 1810).
Courtney J., Diary 1759-67 and 1788-1805, MS. Brynmor Jones Library, University of Hull.
Dwarris F. & Rumball S.A., *A Report on the Inquiry into the State of the Corporation of Scarborough* (Hull, 1834).
Green J., *Poetical Sketches of Scarborough* (1813).
Hatfield J., *A New Scarborough Guide* (1797).
Hinderwell T., *The History and Antiquities of Scarborough* (York, 1798; 1811; 1832).
McIntyre S.C., 'Towns as Health and Pleasure Resorts', D.Phil. unpub. thesis, Oxford Univ., 1973.
Scarborough Corporation Records, DC/SCB, North Yorkshire County Record Office, Northallerton.
Schofield J., *An Historical and Descriptive Guide to Scarborough* (York 1787).
Seward A., *Letters 1784-1807* (1811).
Short T., *The History of Mineral Waters* (1734).
Smollett T., *The Expedition of Humphry Clinker* (1771).
Whitehall Evening Post.
Whittaker M., *The Book of Scarbrough Spaw* (Buckingham , 1984).
York Courant.
York Herald.

CHAPTER 10

Baines E. (ed.), *History, Directory and Gazetteer of the County of York,* II (1823).
Buckley J., *The Outport f Scarborough 1602-1835* (Scarborough, 1951).
Commons Journals.
Dictionary of National Biography.
Duckham B.F., 'The Fitzwilliams and the Navigation of the Yorkshire Derwent', *Northern History* II (1967).
Dwarris F. & Rumball S.A., *A Report on the Inquiry into the State of the Corporation of Scarborough* (Hull, 1834).
Hinderwell T., *The History and Antiquities of Scarborough* (York, 1798; 1811; 1832).
Hutton W., *The Scarborough Tour in 1803* (1804; 1817).
McIntyre S.C., 'Towns as Health and Pleasure Resorts', D.Phil. unpub. thesis, Oxford Univ., 1973.

Robson D.C., 'Scarborough in the Reign of George III: the Town, its People and Trade', MA unpub. thesis, Leicester Univ., 1974.
Scarborough Corporation Records, DC/SCB, North Yorkshire County Record Office, Northallerton.
Tindall C., *The Tindalls of Scarborough* (1927).
Towse, A., 'A History of the Development of the Port and Harbour of Scarborough', unpub. thesis, North Riding College of Education, Scarborough, 1970.

CHAPTER 11

Aveling H., *Northern Catholics: The Catholic Recusants of the North Riding of Yorkshire 1558-1790* (1966).
Baines E. (ed.), *History, Directory and Gazetteer of the County of York,* II (1823).
Baker J.B., *The History of Scarbrough* (1882).
Buckley J., *The Outport of Scarborough 1602-1835* (Scarborough, 1951).
Cole J., *Thomas Hinderwell: Memoirs of his Life, Writings and Character* (Scarborough, 1826); *The Scarborough Souvenir* (Scarborough, 1827).
Dictionary of National Biography.
Fawcett J., *A Memorial of the Church of St Mary's, Scarboro'* (1850).
Hinderwell T., *The History and Antiquities of Scarborough* (1832).
Ollard S.L. & Walker P.C. (eds), *Archbishop Herring's Visitation Returns* III, YASRS LXXV (1929).
Rowntree A. (ed.), *The History of Scarborough* (1931).
Scarborough Corporation Records, DC/SCB, North Yorkshire County Record Office, Northallerton.
Scarborough Gazette. St Mary's parish registers, 1687-1900, 9 vols, printed transcripts, Scarborough Central Library.
Theakston S.W., *Guide to Scarborough* (Scarborough, 1840).
Turnbull C.F., *The History of St Martin's Grammar School 1872-1922* (1960).
Wood J., Plan of Scarborough 1828.

CHAPTER 12

Ainsworth W. (ed.), *A List of Persons Entitled to Vote* (Scarborough, 1832).

Bye J. (ed.), *The Works of Sir George Cayley,* n.d.,Scarborough Central Library.

Dwarris F. & Rumball S.A., *A Report on the Inquiry into the State of the Corporation of Scarborough* (Hull, 1834).

Hopkin N.D., 'Scarborough Corporation in the Early Nineteenth Century', unpub. B.A. diss., Univ. of Leeds, 1964.

Namier L. & Brooke J. (eds), *The House of Commons 1754-1790,* 3 vols (1964).

Proctor K.H., 'Triumph of Reform in Scarborough', unpub. essay, n.d., Scarborough Central Library.

Sedgwick R. (ed.), *The House of Commons 1715-54,* 2 vols (1970).

The Burgess.

Thorne R.G. (ed.), *The House of Commons 1790-1820,* 4 vols (1986).

CHAPTER 13

Buckley, J. *The Outport of Scarborough 1602-1853* (Scarborough, 1951).

Fawcett, J. *A Memorial of the Church of St Mary's, Scarboro'* (1850).

Granville, A.B. *The Spas of England: Northern Spas* (1841).

Hinderwell, T. *The History and Antiquities of Scarborough* (1832).

The Scarborough Gazette, 1845 -.

The Scarborough Herald 1839.

Theakston's Guide to Scarborough (Scarborough 1840, 1841, 1847).

Tyson, A.G. *A New and Accurate Plan of Scarborough* (Scarborough 1842).

White, W. *History, Gazetteer and Directory of the East and North Ridings of Yorkshire* (Sheffield, 1840).

Whittaker, M. *The Book of Scarbrough Spaw* (Buckingham 1984)

I am greatly indebted to the late Mr A. Gambles who allowed me to study his unofficial manuscript of the accounts of Scarborough's serjeants-at-mace and constables 1812-49.

CHAPTER 14

Alexander, W. *On the Seabathing of Scarborough* (Halifax, 1882).
Anderson, J & Swinglehurst, E. *The Victorian and Edwardian Seaside* (1978).
Census of Great Britain, 31 March 1851, 7 April 1861: Population Tables: Yorkshire. Census of Great Britain, 1851: Religious Worship in England and Wales (1854).
Debenham, L.S. 'Scarborough's Water Supply' *Transactions of Scarborough Archaeological Society* (1972).
Hey, D. *Yorkshire from 1000* (1986).
Ordnance Survey of Scarborough 1852.
The Scarborough Gazette 1845 -.
The Scarborough Mercury 1855 -.
Scarborough Public Market Act, 15 Vict, 1852; 17 Vict. 1854.
Scarborough Water Act, 8 Vict. 1845.
Theakston's *Guide to Scarborough* (Scarborough 1847, 1852, 1854, 1858, 1860, 1865, 1871).
Theakston's *Handbook for Visitors in Scarborough* (Scarborough 1868). Walvin, J. *Beside the Seaside* (1978).

CHAPTER 15

Baker, J.B. *The History of Scarbrough* (1882).
Black's Guide to Scarborough, Whitby and Harrogate (Edinburgh, 1866).
Fawcett, J. *A Memorial of the Church of St Mary's, Scarboro'* (1850).
Foord, S. *Scarborough Records* (1970).
Horn, P. *Pleasures and Pastimes in Victorian Britain* (Stroud, 1999).
Kelly, E.R. *Directory of the North and East Ridings of Yorkshire* (1879).
Local Government Board: Return of Owners of Land, 1873 (1875).
Magnus, P. *King Edward the Seventh* (1964).
Miller, W. *Our English Shores* (1888).
Rushton, J.H. *Scarborough: The First Thousand Years* (Scarborough, 1966)
The *Scarborough Gazette,* 1845-.
The *Scarborough Mercury* 1855-.

Scarborough Valley Bridge Company Act, 27 & 28 Vict, 1864.
Scarborough Marine Aquarium Act, 36 & 37 Vict, 1875.
Scarborough Improvement Act, 52 & 53 Vict, 1889.
Theakston's Street Plan of Scarborough, 1875.
Walton, J.K. *The English Seaside Resort* (Leicester, 1983).
Whittaker, M. *The Book of Scarbrough Spaw* (Buckingham, 1984).

CHAPTER 16

Bulmer's *History, Topography and Directory of North Yorkshire,* ii (1890).
Census returns, 1881, 1891, 1901, 1911.
Dade, E. *Mariner's Mirror*, 18 (1932); 19 (1933).
Heywood, A. *Guide to Scarborough* (Manchester, 1870).
Heywood, J. *Illustrated Guide to Scarborough* (Manchester, 1890).
Hood, J.D. *Scarborough, Past and Present* (Driffield, n.d.).
Kelly's *Directory of the North and East Ridings of Yorkshire* (1872, 1879, 1893, 1905, 1909, 1913).
Lord, G. *Scarborough's Floral Heritage* (Scarborough, 1984).
Newspapers: *Scarborough Daily and Weekly Post 1876-1914, Scarborough Express 1865-83, Scarborough Gazette 1845-1914, Scarborough Mercury 1855-, Scarborough Evening News 1882-.*
Ordnance Surveys 1892, 1912.
Robinson, R. *A History of the Yorkshire Coast Fishing Industry 1780-1914* (Hull, 1987).
Smith, G. & Williams, A (eds), *The Rise and Fall of British Coastal Resorts* (1987).
Smith, H.W. *Catering for the Wants of the Holiday Maker* 8 May 1915 (Scarborough Room pamphlet, 363).
Waller, P (ed.) *The English Urban Landscape* (Oxford, 2000).
Walton, J.K. *The English Seaside Resort* (Leicester, 1983);
The British Seaside: Holidays and Resorts in the Twentieth Century (Manchester, 2000).

CHAPTER 17

Adshead S.D. & Overfield H.V. *The Further Development of Scarborough* (1938). *Centenary Souvenir of the Spa1827-1927* (1927).
Cloud Y. (ed.) *Beside the Seaside* (1934).

437

Foord S. 'Harry W.Smith, Borough Engineer and Surveyor of Scarborough 1897-1933. An Appreciation' (1970) unpub. typescript, Scarborough Room.
Kelly's Directories 1921, 1939.
Linton S.F. *Annual Reports of Scarborough's Medical Officer of Health* (1923-37).
Marsay M. *Bombardment* (Scarborough, 1999).
National Union of Teachers Conference Souvenir 1935 ed. F. Drake.
Pimlott J.A.R. *The Englishman's Holiday: A Social History* (1947).
Revised Scarborough and District Directories 1933, 1935, 1936.
Scarborough Directories 1914, 1915, 1923, 1925, 1930.
Scarborough Evening News 1914-1939.
Scarborough Mercury 1914-1939.
Shaw G & Williams A (eds.) *The Rise and Fall of British Coastal Resorts* (1997).
Stallibrass H.C. 'The Holiday Accommodation Industry', PhD thesis, Univ. of London (1978).
Waller, P. (ed.) *The English Urban Landscape* (Oxford, 2000).
Ward, Lock & Co. *Guide to Scarborough* 1921, 1935.
Whittaker, Sir Meredith *The Book of Scarbrough Spaw* (Buckingham, 1984).

CHAPTER 18

Annual Reports of Scarborough's Medical Officer of Health, 1939-72.
Corrigan E, *Up and Down and Roundabouts* (1972).
Dixon P A, 'The Evolution of Scarborough' B.A. diss. Liverpool Univ. 1965.
Jones K W, 'Wood End Natural History Museum' *Yorkshire Illustrated,* Jan. 1952.
Kelly's *Directory of Scarborough* 1952, 1956, 1958, 1960, 1962, 1964, 1966, 1968, 1971, 1973, 1975, 1976.
Laughton T, *Pavilions By The Sea* (1977).
Percy R J, *Scarborough's War Years Scarborough in the '50s and 60s* (1994).
Scarborough Evening News. Scarborough Mercury.
Shaw G & Williams A (eds), *The Rise and Fall of British Coastal Resorts.* (1977).

Stallibrass H C, 'The Holiday Accommodation Industry' PhD thesis, London Univ 1978.

Towse A, 'A History of the Development of the Port and Harbour at Scarborough' North Riding Coll. of Ed. 1970.

Turner H E 'A Sitwell Home Restored', *The Field,* 5 Apr. 1952; 'A Museum Restored', *Country Life*, 29 Apr 1954.

Walton J K, *The British Seaside: Holidays and Resorts in the Twentieth Century* (Manchester, 2000).

Whittaker Sir Meredith, *The Book of Scarbrough Spaw* (Buckingham, 1984).

Ziegler P, *Osbert Sitwell* (1998).

CHAPTER 19

Burton P. (ed.), *Six Inches of Bath Water: One Hundred Years of Scarborough College. 1898-1998* (1998).

Crouch D., *Orleton School: A Brief History* (1991).

Land P., *Bramcote School: The First Hundred Years* (1993).

Scarborough Borough Council :*Annual Reports and Abstracts of Accounts 1981-2000.*

Scarborough Evening News.

Scarborough Mercury.

Shaw G & Williams A (eds), *The Rise and Fall of British Seaside Resorts* (1997).

Theroux P., *The Kingdom by the Sea* (1983).

Whittaker M., *The Book of Scarbrough Spaw* (1984).

Index

Entries in bold refer to illustrations

Aberdeen Walk, Picture House, 349; Gaiety Cinema/Bingo, 381

Acclom, John I, 34, 35; John II, 35; Robert I, 34; Robert II, 35

Acts of Parliament:
Balfour's Education Act (1902), 308, 351
Ballot Act (1872), 232, 315
Butler's Education Act (1944), 359, 410, 411
Corrupt Practices Act (1883), 232, 318
Fire Precautions Act (1971), 380
Fisher's Education Act (1918), 351
Forster's Education Act (1870), 306, 309
Great Reform Act (1832), 133 219, 314, 351
Hearth Tax Act (1662), 113
Local Government Act (1972), 387
Mundella's Education Act (1880), 307
Municipal Corporation's Act, 223, 228-9, 237
Poor Law Amendment Act (1834), 246
Prisons Act (1878), 270
Public Libraries Act (1850), 354
Railway Act (1844), 256-7
Reform Act (1867), 315
Representation of the People Act (1918), 415
Scarborough Electric Trams Act (1902), 303
Scarborough Improvement Act (1805), 161 (1889), 294
Scarborough Marine Aquarium Act (1875), 280

Scarborough Public Markets Acts (1852, 1854), 264-6
Scarborough Valley Bridge Company Act (1864), 272
Scarborough Water Company Act (1845), 257-8
Technical Instruction Act (1889), 308
Test and Corporation Acts (1661-5), 85, 87
Toleration Act (1689), 86, 91
Turnpike Act (1752), 176-7
Wheatley's Housing Act (1924), 339
York-Scarborough Railway Act (1845), 258
Adrian, Mrs, 199
Adshead, S D, 356-8, 370
Ainsworth, W, 354
Aislabie, T, 92-3, 313
Albemarle (Aumale), see William le Gros
Albert, Prince, 284
Albion Road, **289**
Alexandra, Bowling Centre, 407-8; Field, 283, 299; Gardens; 303, 314; Hotel, 290; Princess, 283
Allen, A & J, 119
Allison, J, 393
Alward, G, 325
Amicable Society, 201-2, 206, 209, 250, 306

Anderson, and Flintoff, 394; Sir John, 97-8
Anlaby, M, 92
Anne, Queen, 131
Apple Market (King Street), 108, see also Rievaulx Lane
Appleyard, A, 322
Apprentices, 111-12, 196
Aquarium (People's Palace, Gala Land), 280-2, 349, 356, 364, 382
Armstrong, M, 151
Art Gallery, 366
Arthur, Prince, Duke of Connaught, 304
ASDA, 394
Ashley, Mrs, 345
Asquith, H, 296, 333
Assembly Rooms (Huntriss Row), 261-2, see also Long Rooms
Astley's Circus, 346
Athletic Ground (McCain Stadium), 313, 422
Athlone, Countess of, 261
Atkins, J, 158
Atmar, M, 66
Auborough Bar, 168
Ayckbourn, Sir A, 409-10

Baker, J B, iii, 122, 311
Baines, E, 181, 191
Balgarnie, Rev. R, **287**
Baptists, 205, 253, 267, 288
Barker, T J, 283
Barrowcliff, estate, 355, 356; Plantation (Wilson's Wood, The Glen), 274, 343
Barry, A, 117; builder, 260

Baston, R, 28
Baths:
    Champley's, 171,
    240, 244, 279; Friars'
    Way Slipper, 376;
    Harland's 171, 240-1,
    279; McBean's, 279;
    Medical
    (Londesborough
    Lodge), 367, **383**;
    Public (Foreshore
    Road), 279; Royal
    Northern Sea Bathing
    Infirmary (St Thomas
    Hospital), 279;
    Travis's, 171, 240;
    Vickerman's, 241;
    Weddell's, 171, 241,
    242, 279
Batty, P, 199; T, 47; W, 151
Baxtergate, 20
Baynes, M, 249
Bean, J, 165, 166-7 (Gardens),
208; W, 212
Beatty, admiral, 333
Becket, T, archbishop, 13
Beeching Axe, 382
Beeforth, Lord G, 300
Belgrave Road (Love Lane),
290
Bell, J, 266; R, 217
Belmont Terrace, 260
Belvoir Terrace, 229, 234
Bevan, D W, 308, 309
Beveridge Report, 359
Beswick, A, 223; S, 244
Bilb(o)rough, Hill, 127; R, 127
Binns, A L, 7
Bird Yard, 205

Black Canons (Augustinians),
40, 44
Black Death, 32, 33, 37, 76,
134
Black Friars, see Friars;
Blackfriargate (Beast Market,
Queen Street), 108
Bland, J, (Bland's Cliff), 138,
155, 159, 203
Bleach House, 225-6
Blenheim Terrace, 274
Blitz, 362-3
Blunt, Rev R F L, 310
Board Schools, 306-8
Boats, 124, 322-5
Bodley, G F, 286, 310
Boer War, 320-1
Bolts, 174
Bombardment, 330-5, 329, 331
Borrowby, J, 51
Bosomworth, E, 390
Boteler, N, 92, 198, 199
Botterill, M, 151-2
Bottomley, S, 202
Bowland, A, 123
Bowls, lawn, 64, 145, 313-14
Boyd, F, 380
Boynton, Sir Matthew, 73, 74,
76, 83; Colonel Matthew, 77-
80, 94, 95-6
Boys' High School, see
Schools
Bracken Hill, 109
Bradley, R, 390, 391
Breckan, S, 91
Bridgewater, earl of, 49
Bridlington Priory, 40, 44, 49
Brindley, L, 393
Broadrick, G, 169, 178-9

Brodrick, C, 273
Bronte, A, 261
Brown, T, 204
Broxholme, 235, 356, **383**
Bruce, R, 32
Brunswick, Pavilion, 394;
Place, 234; Terrace, 166, 395
Buck, S and N, 149, 171
Bull Lane, Westover Road, 90,
203; Aberdeen Walk, 235
Burgh, John de, 29
Burniston Barracks, 321, 333,
342
Burton Group, 394-5
Burton, R, 98
Burtondale, 29, 47, 65, 109
Bushell, B, 68, 72, **81**, 82
Butler, 'Billy', 344
Butlin, Billy, 379; Butlin's,
419, 421
Butter Cross, 105, **375**, 376
Byng, J, 146
Byron, H, 224; S, 223-9
By(w)ard Wath (Scarborough
Mere), 25, 121, 237

Cadwell, J, 173
Cafés, 343, 369
Cardow's Cadets, 300
Carleton, E, 84
Carlisle, Lord, 153
Carmelites (White Friars), see
Friars
Carmichael, I, 381
Carnegie, A, 354
Carr Street, 138
Car(r)gate (Carr Street, Cross
Street), 28, 29, 109, 115, 205,
266, 339, 340

Carter, A R, 33; H B, 249, 286,
366
Castle, 15-19, 21, 22, **23**, 26,
32-3, 37, 42, 51-2, 65, 68, 73-
7, 78-80, 83, 89-90, 156, 195,
312, 422
Catherine of Braganza, 62
Catlin, W, 299, 330, 349, 352
Cattle, R, 210, 212
Cayley, Arthur, William, 92;
Sir George, 220-2 **221**; Sir
Kenelm, 350
Cayton Bay, 258; Cayton Low
Road, 422
Cemetery (Dean Road), 266
Chadwick, E, 259
Champley, R, 278
Chapman, Joseph, 240;
Richard, 45, 51; Rodney, 365;
William, 187-8
Chapman's Pasture 266
Chapman's Yard, 237, 395,
422
Charles I, king, 43, 44, 62, 63,
69-70, 94
Charles II, king, 62, 64, 78, 85,
91, 95
Charters, 18-19, 21-2, 24-6,
41-2
Cholmley family, 116; Lady,
103; Sir Richard, 51-2; Sir
Hugh, **67**, 68-77, 95, 156; Sir
Hugh junior, 92, 128
Churches:
　　　　Anglican, Christ
　　　　Church, 167, 208-9,
　　　　251; St Martin's, 234,
　　　　286; St Mary's, 19-
　　　　20, 36, **46**, 47, 48-51,
　　　　49,

53-4, 75, 80, 82, 197-9, 251, 267, 285-6; St Thomas's (East Sandgate), 251-2 Pre-Reformation Catholic, Holy Sepulchre, 20, 27, 47, 48, 54, 64; St Thomas the Martyr, 20, 29, 30, 47, 48, 54, 75, 80.
Baptists: Longwestgate, 205, 253, 267; Albemarle Crescent, 288; Bethel, Sandside, 253.
Congregationalists: South Cliff, **287**, 289; Bar, 288; Eastborough, 288.
Independents, 253.
Methodists: 204-5, Claremont, 288, 372; Queen Street, 252; Jubilee, 288; St Sepulchre, 288; Westborough, 288.
Plymouth Brethren, 253.
Presbyterians, 202.
Roman Catholics, 204, 253, St Peter's, 286.
Churchill, W S, 334
Christian, E, 285
Cibber, C, 142
Cistercians (White Monks), 20-1, 27, 28, 29
Citeaux, 19-20, 29, 40
Civil Wars, 13, 31, 43, 63-84

Clarence Gardens (Tintinholms), **276**-7, 298-9, 314, 343
Clark, Rev. W, 170
Clarke, A and C, 118
Clarke's Company, 348, 399
Clayform Properties, 394-6
Cliff Bridge Company, see Spa(w); Cliff Bridge, 1827, **211**
Clowes, W, 252
Cockburne, G, 216
Cockcroft, Mrs, 273
Cockerills, 151, Anna, 126, Culmer, 158, 159, George, 127, James, 93, 126-7, Thomas, 158, 159
Cockerton judgement, 308
Cole, J, 354
Colleges: North Riding (University of Hull), 414 Scarborough, 310, 413-14 Sixth Form, 412 Yorkshire Coast (formerly Technical), 412-13
Collingwood, R G, 3
Columbus Ravine, 237, 345-6
Conduit Row, 115
Conyers, C, 48
Coode, Sir J, 303
Cooke, T, 47-8, 60-1
Cook's Row (Low Conduit Street), 203, 204, 206
Cooper, E A, 414; Edwin Sir, 336, 347, 413; Mrs 414; W, 72
Corner Café, 343

444

Corrigans, 381-2
Cossins, J, 138, 140, 193, 313
Cotterill, C, 149
Coulson, C, 224
Courtney, J, 172, 175, 178
Coverdale, C, 109
Cowlam Hole, 404, 406
Crathorne, Mr, 179
Crescent (White Bread/Great
St Nicholas Close), 167, 234-5;
House, 366
Crest Nicholson, 421-2
Cricket, 311-13
'crimps', 325
Crompton, W, 154
Cromwell, O, 9, 63-4, 79
Crosby, 278
Crosland, Sir Jordan, 87, 89,
90, 128; Henry, 92
Cross Street, see Car(r)gate

Damyot (Damgeth), 18, 27,
237
Darcy, Sir Conyers, 155
Davies, G, 223, 226
Dean Road, 268, 297
(Cemetery Road), 318, 342
Deane, Dr E, 93
Debenham, 394
Deeton, R, 118
Denisons, 367; Joseph, 162; W
F H 315, see Londesborough
Dennis, E T W, 320, 362, 371
Denton, J, 72, 82
Derrflinger, 332, 333
Derventio (Malton), 2, 6
Deutsch, O, 350
Dewsbury, T, 224
Dickens, C, 262

Dickinson, Dicky, **141**, 135-49,
159, 348; Mrs Anne, 139;
'Peggy', 139, 148
Dighton, R, 84
Digle, O, 108
Disraeli, B, (Beaconsfield),
270, 296
diphtheria, 337, 364, 374
Dobson, W, 95
Docker, H, 198, 200
Dodgson, J, 162-3
Dogger Bank, 20, 109, 124,
334
Domesday Book, 8, 12, 15, 18
Dominicans (Black Friars,
Friars Preachers), see Friars
Don, M, 390
Donner, E, 175, 222, 223, 226,
261; E S, 272
Downe, Lord, 410
Drake, F, 338-9
Driple Cotes, 76, 134, 136,
148, 149
ducking stool, 117
Duesbery, B, 121; T, 212;
Duesbery's Walk (North
Terrace), 201
Dumple (Street), 105, 160,
266, 338, 339, 340
Dunn, Dr J, 259-60
Dwarris, F, 223-225

Eastborough, 226
Eastfield, 373, 375, 388, 389-
90, 420
East Mount, 353
East Sandgate, 126, 180
East Villa, 235 (White House),
356

Eboracum (York), 2,4,5,6
Edison, W, 325
Edward, A, 163
Edward I, king, 15, 27; II, 29,
32-3; III, 31, 40; VI, 43, 45
Edward, Prince of Wales, 262,
283-4
Edwards, M, iii
Elizabeth I, queen 44, 51, 54-5,
124
Elriggs, 109, 110
Emerson, W, 347-8
emigrants, 373
Esplanade, 236, 260, 347
Evans, B, 253; P, 162; Dr W
G, 374, 377-8

Fairbank, J F, 275
Fairfax, Lord, 68, 73, 78; Col.
Charles, 94
Falconer, Dr J, 165, 167-8,
208, 234
Falsgrave, 8, 11, 12, 18, 21, 22,
23, 25, 27, 40, 45, 65, 75, 105,
107, 110, 114, 161-2, 239, 299,
304
Farrer, J, 47, 62, 94, 118; Mrs
Thomasin, 93-5, 105, 134-5,
238; Farrer's Aisle, 80-1, 199;
Farrer's hospital, 376
Farside, R, 175
Fawether, F, 72
Fenton, T H, 367
Fiddes, J, 158
Fiennes, Celia, 125, 134, 175,
177, 184, 203
fishing, 20, 38-9, 54, 124-5,
190-1, 321-6, 336, 373, 382-3,
401
Fitzwilliam, Lord, 216

Fletcher, G, 105-6
'flithers', 323, 325
Floral Hall, 300, 330, 406-7
Fol de Rols, 330, 406-7
Foord, T, 91; W, 88, 118
football, 313, 422
Foreshore Rd, 282
Fowler, B, 320; H, 209, 223,
229, 244, 272; M, 119; V, 152,
224
Fox, G, **88**, 87-90, 95, 156
Franciscans (Grey Friars), see
Friars
Friars: Carmelites, 28, 45, 51
Dominicans, 28, 33,
45
Franciscans, 27-8, 34,
45, 51, 64, 252
Friends, Society of, see
Quakers
Futurist, 349, 371, 407, 408-9
Fysh, G, 198, 200-1; M, 118;
Thomas, 115;
Timothy, 197;
Tristram, 82-3, 87;
Robert, 115; William,
58, 61, 109, 115

gablage (husgabel), 19, 20
Gallows Close, 26, 116, 396
Garencières, T, 195, 197, 198,
199, 202
Garlands, 65
Gates, Sir Henry, 52, 57-8;
Edward, 52-3, 58-9;
Henry, 59
Gaveston, P, 32-3
'Geddes Axe', 351
Gent, T, 95

446

George, king, I, 131; II, 131,
          159; III 131,159,196;
          IV, (Prince Regent),
          131, 196
Gibson, A, 271
Gilbert, A, 123
Gilderscliff (Gilduscliff,
          Gildhouse Cliff,
          Spring   Hill,
          Falsgrave Park),   25,
          27, 161, 237
Gill, T, 83
Gilson, C, 106
Gladstone, W E, 296, 318;
          Road, 237;
          Street/Lane, 296
Glauert, E, 352
Glen (Barrowcliff Plantation,
          Wilson's Wood), 343;
          Bridge, 345
Globe Street, 339
Goland, F, 149, 152, 154
Golden Grid, 401
Goldsborough, 5-7
golf, 313, 342, 343, 344
Grace, W G, 312
Graham, C C, 332, 335, 353
Granby, Lord, 216-17
Granville, Dr A B, 239-43,
348; Lord, 296; Mrs, 102-3
Greathead, H, 189-90
Greengate Lane (North Marine
          Road), 168, 207
Grindal, archbishop, 118
Grove Villa, 235

Hackness, 58, 220
Hague, W, 205
Hal de, Simon, 22, 24, 26
Hall, J W K, 372

Hallstatt, 1
Hanbury, Mr, 137, 138
Hannay, W, 202
Hanover Place, 260
Harcourt Place, 212
Harding, R, 165-6
Hardrada, king Harald, 3, 9-12,
17
Harold, king, 9, 10-12
Harrison, Col. James, 354, 355,
          368; Christopher, 151,
          153; John, 61, 83,
          113, 151; William,
          115
Harthropp, R, 118
Harvey, Mrs, 376
Harwood, A, 117; J, 190; M,
45
Hatfield, J, 171, 176, 178
Hatterboard, 27
Hawksmoor, N, 142
Hay, T (Lord Duplin), 150-3
Haynes, J, 140, **143**, 148
Headley, G, 47
Hearth Tax, 112-14
Hebden, Edward, 209, 210,
          212, 223; Edward
          Hopper, 284; James,
          149, 152, 153, 154
Helperby Lane (King Street),
160-1
Henderson, J, 229; W, 176
Henrietta Maria, 62, 69-70
Henry, king, I, 13, 16; II, 13,
18-19, 26, 36; III, 15, 22, 24-6;
IV, 40; V, 32; VII, 43, 60;
VIII, 40, 43, 44
herring, 20, 24, 38, 108, 122,
124, 321, **323**, 323, 324, 382-3
Herring, T, 193-4

447

Heseltine, M, 390
Hesp, J, 223, 229, 265
Hickson, E, 110; J, 128
Hildesley, bishop, 160
Hill, J, 145, 150, 215
Hinderwell, iii, 166, 169-70,
171, 172, 173, 174, 176, 181-2,
187, 189-91, 194, 195, 201-2,
204, 205, 206, 208, 209
Hipper, admiral, 333, 334
Hispaniola, 369, 401
Hoby, Lady Margaret, 53; Sir
Thomas, 53, 58, 61,
62
hockey, 313
Hodgson, E, 88; P, 84, 87-91
Hol(e)beck, 65, 110; Gardens,
300; Hall, 148; slide, 400
Honorius, emperor, 7
Hopwood, J L, 330; Mrs, 179
Horrocks, G, 344, 368-9
Hospitals: medieval, Saint
Nicholas, 20, 29-30,
47; Saint Thomas, 20,
29, 47, poorhouse,
206-7; St James, 47;
Farrer's, 376 modern,
Elders Street, 340;
Friars' Entry/Way,
340, 341, 372, 376;
Woodlands
(Scarborough
Hospital), 340-1;
Cross Lane, 364
Hotham, Sir John, 69, 95;
Captain John, 84; Sir Charles,
198, 203
housing, 114-15, 246, 338-40,
374-7
Houson, J, 222, 223, 238-9

Hudson, G, 255, 256
Hunman, A, 119
Huntcliff, 5-7
Huntriss, J, 130, 149, 151, 152,
165-6
Hutchinson, Edward, 61, 93;
Isabel, 61, 93;
Stephen, 61, 62, 93;
Thomasin (Mrs
Farrer), 61
Huttons, Catherine and
William, 99, 106, 162, 163,
170, 173, 174, 176, 179, 183,
184, 191

Iceland, 38
Ingrift (Peasholm Beck), 109
Inns and Hotels: Albion 262,
Albert, 262;
Alexandra (later
Clifton), 290;
Balmoral (formerly
Pied Bull, Bull,
Houson's, Reed's),
165, 188, 222, 223,
245, 247, 261, 268,
379; (Blue) Bell, 177,
178, 179, 238, 240,
243, 245, 265, 274,
397; Blacksmith's
Arms, 177, 205, 238;
Blanchard's, 274;
Cambridge, 289, 290,
292, 379; Castle, 262,
314, 397; Cecil, 379;
Crown, 261, 262, 274,
289; Crown and
Sceptre, 177;
Elephant

448

and Castle, 265;
Fountain, 239, 265;
George, 177, 246,
265, 274, 397;
Gibson's, 396; Grand,
273-4, 280, 330, 332,
363, 397; Huntsman
(formerly Nag's
Head,
Miller's, Old Bar),
397; King's Arms,
239, 246; Letters,
265; London Inn, 246,
265, 314; Mariners'
Tavern, 266; New
Inn, 177, 239, 248,
265; North Riding,
290; Pavilion, 290,
292, 314, 350-1, 379;
Prince of Wales, 289,
396; Princess Royal,
262; Queen('s), 260,
262, 266, 274, 311,
362, 363; Railway,
262, 274; Ramshill,
289; Royal (formerly
Long   Room,
Donner's), 144, 240,
241, 261, 285, 351,
363, 379, 395, 422;
Ship (Falsgrave), 268;
Stag and Hounds,
265; Star (King
Street), 239, Swift's,
262; Talbot, 238, 239,
245, 247, 274, 397;
Temperance, 263,
316; Thornhan's, 263;
Three Mariners, **39**,
422; Victoria, 262,

350, 397; Wessex,
379; Wheatsheaf, 265;
White Bear, 239, 265;
York Temperance,
263, 274
Irish Home Rule, 318-20
Iron Age, 1-2, 3
Irton, J, 265
Irton Moor, 356
Irvin, T, 200-1
Irwin, Lord, 101
Italian Gardens, 300

Jackson, T, 246
James, D, 395
James I, king, 44, 55, 59, 65;
II, 85-6, 91, 92
Jefferson, Mrs, 260-1
Jeffrey, T, 165, 169
Jellicoe, admiral, 333, 334
Jenkinson, D, 381, 388
Jenks, Sir M, 345
John, king, 13, 15, 21-2, 109,
387
Johnstone, Sir H, 312; Sir J,
209, 212, 220-2

Keld, C, 98
Keregan, T, 144, 173
Key, J, 128
Kinderland, 403-4
King, R, 353
King's Cliff, 110
King's Hussars, 333
kipper, 323
Kirk, J, 198, 200, 208
Kitchener, Lord, 334
Knowles, G, 256, 262
Knowsley, J, 91
Kolberg, 333

449

Kormak, 7-9

Lancaster, J, 205
Langdale, H, 49; Road, 296
Laughton, Charles, 310, 350-1;
        Robert, 314, 350;
        Thomas, 310, 350-1,
        363, 379
lawn tennis, 313
Lawson, admiral, Sir John, 77,
        80, **83**, 84, 107, 123,
        205; Lady, 123-4;
        William, 53, 90, 128
Lazenby, M and R, 162-3
Leading Post Street, 266
Leeds, duke of, 145, 150, 152,
153
Legard, Sir Charles, 312; Sir
        John, 90, 92
Lelam, engineer, 154, 185
Leland, J, 29, 41, 44, 45, 47, 48
libraries, 174, 354-5
lifeboat, **189**-90
lighthouse, 188, 332, **329**
Linton, Dr S F, 337, 340, 341,
342, 364
Lloyd George, 321, 339
Local Place, 237
Londesborough, earl and
        countess of, 283, 312,
        330, 381; Lodge, 235,
        284, 330, 391; Road
        (Stoney Causeway),
        290, 304; Theatre,
        349, 381
Long Greece (Steps), 126
Long Rooms: Low/Nether
        Westgate (Princess
        Street), 144, 174;
        Sandside, 174-5; St

Nicholas Gate/Street,
        Donner's old, 144-5,
        175, 212, 241;
        Newstead's
        new, 168, 175
Long (Upper) Westgate,
117,205, 206
Lonsdale Road, 296
Love on the Dole, 357-8
Low/Nether Westgate
        (Saturday Market,
        Princess Street), 144
Luff, R, 408
Luna Park, 401
Lutz, Meyer, 347

Macky, J, 144
Maclean, A, 347, 348
Maling, J, 224
malnutrition, 338
Manchester, duchess of, 170
Marche, W, 35
Marine Drive, 303-4
markets, 24-5, 76, 121-2, 163-
4, 264-6
Marlborough, duchess of,
        Sarah, 136-8, 170,
        177
Marsden, H, 353, 411
Marshall, H, 401; R, 47; and
        Snelgrove, 394
Marston Moor, 63, 71
Marvel's, 402-3, 406
Mary, Tudor, queen, 44, 51
Mary, Queen of Scots, 44, 51,
52
Mason, F, 366
Matilda, empress, 13
May, J, 372
Mayhew, H, 350

McCain Foods, 410, 422
McCarthy, C, 410, 422
McMillan, 280-1
measles, 337
Meaux abbey, 27
Mechanics' Institute, 354
Meldrum, Sir John, 72-4, 75, 76
Members of Parliament:
    Acclom, John I, 35, John II, 35, Robert I, 34 Robert II, 35; Anlaby, J, 84; Becket, Sir W G, 415-16; Boynton, Sir Matthew, 84; Caine, W S, 316, 318; Cayley, Sir George, 220-3; Cholmley, Sir Hugh, 68; Cooke, Tristram, 60-1; Crosland, Sir Jordan, 87; Denison, W F, 315; Fysh, W, 58, 61; Gates, Sir Henry, 52, Edward, 53, 58; Handasyd, R, 216; Harrison, J, 61; Herbert, Sir Sidney, 416; Hoby, Sir Thomas, 58; Hutchinson, Edward, 61, Stephen, 61; Johnstone Harcourt, 315, John, 220, 314-15; Lascelles, E, 216; Latham, Sir Paul, 416 -17; Legard, J, 87, Charles, 315; Major, J, 216; Manners, G, 216, R W, 217; Mulgrave, earl of , 315; Osbaldeston, F W, 215, G, 215, W, 215, 216; Pennyman, J, 217; Phipps, Charles, 217, Constantine, 218, Edmund, 218, Henry, 218; Quinn, L, 415; Rea, W R, 315, 415; Rickett, JC, 316; Robinson, Luke, 84, 86-7; Shaw, Sir Michael, 417-18; Sitwell, Sir George, 315, **317**, 316,320, 332; Somerset, C H, 209, 217; Spearman, A, 366, 417-18; Strickland,W, 150; Sutton, C M, 217, 230: Sykes, J, 415, 418; Thompson, F, 87, William I, 61, William II, 87, William III, 87; Trench F W, 220-2, 225, 249, 314

Mercer's raid, 34
Merchants Row, 179,238,266
Mere (Scarborough), 237, 298, 302, 369, 401-2
Merry, W, 249-50, 309
Merrydale, M, 117
Mickledale, 344-5
Milbanke, Sir Ralph, 155
milk, 337-8
Millbeck, 155, 168-9, 185, 237, 277

Miller, Rev M H, 251
miniature railway, 344
Mompesson, T, 59
Montague, M, 398
Moody, J J P, 272
Moore, A, 344
Morcar, earl of Northumbria, 10-11
More, A, 127
Morgan, W, 281, 314
Morfitt, J, 195, 198
Morrison's, 394, 396
Mortimer-Wheeler, R E, 3
Mosdale, J 37; Hall, 156, 174, 332
Mostyn, S, 153
Mount Pleasant, 168
Mulgrave, Lord, 162, 209; Terrace, 219
Murray, Dr P, 229

Naseby, 63, 74
Naval Warfare, 369
Neil, A, 273
Neptune, 344
Nesfield, W, 84, 118; George (brewer), 209, 212
Newborough, 22, 30, 112, 114, 116; Bar, 117, 155, 163, 165, 178, 303, 316; Gate 116, 126; Gates, 163; Street, 160, 161, 163, 178
'New Brighton' (Cornelian Drive), 355
New Buildings (St Nicholas Cliff), 165, 178
            New Dyke Bank (St Thomas Walk), 110, 145, 155

New Olympia, 356
Newspapers:
        Daily Gazetteer, 149
        Daily Mail, 335
        Daily Mirror, 335
        Daily Sketch, 335
        Leeds Mercury, 222
        London Daily Post, 149
        Mercurius Britanicus, 72
        Mercurius Melancholicus, 79
        Mercurius Publicus, 96
        Moderate Intelligencer, 79
        Parliamentary Intelligencer, 96
        Scarborough Evening News, 318, 332, 346, 365, 407, 415, 417, 419
        Scarborough Gazette, 256-7, 260, 261, 277, 286
        Scarborough Herald, 238, 239, 245, 260
        Scarborough Mercury, 320, 346, 351
        Scarborough Post, 312, 318
        The Burgess, 227-30
        The Times, 393
        York Chronicle, 165
        York Courant, 179
        Yorkshire Gazette, 212
Newstead, W, 175

Newton, S, 235; W 49
Nicholson, F, 366; H, 114
Normanton Rise, 391
North, J, 198
North Bay, **405**; Cliff Lift, 343,
391, 406; Pier, 275-7; Pool,
346, 364, 392, 403; Beach, **402**
North Leas, 65, 109
North Marine Road, 236, 274
Northstead, 62, 110, 123, 237,
299, 301, 341, 345, 356, 371,
421
Northway, 346; clinic, 378
North Wharf, 304
Nottingham, earl of, 58

Oddfellows' Hall, 234, 297,
354
Odeon, 350-1, 409-10
Oldborough, (Auborough) 22,
112, 114; Bar, 155, 168
Oliver's Battery, 169
Oliver's Mount/Hill, 9, 169-70,
237, 247, 337, 365
Olympia, Picture Palace, 349;
Funhouse, 399-400;
Leisure, 400
Open Air Theatre, 344-5, 370,
380-1, 406
Opera House, 330, 407, 408
Osgodby, 8, 51, 92
Overfield, H V, 356-7, 370
Overton, colonel, 95

Page, W, 223, 225, 226, 227
Palace Hill, 178
Paradise, 64, 110 114; Close,
198; House, 126, 221, 353
Parisi, 1,2
Park, Mrs, 173

Parliament, see Members of;
27, 65, 83-4, 86-7, 150-3, 215-
19, 314-21, 415-18
Parr, R H, 310
Paxton, Sir Joseph, 263, 298
Peacock, the miner, 161; P,
105
Pearson, G, 110
Peasants' Revolt, 32, 34-5
Peasholm Beck, 26, 76, 237;
Fort, 169; Gap, 237;
Park 300-1, 343, 369-
70
pedestrian precinct, **396**
Pennant, T, 181, 183
Penston, W, 80, 84, 199
Percehays of Ryton, 45, 46
Percy, W, 26-7
Pester, J, 377
Phillips, J, 199
Philpotts, Dr, 352
Phipps family, see Members of
Parliament
Pickering, forest, 24, 25, 40;
Lythe, 68
Picture Palladium House, 330,
349
Piers: Old, 24, 40, 47-8, 54-5,
56-7, 117, 125, 154-5;
Vincent's, 185, 186,
188-9, 226; East, 185-
7; West, 188-9
Pilgrimage of Grace, 43, 51
Pillory Hill, 109
Pindar, G K G, 366, 371-2;
Group, 422; School,
411
Piper, J, 366
Pitts, M, 418
Place, F, 136, 366; F, 268

Plague, see Black Death
Plan of Scarborough, 1811, **159**
Plantation (People's Park, Valley Gardens), 168, 234, 272, 298, **299**
Plaxton's, 330, 348, 371, 394, 422
Pontin, F, 379, 403
Population, 32, 36-7, 43, 55, 57, 59-60, 64-5, 82, 193-6, 341-2, 364, 373-4, 378, 388
Porrett, G, 163; W, 127
Porritt's Lane, 127
Port, 24, 34, 37-8, 40-2, 54-5, 56-7, 60, 66, 69-71, **86**, 125-7, 184-9, 191, 372-3 see also fishing, piers, ship-building
Post Office, 332
Potter, J, 118; W, 249; Lane, 362
Powell, W, 110
Pratt, J, 163
Princess Street, 108, 174
Prisons: Newborough Bar, 163, 178, 226; House of Correction, 226, 247, 248; Castle Road, 236, 269; Dean Road, 269-70
Pritchett, V S, 357
Prospect Mount, 356
Proctor, H, 417

Quakers, 87-9, 202-4, 395
Quay Street, 24
Queen's Parade, (Peasholm Lane), 275, 298
Queen Street, (Blackfriar Gate, Beast Market), 108, 164, 168, 178, 179-80, 205, 230, 249, 358

Railways, 255-7, 262, 271-2, 294, 304, 322, 330, 379, 382
Raincliffe Spring, 237
Ramsay, earl of Holderness, 61
Ramsey, T, **147**
Ramsdale, 22, 25, 75, 109, 110, 138, 167, 168-9, 234, 236, 298, **299**
Rasen (Rasyn), H, 46-7
rats, 342, 364-5, 377-8
Raven, T, 311
Ravenscar, 5-7, 25
Ravenser-Odd, 24
Rawling, G B, 346
Rawlinson, E, 324
Ray, J, 125, 158
Readman, M, 248
Reed, Mrs, 241, 261
Reginald, the miller, 27
Richard I, king, 13, 20, 21; II, 31, 32, 35, 40, 45; III, 40-2, 236; House **41**
Rievaulx/Lane, 20
Rillington, R, 34, 3-6
Robinson, Don, 380, 402, 403, 408; John, 118; Luke, 77, 86-7, 95, 119; Thomas, 235; Widow, 119; William, 118
Rock Gardens, 274-5
Roger, the vintner, 19
Roman Catholics, 204, 286, 412
Roman signal stations, 5-7
Roos, Lord John, 97
Roscoe Street clinic, 366
Rose Gardens, 300

Rotunda Museum, 117, 155, 212-4, **213**, 241, 262, 354, 368

Rowntree, *History*, iii-iv, 3; Store, 394; Howard, 416; John, 203, 204, 229; Joshua, 309, 318-21; J W, 314-16, 418; William, 272, 307

Royal Albert Drive, 303

Royle's Fol de Rols, 300

Royle, G E, 336, 406

Rumball, S A, 223-4

Rupert, Prince, 63, 70

Rutland, duke of, 162, 209, 234; Terrace, 219

Safeway, 26, 396

Sage, Sir Adam, 28; Thomas, 42

Saint Catherine Close, 208

Saint Helen's Square 28, 266

Saint Nicholas Cliff, 135, 155 160, 164, 176, 178, 227-8, 298; Gate, 60; Gardens, 300

Saint Sepulchre Gate/Street, 160, 163, 178, 202, 203-4

Saint Thomas Cross, 105; Gate, 108; Poor House, 207; Yard, 162

Sandside, 111, 126-7, 174-5, **245**, 400-1

Sarony, O, 283

Saunders, N, 91; W, 119

Saunderson, W, 114, 115

Scalby, 8, 22; Manor, 392; Mills, 344, 356, 364, 370, 404-6

Scarborough, Building Society, 422; Fair, 24, 38, 424; Fare, 423; Philosophical Society, 212-3, 220, 354; Salt(s), 159; Seas 424; Warning, 25-6, 424-5; Whey, 158, 159

scarlet fever, 337, 364, 374

Schofield, J, 161, 167, 171, 174, 175, 177, 178, 180, 194, 235-6, 297, 354

Schools, 249-50, 305-11, 410- 14; Adult, 318; Amicable Society, 201-2, 206, 209, 250,306-7; Bramcote, 363, 413;Central,307; Convent, 411, 412; Fairbank's, 309; Friarage, 307, 338; Girls' High, 352, 410-12; Graham, 412; Graham Sea Training, 353-4, 412; Grammar/High, 46, 50, 53, 197, 199-201, 249-50, 251, 286, 309; High School for Boys, 352, 410, 411-12; Lancasterian, 205-6, 250-1, 305-7; Lisvane, 414; Municipal, 307-9, 351-2, 411; Northstead, 342; Orleton, 364, 414; Pindar, 411; Queen

455

Margaret's, 362; Raincliffe, 411, 412; St Augustine's, 411, 412; St Mary's National, 236, 250, 305, 337; St Martin's Grammar, 310-11, 352; St Peter's, 306, 338; St Thomas, 305, 337; Scarborough College, 310, 413-14; School of Art, 412-13; School of Industry, 307; Sixth Form College, 412; Technical College/Institute, 412-13; Wachter French Ladies, 309; Wesleyan Day, 305, 307; Westlands, 351-2; Wheater's Academy, 310

Schreiner, C, 320
Sea-bathing, 98-100, 170-2
Sea-Life Centre, 392, 405, 406
Seamen's Hospital, 207
Seamer, 51, 53, 57-9, 120, 255
Seaward, A, 160, 161
Sedman, T, 110, 199; W, 121
Sellers, J, 322, 324; R, 90-1
Setterington, J, 140, 142-3, 170
Settrington, J, 28
Shafto, J, 28; J, 140, 142-3, 170, 185
Shafto, J, 216
Shambles, 204-5, 265
Sharp, 208, 209, 213
Sharpin, J F, 261-2
Shaw, Dr P, 149, 158-9

Sheppard, W, 117
Sheridan, 173
Short's Gardens, 298
Shipbuilding, 181-4, 243-4
Shuttleworth, A, 300
Simpson, F, iii, 3-4, 6, 7; W (vicar), 50, 84, 87, 120; W (physician), 94, 100-4, 105
Sitwells, 367: Edith, 367; Sir George, 315, **317**, 332, 367-8, 415-16; Osbert, 329-30, 366-8, 415-16; Sacheverell, 367
Skarthi (Thorgils), 7-9
Skelton, J, 201, 250; R, 244, 322; T, 152
Slarke, I, 388
Slee, W, 118
Slingsby, T, 92
slum clearance, 339, 374-6
smallpox, 378
Smeaton, J, 186-7
Smettem, W, 354-5, 367, 368
Smith, Harry W, 297, 300-2, 336, 340, 342-6; J, 388; W, 212, 214, 237, 268; W H, 354; S, 372
Smithy Hill, 126, 127
smoking, 374
Smollett, T, 171-2
smuggling, 146, 164, 247-8
Snorri Sturluson, 10, 11-12
Sollitt, C, 87, 199; F, 87, 112, 117; J, 127
'Sons of Neptune', 404-6
South Bay, **398**

456

South Bay Pool, 301-2, 391, 400
South Steel battery, 68, 156, **242**
Spa(w), 93-8, 100-3, 157-60, 239-42, 282-5, 346-8, 365-6, 398-400
Sports Centre, 392
Spragge, admiral, 90-1
Spread Eagle Lane, 304
Stafford, Sir T, 51, 424
Standing, F, 390
Standish, R, 35
Stephen, king, 13, 16, 17
Stephen Joseph, 409; Theatre, 393, 410
Stewart, W B, 269, 279
Stockdale, Mrs, 154
Stockill, J, 403
Stokoe, Dr J, 376
Stoney Haggs, 162
Stonehouse, W, 91
Stowsley, R, 110
Stubbs, I, 390
Styan, G and H, 268
Sullivan, R J, 170
Swales, J and M, 203
Swalwell, T, 309
Swift, J B, 372

Tanner (St Thomas) Street, 168, 173, 178, 227, 230, 236, 241
Taylor, A, 269; AJP, 328; J, 143-4, 177, 203, 204; Dr J W, 378; W, 52
Tempest, R, 37
Tesco, 395, 396
Tetley, A S, 308

Theakston, S W, 214, 243, 249, 259, 260, 354
Theatre in the Round, 409
Theodosius, 4-5
Thomas, Browne, 72
Thompsons, 65, 71, 76, 82, 87, 128, 198; Christopher, 61, 82, 93; Francis I, 61, 82, 107; Francis II, 87, 93, 128, 199; Richard, 61, 82, 107; Stephen, 50, 61, 76, 82-3; William I, 61, 62, 75, 107; II, 87, 90, 93, 113, 128, 152, 198; III, 200, see also Members of Parliament
Thorgils, see Skarthi
Thornburgh, Sir John, 59
Thornton, A and W, 96; William, 209, 223
Throxenby, 8
Tindalls, family and shipyards: 168, 182-4, 203, 243, 253, 288; Ann, 127; James, senior and junior, 167, 182, 243; John, 182, 183-4, 203; Mary, 127; Robert, senior and junior, 182, 183, 208, 212, 243, 272; William I, 126, 127; William II, 182, 243
Tintinholm(e)s, 76
Tonks, 394
Tostig, 9-12
trams, 302-4, 345, 392; South Cliff, 302; Central,

302; North Bay, 343,
391, 406
Travis, J, 171, 191; Nathaniel,
242; Dr William, iii,
223, 229, 343, 391,
406
Trebble, J, 390, 394
Trinity College (King's Hall),
Cambridge, 40, 154,
185
Trinity House, 124, 201, 207-8
Triton, 344
tuberculosis (pulmonary), 338,
374
Tucker's Field, 301
Tugwell, A J, 318, 320
Tunstall, Dr George, 101-2
Turnbull, C F, 310-11
Turner, J M W, 366
Tuthill, 178
Tyler, Wat, 35
Tymperton, Captain W, 149,
153, 157
Tyson, A G, 244, 249

Ughtred, R, 20
Undercliff, 110, 112, 114
unemployment, 295, 301, 327-
8, 342, 359, 380
United Bus Company, 303, 348
University of Hull,
Scarborough Campus,
414
Uppleby, J, 229
Urquhart, Mr, 199

Valley Bridge, 271-2, 345, 371
Value Added Tax, 380
Vegetius, 6
venereal disease, 102, 374

Verity, T, 284-5
Vernon, archbishop, 212;
Place, 166, 212, 234
Vertue, G, 140
Vescy, Isabel and John, 28
Vickerman, T, 152, also see
Baths
Victoria, queen, 281, 284;
Road (Common
Lane), 266; Street,
192
Vincent, W, 149, 150, 155-6,
see also Piers
Vipont, Mr, 144, 146
Von der Tann, 332, 333
Wales, prince of, Edward, 262
283, 284, see also Inns
and Hotels
Walker, T B, 243
Wallis, Dudley, 403
Walmsley, E, 118-19; brothers,
296
Walshaw, J, 277-8; Gardens,
298
War Memorial, 336-7, 365
Ward, W, 49
Wardale, R, 46
Warwick House,
(Londesborough Lodge) 235
Wasthouse, R, 29
Water, 17, 18, 27-8, 105-6,
161-2, 237, 239, 257-8, 266,
376
Waterhouse Lane, 268, 395
Wawayn, R, 33
Weaponness, 9, 22, 25, 109,
110, 123, 169-70, see
also Oliver's Mount
Webb, Captain, 281
Weddell, T, 255

Wentworth, Sir T, 62
Wesley, J, 204-5
Westbourne Grove, 351
Westfield Terrace, 260, 346
Westmorland, earl of, 51
Westover Road (Folly Lane),
290
West Sandgate, 117, 138
Westwood, **192**, 308, 353
West Yorkshire Territorials,
332
Wharton, J, 229
Wheat (White)croft, 65, 92,
109, 184
Wheater, J, 310
Whin Bank, 237
Whitby Strand, 68
White Nab, 26, 109, 186, 237
White's *Directory*, 243-7
Whitehead Hill (Shilbottle
Lane), 110, 204
Whiteside, J W, 267
Whittakers, 320, Thomas 263,
319, 316-19; Meredith I, 297,
307, 336, 342, 345-6, 355, 366,
415; Francis, 304-5, 355, 365;
Meredith II, 417-18
Wilkinson, H, 248
William le Gros
(Albemarle/Aumale,
count of,), 13, 15-18
William of Filey, 33
William of Newburgh, 16-17
William of Orange, king, 85-6,
93, 125
William Street, 265-6
William the Conqueror, 3, 9,
17
Williams, Charlie, 407

Williamson, J, 212; R, 271-2;
T, 52

Willis, G, 244
Wills, H O, 261
Wilson, R, 236
Wilson's Wood, see
Barrowcliff Plantation
Windmill, 400
windmills, Albion, 236;
Common, 235-6;
Greengate, 236; South
Cliff, 234, 289
Wireless Station (Sandybed
Lane), 333, 334, 364
Withers, E, 139, 142, 146, 177
Witt de, admiral, 125
Wittie, Dr R, 89, 94-102, 105,
135, 138, 170, 278
Wolfe, J, 53, 54; N, 109
Wolseley, W, 92-3
Wood, Miss, 351
Wood, W, 260
229, 311; John, junior,
223, 241, 258, 274,
284, 286, 296, 300,
320; C W, 320
Woodalls, 312, John, senior,
212, 217, 223, 226,
Wood End, 235, 256, 356, 367-
8
Woodger family, 323; H L,
324
Woodhead, Miss, 351
Workhouse, 246, 268-9; Yard,
237
Worlington Grove, 200
Wret, W, 120-1
Wrea Lane, 236, 265, 268, 269

Wyatt's Gothic Saloon, 239, 242, 263, 298
Wykeham Street, 237
Wynd, G, 114
Wyrill, H, 323, 324
Wyvill, J, 51, 92, 93

yawl, 244, 322, 324
York Place, 166, 212, 234, 249
Yorkshire Coast College, 413
Yorkshire Water, 404-6
Young, A, 175
Young Pretender (Bonnie Prince Charles), 155-6

'Zenith', 421
Zoo and Marineland, 402

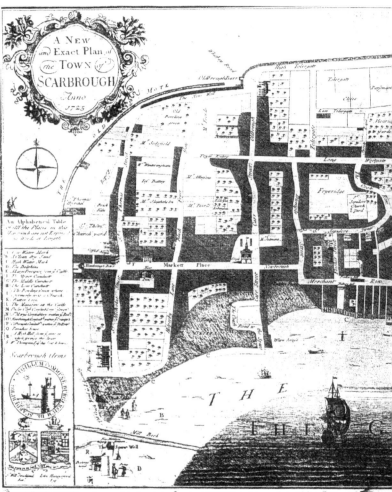

A NEW
and Exact Plan of
the TOWN of
SCARBROUGH
Anno
1725

SCARBOROUGH a large well built rich & Populous TOWN, is Scituate in the North Riding of y Country
To the Serene &c Healthfull Formerly it was Fortifyd by a Strong Castle &c for its Natural Scituation Surpasses most This Town is
are Upwards of 500 Saile The Peer very strong built of large Stone This Place by a Moderate Computation Appears to Contain
for y Use of y Medicinal Spaws. Lat 54 21 Distance from London 100 Miles, from York & Hull 30